PELICAN BOOKS

ARCHITECTURE IN AUSTRALIA

John Maxwell Freeland is Professor of Architecture
at the University of New South Wales. Born in
Tasmania, he attended school in Melbourne and
took out his degree of Master of Architecture and
Diploma of Town and Regional Planning from the
University of Melbourne. He was in private
architectural practice from 1951 to 1955, when he
was appointed Associate Professor of Architecture at
the University of New South Wales, where he took
the Chair in 1960.

Professor Freeland is the author of a number of
books on Australian architecture and architects;
these include: *Melbourne Churches 1836-51*,
The Australian Pub and *Architect Extraordinary:
The Life and Times of John Horbury Hunt.*

ARCHITECTURE IN AUSTRALIA

A History

J. M. FREELAND

PENGUIN BOOKS

Penguin Books Ltd, Harmondsworth, Middlesex, England
Penguin Books Australia Ltd, Ringwood, Victoria, Australia

First published by F. W. Cheshire Publishing Pty Ltd 1968
Published in Pelican Books 1972
Reprinted 1974

Copyright © J. M. Freeland, 1968

Made and printed in Australia for Penguin Books Australia Ltd
by Alexander Bros, Mentone, Victoria

FOR MY MOTHER MARY GRANT FREELAND

ACKNOWLEDGEMENTS

Virtually all the photographs illustrating this book are, intentionally, of buildings which still stand and which therefore can be visited by people interested. Dates as given in the captions are, for the most part, dates of completion.

The author is indebted to the following holders of copyrights who have generously supplied photographs and given permission for their reproduction on the pages following their names:
Messrs Allen, Jack & Cottier—page 306 (above): Messrs Ancher, Mortlock, Murray & Woolley—pages 261 (above and below) and 307 (above): The Armidale Newspaper Co. Ltd—page 189: The Australian and New Zealand Bank Ltd—page 130 (below): The Australian News and Information Bureau—page 242 (right): The Bank of New South Wales—pages 169 (above) and 258 (left): Messrs Bates, Smart & McCutcheon—page 297 (below): Miss M. Bruce—page 11: Mr Walter Bunning—page 278: Messrs Clarke, Gazzard & Partners—page 289 (above and below): Mr Marshall Clifton—page 287 (below): Messrs Curro, Nutter & Charlton—page 297 (above): Mr John Dalton—page 306 (below): Mr G. E. Drinnan—page 115: Mr Charles Duncan—page 307 (below): The English, Scottish and Australian Bank—page 258 (right): Mr Roy Grounds—pages 274 (below), 275, 288 (above) and 290: Messrs Hayes, Scott & Henderson—page 306 (centre): Messrs A. Kann, Finch & Partners—page 284 (below): Messrs Lund, Hutton & Newell—page 288 (below): Mr Neville Lund—page 208 (below): Messrs McConnel, Smith & Johnson—page 303: Mr Gerard B. McDonell—page 262: Messrs McKay & Cox—page 308: The Maritime Services Board of New South Wales—page 239 (above): Messrs Morrow & Gordon—page 284 (above): John and Phyllis Murphy—page 292 (above): Myer (Emporium) Ltd—page 256: The National Trust of Australia (New South Wales)—pages 22, 25, 32, 39, 40, 44, 56 (right), 58, 69, 74, 78, 80, 82, 90, 94, 96, 98 (above right), 101, 105, 107 (above), 116 (above), 122, 167 (below), 173 (above) and 224: The National Trust of Australia (Tasmania) and Platypus Publications jointly—pages 51 (centre), 65, 100 (below), 155 (above and below) and 240 (below): The New South Wales Government Architect—pages 296 and 310: Dr E. Graeme Robertson, Mrs E. N. Craig and Georgian House Pty Ltd—pages 77, 81, 100 (above), 165, 239 (below) and 241: Professor Frederick Romberg—page 274 (above): The Royal Australian Institute of Architects—pages 244 (centre), 295 and 300 (above): The Royal Australian Institute of Architects (Queensland Chapter)—pages 133 (above), 154, 196, 208 (above and below left), 218, and 237: Messrs Harry Seidler & Associates—pages 272, 296 and 304: The State Planning Authority of New South Wales—pages 38, 43, 46 (centre), 56 (above), 75, 76 and 79: Messrs Stephenson & Turner—page 300 (below right): The Tourist Development Authority of Victoria—pages 124 (above and below), 126, 128 (above), 175 and 191: The Western Australian Government Tourist Bureau—page 234: Messrs Woodward & Taranto—page 312: Yuncken, Freeman Architects Pty Ltd—page 294.

The author also gratefully acknowledges the following photographers:
Mr Ronald H. Armstrong—page 300 (above): Douglass Baglin Pty Ltd—page 300 (below right): Beatties Studio—page 155 (below): Mr Lester G. Clark—page 173 (above): The Commercial Photographic Co. Pty Ltd—page 274 (above): Mr G. Douth—page 306 (below): Mr Max Dupain—pages 69, 78, 80, 82, 96, 98 (above right), 101, 122, 261 (above and below), 272, 284 (above), 290, 296, 297 (below), 304, 307 (above), 308 and 310: Mr Arch Frayley—pages 201, (below) and 288 (below): L. & D. Keen Pty Ltd—pages 133 (above), 154, 157, 170, 196, 208, 218 and 306 (centre): Mr Fritz Kos—pages 103 (above) and 200: Mr David McCowan—page 287 (below): Mr Gerard B. McDonell—page 262: Mr Graham Martin—pages 46 (centre) and 58: Mercury Photo, Hobart—pages 51 (centre), 65 and 100 (above): Mr David Moore—pages 284 (below), 289 (below), 303 and 306 (above): Dr E. Graeme Robertson—pages 77, 81, 100 (above), 147 (above), 165, and 239 (below): Robert Pockley Studios—page 115: Mr L. H. Runting—pages 274 (below) and 275: Mr Benjamin A. Sheppard—page 240 (below): Mr Wolfgang Sievers—pages 170 (below), 258 (right), 300 (below left) and 292 (above): Mr Harry Sowden—page 289 (above): Mr H. Warr—pages 38, 43, 44, 56 (above), 75, 76 and 78: Whitelaw's Studio—page 115 (above): Mr James Whitelock—pages 25, 39, 40, 56 (below), 74, 90, 94, 107 (above), 116 (above), 167 (below) and 224.

CONTENTS

Acquiring a knowledge of history is a pleasant and safe pastime for the dilettante. Developing an understanding of history is an essential for those who would influence the future. It is not only on the lessons that history has to teach, valuable though they are, that this claim lies. Rather is it that by making us aware how we arrived where we are today history gives us our bearings so that, like any traveller, we may venture into the unknown confident of our direction at least. When we meet the future by reacting to the present, how we react is largely determined by the past—our history.

A country's architecture is a near-perfect record of its history. Every building captures in physical form the climate and resources of a country's geography, the social, economic, technological and political conditions of its society and the moral, philosophical, aesthetic and spiritual values of its people. Every building records, describes and explains the time and the place in which it was built.

Because of the all-embracing nature of the multitude of factors which contribute to the form and character of any building, the history of architecture is fully-rounded in a way that is unique amongst fields of historical study. The history of the architecture of a country is, in fact, the history of that country. Buildings are original historical documents. Unlike the original sources on which most historical fields depend, those of architectural history, in the main, are not buried under the ground or locked up in closely-guarded libraries and archives and cautiously made available to a few crusty scholars. The documents and evidence of architectural history are everywhere around us, openly and freely available and readily accessible to anyone who has the skill and the mind for it to study, to read, to interpret and to understand. Buildings carry more history than a library of books—and it is not second-hand.

The purpose of this book is to sketch, in broad outline, the path that has been travelled by Australian architecture during the century and three-quarters since the first European settlement was made at Sydney Cove. By world standards of time it is not a long story, but in its short span it is a rapidly changing story. Even in such a general coverage as this it is not possible to deal with it in blocks of fifty or one hundred years and still make sense. Because of this rapidity of change Australian architecture has never known the glories of a golden period in which, as the culmination of a period of steady development, ideas come to full flower. There are no high artistic peaks. Like the story of world architecture over the same period it is largely the story of increasingly rapid artistic disintegration under the steadily growing impact of machines.

This is not the story of an architects' architecture but of a society's architecture. In the domestic sphere, for instance, it is the tastes and ideals of the layman which are dominant and determinant; albeit these may be led and indirectly formed by a few professionals. Until the 1840s, when architecture was still fairly stable, the differences between architects' architecture and laymen's architecture were largely a matter of degree. After that time, when fashion became increasingly important, the two drew apart by about ten years and the difference gradually became one of kind. Until the 1920s, because of the still leisured pace of life in general, the lag was not of great significance. But during the last fifty years, with changes happening ever more quickly, the separation has taken on new importance so that a decade, during which the total of knowledge doubles and which separates the thinking of the professional architect from the public's acceptance of it, is one that has created the impression that present-day architects are a rabidly unreal lot rather out of touch with the society they are supposed to serve.

Throughout the book the aim has been to follow the main crest of each architectural wave as it flowed across the surface of Australian society rather than to ride at its very foremost edge or to follow it into the trough trailing behind. Only where it is essential to give depth and dimension to the general picture have specific matters been picked out in detail.

In general the story centres on Sydney and Melbourne. They are the magnets which have drawn both people and ideas from overseas and from which local influences have spread to affect the rest of the nation. While local factors have played a large part in determining Australia's architecture it is nevertheless true that the major developments have come as a result of changes on the other side of the world.

With an ever-shrinking time lag, which used to be twenty years but is now about three, new ideas, new knowledge and new approaches arrive at the two large metropolises and thence, with a further time lag, which used to be five years but is now about one, to the other state capitals. Consequently, in telling the story of Australia's architecture in broad terms, in order to avoid tedious repetition and details of only parochial interest, New South Wales and Victoria loom large. If this attention seems disproportionate it is not in fact. It is because that is the way it was—and still largely is.

There has not been a great number of books written about Australian architecture but those that have been written are of a consistently high standard. For readers who find the broad story of Australian architecture of interest and wish to know more about it, a list is included of books which delve deeper into various times, aspects and people than has been possible in this book. To the author of each of them the writer unreservedly acknowledges his dependence upon and indebtedness to the fruits of their labour and recommends them to his readers. The writer is also indebted to Mr Richard Apperly, who generously made available the results of his research into the importance of the Californian bungalow, Redwood, in Gardener's Road, Rosebery, and the life of Alexander Stewart Jolly.

J.M.F.

1

In the early morning light of Sunday 13 May 1787, eleven ships sailed quietly out of Portsmouth harbour and onto the high seas, leaving the citizens of the town much relieved by their departure. The two naval ships, six transports and three store ships, totalling less than 4,000 tons burthen carrying stores, provisions and 1,480 souls, were being sent to the other side of the world to found a colony.

The people who made up the expedition's complement reflected the society that was sending them forth into the unknown. In charge was a small enlightened rational-thinking elite of military and civil officers; to serve them was a group of solid, stolid, unambitious, professional marines and hard-drinking sailors; to give them a purpose was a scabrous and distasteful collection of some 750 male and female convicts—murderers, gamblers, embezzlers, forgers, thieves and prostitutes, to whom, through generations of conditioning, idleness, intemperance, debauchery, lewdness and dissipation were the norms of living.

The law that was exiling them was a grotesque, severe and bloody code designed to protect a society in which property was more important than life. It was a society in which a yawning empty gap separated the wealthy, educated upper class from the mass of the depressed, disease-ridden, bovine poor to whom life offered a single choice only—theft or starvation. Over 160 crimes, ranging from murder to theft of any article worth more than a shilling, carried the death penalty. Only in the worst or habitual cases was the ultimate payment exacted. In practice the sentence was usually commuted to transportation to the colonies for seven years, fourteen years or life. After the loss of the American colonies, British gaols had become severely over-crowded. No longer could convicts be sold to avaricious traders in human life for transport as cheap labour to the New World. Old buildings were converted into gaols. Ships no longer seaworthy and barges were anchored in the Thames and pressed into service as emergency places of confinement. As these, in turn, became choked with the refuse of society, the British Government was faced with the choice of sending the overflow overseas or underground.

Remembering a glowing report of places in the Pacific made in 1771 by Captain James Cook, and on the suggestion of Sir Joseph Banks, the Government decided to relieve the pressure by sending the worst of the law-breakers to establish a penal colony on the east coast of New Holland. Captain Arthur Phillip, a forty-eight year old retired naval officer of mixed British and German descent, was commissioned in 1786 to organize and command the venture. He was a conscientious, even-tempered and humane man, ideally suited for the task. In the face of official inefficiency, unofficial disinterest, personal frustration and public scorn and sarcasm, he managed to put together a creditably prepared and equipped expedition.

As the fleet turned into the rising sea on that Sunday morning and headed towards the future, it turned its back on an England which, in many ways, was more civilized than it had ever been before or has been since. It is true that wealth and poverty, refinement and crudity, beauty and ugliness, enlightenment and ignorance existed side by side. It was a society of contrasts in which ladies and gentlemen, elegantly clad in the finest of exquisite clothes, avoided spattering their buckled and brocaded shoes with the muck of the streets by riding securely in sedan chairs borne by fustian-clothed clods, and, on alighting, stepped fastidiously over gin-sodden derelicts lying unconscious on the ground; where buildings of extraordinary purity of design were erected by craftsmen who themselves returned at night to sleep in the meanest of hovels; where religion, beleaguered by the highly heretical *Treatise on Human Nature* written by a home-grown philosopher, David Hume, was outwardly supported as an indispensable tool by those who, while privately agreeing with Hume, were charged with maintaining the superiority of the British system.

It has been truly said that if the twentieth century is the age of the common man the eighteenth century was that of the uncommon man. The Georgian lived in a climate of optimism, excitement, enthusiasm and confidence. He enjoyed life frankly, lustily and without apology. There was no false modesty with the Georgians and where this is so there can be no pornography. Honesty was the quality that ran like a golden thread through everything—manners, behaviour, design, art—and self-criticism. Sheridan saw it as a trifling age by comparison with that of Queen Anne when merit was encouraged and genius was favoured. Hogarth could draw savagely satirical and cutting indictments of the affectation and folly that he found and be fêted for it. Rowlandson could capture the grossness in the streets and be applauded. For while the eighteenth century in Europe was the Age of Enlightenment it was, as one of its foremost philosophers, Immanuel Kant, observed, far from being an enlightened age. The virtues of reason, good sense and humane regard for one's fellow-man preached by its spokesmen were a long way from being achieved in practice.

A social conscience that found the disparity between the classes that abounded everywhere a disturbing thing was, thank God, the concern of those erratic and volatile French. Rousseau's *Discourse on the Origin of Inequality* was soon to bear fruit in a savage blood-bath across the channel, but the same twinges, if not the results, were still a century away in England. In eighteenth century England there was no cant about equality. Johnson rationalized it to Boswell as the best arrangement anyway—equality would do nothing other than breed misery and degeneracy. Subordination is essential and most conducive to the happiness of society. There is a reciprocal pleasure in governing and being governed, in commanding and obeying. 'If we were all upon an equality none of us would be happy,' he said. They were the views of a man who was aware that the wave on which he was riding reached higher than waves had ever reached before. And it was a fact. While the troughs on the surface of English society were wide and low, the crests that divided them were dizzily and exhilaratingly high. Those who rode them were conscious that they were in a Golden Age and that Georgian England was a supremely civilized nation. The English language, after two centuries of wonderful and creative development, came to maturity and achieved, for the first time in its long history, a certain balance and equilibrium that was distinguished by sincerity, clarity and vigour. Robustness and virility combined with a deft touch for fitness, a fine sense of style, infallible judgment and impeccable taste to produce a society marked by an easy grace, elegance and refinement.

While the foundations had been laid in the Italianizing of England, and London in particular, by the court of Charles I and Inigo Jones during the quarter century preceding the Civil War, it had really started in 1660 when, after the bleak austerity and repressions of the Puritan Commonwealth, the loyalist exiles returned home with Charles II. The Restoration was not the restoration of a king only—it was the restoration of a culture and a class. They brought with them the tastes, knowledge, fashions and standards of France and Italy, the most sophisticated countries of the world. They also brought back with them material wealth and a complete and exclusive belief in the powers of reason. It was the most educated and cultured of England's classes that had followed their king into exile, and as wealth and culture went hand in hand their return gave a fresh impetus to the arts as their tastes became those of England. An educated patronage of the arts ensued. Over the next 170 years a flowering of the arts took place which resulted in a delightful urbanity that stood in sublime contrast to the hypocrisy and vulgarity of the Victorian period and the sterility and stridency of the twentieth century.

However, the blooming was largely restricted to the visual aspects of society and art. Georgian England produced no composer to stand with Bach, Haydn, Mozart or Beethoven and her most important composer, Handel, was, like her king, German born. Hume was a pale shadow beside Voltaire or Kant. There was no Englishman of the genius of Goethe. She had few poets of first rank and their lines, even when writing of the abstract, were cast in visual terms. Pope's 'Essay on Criticism' and Gray's 'Elegy in a Country Churchyard' are full of pictures and visual analogies. The major science of the period, astronomy, which Newton had rationalized in a lightning flash of mathematical clarity forty years before the Hanovers arrived, was essentially observational. But Reynolds and Gainsborough painted better and more elegantly than Boucher or Fragonard, if not Goya; the furniture of Chippendale, Hepplewhite and Sheraton was greatly superior in design and construction, not to mention practicality, to the clever, ornate and elaborate work of Oeben, Roentgen and Riesener; and the buildings of James Gibbs, the Dances father and son, and the brothers Adam, while highly imaginative, were under much tighter control and, consequently, in far better taste than those erected by their contemporaries in France.

For half a century or so after Newton's triumph, society, having had the essential simplicity of the previously mysterious universe so brilliantly demonstrated, placed a blind and exclusive trust in the scientific method. Everything, it was believed, must be precisely expressible in rational terms and be able to be exactly and mathematically formulated. Feelings were the falsest of prophets. But by the mid-eighteenth century the scientists had become atrophied in the amber of the limitations of their own system—a situation that was to last over a century. In non-scientific and cultural circles a reaction to the wholly rational set in and emotions were restored to a place in life. Preaching a creed of the absolute relation between cause and effect, with its own set of empirical values, and speaking its own new language, the world of science moved along a divergent path from the bulk of society. The breach that took place between science and the arts in early Georgian times has grown wider until it has become a fundamental chasm with only a few easily fractured gossamer bridges linking its two sides.

The reinstatement of emotions and the concern for visual pleasure were tempered at first, however, by the habits of rational thought, systematization and formulation that had proved so patently workable. Emotional concern was rationally based. In this frame of mind every aspect of the visual world was subjected to the most careful consideration and refinement. The results—the sensitively decorated ceilings and walls and the equally sensitive fireplaces of Robert Adam, the delicate grand pianos and elegant travelling harpsichords of Josephus Merlin and the beautiful and tasteful pottery of Josiah Wedgwood—were without peer. Silver candlesticks, brass door knockers, enamelled shoe buckles, tapestried fire-screens, moulded picture and mirror frames, vases, cutlery, clothes and anything which, by its visual qualities, might offend or delight the eye were meticulously and sensitively designed. And always the result was recognizably and distinctively English. The inspiration came from Greece or Rome to be sure, but, in a process and at a time when it seemed that neither designers, craftsmen nor patrons could put a foot wrong, the products were uniquely Georgian. Orderliness, common sense, a wonderful sense of proportion and balance and a delight in decoration always under complete control were the watchwords. Even when the Georgians produced something that was conceited, fanciful, eccentric or even downright foolish, the result was never ugly or ungraceful.

The epitome of things Georgian was its architecture. It had received its first impetus and one of its most important modifying influences out of the ashes of the fire that had devastated London in 1666. The boost came from the tremendous amount of building that was necessary to replace the mediaeval city which had been gutted. The times produced the man. Sir Christopher Wren was a mathematician and an astronomer with a bent for science and, occasionally, an amateur architect. All educated people of the times were familiar with architectural precepts of taste, proportions and the Classic Orders. After the 'Gothic barbarity', as it was described, men of the Renaissance had re-discovered the intellectual basis of design. Not merely copying the visual forms and patterns of Roman civilization but taking the underlying structure as well and touching it with their own genius, they produced a new architecture of beauty and grandeur.

And Wren was an architect of uncommon genius. Part of Greenwich Hospital and the library of Trinity College amongst others came from his mind, but it was the fifty-two city churches with their delicate floating towers and spires and his masterpiece, St Paul's Cathedral, that transformed the old London into a sort of New Jerusalem and pointed the direction to be followed by others. Together with his pupil Nicholas Hawksmoor and Sir John Vanbrugh, only slightly less in architectural stature, he led a succession of well-grounded and sensitive architects which stretched well into the nineteenth century. James Gibbs, the Dances, the Woods, William Chambers, the Adams, Henry Holland, James Wyatt, John Nash and John Soane passed the flame along for a century and a half, refining, changing and modifying until it was scattered and extinguished in the Revivalist controversies which came in the wake of the Romantic reaction which inevitably followed the Age of Reason.

A host of lesser architects well versed in the skills and limits of the masters turned out a huge number of minor gems. Many of them were designers casually, temporarily and for love of designing—amateurs in the true sense. Horace Walpole was one of them and summed up the credo to which all paid homage when he said, 'Fitness for uses to which a building is designed must always be the source of architectural beauty.' This is one aspect of 'appropriateness' and if there is any one word that contains the whole essence of Georgian architecture it is that.

It was people like Walpole who made it their business to foster the artistic climate of the times. They included such men as Alexander Pope, who consistently championed good design and attacked extravagance, and Richard Boyle, third Earl of Burlington, who revived and stimulated an interest in Palladio when taste for the imaginative extravagances of the Baroque started by Vanbrugh were threatening to get out of hand. Highly and broadly educated members of a wealthy and cultured class, they were dilettantes in its best sense. They took the whole of the visual world for their domain, probing, criticizing, demanding and encouraging better design in everything from the largest to the smallest item.

Not only buildings and the things within the buildings but the whole of the natural setting as well came under their aegis. Architects such as Lancelot ('Capability') Brown, who had worked with Robert Adam and built up a considerable reputation as an architect, turned their attention to the improvement of nature. The landscape in which their buildings were set was designed and changed with a subtlety and sensitivity to perspective and vista which was its own disguise. Groups of trees, lakes and green swards, all artificially and artfully placed, created a precisely casual world of controlled beauty.

By the time the First Fleet sailed from England the cycle had reached its apogee. Decay was incipient, and the Georgian flower was soon to fade. The society was to become complacent with its achievements and find itself anaemic and insipid. In a reaction to the super-rationalism of the seventeenth and early eighteenth centuries an intense interest in feeling and emotion developed. The leaders of taste were jaded with the Classic basis of Georgian architecture. Their Romantic eyes saw beauty in the Gothic churches, cathedrals and ruins. A 'Committee of Taste', urged on by talented architects such as Richard Bentley, considerably influenced the spread of a taste for Gothic. When John Chute, a Gothic enthusiast, assisted Horace Walpole to design Strawberry Hill with its mock ruins in the style, classic Georgian was seriously undermined. But at this stage the movement affected only the very upper stratum of society and only a small part of that. Georgian had never reached its highest peaks in the public buildings, the palaces and the mansions anyway. It was essentially a domestic architecture and its glory was greatest in buildings whose physical size was not such that its domestic scale was killed.

Like everything else on the Georgian scene, its domestic buildings were basically honest in form, materials and decoration, relying on good manners and good taste achieved by an evolutionary process in which proportions and texture were refined and then further refined. Their form was the simplest—uncomplicated two-storeyed boxes topped by an overhanging hipped roof. Their material trademarks were brick walls and rectangular twelve-paned double sash windows arranged with strict symmetry in the walls. Decoration was restricted to stone quoins, stone window dressings Classically moulded and a dentil course and simple cornice mouldings at the roof eaves line. The centrally placed doorway was the focal point on which the whole symmetrical arrangement of wall openings, roof line and chimneys pivoted and concentrated. Stone surrounds topped by a triangular or arc pediment often extended from the face of the building as a porch, with a noble flight of steps, enclosing broad generous doorways of exquisitely and finely wrought timber frames with solid four panelled doors, glazed sidelights and delicately patterned fanlights.

The use of brick and the distinctive windows were not the result of whim. Although flat Roman-type bricks had been used in Roman Britain, their use had virtually died out in favour of stone until their re-introduction from the Continent under the influence first of the Flemish refugee craftsmen, and then of the trading activities of the Hanseatic League. The Flemings brought with them the Old French words *brique* and *briche* to replace the previous words *tegulae* and *waltighel*. Hull, the foremost contact for the League in England, was first to be affected in the fifteenth century and became a town of brick. But elsewhere bricks were restricted to use in inferior or 'unimportant' buildings. Brick sizes varied widely and this was the main reason for their limited popularity. When Queen Elizabeth granted a charter to the Tylers and Bricklayers Company in 1571, it was laid down that within the limits of the Company's jurisdiction, a fifteen mile radius of London, bricks were to measure a uniform $9'' \times 4\frac{1}{2}'' \times 2\frac{1}{4}''$. Outside the geographical limits of the force of the charter a tendency to decrease the size without reducing the price brought a proclamation by Charles I, in 1625, that the London size was mandatory not only for London but also for 'the confines of the same'. The reverse effect took place when George I levied a tax on bricks. The tax was made on the number of bricks irrespective of size. To alleviate the hardship of the levy, bricks increased in size. In 1725 an Act limited London bricks to $9'' \times 4\frac{1}{4}'' \times 2\frac{1}{2}''$ and those for the rest of the country to a maximum of $10'' \times 5'' \times 3''$. A further slight reduction was made by Act to London brick sizes in 1729 and again in 1769, when the 1725 London size was enforced throughout all England except London. In 1776, under George III, $8\frac{1}{2}'' \times 4'' \times 2\frac{1}{2}''$ became the standard size for all bricks throughout England and Scotland. With each step in the standardization of brick sizes the popularity of the material increased. Freed from the greed and tax-dodging capriciousness of brickmakers, the uniformity of the material appealed to the Georgians, for whom uniformity had a great aesthetic value. The warmth, the intimacy, the scale, the proportions and the texture of the material were directly in line with the values that they sought in their world of visual delight.

The unique Georgian windows were likewise the outcome of a blend of practicalities and aesthetics. Until the late seventeenth century flat glass for windows had been scarce and expensive. What glass there had been was usually thick (because of its casting manufacturing process), cloudy grey and with rough surfaces. Colour-stained and set into wall openings it made glowing pictures and patterns but it let through very little light. If light were wanted the wall openings were made small to prevent the rooms from becoming too draughty and left open or protected with thin horn, oiled paper or shutters, all of which cut down the light that entered. Rooms were dark and gloomy. Small wonder that such draughty apertures were given a name derived from the Scandinavian for 'wind eye'.

In the early eighteenth century a technique of glass blowing known 600 years before was re-introduced and thin flat glass became widely available. In this 'crown glass' process a bubble of glass was blown on a heavy pipe. With the bubble still hot a metal rod, a punty, was attached by a molten blob of glass to the bubble diametrically opposite the pipe. When the bubble cooled to solidification the pipe was broken free, leaving a hole in the bubble opposite the punty. Reheated to plasticity short of molten, the punty was rolled along a table edge spinning the bubble which, under centrifugal force, flipped out into a flat thin disc. The punty was detached and when the disc cooled and annealed the glass was cut into panes. As the maximum size of disc that could be blown was about three feet in diameter, the normal size of the pane that was available was about ten inches square. The central part of the disc containing the raised knob where the punty had been attached was used decoratively, often in fanlights. The glass thus produced was distinguished from that of later techniques by a sheen on the surface and a slight bluish tinge.

At the same time that crown glass became commonly available in Queen Anne's reign, the sash window, a Dutch invention which had been known for some time, became increasingly popular and the previously used casement dropped rapidly out of fashion. Well-lighted rooms were needed in the Georgian scheme of things. Light was both a material to be controlled and moulded like any other and a necessity where visual things were all important. Accordingly, their windows were large, protected from the weather by sashes built up of a number of the small flat clear glass panes. Under the influence of the search for perfection based on proportion the panes became rectangular and, with greater skill in glass blowing, the size of panes increased; but the maximum size did not reach much more than twelve inches square.

By the mid-eighteenth century small and medium sized houses were refined and elegant, in the manner of the houses of Wren, but a change had come over the wholly domestic quality of the larger homes and mansions. In an open and unashamed bid to impress, entrance porches were emphasized so that they took on a grandeur that had been absent before. Triangular pediments sat atop giant columns two storeys high. The pediment would have broken through the eaves overhang had it still been there. But this had vanished behind a parapet as walls were carried up past the eaves lines, and the roof, once the perfect expression of shelter and protection, peeked unwantedly from behind the screen.

While the parapets on the country houses had no better foundation than fashion, it was a fashion that had a powerful motivation behind it. It followed the all pervading influence of London. And in London the parapets were not the result of caprice but of sound, solid practicality.

When four-fifths of mediaeval London disappeared in a holocaust of smoke and flame in 1666 the large extent of the destruction was caused by the building practices of the times. Half-timbered walls and thatched roofs were veritable tinder boxes. Upper floors, cantilevering beyond lower floors until occupants of third floors of houses on opposite sides of narrow streets could often shake hands, led the fire across a practically unbroken carpet of inflammable roof tops. To prevent a repetition of the catastrophe London buildings were controlled by a series of Building Acts starting in 1667. House heights were limited by streets to two, three or four storeys plus a basement—the number of storeys reflected the social importance of the street.

The main purpose of the Acts was fire control but the result on architectural form was violent. Timbering was out and walls had to be made of fire-resisting brick or stone only. Party walls between adjacent buildings, and even those between buildings closer than thirty feet, had to be carried up as a parapet at least one foot six inches above the roof. The disposition and construction of fireplaces were controlled. Amending Acts in 1707 and 1709 prohibited the use of any timber closer than four inches to the face of a building. As a result, door and window frames were pushed back from the wall plane and into the naked reveals instead of being flush with the outside as they had been before. An incidental effect was a pleasing indication of solidity. Much more importantly, eaves overhangs, with their necessary rafter projection and timber lining, were no longer possible. The same Act required buildings to provide a rainwater gutter on the street face of buildings to prevent deterioration of footpaths. The only answer to these two conditions was to carry the wall up to form a parapet. It was also found that by doing so another unintended benefit came to passers-by, who no longer ran the risk of being bombarded with a deluge of hard snow sliding unexpectedly off roofs in a thaw. A vestige of the timber eaves cornice remained where a purposeless stone cornice marked the line of the roof behind. Buildings crowded hard up to each other on narrow subdivided strips of land and rose three or four storeys high to make the most of limited ground area. Rows of such buildings lined the streets. Because of the restrictive regulations they had an unavoidable relationship to each other—a uniformity that was often deliberately used to advantage by speculative builders developing a whole length of street and designing the whole series as one related piece.

The London Georgian that developed under these conditions was a distinctive style. The two-storeyed, solid, squat, in-the-round modelled Country Georgian was translated into a two-, three- or four-storeyed narrow-shouldered, peculiarly flat-faced perpendicular style in which the success of the one face presented to public view depended more than ever on pleasing texture and good proportions. Instead of being related to a landscape of trees, lawns and water its good manners were displayed in its acknowledgment of its neighbours.

Most of these buildings were erected as speculative ventures by anyone with enough courage, knowledge, interest or ambition to try. While all types of people, high and low, could and did contribute to it, it was the craftsmen, particularly bricklayers and carpenters, who were at the fore-front in creating the face of Georgian London. The London craftsman of the times was 'a man of considerable skill and status—proud, conscientious and expensive,' according to Sir John Summerson, the biographer of Georgian London.[1] He was a member of a proud class, literate and, in the tempo of the times, burningly ambitious. This, combined with the opportunity of building a burgeoning London, led him to aim for the goals of either social status or material wealth. With the educating help of innumerable books of building design which were published especially for their benefit, those who strove for the former became, by the mid-eighteenth century, professional architects and those chasing the latter, master-builders. It was an unnatural cleavage which has been a burdensome cross for building ever since. It is an unfortunate fact of the life cycle that all great achievements, one of whose hallmarks is a quality of integration and unity, carry within themselves the seeds of their own destruction. So it was that the high summer of Georgian England spawned the division of architecture and building just as it did that of science and art.

The Georgian building tastes, whether in London, the towns or the country, were the purview of the upper class—the sole arbiters of design. Something like fifty years separated their standards from those of the lower class. It took this time for the decisions of their superiors to percolate into the humble homes of the bulk of the populace. They did so via the second-hand shops selling cast out furniture or clothes and by imitation in which a new generation could accept a change of manners, speech or building because it had been brought up with it. They were no longer innovations but traditions. By the time the third George reigned even the humblest house accepted arrangements of glazed sash windows symmetrically balanced either side of a central doorway, brick walls and hipped roof. Thus, with a time lag, the ideas discussed in the salons of the fine homes, at the meetings of the Dilettanti Society or the Architects' Club or promulgated by the Earl of Burlington whose home, Burlington House, was itself an exemplar of its owner's ideas, reached out into the whole of England. On their journey down the social ladder the finer edges were often lost or blurred, became debased by crudeness or lack of understanding; but the essentials remained. Because the original decisions were so very right for their time and conditions, Georgian England was suffused in a golden harmony of supremely good design.

Such was the England by which 750 or so men and women were cast out. Eight months later the coast of New South Wales appeared as a smudge on the horizon. After a tedious but safe voyage they were almost at their journey's end. The bulk of the convicts, for the most part the dregs of British society, neither knew nor worried about what lay ahead. They lived for the day only. The unknown held few terrors for them because, no matter what it was, it could not be worse than the sordid world they had known before. The officers, however, were from a different social level. They had heard the stories based upon the reports of the early French and English explorers of the South Seas about the noble savage. Building upon the rose-tinted pictures painted by Joseph Banks and the versatile Denis Diderot, the supplementary chronicler of the travels of Louis Antoine de Bougainville, a Rousseauesque cult had sprung up in the drawing-rooms and coffee-houses extolling the idyllic life of unsullied leisure, grace and purity led by the dark-skinned Adams and Eves of this antipodean Eden.

Unencumbered by material possessions, unworried by a desire for them, these unfettered children of nature were pictured as living in a tranquil Arcadian paradise of sunshine, green fields and crystal streams where ferocious or dangerous animals and disease were unknown, spending their days strolling through cool, shading woods or fishing idly in sapphire waters teeming with fish, and their nights feasting on unlimited mountains of delicacies and making innocent love under an unbelievably brilliant and scintillating canopy of stars. It was, however, not merely a primitivist's dream. Diderot's Tahitians were rational and highly-civilized men who, far from swaying to the promptings of Nature, studied and analysed it, took what was best from its lessons and tried to live accordingly. It was a picture that held great appeal for the Georgians who, yearning for Utopia, saw in it a heightened version of their own excellences without the sordidness and inequality which formed such a large part of their own world.

Cook's own glowing report of 1771 was in no small way responsible for the vision. As well as giving a romantically transmogrified picture of the lean naked Australian aborigines he enthused fulsomely of the country where 'it can never be doubted but what most sorts of Grain, Fruits, Roots etc of every kind would flourish' and where 'here are Provender for more Cattle at all seasons of the year than can be brought into this Country.'

Consequently, to the civil and military officers on the ships, the dark line on the horizon gradually taking more definite form was an exciting thing. Lush fields, verdant pastures, warm rich earth watered by copious rivers, tall stands of timber and handsome courtly savages awaited them. The best they had brought with them would merge with what was already there and both cultures would be enriched; the unfortunate worst, the convicts, would be regenerated and rehabilitated by 'the soft harmonizing arts of peace and civilization', as Lieutenant David Collins noted. It was a heart-quickening prospect hardly touched by apprehension.

As the coastline became cliffs and the ships sailed through a gap into the calm broad expanse of Botany Bay sails were furled, chains rattled and anchors splashed. They had arrived. It was 19 January 1788.

[1] Summerson, John, *Georgian London*, Pleiades Books, London 1945, p. 53.

2

The reality was far from the expectation. To the dismayed eyes on the ships the prospect of Botany Bay was unbelievable. Bare sand dunes and flat seas of sword grass and swamps constituted the area so strongly recommended by Sir Joseph Banks. It hardly needed an exploratory party to confirm that this was an unsuitable place for a settlement.

When a party did scout the area and returned with the depressing information that there was only the merest trickle of fresh water and no building material to be found, Phillip immediately decided to search for something better. A few miles up the coast he found, where Cook had surmised there might be 'an anchorage for a boat', a deep well-sheltered 'paradise of waters . . . a noble and capacious harbour . . . capable of affording security for a much larger fleet than would probably ever seek shelter in it.' The natural rock quays could take the longest ships in perfect safety. Some seven miles from the entrance to the harbour, which he named Port Jackson, Phillip found a small freshwater stream feeding into a small well-wooded bay with dusty ageless gum trees crowding down to its rocky edge. He fixed on it as the site for his settlement, named it Sydney Cove after the Home Secretary and brought up his ships. Six days after arriving at Botany Bay the First Fleet rode at anchor at Sydney Cove.

On 26 January 1788 in the oppressive heat of a mid-summer's day the building of a nation began. Marines paraded while convicts toiled and swore, felled trees, cleared ground, set up a forge, landed provisions and erected the first structures in Australia—tents and marquees for the officers and guards. By 6 February canvas accommodation was sufficiently established to land the women convicts, and the next day Phillip was sworn in in the terms of his commission as Captain-General and Governor-in-Chief of a domain covering seven and a half million square miles.

With the first emergencies met and the formalities completed the confusion of the first week gave way to order and the real business of the venture got under way. It had been planned not only to punish the convicts by banishment but to use their labour to establish another colonial monument to the power and greatness of the British way of life. The aboriginal inhabitants were to be given the benefits of civilization in exchange for which it was expected they would take a respectful position of servitude on the lowest rung of the social ladder. But the aborigines, the noble savages, spurned the opportunity. They showed a disinterest amounting to disdain for the knowledge, customs, goods and trinkets of civilization and refused to co-operate. The convicts, who were what they were because they had already declared for gambling, thieving or forgery in preference to honest labour, remained unconverted in their outlook. Their aversion to work of any kind was so inbred that most of them remained unswayed by fear of the lash, solitary confinement or starvation rations. The humane Phillip soon found himself, against his will and inclination, forced to make an example of one rebellious malcontent by sending him to his Maker on the end of a rope. Despite the high hopes, the worst aspects of Georgian society had survived the sea trip and were the first parts to show themselves in the new land.

Apart from the tents and what has been described as a prefabricated timber and canvas structure bought by Phillip out of his own funds and intended as a government house, a structure which he found 'neither wind nor water-proof', the expedition had brought practically no building materials. It was intended that the countryside should provide the raw materials and the convicts the labour. It was soon found that they had come lamentably equipped with tools also. Many necessary items were missing altogether and those which they did have were of such inferior quality that they were soon bent, twisted or blunted—useless for working the hard local timber. One of the first requests sent home by Phillip was for a large supply of axes, saws, chisels, augers, gimlets, nails, paint, lead and glass. When these eventually arrived, some two years later, their quality was no better than of those they had brought with them. In the meantime the settlers had to make do with what was to hand. Tools were constantly being repaired or refashioned and tradesmen often found it best to have new implements made at the forge with scrap metal from the ships.

The site chosen for the settlement had fine stands of timber. Some of the trees were of 'monstrous bulk' measuring up to twenty-seven feet around and taking sixteen men six days to grub out the stump. But the wood was too hard for the inferior axes and warped and split in the heat of the sun. In the valleys between the hills at the back of the settlement, however, they found the cabbage-tree palm whose trunk was long and straight with little natural taper, and which split easily into shingles and, most importantly, was soft enough to be worked with the tools available.

Convicts were set to work cutting down the trees and adzing or pit-sawing them

A slab and bark hut (restored) at Advancetown,
via Nerang, Queensland

into sizes suitable for building. It was unpleasant work. The log to be sawn was manoeuvred by smaller log rollers, levers and wedges over a long pit some six feet deep until it lay lengthways along the pit supported on halved cross-logs laid flat side down. Two men operated a heavy double-handled pit-saw. One stood in the pit below the log and pulled the saw downwards, getting showered with sawdust which stuck grittily to his sweating body for his pains. The other bestrode upright on the log itself and, in exchange for being spared the sawdust baptism, had the more skilled and heavier part of the job—starting the cut in a notch axed in the end of the log, guiding the line of cut and dragging the heavy saw upwards. He was called the top-notcher, a term that has passed into the Australian vernacular to denote the best, most expert or foremost in anything.

A search through the convict lists produced twelve carpenters who, together with sixteen ships' carpenters pressed into the work, were charged with erecting the first proper buildings. Amongst Phillip's official retinue of officers was Henry Brewer, who held what was the purely nominal rank of midshipman. Brewer was, in fact, an old crony of Phillip's and had been associated with him as a sort of friend and personal servant both in and out of the navy since 1778. Brewer seems to have been a very likable individual with a warm personality and a full complement of human strengths and frailties. A contemporary who knew them both in their pre-First Fleet days said he, Brewer, was 'an excellent scholar . . . and a very great assistant to the lieutenant' and that while it would not be possible to find 'a more disinterested or honester steward' he was unfortunately 'addicted to liquor and strong language'. Brewer had been born in London in 1743 or 1744 and is thought to have trained first as a carpenter and then found work as an architect's clerk. When the intended Provost-Marshal of the venture failed to join the expedition before the fleet left Portsmouth, Phillip appointed Brewer to the post in a temporary capacity and confirmed the appointment on 26 January 1788. Because of his building experience, limited though it was, Brewer also served as the first, but unofficial, Superintendent of Works. It was an exacting job in the circumstances but until the official appointment of James Bloodsworth (often spelled Bloodworth) to the position Brewer exerted his influence as well as he could on the exigencies of Sydney's birth. When he died in Sydney as a result of the privations of the colony and his weakness for strong drink, on 26 August 1796, he left no directly attributable buildings. The standard building that evolved from the hands of convict and ships' carpenters under the guidance of Henry Brewer used materials readily to hand, was put together with the maximum of speed and was primitive in the extreme. Recognizing only the immediate need to provide shelter, the form was the simplest with which the builders were familiar—the plain hip-roofed box still to be found throughout the rural areas of the Grampians, the Midlands or the Cornish countryside of Home. Only the nature of the materials used gives it any individuality.

In New South Wales heavy posts six inches square were set directly into the ground for the corners in a rectangular plan about twelve feet by nine feet. Other squared posts were then set directly into the ground three feet apart around the wall lines. Sawn timbers were fixed as plates to the top of the posts and on these were erected an open-couple roof system of unsawn rafters cut from slim saplings. Lengthwise across the rafters were tied triangular-sectioned battens—the outside off-cuts from the logs of the saw-pits. With the frame completed short lengths of saplings with shaped ends were slipped into vertical grooves worked into the side faces of the posts. The whole of the outer face of the building was then given a heavy coating of mud, applied with a spade and smoothed off with a trowel, to keep out the wind and the rain. Then, to try to preserve this perishable finish, the mud was coated with pipe-clay found abundantly in the nearby bays, or white-washed with lime made by burning oyster shells collected by the convict women.

The roof, invariably of hipped form, was thatched with reeds cut from nearby swamps such as those in the area preserved in the name of Rushcutters Bay.

Holes were left in one long wall for a central door flanked by two unglazed windows. To conserve precious materials the pitching line of the roof was kept to about seven feet. Consequently, doorways were six feet or even less in height. Doors were of the most simple ledge-and-brace construction hung on leather hinges, while windows were protected by shutters of latticed wattles sliding in grooved rails fixed to the outside face of the wall. A fireplace of heavy mud with a sandstone-flagged hearth provided for cooking and heating. Chimneys were built from timber heavily parged with clay inside and finished in the same fashion as the rest of the walls outside. A trampled earth or packed clay floor completed the building.

So, with the minimum use of skilled labour, the minimum wear and tear on poor but nevertheless valuable tools and a minimum expenditure of equally precious nails, temporarily sufficient single-celled shadeless shelters were provided. In their miniature size, their spartan simplicity and their facial arrangement of central nose-like doorway and two eye-like windows, they had a naive child-like air. But these very qualities together with their overall similarity gave a homogeneity and consistency that in itself was not unpleasing and held the echo of a cultivated background. However, erection of even these simple structures had to await the carrying out of more urgent work such as clearing the ground for crops. By June 1788 only four of the officers had huts and the principal business of the settlement had become the erection of huts for the marines and convicts. The rainy season had commenced and it was realized that 'living in tents is truly uncomfortable and likely to give a severe trial to the strongest and most robust constitution.'

Within months these early efforts began to deteriorate. The mud washed from the walls in Sydney's heavy downpours and the thatching proved inadequate. The supply of the easily worked cabbage-tree palm was cut out but a new and better material was found in 'a species of pine'—the she-oak which grew thickly in the area. Its bark had better qualities for covering roofs and walls than the rushes and its timber split easily and satisfactorily into shingles. Bark held down by transverse saplings to prevent curling or shingles fixed by wooden pegs fashioned by the female convicts began to replace the thatching on the roofs. Broad slabs of timber set directly into the ground with cracks pugged with clay replaced the so-called wattle-and-daub wall construction of the first houses. Such buildings were still inadequate and an alternative soon became a pressing necessity.

By April 1788 a bed of clay suitable for making bricks was found on the far side of the steep hill to the south of the town, brickmaking equipment was found in the stores and James Bloodsworth, a brickmaker by trade, was found amongst the convicts. Three months after the fleet's arrival at Sydney Cove the first bricks were available.

The brickmaking process was the traditional one that had been used in England and Europe for hundreds of years. It was modified only by the limitations of the materials and skills available and the urgency for turning out bricks. Clay was ground by pummelling and pounding the raw lumps with heavy tree-trunk pestles in natural rock depressions. There was neither the time nor the equipment to obtain fine grinding of the clay, which was left coarse and gravelly. Water was added and with bare-legged convicts tramping around in the mess a sticky pug was worked up. Allowed to stand for a few days instead of the two to three months that it would have been given in England, it was hastened to the moulding table. This table, about six feet long by three feet wide and high, was made of wood. It was moved to the clay and for this reason was often fitted with rough wheels. At one end of the table was set a trough of water and at the back of it, or on the ground beside the moulder, a barrel of sand. To the top of the table was fixed a 'stock'—a flat board one inch thick and the size of the largest face of the brick. The word itself comes from the Teutonic word for 'board'. The mould was made of one inch thick timber the size of the brick to be made plus the depth of the stock over which it fitted snugly. The top edges of the mould were protected from wear by strips of metal.

To make the brick the stock was dusted with sand, the mould dipped in the water and similarly sanded and slipped into position over the stock. A clod of pug a little larger than the required amount was thrown into the mould and pressed by hand well into the corners. The excess material was removed and the top surface levelled by drawing a ten inches by two inches by three-quarter inch wooden 'strike' across the top of the mould. If the brickmaker found the clay not tight into the corner he would sometimes press it into shape with his thumb, a practice which has given rise to the false story that thumb prints were a tally mark of a man's production made for the benefit of the overseer. The mould containing the clay was removed from the stock and the formed brick, slipping on the sand lining, discharged on to another flat piece of board or pallet. With three bricks on it the pallet was removed and the bricks stacked in an open grille pattern to allow air to circulate and dry them. The pile of bricks was covered with rushes or, later, straw to prevent too-quick drying. In Sydney's summer two or three days were sufficient for this but in the first few months even this time was cut to a day. Then the bricks were fired. The first ones were fired in a rough kiln, itself made of unburnt bricks, but once the first burnt bricks were obtained round kilns were properly constructed. The fuel used was wood cut from the slopes around the pits. The heat was built up slowly and a week later the kiln was broken open. The low burning temperature of the wood and the too-short burning time resulted in what were, by later standards, poor quality bricks—soft and porous. The underburning was also responsible for the pleasant light brown or salmon colour which gave to them the name 'samel' or 'sandal' bricks. It is recorded that in England in 1763 working this way a man by himself could turn out one thousand bricks in a fourteen-hour day. With another man to work up the matrix and another to carry the pallets away he could produce at least two thousand or, if a willing worker, three thousand in the same time. By comparison, in a gang of twenty-two the early Australian brickmakers turned out forty thousand bricks and roof tiles in a month. The first Australian bricks, being made from government-supplied equipment, were probably close to the size laid down by the British laws.

This description of the first brickmaking has been given in some detail because in its essence it was the method used to make all bricks until 1870. Improvements in the technique came as the country became more sophisticated and the demand for quality became more important than speed and quantity. Machines, either hand or steam powered, were used to grind the clay finely, horses instead of convicts squelched through the pug; later, powered mechanical mixers, moulds turning out two or four bricks at a time and heavy presses to force the clay into denser bricks (hence allowing less water to be used and less distorted bricks to be turned out) were developed; the raw bricks were stacked longer and turned frequently; coal and then coke were used for fuel, thus burning a harder and more impervious brick. But these were refinements only. The brick of the 1860s was a better and more reliable product than that turned out by the first convict moulders working under the guidance of James Bloodsworth on Brickfield Hill in 1788, but it was made the same way.

The workers in the brickfields also turned out burned clay roof tiles. Flat shingle slabs, they were fixed to roof battens by timber pegs whittled by the convict women. However, they were too thin and of poor quality. Lying unprotected on the roof they soon rotted into powder and for this reason were never popular.

Because of the scarcity of building materials those of any quality—bricks, tiles, stone and lime—were at first reserved for official works. The first worthwhile batch of these was earmarked for a residence for the Governor. With it the first building with any pretensions to architectural quality was erected on the brow of the hill on the eastern side of the stream along which the community clustered and with a commanding view over the settlement and the ships in the Cove. The date was July 1788, just six months after arrival.

The Governor had laid a foundation stone in May for a residence which was to be on the western hill overlooking Long Cove (Darling Harbour), but disagreement with his Lieutenant-Governor, Major Robert Ross, the senior army officer, had caused him to hand this site over to his second-in-command and select a new one for himself.

The materials were rough, the skills of the tradesmen were mediocre and the design was unlettered, but with them James Bloodsworth managed to erect what one officer of marines described as 'an elegant brick house'. Only by comparison did it deserve the adjective. It was rude and crude in all ways except for its innate quality of proportions and simplicity bred of the Georgian conditioning of all those involved with it—an unconscious sense of fitness and design that even twelve thousand miles could not eliminate.

It was originally intended to build a single-storeyed three-roomed cottage but when the foundations were found to be sufficiently firm it was decided to increase its size. Measuring fifty-three feet by twenty feet on plan, it eventuated as a two-storeyed building of brick set in lime and hair mortar on a stone base and with stone quoins at the corners. (There are no indigenous long-hair-bearing animals in Australia and the hair for the mortar came from sheep the expedition had brought from England and the Cape of Good Hope. The flock of one hundred sheep was meant to provide the settlement with fresh mutton and the animals were of a type that grew hair, not wool. But nothing was wasted in the material-desperate colony.) A hipped tile-covered roof protected the building and sat tightly on the walls with a mere few inches overhanging at the eaves. Double-hung glazed sashes brought out with the fleet were set in the window openings. The sashes were five panes high on the ground floor and four panes high on the upper floor, arranged symmetrically and evenly spaced either side of the building's only conscious architectural feature. This was a central portion of the front wall some nine feet wide, projecting a brick thickness in front of the line of the face of the rest of the wall, with stone quoins at the angles and capped by a gable roof. On the axis of the panel were mounted the main doorway with its six-panelled door, a semi-circular fanlight and glazed side lights, all embraced within a round-headed opening. Above the entrance a four-pane high double-sash window lined up with the other first floor windows and at the top, in the gable, was the only purely decorative fancy that the designer allowed himself—a blind roundel surrounded by a margin of unmoulded smooth-faced stone.

The building would have drawn nothing but disdainful looks in England but in the six-months old colony it won plaudits and approval. Even the aborigines, who were not impressed by any of the other wonders of the white man, were astonished by the miracle of the staircase. When Phillip, having at last made contact with them by forceful abduction of one of their number in a shameful piece of deceit and trickery for which he justly received a spear in the shoulder, showed his captive the delights of civilization, only the spectacle of men walking around above the heads of other men moved him to amazement. The building served as Government House for fifty-six years. Frequently enlarged and altered and continuously repaired, propped up and replaced, it was vilified, spurned, complained about and unwillingly occupied by successive dissatisfied governors until Governor Bourke convinced London that it really was 'extremely inconvenient, subject to bad smells and irreparable'. In the middle of 1845 Governor Gipps moved into

Above Slab buildings near Perthville, New South Wales, showing the two types of slab construction
Below A slab hut near Vineyard, New South Wales

a new Gothic castle leaving the first Government House to the disgruntled shades of his predecessors.

As bricks started to come from the kilns in quantity other permanent buildings arose—a dry-store near the wharf on the south side of the Cove, a military barracks for the soldiers on the western hill and houses for the civil officers. Bloodsworth was responsible for designing, making most of the materials and erecting them. The Governor valued his contribution in the vital field of building so highly that in 1790 Bloodsworth was granted a pardon which returned him to the ranks of respectable men. When he died in 1804, widely esteemed and regretted, he held the official position of Superintendent of Buildings and had been responsible for many of the private and most of the public buildings in Sydney.

Within a year of its foundation, then, Sydney's buildings were being built of brick. The better ones were roofed with clay tiles while grass or reed thatching, timber shingles or bark protected the others. But building continued to be a discouraging business. The shortage of lime was desperate. While the vicinity was plentifully supplied with sandstone there was no limestone to be found. Only by the slow and laborious process of collecting shells around the shore and burning them could a little lime be produced. There was none to spare for private building. As a result bricks had to be set in clay and mud reinforced with grass or hair. In the heavy rains the mortar softened or washed out. In an attempt to combat this, walls were increased to extraordinary thickness. Even so their precarious instability restricted wall heights to less than twelve feet. Consequently, all buildings with the exception of the Governor's house were single storeyed.

For several years some buildings continued to be erected with wattle-and-daub or timber-slab mud-plastered walls when money was scarce. But even the poorest houses had brick fireplaces and chimneys. The early techniques persisted in the developing areas for seventy years or more with very little variation. In 1826 Surgeon Peter Cunningham told intending settlers that the skeleton of a 24′ × 12′ building of this type with an attached 24′ × 7′ skilling could be erected for eight pounds and fully finished with its windows, doors, thatching and whitewash for twenty pounds. The roof was usually thatched if suitable 'blady grass' was available as it was found that its heat insulating properties were greatly superior to those of bark. Considering the low cost involved in replacing the building should it burn down, the disadvantage of the greater fire risk was probably worthwhile. A sawyer who contracted to build a new farmhouse in 1830 described the way he went about it.

> The first step of its erection was digging post-holes, of about two feet deep, at various distances around the circumference, and along the interior divisions, in which were placed posts ten feet high, squared on the four sides with the axe, excepting the two feet let into the ground, where the whole strength of the timber was left. Along the ground between these, as well as along the tops, wherever there was to be a wall, were laid ground-plates and wall-plates, of about the same size, and squared on the sides facing each other, and having a groove of about an inch and a half wide and two inches deep mortised into the flat sides their whole length. Into these grooves were fitted the two ends of the eight-feet slabs we had split with the maul and wedges. The roof was made much in the usual way only, being for some time to come to continue covered with bark, the battens were not put so close together as they would have been if the roof had had to be shingled. The floor-boards, according to the custom of the country, were six inches wide and one thick; timber being used so green, and the heat being so great, boards of any greater width turn up at the edges. The rooms were all joisted at top and on the joists was spread a floor of bark, so as to form, over the whole top of the house, the settler's

first rude granary. Squares of a couple of feet each way were left open on the wall in various places for windows; at present, however, they were only fitted with shutters. The chimneys were large, like those of old farm-houses, and for security, had a little wall of rough stone and mortar run up inside about three feet; and in the middle of the fireplace was a large flag-stone, of a sort capable of resisting the fire, which constituted the hearth and baking-place.[1]

Basically the same thing was built in Sydney during the first ten years. The Reverend Richard Johnson, whose endeavours to carry out his Christian duty met with little encouragement from the rationalist Phillip and his officers, having been denied government funds to build a church, had to finance it out of his own pocket. Consequently, he had to resort to the cheapest method, wattle-and-daub, when he built Australia's first church in 1793.

All the earliest building techniques met with disheartening results. Whether brick, wattle-and-daub or slab, the buildings were unstable affairs. The mud of the mortar covering the wattles washed out easily in Sydney's heavy rains. For years later walls sagged and chimneys collapsed. In November 1803 the *Sydney Gazette* told its readers with a touch of relief, 'The late very heavy weather has not been attended with any material accident that we can learn. A few pannels of houses built upon the principle of ancient colonial architecture were washed down. One family was persecuted by this species of disaster; for on Monday night the falling in of a whole side left them shelterless, and obliged them to remove to an opposite house next morning, but at between eight and nine at night the crash of decaying wattles was repeated.'

For years similar items continued to appear in the *Sydney Gazette* after every heavy downpour. The paper constantly pressed for better construction in the colony particularly in those buildings belonging to what it was pleased to call 'the lower orders'. It pointed out the dangers associated with the 'slight construction' of wattle-and-daub or slab buildings; it printed articles on the shortcomings of grass thatching—the excessive weight caused by its necessary thickness, its poor waterproofing, its smell, the danger of spontaneous combustion and the refuge it offered for birds, lice and vermin—and urged people to use wooden shingles or at least dried straw instead of green grass for thatching. Poor construction was to plague the colony for many years. In 1802 a severe earthquake rippled through Parramatta and found many of its buildings wanting. In 1804 the heavy walls of a large stone building being erected near Hospital Wharf for Isaac Nicholls were blown down during a storm. In the same year the house of Samuel Terry caught fire when a beam which had been built into a chimney during the addition of a room 'cherished a spark, which accumulating strength . . . nearly burnt the house down.' Until after 1810 never a week and seldom a day went by without at least one house being burned down from a fire starting in the chimney.

From the very first day attempts were made to use the local timbers for building and naval purposes. While some of them, such as ironbark, were adjudged better than oak for shipbuilding, their extraordinary hardness was discouraging to builders with poor tools. At Parramatta two government stores were built with a timber frame and sheeted with planks cut from huge red-gums. But after their completion in mid-1788 the boards had twisted and split so badly that they were useless and 'in a Tottering condition', according to a report written in November of the same year. The timber had to be used green in all the first buildings and this was a constant source of trouble. Consequently, all authorities on timber soon voted the wood of all gum trees as fit only for burning.

The site of Parramatta had been discovered within a few months of the arrival at Sydney Cove. Fourteen miles further up the harbour where it narrows to a river, it had magnificent stands of tall straight trees, softly undulating country, clayey soil highly suitable for growing vegetables and grain and was free of rock—very different from the steep craggy site of Sydney with its thin covering of poor soil and stony surface. In November 1788 Phillip had named the area Rose Hill after the Secretary of the Treasury. A year later, with the colony in the grip of famine, the Governor decided to test his theory that a man working freely for himself was a better social asset than one slaving unwillingly for the Government and that an industrious man could be self-sufficient on two acres of good land. He chose James Ruse, granted him his freedom and land at Rose Hill in January 1790. Within twelve months Ruse had proved Phillip right. In the meantime it was decided to develop the area as a second town. In July 1790 the lines of a town were laid out by Lieutenant William Dawes and the establishment of a town proclaimed by the Governor.

Dawes produced Australia's first effective town plan. He was a well-educated man of ability and ingenuity with a reputation for studiousness, cheerfulness, kindness and religiousness without sanctimony which his contemporaries found 'most admirable'. He was the son of a clerk-of-works at Portsmouth and from his father he had acquired a knowledge of building and engineering which made the young naval officer a valuable man in the colony. Almost immediately after the arrival of the First Fleet Dawes was appointed Engineer and Artillery Officer and in this capacity was responsible for several defensive batteries protecting the settlement. His rough erection on the western point to Sydney Cove with its guns pointing down the harbour, known as Dawes Battery, has long since disappeared; but children clamber over some of the guns set in a lawn landscape under the shadow of Sydney Harbour Bridge as it leaps across the water from Dawes Point.

As one of his first duties Dawes was required to design the plan for Parramatta by building on a survey that had been carried out by the Surveyor-General, Baron Alt, at Phillip's direction. The result of Dawes' work was 'a plan of grace balance charm and utility', in the view of a contemporary. It was a grid road system running north and south with the town edging on to the south side of the Parramatta River— a fine Renaissance scheme in the best Classic manner. In Dawes' plan the main thoroughfare, the present George Street, was a 205 feet wide avenue running straight east and west between a Government House set in parklands on the brow of a gently rising slope and the Government Store at the riverside. The main cross street, the present Church Street, was 143 feet wide with a grand vista to the Town Hall, which was to be set in a generous plaza and gardens at the river's edge. The other streets were 118 feet wide and service lanes were 76 feet wide. Throughout the scheme vistas were centred on important buildings of the future. Provision was made for such buildings as a school, a courthouse, a church, barracks, a market, a hospital and two inns, together with ample parks and open spaces, all symmetrically arranged around the two main axis streets.

Phillip had seen the need for a controlled development of Sydney. Accordingly, within a few weeks of the landing, he had set Baron Alt to drawing up a plan for the future development of that town. The Surveyor-General conceived an orderly arrangement of wide streets running along the contours and sited to catch the cooling breezes blowing along the gully. The streets were to be lined with 60 feet wide blocks of land 150 feet deep with each block holding one house only. Provision was made for public buildings. Circumstances worked to frustrate the plan from the beginning and it was never even adopted let alone effective. The only vestige of that first aborted town plan that still exists, but by chance not design, is the narrow Lang Street running obliquely between Grosvenor and York Streets. Other more modest plans for Sydney were produced in the early months of 1788. In March Captain Hunter drew up what was essentially a military camp and in April Francis Fowkes, a convict, tried his hand. Neither got any further than the paper on which they were drawn. Drought, crop failure and the threat of starvation loomed as a major and ever present problem for the first two years and the sheer struggle to survive occupied everybody's mind. Ready accessibility to water was essential for people in these circumstances and buildings clustered along the banks of the town's water supply. It was the magnet of the Tank Stream and the scarcity of water, not the will of a planner, that determined the form and layout of the Sydney streets of today as they ran along the banks of the stream or led down the hills to it.

At Parramatta the self-interest and avarice that were to plague the colony when the spectre of starvation subsided were already stirring. The lines of Dawes' plan were soon being breached. As Phillip was the only person in the colony who cared for the legacy they would leave to posterity, the plan finally broke down completely on his departure. The élite of the New South Wales Corps played havoc with the nobly conceived if modest dream. Buildings crept towards the centre of the streets or ignored them altogether in accordance with the personal convenience of land-owners. Streets became narrow, alley-ways developed. The town became cramped and mean. When, in later years, attempts were made to clean up the mess things had gone too far for even the bones of Dawes' plan to be recaptured. In 1811 Surveyor Meehan, in a slovenly job of planning, allowed Church Street to leap across the river at its northern end instead of terminating at the Town Hall as proposed by Dawes and gave it an ugly kink at its south end to link up directly with the road coming from Sydney.

In December 1792, sick in body, disillusioned in mind but still hopeful in heart for the future, Phillip left the colony he had guided through the shoals of hardship, difficulty, incipient chaos and failure into the deep waters of comparative safety. He took with him the affection and respect of all those whose lives had been in his calm, warm hands for five years. Before he left he had seen that while the settlement remained a penal camp depending on the efforts of thieves and their guards the growth and development that he believed possible could not come about. He believed that the natural potential which he saw about him could only be realized by the introduction of free settlers, the emancipation of worthy convicts and the granting of land to them to be worked with the help of assigned convicts. Two free settlers, Henry Dods, Phillip's personal gardener, and a transient passenger en route for China named Smith who had decided to stay, had arrived with the First Fleet. Both men had proved themselves able to offer valuable services to the community. The experiment of emancipating Ruse had proved a success. Both events had confirmed Phillip in his belief.

Phillip's ideas had been strongly opposed by the army led by his Lieutenant-Governor. To them the settlement was, and should remain, purely a military punishment camp for the correction of the wayward and the exaction of society's penalty. Any benefits to be milked from the venture should belong to those forced to suffer its privations without just cause—the military, particularly the officers and their civil counterparts. Free settlers and any thoughts of economic develop-ment were both unnecessary and a hindrance. Therefore, it was left to Phillip's successor, Major Francis Grose, an amiable man but one of considerably less talent than Phillip, to throw the land open for development. But he adopted a very different means for achieving it than Phillip had in mind. Under Grose land grants were made to the military officers. Grose undertook to supply convict labour to work the grants productively and to purchase the surplus produce for the Govern-ment stores. He also gave the officers a monopoly to purchase the cargoes of ships which began to call at Sydney and to sell their purchases at their own prices. In addition, Grose permitted convicts to work for wages after they had completed their regulation daily stint for the Government and also for the wages to be paid in rum.

As a result of Phillip's submissions to the Secretary of State, free settlers began to trickle into the colony. They brought with them the wants, needs and drive of free men prepared to suffer present hardship for a future fortune. With this growth of activity—the arrival of shipping, trade, private enterprise and the demands of settlers—standards expanded and improved. Grose could exercise little restraint on the selfish and high-handed arrogance that enveloped the community as the elite tore at the carcass of the community for their own gain. The shortage of currency was both acute and chronic. Rum became the sole medium of exchange and control of its purchase was firmly in the hands of the officers. Taking it in turns to purchase the cargoes that arrived, they gained a throttle-hold on this vital commodity and hence on the whole settlement. Everybody wanted rum—the officers and settlers because it was their normal currency, the convicts who had ambitions for the future because it represented wealth and capital and the convicts who had none because it afforded release and oblivion from a hopeless and depressing present. When Governor Hunter arrived to take charge in 1795 he found the New South Wales colony swimming in spirits with all the rampant troubles of a rum-based economy.

The result of the expanded concept of the purpose of the settlement, the change of direction that followed the broadening of interest, was soon clear. Government building practically ceased as the emerging élite began to accumulate wealth and surround themselves with the privileges that their position warranted. When Phillip departed even the military officers were living in thatched wattle-and-daub hovels. Eighteen months later they were housed in comparatively comfortable and substantial stone and brick barracks. However, most of the community's energy was channelled into developing the private holdings and fortunes of the few free settlers and the officers. Out of the towns, tree-covered land grants were cleared and serious efforts were made to extract wealth from the soil by enlightened and determined, rather than desultory, agricultural practices.

The first plough in the colony which broke the ground at Parramatta in 1795 symbolized the spirit of the times. The plough was brought out by Captain John Macarthur whose fortunes, while a pinnacle of their class, nevertheless exemplified what was happening. Macarthur had come to Australia as a lieutenant with the New South Wales Corps when it arrived to relieve the marines who had accompanied the First Fleet. The marines had found the conditions in New South Wales far from their liking. Dissatisfaction had reached such proportions that a special volunteer corps had been raised to take over their duties. As a result it was composed of all the misfits, cowards and bullies of the regular units of the British Army. Generally the officers were men for whom personal ambition outweighed normal military considerations. Macarthur was a man with a lively mind and an aristocratic touchiness. On a grant of 250 acres at Parramatta, which he named Elizabeth Farm in honour of his wife, Macarthur developed an efficient and prosperous farm. Working a hundred acres of it with the labour of convicts, whom he ruled firmly, exactingly, uprightly and justly, and leading an impeccable private life, he laid the foundations of a vast personal estate and influence—a model for his slovenly contemporaries.

In 1794 Macarthur moved into a farmhouse he had caused to be built on the picked position of his land facing north and overlooking the Parramatta River. It was a single-storey building, rectangular in plan, consisting of four rooms, two either side of a large central entrance hall, and measuring sixty-eight feet by eighteen feet. The walls were of brick and the hipped roof was covered with swamp-oak shingles cut from local trees. In the fashion of the times the eaves were close cropped to the walls, the glazed windows were symmetrically disposed around the generous central doorway. The influence of a hot climate was not yet being manifested even in the country farmhouse where it was first to exert itself. A verandah with rooms at the corners ran along the east front but its purpose was that of an external passage—to give access to the rooms rather than protection from the rain and the heat of the sun. The kitchen, laundry, meat-house and servants' quarters were gathered in another building well and appropriately separated at the back. In its linear arrangement of rooms which allowed effective cross-ventilation and quick cooling by the evening breezes of the stifling air inside during high summer, Elizabeth Farm was the primitive prototype of Australian country farmhouses in New South Wales. Extended and altered over the years, it still serves as a pleasant private home—the oldest building in Australia.

By the late 1790s better standards of building were coming to the towns of Sydney and Parramatta. Footings and thresholds were made of local sandstone and walls were brick. The stone was obtained from random quarrying of the outcrops that occurred everywhere on the western ridge of the town, particularly that part now known as the West Rocks area. It was taken from or near the surface and consequently was usually soft and weathered and did not stand up well. The good stone was deep and the effort to obtain it was not worthwhile. Floors were made of pit-sawn planks six inches wide and one inch thick fixed to joists set directly into the earth with their upper faces flush with the soil surface. Internal walls were plastered with a mud reinforced with grass or hair for adhesion and cow dung to stop cracking, and painted. Ceilings closed off the roof space which served as a store and a heat insulating buffer. The ceilings were made of hessian fixed to the underside of joists and whitewashed or of bark laid on top. Door and window openings were spanned with timber lintels to carry the overhead brickwork. There was still no time, or skill, to build flat arches. Cottages were built bigger than before. They continued to be the plainest of buildings but, measuring no less than

Elizabeth Farm in Alice Street, Parramatta, New South Wales: 1793-94

twenty-four feet by twelve feet, even the most humble contained two rooms formed by one cross partition—one room for sleeping and the other for cooking, eating and general living. The central doorway opened directly into the living room in the end wall of which was built a wide stone fireplace for heating, cooking and comfort or discomfort, depending upon the season. Doors and window shutters, ledged and braced, had metal hinges and latches and glazed sashes were used more often than not.

The struggle to overcome the shortcomings of mud-mortar led to the development of an unusual half-timbering technique. By means of iron plates and bolts sturdy timbers were fixed together in one- or two-storey frames and filled with panels of brickwork instead of the all-too-impermanent wattling. The outside face was sheeted with weatherboards nailed directly onto the frame or fixed to battens on the brickwork. The boards were sometimes of local she-oak split with a tapered profile, but were frequently imported from Singapore or from the islands of the Pacific. While such buildings had all the external appearance of a weatherboard building of today, their inside walls were brick and could be plastered in the traditional manner. David Bevan's two-storeyed Union Hotel, opened in Sydney in 1798, was such a building. It was a method that was thoroughly satisfactory and had many advantages including heat insulation, provided the weatherboards did not split which, until the cedar forests around the Lane Cove, the Hawkesbury and the Hunter Rivers and later, the Illawarra were tapped, they often did. This 'weatherboard veneer' construction was the normal, and in fact only, weatherboard construction used throughout Australia until the timber frame technique was introduced from America with the migrants of the gold-rush period after 1850. Many buildings in the country such as the old Klensendorffe's Inn at Tahmoor, erected in 1825, are of this type and are still sound. It is interesting to note that in 1948 when the Commonwealth Experimental Building Station was faced with the task of finding new techniques of buildings in the postwar period it recommended 'weatherboard veneer' as a possibility. However, as it suffers from one of the main disadvantages of all timber buildings—high maintenance costs—its revival did not eventuate.

By the turn of the century the demands of the free settlers whose dreams were materializing, of the few emancipated convicts who were becoming men of substance, and of the 'pure merinos' of the Macarthur class created a need for houses larger and better than the cottages of the early years. The supply of materials increased to meet it and by migration and emancipation the pool of skilled labour increased to use them. These better-class homes had floors raised clear of the ground and an underground cellar; dust-proof tongue and grooved flooring made by grooving both edges and inserting a separate slip-tongue between abutting boards; walls smooth plastered with a rich lime setting-coat on top of a dung and hair-plaster base; ceilings similarly plastered onto a ground of thin closely-spaced wattles or lathes; cedar joinery, Georgian glazed sliding sash windows, tile or oak shingled roofs and a main doorway with a six-panelled door and glazed head and side lights. Glass was available in common sizes, $11'' \times 9''$ and $9'' \times 7''$, from the merchants and house-shops at a cost of a shilling for the larger and $9\frac{1}{2}$d for the smaller panes. The windows had delicate metal catches and recessed hinged lifts while the doors were hung on brass or wrought iron hinges fixed with hand-cut untapered screws and secured, not by a heavy wooden latch bar, but by cast brass locks and handles. Many of the houses were two-storeyed. All the available, but limited, cunning of the joiner's art was lavished on the main doorway and the staircase. Stairs were made simply with straight lengths of rounded handrails, plain one inch square baluster rods and square chamfered and nicked newel posts. Plain though they were, together with the doorways, were the most sophisticated parts of the building.

While the ordinary houses of the time were going through the struggles of shedding their thatched roofs and mud walls and gradually clambering towards an architectural respectability that was to be a chrysalis which would eventually emerge as a truly beautiful butterfly, government building resumed. After a five year hiatus following Phillip's departure, Governor Hunter launched an ambitious building programme. Grose's policy of the assignment of convicts to individuals had left the convict labour cupboard bare for government work. Hunter had to turn to hiring free men and even soldiers to carry his programme through. Under a contract system and with the supervision of Superintendent of Buildings Bloodsworth, he enlarged the Government House and built a storehouse, quarters for the hospital surgeons, a windmill, a particularly ungainly round-towered barnlike stone church on Church Hill and, in a flash of civic pride, a 150 feet high clock tower nearby. At Parramatta he caused to be built a two-storeyed brick Government House to replace the original primitive brick cottage built by Phillip; and St John's Church, a duplicate, except for the tower, of the St Philip's monstrosity on Church Hill. The architectural quality of these works varied greatly indicating the hands of several designers at work. However, except for the clock tower which has been attributed to Bloodsworth and which displayed a fine and elegant sensitiveness, the buildings were solid, stolid and aesthetically barren— basically military engineering rather than architectural in concept.

The pleasant amiable Hunter was no match for the wily hardheads fighting ruthlessly for their own personal empires in Sydney. His attempts to curb their excesses were flippantly brushed aside as a mere irritant by the monopolists who, with cheeky nonchalance, out-manoeuvred him by writing Home accusing him of the very crimes they themselves were so blatantly committing. Despite a pathetic explanation to Whitehall, Hunter was dismissed. Bewildered and relieved, he handed the reins to Philip Gidley King in 1800.

Governor King, gruff and bluff, soon found himself at loggerheads with his arrogant officers and many of his republican-minded subjects who delighted in bedevilling His Majesty's representative with such double-edged taunts as drinking 'Damnation to all kings'. Under King the colony slowly but unspectacularly expanded. Coal had been found at the Coal River, a hundred miles north of Sydney, in 1796. Hunter established a settlement of Sydney's criminals at what is now Newcastle both to mine the coal and get the recalcitrants out of the way. King despatched Lieutenant Bowen with a further batch of offenders to Van Diemen's Land in 1803 to establish the rule of His Brittanic Majesty in that island. Bowen landed on the east side of the Derwent River at Risdon Cove. Hardly had he erected his tents than David Collins, who had been sent out from England to establish a colony at Port Phillip but failing to find water had taken his expedition to the Derwent, took over command from Bowen, condemned Bowen's choice of site and moved the whole company to a small bay, Sullivan's Cove, on the opposite side of the river and founded Hobart.

Both the settlements at Newcastle and Hobart were prudently provided with prefabricated timber buildings but, as with all pioneering ventures, both found themselves in fact dependent on local materials for timber, lime, bricks and roof coverings. Talking of a prefabricated house which had been shipped to Newcastle the *Sydney Gazette* in 1804 said it was '24 feet by 12 . . . the whole morticed, tennanted, and ready for putting up when landed; the doors, windows, and roofing accompanied the frame, together with sufficient bricks for the erection of several chimneys. The work was executed at Parramatta in less than one week.'

At Hobart the first building, a house for Lieutenant Lord, was a thatch-roofed wattle-and-daub hut with a chimney built of sandstone obtained from an outcrop on the eastern head of the bay. As in Sydney bricks and roof tiles were being produced within five months of arrival. Collins believed they would prove the

Old Government House at Parramatta, New South Wales:
1800. Architect, James Bloodsworth (?);
porch and fanlight 1816 by Francis Greenway

best material for building but poor burning resulted in clay packs that were little better than sponges. It was noted by visitors that in houses built of them water could be seen running down the inside face of the walls during rainy weather. The trials and tribulations of inadequate building knowledge and materials that afflicted Sydney were part and parcel of the story of the early struggles in the scrape-and-make conditions of every new settlement for the first hundred years. Towards the end of 1804 an expedition was sent under Lieutenant-Governor Paterson to found a settlement at Port Dalrymple near the mouth of the Tamar River in the north of Van Diemen's Land. In his first report to Sydney Paterson joyfully told of the discovery amongst other building materials of abundant quantities of limestone in the area—'a boon hitherto denied the Territory'. Henceforth lime for mortar was much more readily available to everyone both in Van Diemen's Land and Sydney.

In Sydney, under Governor King, the town was swelling. By 1804 it consisted of 675 houses and 2,100 inhabitants. But building was still primitive and amateurish.

Government building was as rough and ready as any. The primitive conditions of the community and building are reflected in the following notice which appeared in the *Sydney Gazette* on 10 February 1805.

To be Erected at Sydney by Contract

A Court House of the following dimensions viz. 60 Feet long by 26, in the Clear, and the Wall 12 feet high from the ground floor; 4 windows in front, 2 at the back, and a fire place and one window at the end; the floor of the lower room to be boarded, and a room above of the same dimensions; no partition wall either in the lower or upper rooms: A Varando in front, with a small room at each end.—The Bricks, Iron-work, and Nails to be furnished by the Government, and the Timber carried to the pits at Government expence.

Any eligible Bricklayer and Carpenter, willing to treat for erecting the above Building on the Ground where the Guard-house now stands, to deliver sealed tenders, together with their plan, on Thursday the 7th of February, to me at Sydney, for the purpose of laying the same before the Gaol Committee.

The Carpenter who engages to do the work will contract at the same time for the Sawing and Shingles.

Good security will be required for the performance of the Contract.

By Command of His Excellency,

(signed)   J. Harris.[2]

It was still considered a sufficiently important selling point to mention in newspaper advertisements that a house for sale was fully glazed and shingled. Glass was a valuable enough commodity to steal out of window-sashes in houses. Several culprits were given stiff penalties including lashings and labour in the Newcastle mines for this not uncommon offence in the early 1800s. Another attraction thought worthy of mention was if a house had a malthouse complete with a full set of brewing equipment attached to it. There was no control over the brewing or selling of beer. Domestic manufacture was in fact encouraged as a counter to the evils of the rum fumes and as an encouragement to agriculture, particularly the growing of barley.

The first stone private dwelling appeared in 1803 but it was an excessive extravagance. When in April the next year the well-to-do merchant James Underwood laid out a fifty-three feet by twenty-three feet three-storeyed house facing the Parade in Sydney he considered it sufficient to face the ground floor brickwork with dressed stone and leave the brickwork exposed on the upper and attic floors. By the end of 1805 stone houses were still rare enough for the *Sydney Gazette* to report that two of them, remarkable not for architectural quality but for materials, were being built near the new bridge across the Tank Stream.

The better homes tended to be self-contained so that even in the heart of the town there was a rural flavour. An established vegetable garden, fruit trees, enough pasture for a cow, self-sufficiency in water from an independent well together with a separate kitchen, bakehouse and malthouse were the appurtenances of a well-found home. And the houses, even the small two room ones, of the latter part of the first decade of the nineteenth century were taking on little conscious touches of stylism and luxury. The central doorway frequently was crowned with a semi-circular fanlight occasionally fretted out of a solid block of cedar. Two chimneys, one on each of the end walls, were added not only for the comfort of heating in each of the two rooms but also to complete the rigid symmetry of the main elevation. They were becoming Georgian and Colonial.

Despite the increase in architectural pretensions the quality of the materials and the standards of construction remained low. Nearly all buildings had to rely on a heavy coat of whitewash to be reasonably waterproof. The cheapest and least effective whitewash was made from a simple mixture of lime and water; a much better one and the one most commonly used was a boiled mixture of slaked-lime tallow and salt water; an even more effective one substituted milk for the salt water while the best of all used ground-up milk curds instead of milk. The curd mixture had the added advantage of drying quickly so that two coats could be applied in one day. In the country a satisfactory whitewash was also made by mixing apple-tree ashes with milk; while in those areas such as Bathurst or the upper Hunter River where gypsum was found in inch-thick veins or lying in nodules on the ground, and around Sydney where fine quality pipe-clay was available, these naturally-found materials formed the bases of cheap but effective whitewashes. Earth pigments could be added to any of the washes but most buildings were coated with untinted washes and Sydney generally was a white town. Joinery timber was painted with oil paint using imported linseed oil or seal oil or elephant oil obtained from the seals and sea elephants hunted in Bass Strait.

Having failed to control the abuses and highhanded exploitation that were rotting Sydney, King was relieved of his governorship. In 1806 William Bligh, with two mutinies already behind him, arrived to impose his hot-tempered and domineering will on the oligarchy that held the colony in thrall. Within two years he had three mutinies to his credit. After early expressions of loyalty and goodwill his rash efforts led him into the bitterest conflict with those he had come to tame. Primed with a special issue of rum, the soldiers of the New South Wales Corps weaved down and up the valley along Bridge Street, stormed Government House, scattered a dinner party being held there and arrested their Majesty's representative.

For two years the people of New South Wales waited in a sort of suspended

The Presbyterian Church at Ebenezer, New South Wales: 1809.
Architect, Andrew Johnston (?)

animation, dissatisfied with the past and apprehensive of the future. In the two years interregnum that followed, the rottenness that was already everywhere and at all levels eating into the whole society became even worse. To an arrival sailing up the harbour Sydney presented a pretty picture. It was a town of rural dolls' houses of white walls and grey-brown roofs climbing up the rocky hillsides and nestled around a sheltered cove on one of the most beautiful harbours in the world. But, inside the town, there were degeneracy and decay. The tight-knit group of exploiters were uncaringly bleeding the community to their own advantage. The have-nots and the convicts were being crushed further and further into despondency. The town was thick with public houses, unlicensed grog shops of the most appalling type, and brothels. Unmarried couples living together were as common as those respectably joined while the streets and alleys running with slime, grease and filth were the playgrounds of innumerable unwanted children.

The moral decay that everywhere sat on the town was reflected in the fabric òf the buildings. Even though it was a mere twenty years since the first tents had gone up amid the dusty gum trees, the buildings were decrepit and tumbling. In his excellent book on *The Early Australian Architects and Their Work*, Morton Herman succinctly pinpointed one of the main reasons for this state of affairs when he said, 'The town had been cobbled up by amateurs.' The challenge of new and untried materials, shortage of skilled labour, unexperienced conditions and unknown dangers would have extended even knowledgeable and trained architects. When it was pickpockets, forgers, prostitutes and thieves whose lives had been dedicated to avoiding learning anything useful who had to provide the knowledge, the materials and the labour, it is hardly surprising that the results of their efforts frequently were failures. Untutored in mechanical principles or material limitations, they built buildings as best they knew. Even without the drenching downpours of rain, the shrivelling heat of the summer sun—extremes they had never known before—or the silent and hidden depredations of fungus and white ants, the builders of early Sydney would have had a hard job to erect buildings even moderately well; with them they had no chance. Practically every building, from Government House which was honeycombed with white ants to the Store, from the prideful clock tower to the meanest cottage, was forever being repaired, re-roofed or shored up just to keep it standing. Sydney, despite its attractiveness from a distance, was mouldering away.

But even as the colony in New South Wales lay in the penumbra of a short Dark Age awaiting the future apprehensively and fearfully, a new governor with new strength, new ideals, a new and enlightened mind and a new humanitarianism was bringing his own regiment and a new future from an at last awakened Whitehall. Australian history was about to begin.

---

[1] An Emigrant Mechanic [Harris, Alexander?], *Settlers and Convicts*, G. Cox, King Street, Covent Garden, 1852, pp. 78–79.

[2] *Sydney Gazette*, Vol. II, No. 102, 10 February 1805, p. 1, col. 1.

THE AGE OF MACQUARIE 1810–1821

William the First was the first of our kings
Not counting Ethelreds Egberts and things.

3

What William the Conqueror was in English history Lachlan Macquarie was in Australian. The internecine squabbling, the selfish scrabbling for personal gain, the complete unawareness of and disregard for any sort of national future that had marked the first twenty-two years were to be consumed in the fire that Macquarie lit. He was a man endowed with an exceptional breadth and rectitude of mind, a magnificent vision, upright principles and ideals, a noble humanitarianism, an understanding compassion for his less fortunate fellows and a firm belief in the rightness of all British institutions. These qualities, tempered by forty-eight years of harsh worldly experience, moulded him into a pragmatic and first-rate administrator. He was imbued with a creative urge that had found no outlet in his military service. New South Wales was to give him the opportunity to express it. Wielding a broad brush in the grand manner he created a design for his demesne far beyond anything that had been dreamed of before. It was a concept that was to prove too fine and both Macquarie and his plans were eventually to be pulled down by those of lesser vision and meaner ability. But he stayed long enough for many of his ideas to take form and to leave behind sufficient of his thinking and influence to change the colony from a penal camp of the moment to a young nation of the future.

On the first day of the year 1810 the new Governor-in-Chief took up his duties in the noisome mire which he had been charged with cleaning up. Macquarie got down to business immediately after being sworn in. The classes, he informed his people, were to maintain their places and conduct themselves accordingly; immorality and vice were to be avoided; the Sabbath was to be accorded its due by regular attendance of everyone at divine service. The aborigines were to be treated kindly and troubles with them avoided. Houses of ill-fame were prohibited and cohabiting unmarried couples were advised of both their moral and religious shortcomings and the disadvantages in inheritance and support rights that they would suffer if they persisted in their sin. Justice and impartiality were to replace animosity, dissension, jealousy and immorality. Those who took heed would find in him a friend and protector but woe betide those who ignored his words.

Macquarie worked enthusiastically and everywhere. The troublesome trading monopoly of the New South Wales Corps which had been at the root of much of the strife was broken by sending the Corps home. Macquarie's own trustworthy 73rd Regiment took over military duties. Through their own loyalty to their commander and his wariness, they never outgrew their legitimate field. Having laid down lines for the reform of the manners and morals of his subjects and having put trade in the hands of free men, Macquarie demonstrated his sympathy for the ideas of those who wished to see the colony acquire a viable future by his belief and actions in the worthiness, as human beings, of emancipated convicts and the part they could play in bringing it about. His embracing of the rights and dignities of the emancipists was to lead him into conflict with the free settlers—a conflict which eventually sent him home.

Within months Macquarie set out to survey his domain from end to end.

Among the many shortcomings which appalled him was the state of the buildings which, generally, he found in 'most ruinous decay'. He determined to set this right along with everything else. Macquarie firmly believed that the sort of society he envisaged could not grow, let alone flourish, in the random haphazard collection of ill-built, unhealthy, inadequate heaps of bricks and sticks that he found. Urged on by his Lieutenant-Governor, Joseph Foveaux, Macquarie's inner mind was already erecting fine sturdy well-designed houses, hospitals, barracks, wharves, stores and roads even as his eyes saw the dilapidation and decay in front of him. Whitehall was aghast at such extravagance when he informed them of his plans and sternly forbade the madness. But Macquarie was an old soldier. He held power to act without reference to London in an emergency. To him the combination of benighted tight-fisted authorities twelve thousand miles away, the conditions confronting him and the vision in his mind constituted an emergency without doubt. Helped by a cool glibness that easily found justifying reasons that could be put in his reports, he went ahead.

But before he was pushed into this extreme he was acting to raise building standards and the design of the towns. He had been brought up in an England which was vitally alive to the need for town design both in whole and in part. The Woods, father and son, had built the Circus, the Royal Crescent and Queen Square at Bath when Macquarie was a child and the London squares were familiar to him. Numbers of architects, both amateur and professional, were publishing suggestions for town plans and books of building designs of all sorts. John Wood Junior, for instance, had published 'A Series of Plans for Cottages or Habitations of the Labourer' in 1781, 1792, and 1806. John Soane, later to become one of the most famous Regency architects, published a similar book in 1804, as did John Plaw. Mrs Macquarie herself was by way of being a knowledgeable amateur on architectural matters and brought with her a book of plans which helped the Governor in his architectural needs before he found in the penal scrap-heap a properly trained architect to assist him. Not only from having been brought up in a design-conscious society but also from the tastes and interests of the immediate social circle in which he moved, Macquarie's mind was turned to, and enlightened on, architectural and town planning matters. No governor before him was so attuned and none after him enjoyed the power and authority to do anything about it. Only in Macquarie was the spirit willing and the flesh able.

Macquarie made a gentle start on Sydney. He laid down, in August 1810, that Sydney's streets were to be sixty-six feet wide and that no building should be built closer than twenty feet to the street. Verandahs were permitted within this space but it was clearly understood, in the lease, that the twenty feet could be appropriated at a later date without compensation if the land were needed for street widening. Before this, according to Surveyor Meehan, 'people generally built according to their fancy and without arrangement'. He took the opportunity that granting land gave him to insist on a minimum standard of building. During Macquarie's reign any lease of land in Sydney carried a condition that the grantee should build, within three years, a house at least fifty feet by sixteen feet of brick or stone and two storeys high. After visiting Hobart in 1811, he left behind an edict that grantees should build, within three years, either a forty feet by sixteen feet single-storeyed or twenty feet by sixteen feet two-storeyed brick or stone house.

As he tramped and rode through the country Macquarie encouraged better building by word and action. In making grants of land in the country he frequently stipulated that the owner undertake to erect an adequate building within a certain time. Normally he required it to be of two storeys and always of brick or stone and shingled. Aware of the vital part inns would play in opening up the country, he often specified that the building should be an inn. The oldest hotel building in Australia, the Macquarie Arms, was erected under such a condition when, in 1811, Richard Fitzgerald was given a site in the present town of Windsor on condition that he erect a 'handsome commodious inn of brick or stone and to be at least two storeys high.'

Fitzgerald's grant was not made lightly. It was to form a fitting architectural piece in the new town that Macquarie laid out at Green Hills. This was one of the five towns of Windsor, Richmond, Wilberforce, Castlereagh and Pitt Town that the Governor designed and proclaimed in the Hawkesbury Valley on his first tour of inspection. They were the first opportunity he had of giving effect to his ideas of town design. They were not to be permitted to become the huddle of disreputable shanties and crooked narrow streets that made up towns elsewhere. Set on eminences in a broad flat valley, the Macquarie towns had an open square for a heart fed by well-ordered streets. Macquarie symbolized his people's dependence on a spiritual and temporal authority by specifying and giving priority to sites for a church and a court house. He held up the future by declaring an area for the schoolhouse. To ensure that the standards of his towns would not be destroyed by those who could not see what he saw, he promulgated on 15 December 1810 a Government and General Order that laid down: 'The Dwelling Houses are to be either made of Brick or Weatherboard, to have Brick chimnies and Shingled roofs and no Dwelling-house is to be less than nine Feet high—A Plan of a Dwelling House and Offices will be left with each District Constable to which each Settler must conform in the erecting of his Building.'

This was the earliest regulation controlling building in Australia and applied only to the five Hawkesbury towns. When, twelve months later, with uncharacteristic foresight, he wrote similar regulations for Hobart and then for other towns such as Liverpool and Campbelltown, each time geographically limiting their application, he introduced a pattern of local building control that has bedevilled Australian architects and builders ever since. The system has spread so that today each of numerous authorities has its own requirements which not only overlap but are often superimposed and frequently contradictory. The lack of any uniformity of building regulations on a regional, state or national basis is a bane that plagues Australian building still. It is one of Macquarie's least valuable legacies.

Macquarie was a man of action. He pointed out the way he expected his subjects to follow by setting the example. One of his first requests to Whitehall had been for the services of an architect. His request was refused on the argument that as the buildings for which he required an architect's skill were unnecessary in themselves there was no need for the architect either. But the Governor was not so easily discouraged. He gathered together a covey of carpenters and bricklayers and other tradesmen from the ranks of convicts and free men. Under the cloak of his emergency powers, he disregarded the specific ban on his projects that came from Lord Liverpool and commenced to raise a series of essential public buildings and to restore and maintain those he thought worth salvaging. One of the buildings beyond salvaging was the general hospital that had been built on the west side of George Street in 1795 and which had become too small anyway. In November 1810, probably with the aid of his wife and a book of architectural designs she had brought with her, Macquarie signed an agreement with Graham Blaxcell and Alexander Riley, who were later to be joined by D'Arcy Wentworth, for the erection of a large three-block hospital on the crown of the eastern hill in what is now Macquarie Street. The builders were to receive a monopoly to sell 45,000 gallons of rum, on which they would pay three shillings a gallon duty, and some other trading concessions in meat and stone. The arrangement was typical of the practical expediency of which Macquarie was a master. As no money was to change hands, there was no need for the matter to be hinted at in public accounts and the Governor's right to proceed in the name of emergency was safeguarded. There

The General Hospital (Mint Building) in Macquarie Street, Sydney: 1810-15

was no call for London to know what was happening until Sydney had its building. In the event, the agreement was repudiated, the contractors did not receive their monopoly, Macquarie received a torrid roasting, the building received a thorough lambasting for its inadequacies in design and construction; but Sydney got a large imposing hospital.

The Sydney General Hospital (from the circumstances of its erection, it was generally called the Rum Hospital) consisted of three separate rectangular blocks. Two of them, the surgeons' quarters and the store, still stand, used as the State Parliament House and the Land Tax Office; but the main central block was demolished in 1885 to make way for the present stone hospital.

Macquarie's hospital was architecturally naive and those parts of it left eloquently display the struggle between ambition and reality that the Governor had. Grand and ambitious in size, straightforward and militarily blunt as a functional statement, its architectural grammar was uninformed and its antecedents vague while its construction and form were modified by the limitations of its materials and the technical knowledge and rapaciousness of builders primarily bent on accumulating wealth. Part of Macquarie's military life had been spent in India and from that experience he had come to appreciate the virtues of verandahs in a warm climate. Consequently, two storeys of shading verandah shrouded all four sides of the two feet three inches thick brick walls that formed the rectangular box of each block. The two tiers of superimposed verandah columns, each one storey high, which held up the balcony and its roof were turned out of cedar timber in quasi-Doric moulding which shocked the purists. A protecting timber balustrade ran between the columns at the upper floor. The parallels of the hand and bottom rails were divided into pleasantly proportioned horizontal rectangles by means of vertical balusters. These divisions were closed and further elaborated by crossed timbers. The pattern of straight lines forming a series of diagonalled rectangles was, with variations, the basic one for all timber balustrades until the advent of cast iron.

Constructionally the buildings show a vast ignorance of mechanical principles which was symptomatic of the building skill available. For instance, the verandah columns were canted inwards perhaps in imitation of the optical illusion correcting manner of the Parthenon. The adjustment was dangerously and worryingly over-done. Again, the columns were set eccentrically over their sandstone footing which in turn had been so pared in thickness in order to save money that it was a mere shell. These offending matters, together with the columns and the building's general unclassical design, later gave a convict architect the opportunity to condemn the whole building, to predict its imminent collapse and thereby help to have himself installed as the first government architect.

The roof structure of the hospital in particular brought forth scathing comment from those who had more knowledge than the builders and who were given the task of criticizing their efforts. It was an extended version of the method of framing roofs commonly done in the colony. This was a most unscientific business which had developed from the open-couple roofs of the early huts in which rafters were leant against each other at the ridge line and carried their thrust obliquely into the walls. The ceiling joists were set across the building independently of the rafters.

The present practice of using the ceiling joists to tie the feet of the rafters and thereby form a stable truss system did not come into general use for almost one hundred years. Even comparatively thick walls could not withstand the thrust of an open-couple system where the span was more than about sixteen feet. In thinner walls it was correspondingly less. This, combined with the limited lengths of timber that could be cut from local trees, gave rise to the practice of erecting a series of short-span open-couples over areas greater than the walls could withstand in one jump. In section, such roofs were in the form of an M and when seen from the front and sides appeared as being hipped lengthwise along the elevation being

Kirkham Stables, Kirkham Lane, Camden, New South Wales: 1816

viewed. A consequence of this form of construction was a lower roof than would have been the case with a simple large span. The reduction resulted in a visually lighter roof mass and a pleasanter proportion between it and the walls of the building. It was an exceedingly happy occurrence that was responsible for a great deal of the restful character and harmony of Colonial buildings. To achieve a uniform ridge height it was necessary, of course, for the area being covered to be divided into equal spans. As this meant that the valleys seldom coincided with the line of an internal wall the feet of the rafters were supported on a heavy beam. It was the custom to set the beam on the flat rather than on edge, a mechanically much stronger and more economic arrangement—a further example of the lack of structural understanding of the early builders. However, as there was never any dearth of timber the wastage of material was of small account; but when the depth of the beam was skimped, as it frequently was, the valley dipped in the middle and in heavy rain roof leaks were a common complaint. This roofing method was used for many years for all sorts of buildings, from small cottages to large warehouses, when the technical knowledge of architects and engineers was not available.

The form of the roof of the General Hospital was of this type although an attempt was made to gain stability by a little elementary triangulation of the members which were secured with bolted iron plates and pegged or wedged mortice and tenoned joints. In the hospital the hipping, like the verandah, was carried around all four sides. Consequently, while the centre of the main building, the axis of the whole arrangement, was marked by a triangular pediment, the three buildings were 'finished' and designed on all sides thereby avoiding a neglected, unsightly back elevation. In this feature, so uncharacteristic of practically all Australian buildings, except churches, Macquarie's ungainly hospital was unique.

For some four years after his arrival, Macquarie struggled to bring order and an altruistic purpose to the life of the colony. His own expansive thinking fell over the whole community as a spell. Until it became clear that his championing of the rights and worth of the emancipated convicts would not be deflected, the military and civil officers and the free settler classes stood solidly behind him. Success crowned his every effort. The halcyon year was 1813 in which the wave of unity peaked before shattering into a spray of returning factionalism. From that year onwards the Governor found himself increasingly at odds with the respectable members of his society. His Judge-Advocate, Ellis Bent, objected to having Simeon Lord, an emancipated convict of wealth and influence but whose private life was notoriously immoral, foisted on to the Bench of Magistrates. The officers of Macquarie's own regiment supported Bent and sneered at their commanding officer's emancipist policy. By haughtily declining invitations to dine with emancipists at Government House, they made it plain that they in no way intended to associate with social inferiors such as Lord. The colony's senior chaplain, Reverend Samuel Marsden, early found himself unable to support a policy that offended refined sensibilities by giving power and office to ex-felons and joined those in opposition to the Governor. After 1813 the dissension and the wrangling increased. But even after the trouble commenced Macquarie determinedly pursued his goals amid the rising ructions so that the colony he was to leave was vastly different in attitude, outlook and standards from the scrawny emaciated one he inherited.

The same year that saw the first murkiness in the clear golden aura that surrounded the early years of the Macquarie age also saw the arrival of the first trained architect to come to Australia. Daniel Dering Mathew arrived as a free settler with the object of partaking of a share of the heaven-sent opportunities that Macquarie's plans presented. The Governor must have been mightily pleased at what at first seemed like the filling of a serious gap in his plans. He immediately commissioned Mathew to prepare a sketch for a combined town hall and law courts. The result was a disappointing thing to come from the board of a trained architect and perhaps Macquarie was relieved when Lord Liverpool expressly forbade any further work on the proposal. Mathew was more fortunate when he designed a two-storeyed house for the Colonial Secretary down the hill from Government House on the site now occupied by the New South Wales Department of Education. The building combined offices on the ground floor with living quarters for the Colonial Secretary on the upper floor. The kitchen, the gig-house and stores were in a separate building at the back. It was a typical country Georgian house but simplified by the shedding of all extraneous decoration except for a curiously and ignorantly decorated and recessed entrance porch flanked by two queer 'Doric' columns. The windows, door and chimneys were placed symmetrically in unadorned brick walls and the roof was hipped with close eaves.

Mathew's star had started to dim almost as soon as it appeared. His plan for the town hall had been disappointing and now, when his first building was actually completed and it was found to be very poorly built, the unfortunate architect who had loudly and repeatedly proclaimed his competence to the Governor found his star fading fast. It and his hopes were to be virtually extinguished by the arrival in Sydney of two greater architectural lights in the next year.

Francis Howard Greenway had already been sentenced to transportation for life at the Bristol Assizes in March 1812 before Mathew left England, but the unwilling migrant arrived in Australia a year after the architect who came of his own volition. And whereas Mathew is virtually forgotten and bequeathed nothing of value to posterity, Greenway left behind him a magnificent architectural heritage and a name in Australian history that is familiar even to people who know of no other architect.

Greenway had been born in 1777 at Mangotsfield in the West Country of England where his family had been builders, masons, quarrymen and architects for generations. By 1805 Francis, together with his brother Olive, was conducting an office as an architect and landscape-gardener in Bristol. Through misfortune rather than mismanagement he became bankrupt in 1809 and in an endeavour to pay off his creditors he forged a memorandum to a contract between himself and one of his ex-clients. It was a foolish act because by the time the matter came up Greenway had been discharged from bankruptcy. But in the early nineteenth century nothing was more important than a man's honour. The forgery seems to have been prompted by a mixture of vanity, morality and a little professional public relations. For the forgery he was despatched to New South Wales. In February 1814 Greenway staggered off the *General Hewitt* after a nightmare journey in cramped and filthy conditions during which death and sickness had been ever-present.

Greenway had many faults of character. He was headstrong, bumptious, vain, self-confident, aggressive and given to maliciousness; but in his professional work he was a man of superior knowledge, ability and initiative—imaginative, sensitive, business-like and thorough. When anything was wrong Greenway was quick to do something practical to correct it. He had been thoroughly born and bred to architecture. Family tradition and a professional training and practice amid the fine architecture of Bristol combined with his own qualities of mind had made him an extremely sound architect. If he had remained practising in the West Country he would have been no more noteworthy than dozens of other minor figures that were enriching English architecture but in Australia, with its opportunities and lack of competition, Greenway's genius blossomed miraculously to write his name large in the pages of Australian history.

Greenway's path into the right quarters was smoothed for him by a letter from ex-Governor Hunter to Macquarie recommending him as 'an architect of merit'. The incumbent Governor had been taught to be cautious. Having been disappointed with the abilities of Mathew and anxious though he was to press on with the building visions that filled his mind, he was not eager to put them in the hands of anybody incapable of carrying them out to the standards he expected. As a test of this well-recommended convict, the Governor asked Greenway to make a copy of a design that he, Macquarie, had chosen from a pattern book for use as a town hall. Greenway's cocky reply pointed out that, in matters of architectural taste and knowledge, the Governor had a lot to learn from the convict. Macquarie, as a military man and by nature, was not used to insubordination. He curtly but tolerantly censured Greenway for his presumption. The Governor was in a position to enforce his will. Greenway had to make the copy anyway but otherwise went unpunished for his temerity.

The experience made the Governor wary of becoming too involved with the fiery, conceited and tactless architect. Nevertheless, he granted Greenway a ticket-of-leave which enabled him to hang up his architectural shingle in George Street. From that address Greenway conducted an architectural practice that brought him a livelihood. The work included a number of minor domestic commissions, a series of imaginative proposals for the development of the colony and several honorary, possibly sometimes unrequested, consultant commissions for the Government. Eventually Macquarie recognized that, despite his personal shortcomings, Greenway was his man. In March 1816 Greenway was appointed Civil Architect and Assistant Engineer with the duties of planning and erecting all Government public works. His salary was to be three shillings a day. So, hesitantly, charily, almost reluctantly but inevitably, was born the combination of Macquarie, the occasion, and Greenway, the means, that in six short years was to give Australia its finest architectural heritage.

Greenway started by sweeping the field clean of any potential rivals. In reports, verbal and written, he enthusiastically and savagely condemned the work, impugned the integrity and demolished the reputation of his predecessors and contemporaries. He had no need to. His own superiority was manifestly clear but Greenway's vanity was overweening and he brooked no threats.

In six years, in a veritable paroxysm of energy, Greenway, alone and unaided, designed and supervised the erection of an enormous number of buildings from an obelisk to a huge hospital, from a lighthouse to a large school, and had initiated plans and schemes for many more including town sewers, water supply, fortifications and bridges. He even had time to give some thought to and make suggestions for a town plan and building regulations for Sydney.

Greenway found the standards of workmanship and the practices of the industry far below those he demanded. He entered the building industry like a scourge. Never one to let things slide, he set his teeth into the masons, bricklayers and carpenters to achieve what he wanted. Standing over them, continually badgering, directing and instructing them in the techniques and skills of their trades, he eventually drove home the realization that the slipshod work they had been able to fob off before was of no use to him. His first major building, a lighthouse on South Head for which he was the supervisor of construction of a design carried out by Captain John Gill, the Acting Principal Engineer of the Government, for instance, was used by Greenway as a training school for masons at which he gave both teaching and incentives to produce improved work. Gradually and single-handedly, by threats, cajoling and teaching, he raised the quality of workmanship from crude to truly craftsmanlike.

The conduct of building contracts, the happy-go-lucky way in which payments were made before, after, or never, for materials and work that had been, would be or, often, never would be provided, were open to great abuses. Frauds on the Government or private clients were blatantly perpetrated. Collusion between contractors, tradesmen and labourers to give the shoddiest of work for the highest

The Court House at Windsor, New South Wales: 1822.
Architect, Francis Greenway

price was rampant. To combat these practices and put the whole matter on some sort of businesslike basis, Greenway introduced, and enforced, the system of progress payments for work done and materials used after inspection and approval as the building was erected. This insistence on quality and fair dealing made him many enemies over the years. Other architects, such as Mathew and Henry Kitchen, another free settler who arrived in Sydney the same year as Greenway, both of whom were subjected to the lash of Greenway's abuse for their incompetence; contractors and builders whose shenanigans at the Governor's expense were stopped; and a whole array of tradesmen and artisans who had been vilified for lack of skill and thoroughness were to remember and repay their humiliations and frustrations with compound interest when the time, and Commissioner Bigge, arrived.

Greenway designed his buildings in the architectural idiom current around Bristol which in the early nineteenth century was still untouched by the Revivalist controversies raging in London. The underlying thought of rational and strict control of form, decoration and details were Classical in foundation but the total expression was English. They were no mere copies of Italian originals but vital and original creations springing out of the native conditions. To such an approach Greenway added his own highly personal touch of genius. His architecture was both stylish and authoritative. While it was manifestly clear that their creator was thoroughly English, Greenway's buildings were just as distinctively the work of one individual who had marked them as his own.

Greenway's buildings lifted the standard of architectural design to an even greater extent than his demands raised those of constructional standards and practice. Taken in the broad picture they were all greatly superior to anything that had gone before. But within themselves there was a large range of quality. His lighthouse, which took a single Doric column as its inspiration, was structurally bad due to poor materials; its aesthetic weakness, however, was the responsibility of its designer, John Gill, not Greenway. His court house at the west end of St James' Church in Sydney was formless, pedestrian and dully anonymous. For the stables of a new Government House, now the Conservatorium of Music, he stepped out of his accustomed architectural manner by designing the facade in a pointed arch and battlemented Gothic with unfortunate results. His Liverpool Hospital, Windsor Court House and St Luke's Church, Liverpool, are fine, well-proportioned, well-ordered and plainly successful buildings whose merits shine even more brightly in the architectural chaos that succeeded them. It was, however, in his churches, St James', Sydney, and St Matthew's, Windsor, and Hyde Park Barracks that Greenway soared to his greatest heights.

The end of the Napoleonic wars in Europe had brought with it in its aftermath an increase in crime in England and in consequence a greatly increased flow of convicts to New South Wales. This development gave Macquarie, always concerned for the physical and moral welfare of his charges, both the need and the means to erect a barracks in which to house them and churches in which to reform them.

In the latter three buildings Greenway worked a severely restricted palette relying on the virtues of simplicity and proportion to achieve his end. In the churches he had a contrasting and balancing tower and the chance of a spire at St James' and a pepper pot at St Matthew's to add variety to the severity of the simple box-like body of the building. They were clean uncomplicated buildings,

St Matthew's Church of England at Windsor, New South Wales: 1817-20. Architect, Francis Greenway

lightly but firmly designed to meet the needs of uncompromisingly Protestant congregations. Their plain interiors formed a fitting background to the black gown and white bands of the preacher. Elaborate ritual and ornate colourful vestments had no place in a vehemently evangelical society which saw all hope and cause for pride and pleasure in the unchallengeable rightness of the Protestant ascendancy. Built of local brick, their walls were defined by brick pilasters (a thickening of the wall made necessary by the need to support the load of the roof trusses), into a series of bays whose happily chosen proportions were the same as those of the wall itself. It was largely this repetition of the same proportion in the walls, the bays, the windows and the details that gave the buildings their unity and strength. Large generous windows set in recesses pierced the walls, their round arched heads formed of soft rubbed bricks. In the case of St James', the arch brickwork was made of 'samels' whose colour decoratively defined them by contrast with the light brown of the main body of the wall. The roof carried over the end walls where the gable was expressed as a triangular pediment by carrying a cornice across at the eaves line. This Palladian trick enabled the same architectural treatment as on the side walls to be carried around the end walls. It was a device that eventually found

St James' Church of England in Queen's Square, Sydney: 1820-24. Architect, Francis Greenway; additions by John Verge (1834) and Varney Parkes (1893)

its way into New South Wales domestic architecture, one of whose distinctive and less favourable hallmarks is the heavy, ungainly boxed timber gable sticking out beyond the line of its wall—massive, crushing and cumbrous. But in Greenway's churches and barracks there was no building out of the wall face and the pediments sat lightly and gracefully over their pilastered walls.

In the Hyde Park Barracks Greenway, using his skills to the utmost, produced a heady, calculated and fundamental building. Without the excuse or the permission for any non-essentials, he had to rely wholly on proportion and sensitive handling of functional elements, pilasters, windows, chimneys, ventilators and doorways to achieve what is usually considered his masterpiece. By an extreme virtuosity Greenway managed to wring out of these restrictions a building which, while physically not large, was marked by a noble elegance and harmony that was the epitome of refinement and imposing dignity. There are no exceptional feats of workmanship, no extravagant use of materials, no unnecessary enrichment but only an extraordinary command and control of essentials in this building erected to house the convict litter of Sydney. The Hyde Park Barracks is, like the St Paul's Church that Inigo Jones built for the Earl of Bedford at Covent Garden, just a barn—but a very handsome barn. The main building, the dormitory block, stood in a large courtyard surrounded by a wall in which were symmetrically housed

Hyde Park Barracks in Queen's Square, Sydney: 1819. Architect, Francis Greenway cells, latrines, a cookhouse, a bakehouse, guard rooms and guards' quarters. Today really only the dormitory remains—in use as the Law Courts.

The architectural success of Greenway's public buildings brought him the gratitude of the Governor in the form of a free pardon and the increased jealousy of his enemies. Rivals plagiarized his designs and even stole his drawings until, to safeguard his ideas, he was forced to refrain from doing any but essential drawings and then rubbing them from the paper as soon as possible or doing a sketch for the workmen on a piece of stone that was about to be used at the site.

While Macquarie had found in Greenway the right man to translate his ideas for public building into bricks and mortar and set a standard for others to follow, he had also found, on his own staff, another architect to more than adequately support the tireless Greenway in the assignments which that over-worked enthusiast could not handle. John Watts, who had been articled to an architect in Dublin before he joined the army, arrived in Sydney in 1814, the same year as Greenway, as a lieutenant in the new regiment which was replacing Macquarie's own 73rd Regiment. On arrival he was appointed aide-de-camp to the Governor who, impressed with the military background, good breeding and warm personality of his aide, formed a warm friendship for him. Equally impressed by his competence and ability in the field of construction, the Governor grasped the opportunity to further his building needs by setting him to work on various pressing problems. His first commission was a military hospital on Observatory Hill. Much of the building still stands but over the years has been extensively modified and changed. In 1849 it was converted by Mortimer Lewis for use as the National School (the present Fort Street Girls' High School) and embalmed by totally encasing it in its present Classic coffin. However, Morton Herman's painstaking reconstruction of it shows it to have been a more refined and smaller version of the Rum Hospital in Macquarie Street—a plain rectangular brick block with stone quoins one room thick with an M-construction shingled roof, a two-tiered verandah with Doric columns on all four sides and double-hung windows with flat stone arches ranged symmetrically either side of a central six-panelled doorway crowned by a

The Lancer Barracks in Allen Street, Parramatta, New South Wales: 1816-22. Architect, John Watts

semi-circular fanlight. A smaller single-storeyed four-roomed version, identical in its architectural details, served as a surgeon's quarters. The general similarity of the two hospitals indicated that the influence of Macquarie's experience of verandahs in India was strong but the later building showed the sureness and precision of a knowledgeable mind that was missing in the earlier one.

Watts' talent—and it was considerable—was used to build what was strictly an extension but practically a new building to the Government House at Parramatta. Also, in that town, he erected a hospital, a military barracks—the Lancer Barracks, the oldest military establishment still in use in Australia—and the still standing twin, tall, pyramidal-roofed towers for the Church of St John. He executed several other military works including the first work on the Subaltern Officers Quarters of the Anglesea Barracks in Hobart which were eventually completed by John Lee Archer. The standard of Watts' work was that of the sound, thoroughly trained and able, disciplined military designer but one constrained in imagination by his lack of an original spark. His buildings were architecturally precise, correct, rigidly formal, appropriately restrained and constructionally reliable.

The surge of good government building and comparatively fine design that welled up under the aegis of Macquarie communicated itself to the community at large. By means of trade, commerce, farming and enterprise a number of people had become men of substance. They aimed higher, both socially and materially, than any had dreamed of before 1810. The buildings that were erected for them reflected the changing social climate.

Along the streets of Sydney the first few buildings especially designed as shops appeared, their bay display windows made of many panes of crown glass reaching from near the ground to above door height. Shops had first appeared after trading-ships started to call regularly at Sydney in the middle 1790s but retailing had taken place in one room of an ordinary house. Private trading ventures of all sorts were usually short-lived affairs, taken up for the moment when prospects were propitious but dropped just as quickly when they had been milked of a quick penny. Anything so long-term as to justify special buildings was no part of the transient live-for-today immediacy that preceded the stability that gradually unfolded in the second and third decades of the nineteenth century.

Importers erected substantial warehouses for their goods. Robert Campbell, for instance, had come to Sydney in 1798 from Calcutta with the express intention of carving a fortune for himself when all trade was in the hands of the officers of the New South Wales Corps. Having lost a first trial shipment near Bass Strait, Campbell accompanied his second ship to challenge the monopoly of the 'pure merinos'. Within ten years he had erected a three-storeyed stone warehouse on the west side of the Cove behind his own wharves to and from which flowed the merchandise which made him rich. Other merchants followed Campbell's lead. The warehouses were all made of stone. It had been learned by bitter experience that in the soft mud and lime mortar which was the best that was available bricks were easily pried out of their beds and that brick buildings were far from burglar-proof. Heavy blocks of stone were more discouraging.

Macquarie's concern for the moral welfare of his people had caused a clean-up in the public house business. In Sydney the multitude of inns, taverns and alehouses was brought under official surveillance and their numbers reduced. Many illegal sly-grog shops continued to sell their gut-rotting firewater in the alleys of the Rocks and outside the town limits but the regulations that went with the issue of a licence to retail alcoholic liquor resulted in a higher standard from those who wanted to continue to receive the official blessing. In addition, the slowly increasing flow of immigrants and the rise of a moneyed class who travelled between the towns on business or pleasure gave rise to a demand for better service and surroundings in the town inns. Like the shops, the early inns

Rouse Hill House, Windsor Road, Rouse Hill,
New South Wales: 1818-22

had been private homes in which the owner hoped to skim the cream until a better opportunity came along. But under Macquarie buildings purposely designed as inns, offering many of the comforts of home, were erected. They were still strongly domestic in character—a house for the licensee who took travellers into his home—and it was a large inn that had six public bedrooms. With the inns, the few shops, the warehouses and Macquarie's tremendous spate of churches, hospitals, schools and military buildings, Sydney was taking form.

Perhaps the most significant of all the developments that were taking place was in the homes. In the towns, either by regulation or volition, the temporariness of slabs, mud, wattle-and-daub and bark roofs disappeared. Brick walls and shingled roofs became universal from the smallest cottage to the largest mansion. Unglazed windows were no longer fitting for Sydney Town. Lime became more readily available as shipments came in quantity from Van Diemen's Land and large beds of shells around Botany Bay and at Newcastle were dredged to provide the raw material. Good timbers also were coming from Newcastle and the Hunter River—beefwood for shingles, cedar for fittings, pine for flooring, hardwood for roof framing and rosewood for furniture.

Two-storeyed houses became as common as single-storeyed cottages. The best of them were fitted with unexpected refinements imported from England.

Doors had mortice locks and recessed butt hinges, stairs had wreathed handrails, turned balustrades and carved stair ends; fireplaces were elaborated, sometimes in imported marble (local marble had been discovered at Bathurst to the west and in Argyle to the south but because of its quality and transport difficulties no use was made of it, even for the manufacture of lime) and rooms were furnished with excellently made pieces brought out in the immigrants' chattels or imported by Robert Campbell and his colleagues. In some of the better houses the windows were protected by venetian blinds hung on the outside as a protection against the hot summer sun. The interior joinery and the furniture were made of colonial cedar polished like mahogany. Floors were covered with Indian cane matting instead of carpet 'on account of its superior coolness'.

Doorways and windows had sills of stone wrought from the sandstone lying abundantly around and either similar stone lintels for narrow openings or semi-round or flat arches made from rubbing soft-burned bricks into the required taper. However, the skill of carving brickwork, so highly developed in England, was never practised in Australia and even in the high time of the 1830s brick decoration was restricted to features that could be rubbed, built or coloured. One of the popular architectural fashions was to define the brickwork of the arches by using a brick of a different colour from those of the walls. A common, but not exclusive, combination was bright red rubbing bricks and samel wall bricks. A further architectural touch was given to the more important arches, over the front doorway for instance, by building in brickwork a tapered projecting block in the form of a keystone and the apogee and projecting rectangular springing blocks at the extremities. Even the less pretentious cottages were carried along in the wake of the pace-setting houses. A strict symmetry of arrangement of the parts was mandatory, wall openings were flat-arched, the walls were bricked, the roof shingled and often, in imitation of its betters, a cramped little semi-circular fanlight with radial spoke-like glazing bars was pushed into the doorway. Except in the lowliest hovel the furniture was locally made polished cedar even if the workmanship was simple and crude and the seats of the chairs were woven rushes.

One of Macquarie's earliest acts to improve the quality of building had been to open a Government quarry on the north-western side of Fort Phillip hill.

Glenfield farm house at Casula, New South Wales: 1817

It was the first step in forming the most charming existing Colonial sections of present-day Sydney—Argyle Place. Here, digging deeper than the friable surface stone, good hard stone was pried loose at great cost in labour by straining muscles without the aid of gunpowder. Except in foundations, where it was commonly used on all buildings, stone was only acceptable with smooth finished faces—'polished' it was called. This was achieved by the slow and laborious process of chiselling it down through stages—from the rough face it had from the quarry to a dimpled picked surface when it was rubbed and ground by hand to the desired smooth flat finish. It is not surprising, then, that good stone was a very expensive material, that its use was largely restricted in ordinary building to sills and hearths and that generally stone quoins were not used for any but official buildings.

While the town houses of Sydney and Parramatta were becoming consciously styled and acquiring many of the characteristics of their English progenitors, country houses were developing features that were the hallmarks of the Australian Colonial style and the beginning of an all too short-lived indigenous architecture.

The waters of the coast and harbours have a steadying effect on temperature fluctuations around Sydney. While temperature extremes may vary by eighty degrees Fahrenheit they are limited to a very few days in a year. The difference between summer and winter extremes is some twenty-seven degrees Fahrenheit but the change is even and gradual. More importantly, the daily fluctuations are minimal and, with odd exceptions, in any twenty-four hours the temperature is remarkably even. But inland, even a few miles from the coast, temperature changes, both seasonal and daily, can be violent and severe. In the country, then, the climate was a problem that needed an architectural answer.

The answer that was found came second-hand from the tropical countries of the East. The verandah had been used from time immemorial in the enervating heat of the tropics. It had been taken back to the counties of Devon and Cornwall in England by the founders of empire. Thence it came to Australia. Governor King had incorporated a verandah in the extensions he carried out to Government House in 1800 as a covered means of access between the front door and an assembly room that he tacked on to the side of the original building. Even by the time Macquarie arrived in 1810 there were only half a dozen or so verandahs in Sydney; the great majority of the buildings were plain shadeless boxes. But in the country the verandah came into its own very early. John Macarthur's Elizabeth Farm, built in 1793, had a verandah from the beginning. By the turn of the century numbers of farmhouses were following Macarthur's example. Ten years later, practically every new country house had one.

The verandah was not primarily a means of keeping a house cool. As with Governor King's verandah at Government House, it was first of all a means of access. Country houses were built one room thick to take advantage of cooling evening breezes and allow cross-ventilation. In the better standard of house there was a central entrance hall and internal communication by way of connecting doorways between the string of four, six or eight rooms. In the poorer ones the entry was directly into one of the rooms, the parlour, with the same internal connection as the larger homes. In either case to move from one end of the house to the other entailed traversing through each room, with a consequent loss of privacy. To overcome this considerable disadvantage an external means of communication was necessary. The verandah was the result. French doors, either louvered for further privacy or glazed, gave access from the verandah to the rooms.

Because communication was the primary purpose of the verandah it occurred only where it was needed for this. Until its other advantages were appreciated verandahs were used on the ground floor and on one long side of buildings only. Often, again as at Elizabeth Farm, it was terminated at the ends by small rooms

Claremont Cottage, off Moses Street, Windsor, New South Wales: about 1822

The Retreat, or Kelvin, in Badgery's Creek Road, Bringelly, New South Wales: about 1820

Experiment Farm Cottage in Ruse Street, Parramatta, New South Wales: before 1821

protruding from the main box of the building giving a stunted ⌐⌐-shaped room plan but a rectangular roof plan. The outer edge of the verandah was supported on a series of posts which ranged in finish from roughly trimmed tree-trunks to finely worked and dressed columns. The latter were sometimes chamfered at the corners for all or part of their length into elementary mouldings or even had their faces cut and worked in simple groove patterns.

At first the verandah roof was formed by extending the roof about six feet beyond the wall line. Because of the low seven to eight feet ceiling heights, if the verandah had continued outwards in the same plane as the general single span roof it would have been only four feet or so high at its outer edge. Consequently, the roof was changed to a shallower pitch either over or just inside the outer wall line to bring the verandah eaves above eye height. The visual silhouette that resulted was a broken-backed effect and not very pleasing.

By 1820, Macquarie's standards were taking hold throughout the colony and all buildings, including country houses, were being built with new horizons. Even when not required by regulation, ground floor ceiling heights were commonly at nine feet. It was found that the extra volume was distinctly cooler and, when small touches of comparative luxury could be expected, were more pleasant by their generosity. In such single-storeyed country buildings it was possible to form the verandah by extending the roof in an unbroken plane. The consequential simplified form was more in character with the spartan simplicity of the rest of the building and the result was an improvement over the broken-backed roofs of the early verandahed buildings.

At the same time, the verandah suddenly gained ground and popularity in the towns. On the more expensive and tighter land near the towns, houses normally had four rooms on each floor—two front and two back, divided down the centre by an entrance hall and passage. The building was necessarily deep in proportion to its width. An M-form roof structure was thrown over it and resulted in a reduction in the relative visual bulk of the roof volume even when extended into a verandah. When the building was double-storeyed, with living rooms on the ground floor and bedrooms on the upper floor, the verandah, true to its access origin, stayed tied to the ground floor only. The upper floor stuck above the sheltering verandah bare and unprotected.

The rise in popularity of the verandah came from a sudden appreciation of its secondary benefits. Very early on country houses had found that the verandah provided an excellent airy and shady place for cooling the milk and it was now discovered to do the same for people. Firstly, by keeping the direct heat of the sun off the walls it had a considerable cooling effect; but secondly, and more importantly, it provided a sheltered and shaded area for sitting and relaxing when the inside of the house became overheated. With this, the verandahs increased in width to ten or even twelve feet and where space allowed were often extended around the end walls of the house. In the bright Australian sunlight the contrast of light on the ranks of white verandah posts and the dark depths of shade on white or mellow brick walls was consequential—but its visual strength was unignorable. In the better houses it was constructed with an eye to detail and quality. The posts became Doric columns turned out of solid wood and were painted white, the floor was flagged with squared sandstone and the ceiling was lined with boards. The result was a long low building, earth-hugging and horizontal, perfectly in harmony with the landscape.

During the decade after 1815 when the verandah was emerging from its country-side home to become the most important feature of Colonial architecture, a lesser development took place at the eaves line. In two-storeyed buildings and in one-storeyed buildings which either because of lack of room or imagination did not enfold themselves in a verandah, it was found that the bricks and weak mortar were still the Achilles' heel of otherwise good buildings. In Sydney's heavy downpours the rain, running from the shingled roofs in sheets and streaming down the walls, played havoc with the mortar. The trouble was particularly bad near the bottom of the wall where the splash from water that fell directly to the ground quickly ate into both mortar and bricks. To overcome the latter it became normal, even in the most humble cottage, to set the brick walls on a base of stone, a practice that had previously been restricted to public buildings and large houses. To overcome the former and keep roof water clear of the wall, the roof was carried two feet or so past the wall line. Greenway, ever alert to the requirement of local conditions and materials, had used wide eaves for this very reason in his churches and the Hyde Park Barracks. The practice became part of Australian building lore. When the introduction of roof gutters, machine-made bricks and cement mortar made the spreading eaves functionally superfluous, it continued as a standard feature which is still blindly used in the great majority of Australian houses. Like the verandah, the aesthetic richness that came from the deep shadow cast by the overhang on the brick walls was a consequential but highly significant contribution to the quality of the Colonial buildings. As long as roofs remained hipped, it was a noble feature but when, after the 1840s, the gable in various forms became the standard roof idiom for Australian domestic work it raised aesthetic problems which gave rise to numerous attempts, generally singularly unsuccessful, to find a satisfactory transition from the overhang to the gable, as we shall see later.

These two features, the verandah and the wide roof overhang, were developments that were restricted to the settled area centred around Sydney. In Tasmania, where the rainfall is softer, a similar quantity of water falls over a much longer period and the sunshine is milder and never fiercely hot, the milder climatic conditions did not give rise to the same extreme developments. In later years, from the 1870s onwards, when fashion rather than logic reigned in architecture,

Reibey Croft at Freeman's Reach, New South Wales: about 1820

new Tasmanian buildings became verandahed and some of the older Colonial buildings such as Wichford, Bowthorpe and Jessiefield, all near Longford, gained them as additions; but until then, with a few exceptions, they retained what was for them the quite satisfactory unshaded walls and the close-cropped eaves that both they and the New South Wales buildings had in the beginning.

Macquarie left Australia in December 1821. He had been humbled and toppled into ignominy by a mean and mischievous group who, believing themselves to have been unjustly treated in a host of minor ways by the Governor, petitioned the British Government with a list of accusations against his methods. Glad of the opportunity and nothing loth to clip the wings of the man whose grand ideas for the future of New South Wales ran pig-headedly counter to their own, the Government appointed lawyer John Thomas Bigge as a one-man Commission of Inquiry, nominally to investigate the charges but in reality, it has been said, to prove a case. Macquarie reacted pettily to the slur on his honour and determined to defend himself. From the first he had believed, in true military fashion, that every member of the colony owed unswerving obedience to his authority, an attitude which was interpreted as highhandedness by his opponents. But, after 1817, when he had been denounced to London, the redemption of his good name became an obsession that absorbed a large part of his energies. His creative talents dried up. When he could have been reaping a rich harvest from the efforts of his early years of toil, his enthusiasm and drive were being expended on re-establishing his honour and authority. In the last three years before his detractors clawed him down with the help of Commissioner Bigge, Macquarie shrank. The vast visions were replaced by a concern for the sort of unimportant trivia that had occupied the minds of his predecessors. But even when he was no longer able, or cared, to keep up with it, the forward bore which he had started surged steadily on without him until it reached its climax twenty years after he left.

4

The years 1822–1842 were the rich time of the Colonial period of architecture and the ten years of the 1830s were its high summer. Macquarie's reign had prepared the ground, the twenties saw his seed grow lustily and luxuriantly and the thirties brought it to its full and finest flowering.

Sydney's ideas had been chastened by the adverse report of Commissioner Bigge. Governor Brisbane arrived armed with strict instructions that were the antithesis of the powers and policies that had brought humiliation to his predecessor. Amongst other things, he was in all ways to favour free settlers and make the way of the emancipist at least hard and, in some respects such as the holding of public office, impossible. And he was to set his face completely against any highflown governmental schemes, in particular the extravagant public building programmes that had addled the mind of Macquarie. Consequently, except for repairs and extensions, government building virtually ceased for fifteen years. When, by the mid-thirties, many of the early buildings were beyond the help of even temporary maintenance and the growth of the town made it necessary for government building to be resumed, it was curbed and much more restrained in concept, size and architectural thought than it had been in 1815.

While government building in New South Wales was in a hiatus the settlement in Van Diemen's Land started to receive its first good public buildings. One of the best legacies from these years in Tasmania is the utilitarian but spartanly beautiful little bridge, which, in three short stone steps, crosses the Coal River at Richmond outside Hobart. It was commenced in 1823 but there is no record of the name of the person who designed it. Possibly it was Major Thomas Bell, the Acting Engineer and Inspector of Public Works in 1823, who was responsible for the small gem. In 1824 Captain Sydney Cotton, an army engineer, was in charge of its construction. Undoubtedly its direct, no-nonsense purposefulness strongly suggests a military mind behind it. Also at Richmond, a veritable treasure chest of Colonial buildings of all types, is a quaint Regency-flavoured court house. It is highly probable that this odd doll's-house building came from Tasmania's first Colonial Architect, David Lambe, who arrived in Hobart in 1824 at the age of twenty-one. At any rate, it was begun in 1826 during Lambe's term of office and he referred to it in his reports.

An increase in the flow of convicts to the island in the twenties required more and better government work, especially after 1825 when Van Diemen's Land became a separate colony independent of New South Wales. To help erect buildings befitting its position the British Government sent out John Lee Archer to be Colonial Architect. Archer was the son of an Irish engineer. He had trained as an architect under Charles Beazley in London and with John Rennie who built, or was associated with, several docks, harbours, canals and bridges including the London, Waterloo and Southwark bridges across the Thames. Archer too had been involved with these and later when engaged in his own practice in Ireland his work had included several churches, bridges and canals around Tipperary and Killcooley. It was

Above Bridge at Richmond, Tasmania: 1824. Architect, Thomas Bell (?) *Left* The Council Chambers at Richmond, Tasmania: 1826. Architect, David Lambe (?) *Below* Bridge at Ross, Tasmania: 1836. Architect, John Lee Archer

Rennie who recommended Archer to Bathurst as experienced and competent in the 'various Departments of Civil Engineering and Building in General'.

Archer arrived in Hobart in August 1827 and immediately took up his duties. Eleven years later he was sacked by Governor Franklin in the name of economy but in fact as a prelude to a not very subtle bit of nepotism in favour of his wife's nephew. But in the intervening years Archer managed to enrich Tasmania with some of its most precious architectural inheritance.

With the influx of convicts there was urgent need for military and convict barracks, police buildings and stores. Also, because of the number of convicts, there was no shortage of quantity of labour and it was cheap. But, as always, there was a shortage of skill. By strict and driving personal training and demanding supervision, in the same way that Greenway had tackled the same problem in Sydney, Archer managed to design a host of works and to see them through to completion and at an extraordinarily high standard of construction. The Anglesea Barracks in Hobart and the military barracks at Richmond, canteens, drill halls and officers quarters, the elegant bridge with its elaborately carved elliptical arches across the Macquarie River at Ross, a causeway at Bridgewater, the tower of St David's Church in Hobart and half a dozen other churches at Stanley, Richmond, Bothwell, Ross, Newtown and the nave of St George's at Battery Point, court houses at New Norfolk, Hobart and Launceston, customs houses at the two latter, the Treasury and its offices at Hobart, several gaols including

St Luke's Presbyterian Church at Bothwell, Tasmania: 1831. Architect, John Lee Archer

the existing one at Richmond and numerous houses, hospitals, schools and lighthouses at Low Head and Cape Bruny were some of the works Archer managed to wring out of unwilling hands.

His best works, the bridges and the military buildings, were excellent in the direct way of a thoroughly trained and knowledgeable engineer who was also aesthetically sensitive. In their form his lesser works, the churches, were typical of the sort of parish church that had a revival in the southern counties of England during the eighteenth century—a square tower in the middle of the short end of a rectangular nave with the entrance to the church through the base of the tower. Archer gave them a traditional Gothic flavour with pointed arched openings and buttresses but even here he achieved, by necessity and inclination, a spartan simplification that left the basic form stripped of adornment. Their unabashed straightforwardness relied for its success on the factors common to all good Colonial architecture—proportions and texture.

Archer erected his most important structures, such as the bridges, in stone and the least important, such as his houses, in brick. In both cases the results were fine and honest. But in those that were too important for homely brick or not important enough for stone he adopted the technique of plastering brick walls in imitation of stone. Thus his churches are usually smooth and flat surfaced. Combined with the almost total absence of mouldings this produced a finished building of flat cardboard thinness. When Archer was being consciously

Old Trinity Church Tower, Hobart: 1833. Architect, John Lee Archer

St Luke's Church of
England at Richmond,
Tasmania: 1834.
Architect, John Lee
Archer

architectural, as in his churches, he was a long way from being a Greenway; but in his bridges and lighthouses he was without peer.

A few years after Archer's arrival in Van Diemen's Land, and while he was busily improving that colony, another architect who was well experienced in bridge building came to New South Wales. David Lennox was a stonemason by trade who, caught in the building recession that descended on England in the thirties, decided to move to Australia. In 1832 he stepped ashore at Sydney. The country to the west of the Blue Mountains was opening rapidly. Traffic to the outer areas was increasing heavily and permanently. Better roads and bridges were warranted and needed urgently. Governor Bourke appointed him Superintendent of Bridges.

Lennox had it harder than Archer. Instead of the unlimited supply of cheap convict labour that was available to Archer, Lennox found himself desperately short of men. But by dint of perseverance he managed to scrape together a few labourers and, like Greenway and Archer, by personal tuition to train them to a remarkable degree of competence. Between 1833 and 1836 he built the excellent small stone bridges at Lapstone, Parramatta and, his finest work in New South Wales, the graceful 110 feet elliptical span of the Lansdowne Bridge at Prospect Hill. In 1846 he virtually repeated but bettered the Lansdowne Bridge when, as Superintendent of Bridges at Port Phillip, he erected the first Prince's Bridge which leapt 150 feet across the Yarra River at Melbourne.

So, during the twenty years after Macquarie, government building effort was limited to strictly utilitarian churches and the main worthwhile official work was concentrated on a few small but very fine bridges.

During the same time that government building was quiescent, however, private building was vigorous. After a short period of hesitation following Bigge's foray into the colony the free settlers—'the exclusives' as they were known—stepped ahead boldly. Leaders of commerce built large warehouses and saw them not as mere utilitarian sheds but as monuments that both improved the town and proclaimed their owners' importance at the same time. Robert Campbell, for instance, engaged Greenway to design him a three-storeyed warehouse to be an architectural adornment to Sydney and a worthy reminder of its owner's status.

The centre of Sydney lost its rural character and took on that of a busy town as a few allotments were subdivided into smaller areas and shops were erected right up to the street front. Sydney's small population of the first three decades was able to provide a living for proprietors who stocked all and anything that the local market produced or the haphazard shipping arrivals thought fit to bring. Most shops were private homes with the parlour given over to merchandise. By 1825 shops specializing in certain lines were appearing and were being especially designed for their purpose.

The front of the ground floor of such buildings was given over to the shop in which the street wall was a flat plane of window. The windows were made up of a number of small glass panes set in a large frame. The frames were as large as eight feet by eight feet and sat on a low stall-board some eighteen inches high. To give rigidity over such a span the glazing bars were two or three inches deep. To allow the maximum glass area for display, they were only three-quarters of an inch at their thickest and fined down to a thin rounded edge at their outer face.

With government building frozen almost to inaction (only the Law Courts started by Greenway went on in a desultory sort of way) buildings of civic importance came from the interests and driving initiative of groups of private people. In 1821 the Wesleyan Methodists erected in Macquarie Street the first non-Anglican church in the colony. The chapel was a large hip-roofed brick box adorned with plastered quoins at the corners. Two round-headed oversized

Above Lansdowne Bridge at Prospect Creek, New South Wales: 1836. Architect, David Lennox

Right St Thomas' Church of England at Port Macquarie, New South Wales: 1828. Architect, Lieutenant T. Owen

St Peter's Church of England at Campbelltown, New South Wales: 1824. Architect, Francis Lawless

and overscaled windows which flanked a similar sized entrance in the street wall were framed on plasterwork quoins to match the building's corners. It was pure facade design for on the side walls it was an entirely different building. The plaster quoins on the face did not even carry around the corner and two rows of domestic sized windows in the side walls gave the false impression of a two-storeyed building. In 1824 the Presbyterians, under the energetic leadership of the Reverend John Dunmore Lang, erected a small stone kirk in the form of a parish church. In its proportions and with its unbuttressed walls and pedimented gables it was a Georgian building but its architect, Standish Lawrence Harris, set pointed Gothic windows in its rough walls, supposedly the first appearance of the Gothic idiom in Australian building.

Hotels, again especially designed for their job, with six or eight bedrooms on an upper floor and dining and parlour rooms on the lower, appeared on the most propitious sites—the corners and the high ground. The best of them offered the latest of civilization's refinements. In 1825 William Cummings was able to offer a billiard table and 'a Bath capable of being used either hot or cold' to clients, country visitors and new migrants, who stayed at his Pulteney Hotel in Bridge Street. The introduction of a bathroom in the Pulteney Hotel was indicative of the rising standards that came about as the colonists headed towards the thirties. Building costs rose in sympathy with them. In 1826 bricks cost 21/- a thousand, eighteen inch shingles cost 9/- a thousand, brickwork cost £3-8-0 a-rod, sawn cedar was 2½d a foot, lime was 7/- a bushel and a mechanic's wages were 6/- a day.

Between 1825-27 the country lay in the grip of a desiccating drought, but after the rains came it moved ahead, prosperous and confident. The general economic conditions, the rising tide of free settlers and the coming of age of the first generation of native-born currency lads, some of them the inheritors of large family fortunes, created a situation that was ripe for an upsurge of building. It was made possible by the fortuitous decline of building in England at the same time. Numbers of highly skilled out-of-work craftsmen decided, on their own initiative, to try

Cleveland House in
Bedford Street, Sydney: 1823.
Architect, Francis Greenway (?)

Opposite Bligh House in Lower
Fort Street, Sydney: about 1833

St Matthew's Rectory at Windsor, New South Wales: 1823-25. Architect, Francis Greenway

their luck in Australia. Others were urged or assisted by such Australia-conscious leaders in the colony as the Reverend Dunmore Lang to migrate and take their skills where they were urgently required and wanted. Thus both the need and the means for a climax to Colonial architecture came together.

The opportunities that awaited in Australia became the occasion for a spate of advice, most of it gratuitous, from well-meaning people. Addresses were given, pamphlets were printed and books were published by visitors, by those who had experience in India but had never been to Australia and by people who had never left England, telling, with varying degrees of vehemence, how the country should be developed. The ideas ranged from the sane to the silly—from the provision of an inviolable green belt around all towns to the importation of elephants for agricultural purposes, from the advocacy of verandahs and ceiling-height windows to a ban on marble as an unworthy building material fit only for lime burning, from instruction for the construction of a new invention, the water closet, to fanciful designs for a variety of stylistic houses. One critic on the hearth damned the provision of the one hundred feet wide streets that Darling was using as his standard for new towns as neither able to admit currents of cooling air nor able to prevent conflagrations from spreading in such a warm and dry climate. He advocated that main streets should be no less than 450 feet and secondary streets no less than 150 feet wide. He had grand ideas of space as well as the sort of climate and society that existed in Australia. Rooms, he advocated, should have windows on three sides, should measure at least twenty-four feet by sixteen feet on plan and have a minimum height of sixteen feet. Roofs should be compulsorily flat and parapeted, said some; bathrooms should be mandatory, said others.

Town planning was a particularly popular subject for free advice, as it still is. In 1830 a retired officer of the East India Company, T. J. Mazlen, calling himself a 'Friend of Australia', weighed in with a dogmatic assertion that Governor Darling should insist on towns being laid out on a grid pattern of tapered streets, widest

The Richmond Hotel at Richmond, Tasmania: about 1830

at the town centre with the straight edges of the streets being infinitely varied by the line of the building facades, that one style of architecture only should be allowed in each street which should be named after its architectural style. In Mazlen's hypothetical town the main street was to be Composite Street followed outwardly from the centre in descending architectural order by Corinthian, Ionic, Doric, Tuscan, Maresque, Hindoo and Chinese Streets, each with an appendage of North, South, East or West.

But the Governor and the people of New South Wales had little use for gratuitous advice based on uninformed or misinformed idealism. The immediate problems of a burgeoning colony were as much as the Governor could manage to cope with. He set himself the mundane target of ensuring that new towns were given a simple grid skeleton of realistically wide streets before they got out of hand without even this basic framework. From the first attempts to plan Sydney and Parramatta, experience had shown that over-wide streets could not survive no matter how cerebrally desirable they might be.

Darling took a practical interest in town planning and his ideas were based on the realities of conditions in his colony. With the country poised ready to establish a number of new towns he took positive steps to ensure that they would be at least tidy and workable. He was spurred to the task by the projected development of Maitland. Accordingly, on 5 March 1829, he issued a set of regulations for the guidance of the government surveyors who were charged with ensuring that any new town conformed to the requirements. Darling's move was of tremendous importance. These regulations were directly responsible for shaping the character of the great bulk of Australian towns. While they remained in force—everywhere except in South Australia and Western Australia—they imposed a uniform pattern on towns. Even after they were superseded, their basic ideas and principles were incorporated into later Acts and their thinking was accepted unquestioningly so that with a few late exceptions Australian towns are all Darling towns.

Darling's regulations put all towns into one of four classes (Sydney, Sea Port Towns, Towns at the Head of Navigable Waters and Inland Towns); required blocks of land to be one chain wide and five chains deep, corner blocks being two chains by two and one-half chains; allowed any one building to occupy up to four blocks; granted land in fee simple on an annual quit rent of two to six pence a rod; required grantees to construct drains from their property to the public sewers and to 'make and maintain in good repair a flagged footpath in front of their allotments'. All buildings were to be exactly fourteen feet, no more no less, from the footpath. The area in front could be used for 'an open verandah or such planting as may be desired' and the street boundary had to be defined by an open fence or, in the case of shops, posts ten feet apart. There were to be no steps projecting into the streets and, in order to ensure a uniform height of buildings reflecting the street contours, door thresholds were to be one foot above the crown of the road opposite the building.

Darling's regulations had to run the gauntlet of approval by a Legislative Council heavily loaded with self-interest. Some of his clauses did not get into the Act which eventually enforced the regulations and those which did were not of great significance to our story. But Darling's seventh clause was retained and it was the significant one whose effect was to be so momentous. It stipulated that the street pattern 'should always be rectilinear' and that main streets should be at least one hundred feet with eighty feet of carriageway and all other streets eighty-four feet with sixty-six feet of carriageway. Darling was a strong-minded and wilful militarist with a militarist's love of order, but although he appreciated the desirability of open spaces in a town he was realist enough to know that such a requirement had little chance of success in a society that viewed an individual's right of private gain as sacrosanct. He was already at odds with his Legislative Council and many of his most influential citizens to whom he was the blackest of despots. He therefore cast his regulations at a level that had some chance of acceptance. Nowhere in them was there provision for profit-wasting public squares or parklands. And thus, with few exceptions, it happened.

The regulations came just in time to cope with the burst of settlement that took place during the thirties. To forestall any designs that may have been in the minds of the French, Captain James Stirling, in 1829, landed a group of free settlers and a military detachment on the banks of the Swan River in the extreme south-west of the continent to found Perth. In 1835, two rival bands of private adventurers migrated under John Batman and John Pascoe Fawkner across Bass Strait from Launceston to settle illegally beside the Yarra River at the northernmost part of Port Phillip and found Melbourne. In 1836, a highminded and God-fearing group of free settlers dedicated to the virtue of private profit, under the care of Governor Hindmarsh and with the blessing of the British Government, founded Adelaide on the western side of the Gulf of St Vincent. And in 1842 at Brisbane, Moreton Bay, which had remained a tightly closed penal settlement since its founding in 1829, was thrown open to free settlers. Over the same period the inland of New South Wales was opening fast. And in all of these places except Perth and Adelaide the town layout was directly controlled by Darling's regulations.

Melbourne was planned by Robert Russell strictly in accordance with the regulations. When Surveyor-General Hoddle arrived to set his seal on Russell's work and formally lay out the town he widened the main streets and added the 'little' streets as access lanes to the mews at the rear of the properties. Melbourne was the most spectacular result of Darling's influence, but it also shaped Brisbane, Ballarat, Geelong and hundreds of country towns, large and small. Even in far away and independent Perth, Surveyor Hilman adopted the same principles and attitude in laying out the pattern of streets for Western Australia's future capital. When, in 1842, the Western Australian Company proposed to develop 51,000 acres of rolling country at Australind near Bunbury into a town of 20,000 people surrounded by five hundred 100 acre farms, its plan was the standard chequerboard of quarter blocks. However, it allowed for a certain amount of public parkland strategically and geometrically placed—a novel and unique bit of altruism for the times which may be one of the reasons why the project folded up.

Only in Adelaide was there a different story. There, Colonel William Light, the Surveyor General appointed by the South Australian Company, the sponsors of the settlement, conceived a noble town design. By its very fineness it was unique among Australian towns until Walter Burley Griffin gave the nation a scheme for Canberra in 1912. The plan for Adelaide did not come easily. Light had joined the main body of the expedition a month after its arrival at Kangaroo Island. Governor Hindmarsh was impatient at the delay while he waited for the surveyor and packed him off immediately to select a site for the main settlement. Light journeyed up the shores of the Gulf of St Vincent and had a mere ten days to inspect the countryside and decide on a site for the town before he was joined by Governor Hindmarsh and the main party. But his choice did not meet with the approval of the Governor who, as a naval man, found it too far from the harbour for his liking. For the sake of harmony, Light allowed himself to be persuaded by Hindmarsh. But within twelve hours, prodded by the expressed disappointment of his assistant, his better judgement reasserted itself. Falling back on the supreme authority in such matters given him by the Company, he reverted to his original intention and on 31 December formally declared his decision to Hindmarsh. The divided authority that rested between the Governor and the Surveyor-General had its first testing time and the division was irreparable. From that time forward Light was constantly harassed in his work by Hindmarsh and his sycophantic Secretary Stevenson.

The site chosen by Light was centred on the Torrens River where it lay in a broad gently-sweeping valley between two flat-topped hills. For ten days early in 1837 Light walked about his choice studying it deeply, visualizing, remembering and pondering. In his own words he spent the time 'looking repeatedly over the ground and devising in my own mind the best method of laying out the town according to the course of the river and the nature of the ground.' It was the fact that these two factors were uppermost in his mind during the gestation period and because of the way in which he finally used them that Light made his original and most creditable contribution to Adelaide. While Adelaide would still have been the best planned Australian town without Light's considered use of the river and the topography, it would not have been the unique one it is.

The final plan that Light decided on consisted of two sections of building blocks—one on the flat summit of the southern hill and the other on the broken rising slope of the northern hill. The gentle valley and the river banks between the two were left as open parkland. The southern building area he divided into a grid pattern with five widely spaced 132 feet wide streets running north and south, and eleven closer, narrower east-west streets. In the centre of South Adelaide Light provided a large rectangular public space which he intended should be formally landscaped and surrounded by public buildings. Four lesser but still extremely generous squares were provided mid-way between the centre and the corner extremities of the town. Each square was carefully centred on main streets with an eye to vistas.

Across the valley, Light divided North Adelaide into three different sized rectangular sections, each disposed to take advantage of the rising site but thoughtfully related to each other. One medium sized public space was provided in the largest section. Within each section the street pattern was a grid. Together the three sections provided 342 allotments to augment the 700 allotments provided in South Adelaide. The smaller area, the breaking down into three sections and the natural, stepped topography resulted in a more human, less formal and more domestic character than the southern town.

Finally, in a magnificent gesture of courage and enlightenment, Light wrapped his towns in a leaf-green cocoon by declaring the entire surrounding area—a band about a mile wide—a natural parkland.

Adelaide's town plan is an extremely fine one. Light has been awarded by its admirers every complimentary appellation up to genius for his brilliance. Many attempts have been made to trace the plan's origins and the sources of its author's inspiration. Some have seen a direct connection between Adelaide and a couple of other towns which Light had either served in or visited; but the likenesses are more imagined than real. It has even been suggested that Light, as a military man, developed it unaided from his knowledge of the layout of Roman military camps. The truth is probably something much less. The broad principles and ideas used by Light were common town planning cant in the nineteenth century and many of its minor or more subtle virtues were probably no more than accidental or, if foreseen, acceptable consequences rather than conscious or premeditated achievement.

The rectangular grid of streets was universally accepted as the only possible layout for a new town at the time in the English speaking world. In an indirect way it did owe its origins to Roman military camps but its acceptance in the nineteenth century had been an evolutionary process stretching over nearly two millennia. After the burning of Rome in 64 A.D., Nero had set down rules governing the layout and width of the streets and the height, type and materials of buildings that should occupy the half city that had been devastated. Nero based his ideas on experience gained in the orderly camps of the Legions. In the new

Rome the streets were wide and the blocks rectangular. The practice spread to other Roman towns built or rebuilt after that date. With the revival of interest in antiquity in the eighteenth century and the faith it engendered in the rightness of all things Classic, the grid pattern street was accepted along with everything else. Amongst the many people who had something to say about the design of new towns in the colonies, the arrangement of streets and public squares used by Light was universally recommended. The idea had been used, but on a smaller scale, by Dawes for the first plan of Parramatta in 1790.

Light has also been credited for remarkable foresight in having a few broad streets running north-south and many close narrow streets running east-west. The resultant blocks were long and narrow and, having their length east-west, gave the majority of allotments either desirable north or south aspects. The arrangement of narrow east-west streets also resulted in buildings affording each other mutual protection from the hot dust-laden north winds and in well-shaded and hence cool thoroughfares. As Light designed the town in the height of summer, it is unlikely that he would be unaware of climatic problems. However, he may not have arranged things as consciously as the foregoing suggests. It is more likely that climatic benefits were acceptable consequences rather than determinants. This is supported by the fact that Light's allotments were a standard one acre in area. He is unlikely to have foreseen his streets lined with the continuous building that was necessary for these virtues to arise with an allotment of that size. It is further supported by the fact that the streets that Light meant to be the best ones should not have any of them at all. North Terrace, the northern boundary of the site, was intended for the best residences with a lovely view across the river valley to North Adelaide. But it caught the full force of both hot winds and the sun. King William Street, the wide central north-south street, was meant as the main shopping street. It was a funnel for the winds and its east or west facing buildings were blasted by, and unprotected from, the sun. These very conditions forced the

Terrace houses in Johnston Street, Windsor, New South Wales: about 1830

Workers' cottages at Battery Point, Tasmania:
1846. Architect, John Watson

main shopping area to develop in Hindley and Rundle Streets whose present narrow congestion is anything but what Light intended. It has also been claimed that the numerous streets leading west were a functional answer to the probability that the major volume of traffic, coming from the port, would be in this direction. On the grounds of the economics of time and road construction alone, this is so illogical that if it were true it would be a fault rather than a virtue in Light's abilities. Once again, like the street pattern, it was a tenet of town planning of the time that streets should run to the cardinal points of the compass unless the topography prevented it or the use of prevailing winds for cooling made it desirable to do otherwise. When Light was setting out South Adelaide he had a perfectly flat site and after a few weeks he could have had no real idea of the good and bad prevailing winds. Therefore, there was no reason not to conform to the accepted rules. In North Adelaide he departed from the standard orientation for the good and sound reason of the broken topography—and by doing so again conformed to the accepted rules.

The swathe of parkland encircling Adelaide is one of its most valuable features. This idea had been propounded by various people, such as T. J. Mazlen in 1832, but Light seems to have been one of the first to put it into practice. The majority of experts supporting the idea recommended a belt on three sides only, allowing future expansion to take place out the unenclosed side. But Mazlen supported complete enclosure both for health and beauty. As Mazlen's book appeared only four years before Light left England and it was aimed directly at Australia, it is likely that Light had read and absorbed it.

In many ways, then, Adelaide was no more than a testimony to the fact that the Surveyor-General was well versed in the latest thinking in town planning and was well able to apply the rules. But, if he had done this and no more, Adelaide would not have been the remarkable example it is. It was the inspiration to split the town into two and to leave the river and its valley as a parkland, together with the sensitive handling of the ground conditions of North Adelaide, that lifts it from being merely good to excellent. And this, it must be admitted, was due not to the knowledge but rather to the faith, determination and sensitivity of its planner.

In Sydney in the 1820s the problem was not so much to get wide streets as to get streets at all. Without any sort of control or guidance after Phillip's first abortive attempt the town had grown haphazardly with buildings erected practically anywhere until its streets had degenerated into twisted and tortuous alleys. Macquarie's order of 1810 setting sixty-six feet as a standard street width had operated effectively in towns like Liverpool; but in Sydney the line of the central streets was already out of hand by the time his order came. In December 1827 the first building regulations for Sydney were issued as the result of an Act passed in the Legislative Council. Their purpose was to tidy up the streets and to avoid having to later compensate landowners at high prices for land that was alienated in the uncontrolled days. It was not concerned with the building as such but required only that intending builders should inform the Civil Engineer of their intentions 'for the purpose of having the line of front laid down with reference to the street and existing buildings.' The measure was not before time. Under increasing population pressure the demand for space grew. Until 1827 land in Sydney was held on short five to seven year leases. The insecurity of tenure inhibited full-blooded development. But in that year the period was changed to give perpetual leases for small annual sums. The change encouraged the hesitant, the timid and the canny to put their holdings to work. By the early 1830s subdivision of the early sixty feet wide blocks into three or even four smaller lots was bringing the crush of town living into the previously ample and spacious life of Sydney. Land prices climbed spectacularly. A block of land bought by Wentworth for £70 in 1825 was sold by him for £1,250 in 1830—and this was no isolated case. Building activity broke out like a rash in the main streets of the town.

To make the most of expensive ground, buildings crowded up to the boundaries and one-storeyed buildings became a thing of the past—a mark of the primitive early years. Short lengths of street became a continuous series of glazed shop fronts. Generally the windows were flat-fronted but a few used projecting bow windows with recessed doorways to attract attention. On undivided blocks a few attached houses, in pairs, threes or fours, were built speculatively. These early terrace houses were conceived and designed as a single building. By means of strict symmetry of windows and chimneys, tied together under an embracing unbroken hipped roof, they seemed at a glance to be no more than any other large house. Only the separate entrances to the units indicated otherwise. Some of them, such as the pair of houses built by John Dunmore Lang in 1828 as his own manse and a home for his mother, emphasized their unity by a single-storey verandah stretched across the face. Lang's building, diagonally opposite his church in York Street, Sydney, eventually became Petty's Hotel, and now, much altered, forms the central part of the Australian Red Cross Blood Bank building.

All the activity and the buildings pushed right up to the street front brought into being the second set of building regulations in 1833. Once again the building itself was not controlled. The regulations were concerned with the protection and safety of the public, primarily during building operations. As such they unconsciously reflected the free-for-all conditions that had existed before their advent. Conditions were set out to control the erection of scaffolding, blasting, protection to open excavations, the levelling of footpaths, the numbering of buildings, the leaving of materials on carriageways and footpaths, the lighting of obstructions and the covering of open wells. Pigs, whose vicious attacks on the unwary had been a source of serious danger for forty years (a young baby in the presence of its mother had been eaten while still alive by one ravenous brute in 1804) were not to be allowed to wander the streets, nightsoil was to be carted only in the dark of night and especially was it or garbage not to be tipped into the streets.

The regulations also prohibited the construction of cellar windows or door openings under any footpath and required all buildings to be provided with gutters to prevent rain dripping from eaves onto public footways.

Terrace houses in Davey Street, Hobart: about 1835

Terrace houses in Queen Street, Campbelltown, New South Wales: about 1840

Collits' Inn at Old Clwydd, New South Wales: 1825

The extension of cellars under footpaths had grown up in Georgian London during the mid-eighteenth century when the extension was used for fuel storage. Coal was delivered by means of a circular opening closed by a cast iron cover. They were potentially dangerous mantraps and when a respectable citizen suffered a damaged leg one dark night in Sydney the complaints against them were loud. The authorities took the opportunity to ban them when the new regulations were being drafted. Henceforth, access to basements was from the rear of buildings or by goods being shuttled in through low slot openings in the wall at ground level. Numbers of old buildings, particularly hotels, still receive their goods this way.

At the same time that these developments were taking place in the heart of Sydney the Colonial house was reaching its peak of development. In the outer parts of the town, in the countryside of New South Wales and in areas around Hobart, very beautiful homes were being raised for the comfort and pride of those who had passed safely through the first hard struggles of family foundation. The general run of Colonial house was a highly refined edition of the simple boxes that had developed over the previous forty years. Quality workmanship, provided by the influx of skilled tradesmen, was no longer the exception but the norm. Imported Welsh slate was available to those who could afford it. Good supplies of limestone had been found by the thirties in both New South Wales and Van Diemen's Land. Lime as well as other basic materials was readily available and cheap. In 1832 bricks cost eighteen shillings a thousand, lime was ninepence a bushel, cedar was one penny a foot and a tradesman's wages were sixpence a day. Workmen's cottages remained single-storeyed two or four room affairs but even in these the pool of skill available was reflected in the sensitive window and door joinery, in the solid and true brickwork with its openings trimmed by accurately rubbed flat arches in brickwork contrasting in colour with the main wall, in the true and level lines to floors and eaves, in the well-worked sandstone footings, door and window sills and in the well-constructed chimneys.

Middle- and upper-class houses were almost invariably two-storeyed. Single-storeyed verandahs crept around all four sides of the house, thereby increasing the usable outside shaded area and at the same time visually tying the building even closer to the ground. The care that was taken over the disposition of most of the elements in the building composition—the doorways, the windows and chimneys—was often loose when it came to the verandah posts. Whilst on many buildings the verandah posts were evenly spaced and related to the total elevation, they were not infrequently almost randomly placed around the perimeter. Within the same length of verandah in the same building, spans between posts differed by a foot or two for no apparent reason, as though they had been positioned by eye or had their placing determined by the length of timber available for a top beam. Oddly enough, because of the perspective, the variation is seldom apparent and never distracting. In the better buildings, particularly where the house was close enough to a town to make it feasible, verandah posts took the form of turned wooden quasi-Doric columns whose proportions varied from over-attenuated skinny spindles to satisfactorily-proportioned and elegant shafts consistent with their nature and the load they carried. The accuracy of their architectural style varied from the crude and vaguely similar to the refined and strictly correct. However, whatever their academic shortcomings, they were seldom over-robust or ostentatious. In these buildings the ceiling height was commonly ten, and sometimes twelve, feet. In those which were only one-storey high the higher ceilings caused verandah roofs to break free from the house roof instead of being a continuation of it. The main bulk of the house and its roof stood as a clear block above the lean-to verandah. Homes with slate roofing took precautions against the heavy load of the verandah roof by installing sturdy columns or by coupling them in pairs.

The verandah posts were linked by a valence board hanging from the underside of the roof. Sometimes the board was left plain but often the opportunity was taken

Throsby Park at Moss Vale, New South Wales: 1834

to add a playful decorative touch by shaping the lower edge into waves, loops, scallops and pendulous frills in a quite bewildering variety of intricate patterns. The flippant treatment of the valence boards, which were in themselves unnecessary, is not typical of the approach to decoration. In all other respects, when the colonial designers became lighthearted, their efforts were directed to embellishing essential and functional parts of the buildings.

Verandah railings, which were used only when safety required it, were made of wood. The basic design was one that was used widely in colonial buildings when the British Empire was abuilding. It is found in India, Malaya, the Residences of most of the Pacific Islands and Macquarie's Rum Hospital. It consisted of solid hand and bottom rails divided into horizontal rectangles by widely spaced vertical balusters with the rectangles then closed by diagonal members. The light and airy criss-cross pattern, and a multiplicity of variations on the theme, was the

Oak Lodge at Richmond, Tasmania: 1830

standard used in all timber verandah balustrades until replaced at the turn of the century by the heavy Edwardian fences.

Consistent with the improved standards of the times, verandah ceilings, either flat or following the rake of the roof, were lined with boarding and floors were paved with squared sawn flagstones laid in a diagonal chequer-board pattern. Often the same paving was carried inside through the doorway to the floor of the entrance hall.

The verandah was a part of the New South Wales vernacular. It was not significant in Van Diemen's Land. But apart from the verandah there was little difference between the ways in which houses in the two colonies developed. All the wall openings were treated carefully and precisely. The disposition of the windows was apparently symmetrical although, like the verandah posts, not always metrically so. Sills were stone and the flat-arch heads of rubbed, strongly splayed brickwork were contrasted with the wall brick, either by the use of different coloured bricks, or, where these were not available, by plastering and whitewashing. Good quality easily worked timbers, mainly cedar from the Hunter River and from around Illawarra, were readily available. Window frames and sashes, their glazing bars fined down to almost gossamer thinness, became lighter and their mouldings sharper and crisper under the deft touch of skilled and sensitive hands. Occasionally the upper-floor windows were fitted with louvered wooden shutters but generally they were left unprotected. When shutters were used they were usually confined to the ground floor. Their purpose was privacy and security, not sun-protection. Consequently, they were to be found on windows well shaded by verandahs or, in the towns, on street fronts where people might pass by. They were never used on a rear unverandahed wall no matter what its orientation.

It was on the entrance doorway that the main thought of design and skill of execution were concentrated. This centrally placed crucial focus was the preserve of the joiners. Masons, bricklayers and plasterers played no part other than to provide a plain unadorned opening into which was fitted the finest work that the mind and hand of the joiner could produce. The door itself was heavy and solid. Usually it measured seven feet high, three to four feet wide in one or two leaves, two inches thick and had six varying size panels crisply moulded. It was adorned at the centre of the lower intermediate rail with a plain brass knob and at the same position of the upper intermediate rail by a heavy but elegant or fanciful brass knocker designed to entrance or amuse and to give a most solid and satisfying response. Sidelights, sometimes fully glazed to the floor but generally panelled in the lower half and glazed in the upper, flanked the door frame, increased the width and enhanced the generousness of the doorway. Both the door and sidelights were crowned with an elaborate fanlight. Until the middle 1820s fanlights had been robustly semi-circular and the coarse glazing bars were straight and radial. By the thirties the fanlight had become gracefully elliptical. Glazing bars, deep, narrow and knife-edged, were bent and turned into an intricate tracery of delicate geometrical patterns in loops, S-forms, ovals and straight lines—veritable cobwebs of delight. Some of them were imported from England but mostly it was local craftsmen and local materials that wrought these fantasies.

In the humble homes of the labourers where the doorway was the width of a narrow door only and the head of the opening was flat, the same principles and awareness were apparent. The door itself was thick and solid and the composition of the six panels, the handle and the knocker was equally studied. The rectangular

Bowthorpe, near Longford, Tasmania: about 1835

fanlight was playfully elaborated by cheap straight glazing bars into lozenges, diamonds and rectangles and, occasionally, by curved bars into ovals and inter-locking loops. While such fanlights were necessarily tight they were never mean.

The differences between the best Colonial homes and the lowly cottages of the 1830s were basically ones of money—not of taste. Only by comparison with its finer contemporary work was the joinery of the cottages crude—by comparison with what had gone before and what was to come after, it was excellent. It was really only in size that they varied. By qualities of simplicity, directness and honesty the builders of the 1820s and 1830s gave to the most humble house the seemly dignity of a mansion. Because of a strong common outlook, because the same materials were used in the same ways to cope with the same problems, because they took the same physical form and were set in the same environment, the Colonial Style houses with their salmon or light brown walls, their precisely placed sparkling white framed windows, their green shutters and doorways and their grey-green shingle roofs and (in New South Wales) their white posted verandahs, achieved a unity and harmony with their surroundings and each other that were superb.

While the Colonial houses were consciously designed it was a consciousness founded largely on intuition and tradition rather than intellect. Generations of fine design in which good proportions, pleasant texture and harmony with the surroundings, whether urban or rural, were *sine qua non* had made the idiom second nature—almost instinctive. When it was transported across the oceans even the remaining vestiges of superficiality were washed away. When the Colonial Style came to full flower, naive though it was in many ways, it was distinguished by an exemplary regard for an economy of resources and materials used in the best of taste. In this lay its modest glory and supremacy in Australian architectural history.

The design quality of the Colonial Style houses was largely external. So long as there were four rooms on each floor, the plan was conventional enough to be straightforward—a central hall and passage were flanked with two rooms each side. But when, as happened in the larger houses, the number of rooms was more than this the plan often broke down into a tortured collection of rooms and passages, frequently disconnected or leading nowhere, cramped and shoved ill-fittingly into the strict rectangular confines of the outer walls. The internal organization of rooms had little semblance of the control that marked the outside. Being the normal and conventional house of the times with which everybody was familiar, such buildings were in no way fashion conscious. The planning, such as it was, was carried out by the light of a guttering candle with a scrappy bit of paper and a stubby pencil by the prospective owner. His efforts, once they went beyond the known, were crude in the extreme.

The real designing was left to the builders, tradesmen all, who translated the plan they were given into three dimensions innately. The internal details, being in the hands of the craftsmen, were plain but excellent. Ceilings were plastered using closely-spaced thin-sawn oregon battens to form a key. A thick one inch layer of porous hair mortar was finished with a thin setting-coat of rich lime and sand. The finish was flat and very smooth but the materials did not lend themselves to complicated moulding. Walls were usually finished in the same way directly onto the brickwork. Consequently, room surfaces were plain and at the junction of wall and ceiling cornices were simple or non-existent. A few inches from the top of the wall a light timber rail was fixed from which to hang pictures and homily-bearing dishes. Where walls were not smoothly plastered, they were lined with painted cedar boards. The joinery was universally cedar with simple and gracious hand-run moulding—never carved. Window reveals were panelled, often as folding security shutters, door architraves were mitred or butted against square blocks which had square or round dished and bossed rosettes at their centres, skirtings were six to twelve inches high with only the top three inches moulded. Fireplaces received the most attention and were surrounded with cedar in the same general form as the architraves. Staircases, except for the newel posts, were invariably plain but light and firm—straight flights with unmoulded stringers, bullnose treads, plain inch square balusters, gently rounded handrails with finger grooves and square or turned newel posts.

Architects had no hand in designing the ordinary Colonial house. Being fashionable and expensive creatures their services were used only by those who could afford them and wanted a fashionable home. But even the architects often found themselves floundering, producing awkward and distorted plans when the clients' requirements went beyond their experience and capabilities. John Verge, the most fashionable architect in Sydney during the 1830s, for instance, was often found wanting in planning his larger homes.

In the first one-roomed huts built at Sydney Cove, all living, eating, sleeping, cooking and washing took place in this all-purpose room. From the time houses expanded beyond a couple of rooms, it was the practice to use the house itself for the living and sleeping requirements of the family only. The service spaces— the kitchen and the wash houses and, in medium or large houses in the country, the brewhouse, the meat house, the dairy and the servants' quarters—were in a separate block at the rear. The division had several causes. After a couple of summers, it became evident that the heat from cooking made the house almost unbearable for some eight months of the year. As a result, separate kitchens built well away from the main house became the universal practice. The same factors applied to washing and brewing so the three activities were housed under one roof.

In England it was normal for kitchens and servants to be housed in the basement. In Sydney the ever-present sandstone put excavated basements out of the question in most places. But an even more important factor was a quirk of human nature that is as old as time. In New South Wales all employers were free and all servants were convicts. The employers were conscious of, and touchy about, the fact. Few respectable people, even those who until recently had been guests of His Majesty's Government themselves, wanted convicts actually sharing their homes. Hence, servants were housed away from the main house with the wood, the meat, the heat of the kitchen and most of the flies. By the 1830s, however, the service block was joined to the main house by a paved path and a low covered link—a roof supported by posts each side.

Kitchens were important rooms, spacious, with flagged floor and whitewashed walls, lit by small windows set halfway up the wall and barred for security against predators—both black and white. Kitchens were not usually ceiled and ventilation was left to chance and loosely fitting shingles. Wooden work-benches with an open slat shelf midway to the floor ranged along the long walls. In the centre of the room stood a large broad wooden table. Both benches and table were scrubbed to a creamy whiteness with sand, brushes and sweat. At one end of the kitchen was a pantry in which jars, barrels and bags of provisions, often sufficient for twelve months, could be stored. The other end was wholly taken up by a wide fireplace with metal hobs, bars set crosswise and a separate enclosed baking oven at eye height. The various utensils and equipment—the butter churns, the pats, the boards, marble slabs, the pots, pans, cauldrons and choppers—were hung openly on pegs or stored on the benches or shelves.

A few other refinements began to appear in the service block of better homes during the thirties. Mechanical washing machines were available in Australia in 1832 and instructions on how to make one were given in articles written in England for people settling in Australia. One type consisted of a perforated drum rotating on a horizontal axis inside a water-tight churn. A handle turned by hand

Lindesay, Carthona
Avenue, Darling Point,
New South Wales:
about 1835

or, in the case of big ones, by steam or horse power, tumbled the clothes to cleanness—the same principle used in several of the automatic electric washing machines of today. Another type was rocked lengthwise like a cradle while wooden balls rolling to and fro pummelled the clothes into submission. However, as boiling and scrubbing remained the standard clothes washing method in all Australian homes until the 1930s, it is clear that the early machines were neither labour-saving nor efficient.

Water closets were coming into use by the 1830s. One of the blessings spawned by the inventive urge of the Industrial Revolution, they had been given to the civilized world in 1778 by Joseph Bramah. Government House in Sydney had one by 1821. Ten years later they were being installed in many of the better houses. The pans were primitive affairs fashioned out of lead. An inverted truncated cone, to which was fitted a wooden seat, was jointed and sealed to a large hemispherical bowl from which a wide pipe at the upper edge discharged into a septic tank chamber directly underneath. The levels of cone, bowl and outlet were arranged to provide what is today euphemistically called a water seal but in 1833 was more frankly described as a 'stink trap'. Either way the principle is the same. An overhead cistern, filled by a hand pump, flushed the 'stink trap' for as long as a hanging chain was held down and water remained in the cistern.

At the time that the unaffected Colonial style was passing through its best period during the 1830s the leading figures in local society abandoned it as smacking too much of a rude and primitive past. They turned to a consciously fashionable architecture. The demand for it came from the significant growth of a moneyed and educated class to whom a taste for fashion was a normal part of life. It was a group composed of the local élite and leavened by a better class of free settlers who, for the first time, started to arrive in increasing numbers. The former, whose land grants were taking on the aura of estates, were second generation Australian families whose scions were sent Home to acquire the polish, tastes and education befitting their station. The latter were already people of substance when they landed and came not to establish a modest fortune, as had their optimistic but penniless predecessors, but to increase the one they already had. As a class its members sought to establish their superiority by displaying it.

The means came from the affluence and economic growth that buoyed the whole society and of which they commanded the largest share. The way was provided by a rise in the building skill brought out in the migrant ships. This included not only the artisans and journeymen who had been trained in a period in which English domestic architecture was the best it had ever been, but also some who had made the transition to the architectural profession. Both the architects and the craftsmen had been well schooled in the skills and the tastes current in the London circles that Australian society was bent on imitating. Consequently, in Sydney and its countryside, many large homes were erected in a local version of the English Regency style.

Just as the Colonial style was a stripped-down translation of the brick Georgian before 1800, so Australian Regency was an exceedingly simplified version of the style made popular by John Soane under the encouragement and patronage of the Prince Regent.

Because of the class of person for whom they were built, the Regency homes were comparatively large. The aim of the style was to impress—both by means of scale and sophistication of detail. The combined result was that the Regency homes were imposing buildings. Invariably two-storeyed, they were characterized by the strictest formality. Usually the roof continued to cap the building with a wide overhang but in some of the most pretentious ones the roof eaves disappeared as walls were carried up to form a solid parapet screening the roof, whose line was then marked by a bold projecting cornice of straight run mouldings. The centre of the parapet of the front wall was broken by a large, quite non-utilitarian triangular pediment, whose Grecian origin set the theme for the decorative treatment for the whole building. Pilaster strips running the height of the building broke the wall plane into bays, windows increased in size and the openings were surrounded with moulded frames. The verandah was outlawed as an unspeakably uncouth device but the front door was elaborated with an imposing, sometimes pompous, portico of Classic parts. The portico, frequently reduced to the proportions of a porch, was one storey high and consisted of a flat roof projecting from the wall and supported on corner columns. Its details, a heavy box-proportioned cornice and turned wooden columns, were in one of two Classic Orders—usually the simple Doric or its derivatives or occasionally the more complicated Ionic Order. In a few instances, such as at Elizabeth Bay House in Sydney, the portico roof became a balcony reached by french doors on the upper floor. The floor of the porch was usually an inch or two above ground level, but occasionally it was raised well above the ground to give an opportunity to emphasize its Classical roots by providing a sort of three-sided stylobate of accurately squared and dressed steps.

Elizabeth Bay House at Elizabeth Bay, New South Wales: 1832-37.

Architect, John Verge

Finally, the whole building was encased in a coat of stucco marked out in shallow grooves in imitation of stone and painted fawn colour to heighten the masonry illusion. Plastered walls, one of the earmarks of the Regency work, did not of course come in with the style. The practice of smooth-coating and colouring walls had happened with the very first huts erected at Sydney Cove. Government House, built in 1788, had stuccoed walls and the practice had never entirely ceased. But in these cases the causes lay in the highly practical need to waterproof dubiously secure walls. Except for fake stone quoins, little attempt had been made to use the plaster other than functionally. At all times before the thirties brickwork had been aesthetically preferable and had been by far the most popular wall expression. But now the effects which could be achieved by stucco were a necessary and essential part of the new fashion. Not only the wall surfaces but the cornice moulding and window dressings, the portico mouldings and the pediment

Hobartville at Richmond,
New South Wales: 1829.
Architect, Francis Greenway (?)

were run in straight lines of plaster groovings—but there the frippery stopped. The pilasters, flat strips of column profiles complete with entasis and capitals and the tympanum of the pediment were, like the walls, left plain and bare. The delicate garlands and wreaths derived from Adam and popularized by Soane, which gaily and lightly touched the face of English Regency work, were not part of the Australian style.

The interiors of the Regency homes were little different from the standard Colonial house of the same period. Because of their size they usually contained many more than the standard four rooms on each floor. The unaccustomed complexity often resulted in some cramped and contorted planning strongly at variance with the order and control of the exterior. Internal walls and ceilings were flatly plastered and left unrelieved by decorative mouldings. The joinery work, universally cedar, had straight shot mouldings and was put together simply

Douglas Park, near Campbelltown,
Tasmania: before 1835.
Architect, Hugh Kean

but elegantly around doorways, windows and skirtings. Except in those buildings which refused to compromise with colonial experience and conditions, windows had jalousies on the outer face and, often, solid shutters folding into the internal jamb linings on the ground floor. Stairs had either gracefully turned or straight square balusters and wreathed and necked handrails. In the finest cases, the treads were solid slabs of worked stone cantilevered from the walls of the entrance hall. Hobartville, near Richmond, New South Wales, has such a one; and the elliptical stone staircase with its wrought iron balustrade at Elizabeth Bay House is possibly the finest of its kind in Australia. In the Women's Cell Block of the old Darlinghurst Gaol, now used as the Cell Block Theatre of the East Sydney Technical College, the original cantilevered treads have been chipped off flush with the wall to reveal clearly the construction of such self-supporting staircases. Set dry without mortar, each lower slab was cut precisely into the one above. The two met at a splayed face which transmitted the load spirally downwards. When the massive cantilevered rectangular blocks from which the staircase was made were in place the undersides were laboriously cut away to a line passing through the lower meeting point of the splay to give a smooth soffit and a remarkably light stair side.

The staircase at Hobartville

Apart from the stylistic changes the large Regency homes were the first to take advantage of a technical development in the manufacture of glass that produced panes larger than the small panes that came from the crown glass method. The new glass which came in larger panes was known as hand cylinder glass and took its name from its method of manufacture. The process had been known and used from the eleventh century but it was not until the early eighteenth century that it came into more general use and gradually displaced the crown method.

Because it was the general and accepted method of window glass manufacture throughout the world from about 1830 until well into the twentieth century and because there are many misconceptions of the process, a brief description is warranted. A globule of molten glass, up to forty pounds in weight, was blown firstly into a pear shape and then, by further blowing and pulling, into a long sausage shape. The rounded end of the sausage opposite the blow pipe was deliberately blown thinner than the rest of the glass. Trapping the air inside the glass with his thumb, the blower re-heated the bubble until the thin end was blown out by the expansion of the trapped air. The blow pipe and the rounded cap were removed by placing a thread of hot glass around the shoulder and touching

The staircase at
Elizabeth Bay House

it with a cold iron. The cylinder of glass that resulted was split lengthwise by alternate hot and cold irons and then after re-heating gradually eased open until it lay as a flat sheet. Because the difference in the circumferences of the outer and inner faces had to be taken up mechanically the resultant sheet was always dappled or wavy and often slightly bowed. Dirty or over-hot flattening blocks gave the glass a burnt appearance. The early panes produced by the hand cylinder technique were commonly about twenty-four inches by eighteen inches but as skill increased a good blower of the 1850s could produce sheets four feet by two feet and by the eighties sheets five feet by three feet came from the best blowers. In 1896 in the United States a machine was invented which went through exactly the same motions as those of the hand craftsman and produced even larger sheets. Window glass was never made this way in Australia. Until 1932, when the Australian Window Glass Company turned out its first drawn sheet glass, glass used in Australian buildings came from overseas, mainly from England and, from the end of the nineteenth century, from Belgium and America as well. From 1835 until the second decade of the twentieth century it was all cylinder (or Normandie) glass.

Having completed this diversion from the story of Regency architecture, we must now return to the main theme.

Although someone (there are numerous indicators, but no proof, that it could have been Greenway) erected Hobartville in 1829 in a Regency dress for William Cox, the responsibility for popularizing the Regency style in Australia lay largely with John Verge.

Verge was one of those caught by the lack of building work in England during

Camden Park House at Camden Park, New South Wales: 1834.
Architect, John Verge

Hythe, near Longford, Tasmania: about 1831.
Architect, Samuel Jackson

the late 1820s. In 1828 he forsook his wife, his country and, he hoped, the building industry in which he had made his living for the previous twenty-five years. He was the son of a successful London speculative builder and he had spent all his life training with and working for his father when he made his fateful decision. On 27 December 1828 he stepped ashore as a middle-aged free settler at Sydney Cove accompanied by his only surviving son and determined to lead the idyllic life of a pastoralist.

Governor Darling favoured Verge's application for a land grant and in March 1829 he was developing four square miles of virgin country on the Williams River near the present site of Dungog. Inexperience and bad luck doomed his first efforts on the land. Despite his dreams and schemes he was forced by circumstances to fall back on the things about which he knew. Eighteen months after his arrival Verge was operating, reluctantly, as a builder.

In the Sydney of 1830 Verge's building knowledge and skill were outstanding. Clients flocked to him. The colonial aristocracy waited open-handedly for his services to erect for them houses in the style and fashion of England. For seven years, before he once again abandoned building for the land, Mr Verge was the architectural giant of New South Wales. As his work grew he was forced to devote all of his time to designing buildings and to engage other builders to erect them.

With this development, fortune smiled on him by bringing to his door, in 1832, a partly trained twenty-three year old migrant architect, John Bibb. For the next six years Bibb worked in the service of Verge. Bibb supplied what Verge lacked. Verge was a thoroughly skilled builder who had a limited degree of

Panshanger at Lake River, near Longford, Tasmania: before 1838

remembered architectural knowledge. His planning (at Elizabeth Bay House for instance) was weak to the point of being poor and, while his details were refined as one would expect from a well trained builder, his taste and sense of style on a large scale were undeveloped. Bibb was a good planner and knew the subtleties and nuances of both taste and style. Verge's practicality and Bibb's sensitivity combined to make a fine team that produced a host of excellent buildings. Verge had already built 'most of the villas of Woolloomooloo Hill, some of which are worthy of the suburbs of London' (according to the *Sydney Gazette* in 1832) by the time Bibb joined him. Some of them, such as Tusculum in Manning Street and Rockwall in Rockwall Crescent, are still standing. But it was the team that produced their best work.

In the name of Verge the two of them built such beautiful residences as Camden Park at Camden for William Macarthur, Denham Court near Ingleburn on the road between Liverpool and Campbelltown for Captain Brooks and Elizabeth Bay House for Alexander Macleay the Colonial Secretary. The former two are country houses set on rising hills overlooking rolling pasture land. Verge allowed them to retain some of the vernacular of country houses, such as a wide eaves overhang, but below the eaves line they conformed to Verge's brand of stuccoed Regency —sometimes stiff, sometimes awkward but on the whole pleasing and graceful. At Elizabeth Bay House he permitted no such deviationism. Its planning is inept and its central pedimented section, flat and cardboard-like, is weak; but this large elegant suburban residence with all the faults and limitations of which Verge was capable was the epitome of the style that he introduced into Australian architectural history.

Regency style homes appeared in Van Diemen's Land soon after their introduction into New South Wales. A few families who had prospered in much the same way as others had in the mother colony built large homes reflecting the security and material well-being they had earned. Generally the Tasmanian Regency houses, being less affected by climate, were stylistically a purer breed. One of the earliest of them, Hythe near Longford, built about 1831, was the purest Regency; while Beaufront, near Ross, built two years later, was only slightly less so. By the 1840s the closer concern for purity in Tasmania showed up even more clearly as some of the new large homes were dressed as unadulterated Classic models. Killymoon near Fingal, parts of the extensions to Woolmers at Longford, Lake House at Cressy and, best-known of them all, Panshanger near Longford were just a few of the many that were uncompromisingly Classic.

5

The first of January 1838 was an important date in the history of Australian architecture. On that day there came into effect, in Sydney, a comprehensive set of building regulations that virtually spelled doom for the Colonial style. With it the only shoot thrown by the Australian architectural tree that showed promise of developing indigenous qualities and characteristics was abruptly pruned. Only in the ragged fringes of the outback, whose limits have been pushed steadily further inland and where the necessary but deadening hand of bureaucratic control has lain but lightly, have the outgoing natural forces acting on building been free to develop in an organic way.

In July 1836 the Legislative Council in New South Wales decided that control of the growth of Sydney could no longer be left to a couple of sets of regulations that were concerned with ensuring that street lines were recognized and that people were protected from the more obvious inconveniences and hazards during construction of buildings. Within the central area of the town, buildings jostled hard against each other in the struggle for space. As shops, public houses, warehouses and homes crowded right up to the boundaries on the street front and both sides, the dangers of fire were recognized. Accordingly, a Building Act was passed on 8 September 1837 to be operative from the first day of the next year. It was, to all intents and purposes, a straight ingrafting of the London Building Act which had grown out of the ashes of the Great Fire of 1666.

The Act categorized buildings into six 'rates' or classes according to size, not type. First-rate buildings, for instance, included churches, breweries, factories, foundries, warehouses of three storeys or more than thirty-one feet high and all houses with a ground floor area of more than nine squares. It is interesting to note that the idea of a 'square' (that is, one hundred square feet of floor area) was both legally and technically sufficient for the purposes of the times. While it has remained very much a part of lay language, the term has long since ceased to have any other status.

The 1837 regulations were essentially aimed at fire control. They set down thicknesses of external and party walls, required party walls to extend one foot six inches above the roof line, laid down requirements for the construction of fireplaces, chimneys and flues particularly when constructed in a party wall, prevented the construction of fireplaces and chimneys on the street frontage and stipulated the construction of division walls between occupancies in the one building. Roof coverings were limited to glass, copper, lead, tin, zinc, slate or tile. Thatching, bark and wooden shingles were not included in the list of approved materials.

Two further important requirements that had been included in the London prototype in 1709 were transposed to Sydney in 1838. Essentially they were concerned to keep inflammable materials away from external parts of the building where they could easily catch fire. The first of them required all timber to be kept at least four inches from the face of the building, the second stipulated that no bow window was to be built beyond the street line and, more importantly, banned all projections except those 'essential to copings, cornices, fascias, door and window dressings'. Only dwellings, warehouses or stables which stood more than eight feet back from the street and at least thirty feet clear of any other building were free of these restrictions. In the heart of crowded Sydney there were few, if any, such instances.

The effect of these critical clauses, evolved for the cool sunless drizzle of London, was instantaneous poison to the Colonial buildings of Sydney. In one swift clean stroke the bland, flat-faced, cramped and vertical London Town Georgian architecture was imposed on warm sunny Sydney Town. Window and door frames had, by tradition, been set back into the walls anyway so the effect on these parts was not apparent. But elsewhere the effect was visually immense. Verandahs and window shutters were wiped off the face of buildings and roof overhangs disappeared as walls were carried past the eaves line to form a parapet. Where a series of buildings huddled side by side on narrow-fronted allotments, they were visually separated and their narrowness accentuated by the projecting ridge of their party walls breaching the plane of the roof like a series of dorsal fins.

Speculative builders moved in to contribute their rewarding bit by erecting rows of terrace houses. Single, narrow-shouldered, two-storeyed units were repeated from three to seven times. While the repetition of doors and windows resulted in a length of similar buildings, the separateness of the units was made patent by the party walls, sticking through the roof, slicing it into slabs. The simple

Terrace cottages in Burton Street, Darlinghurst,
New South Wales: about 1845

uninterrupted hip roofs of former times had given the appearance to attached houses of a single unified building but now terraces were expressively a series of replicas stacked next to each other. And all of them, whether a lonely single-storeyed cottage standing forlornly by itself or a series of terrace houses, were flanked at the ends by blank gabled blades of brickwork presenting smoothly plastered flat parapeted faces to the passing parade.

The unreasonableness of some of the provisions of the Act and the inappropriateness of others gave rise to a clamour of protest from the press, architects, builders and the public. Within six months of the Act coming into operation, protests caused the Legislative Council to appoint a special committee to investigate the whole matter. Under the chairmanship of K. Snodgrass, a succession of architects, builders, surveyors, bricklayers, carpenters and even a grocer, led by Verge and Bibb, presented opinions and facts against the stupidity of the ban on verandahs, window shutters, the mandatory requirement of parapets and the non-inclusion among the approved roofing materials of the colony's most readily available roofing material, timber shingles. In September the committee presented its recommendations for amending the Act and on 12 October the Legislative Council passed them into law. Verandahs and balconies of hardwood were to be permitted provided they did not go closer to the corner of the building than two feet or were separated from neighbouring buildings by a nine inch party wall; balconies were to be allowed to project three feet two inches over a footpath; roofs could be covered with hardwood shingles provided they were produced from within the colony, thus getting in a blow for the country's development and the balance of trade as well as building sanity.

The Council Surveyor, William Buchanan, gave evidence that shutters and jalousies often blew off in high winds and therefore should not be allowed. However, he was on the side of the objectors as far as the parapets were concerned and gave it as his opinion that, while parapets were justified in London where they protected pedestrians from the perils of thawing snow, they were not necessary in Sydney. In addition, the internal lead gutter that they required was unnecessarily expensive. The committee let him down on both counts. It allowed venetian blinds to be used externally but, while it abolished the need to use parapets on the back and sides of the buildings, it continued to demand them on the street front purely on the grounds of appearance.

While these amendments removed the more irrational requirements of the legislation by restoring verandahs, the type of building that came out of them had little in common with the Colonial style buildings. The visually important cutting up into a number of separate units of each building by party walls remained. Where verandahs were used this effect was accentuated as the blades of the party walls projected the full depth of the verandah on the ground floor in front of the main wall.

Despite the hurried overhaul of the Act the public was not placated. A public meeting was held in the Mechanics School of Arts three weeks after the amendments were announced, to continue the objections 'to many of the clauses which will tend to do serious injury to the Colony', the *Australian* soberly reported. Over the next few years a continuous and heated campaign was waged against what was variously described as a 'notorious, absurd, inadequate, ill-digested piece of legislation' which was 'a great source of annoyance' used to promote shoddy showiness at the expense of sound construction and which encouraged large stores and mansions while persecuting small buildings. Some of the opposition was not as altruistic as it purported to be. The Act restrained much of the anarchy that many people had used to their own free-wheeling advantage. The bridle of control felt uncomfortable where no restraint had existed before.

But the criticism regarding the encouragement of large and flashy buildings

Terrace houses in Burton Street, Darlinghurst, New South Wales: about 1840

Alfred's Terrace in Kent Street, Sydney: 1867

was justified. By dividing the buildings into 'rates' according to size, the Act encouraged people to build to the maximum of the rate of their building. As there was little difference in the restrictions on the first three or four rates, the tendency was to build in the first rate. The costly parts had to be provided anyway so it made better economic sense to build a large building for comparatively little extra expense. But the protests were in vain.

Some of the objections arose from the fact that the 1837 Act was interpreted as independent of, or at least superseding, the 1833 Act. After 1845, when a further amendment made it clear that the two were related and complementary, much of the criticism waned and people learned to accept the restraints. However, frequent predictions that repeal and the substitution of a more sensible Act were imminent were not fulfilled and the Act continued to control Sydney's building until 1879.

While the 1837 Building Act had been introduced to control a tight little area in the very heart of Sydney, its eventual influence was widespread. Its area of application in Sydney was expanded in 1842 to take in what is now the main city area. In 1840, regulations similar in their main and important points to the original 1837 Act of Sydney became operative in Hobart. The first building regulations that were introduced in Adelaide, on 24 August 1849, were an amalgamation of the 1833 and 1837 Sydney Acts. The combining was done to avoid the confusion and troubles that had arisen in Sydney but the individual clauses of Adelaide's Act were almost word for word those of the Sydney prototypes. In 1852, the Sydney Building Act, with a flick of a wand, was transmogrified into a Brisbane Building Act. And so, regulations designed to meet the needs of an old and established city in far away England were imposed, together with their important architectural consequences, on most of the future new centres of population in the very different conditions of Australia.

In Melbourne, however, it was different. Melbourne was incorporated as a city responsible for its own domestic affairs in the same year as Sydney, 1842, but it was not until October 1849 that it got its own separate Building Act. The Act became effective from the first of January the next year. It was a singular and most important landmark in Australian building control. Whereas all the other Building Acts had been mild adaptations of other Acts and, consequently, were very similar to those of London, Melbourne's Act was strongly influenced by local needs and conditions. Its most important departure from its predecessors was fundamental. It expanded its own objectives beyond the concern for fire risk and public safety which had dominated previous thinking on the subject by taking within its purview such matters as the rights of other property owners (e.g. light and air), the health and comfort of the occupants (by setting minimum room sizes and light and ventilation requirements) and the visual responsibility of the owner to the community at large (by setting building heights and approving a list of building materials which varied according to the importance of the street).

In all these aspects the Melbourne Building Act departed basically from the concept of control being for the safety of the public generally to protection of individuals, including the owner himself. Before, this control had stopped short at the outer face of the walls of a building. Now bureaucracy moved inside as well. An owner was no longer an unconfined king within his own walls. In this fundamental matter the Melbourne Act of 1849 set a precedent which all the multiplicity of later regulations accepted without question and used to bind all concerned with the erection of buildings in tighter and tighter bonds.

The unsystematic and often capricious ways in which Sydney's leasehold land titles had been distributed in the past had led to a near chaotic situation by 1832. In that year the government decided to institute a general clean-up of titles.

Until the land's dimensions, the quit rental and the owner's rights had been clearly established and recorded with the Surveyor-General's Office, new building was severely restricted and subdivision and selling prohibited. The result was to dam up the demand created by the ever increasing flow of free settlers. It was not until 1837 that the blockages of the titles clean-up began to be removed and 1839 before the way was really open. As early as 1836 rich merchants were realizing that terrace houses were a sound capital investment and a fertile source of profit. The next year they were becoming free to engage architects to begin planning—at the time that the Legislative Council was passing the building regulations that were to change the face of the town. The first important terrace house block was designed by John Bibb for Samuel Terry—the Botany Bay Rothschild—in 1837. It began building the next year on the west side of Macquarie Street opposite Sydney's Hyde Park. By 1840 the erection of terrace houses became an explosion. As a result of the regulations the terraces presented a face to the world that was either a long flat blank parapeted wall or a series of vertical brick leaves with the individual buildings crouched into the verandahed hollows between. On the unverandahed upper floor they were all the same. By the middle forties the cost of land made it economically necessary to build terrace houses three storeys high. As the buildings rose they dragged a skirt of verandahs up with them. Always, however, the upper floor was left shadeless. Rows of three-storeyed terraces with two storeys of verandah all neatly divided into compartments by slabs of brick fire walls appeared in the choicest domestic areas of the city—on the hills and overlooking the open public spaces.

The plan of the terrace houses was simple in the extreme. Sydney's sandstone made excavating a basement in the London fashion impractical. Only occasionally, and where the natural fall of the ground lent itself, was use made of below ground-floor space for storage or cramped little servants' rooms. The ground floor consisted of a front and a back room with a long narrow passage running down one side directly from the front door to the back. Between the two rooms and off the passage a steep staircase gave access to the upper floor which had two rooms disposed similarly to those on the ground floor. The kitchen and wash house were housed in a single-storeyed block, usually attached as a wing to the rear of the building or in the form of a separated unit some feet away. In either case, there was no direct internal communication between the house and the kitchen and access was had only by going outside. Servants' quarters were normally provided either as additional rooms on the kitchen block or in cramped garrets in the fiercely hot roof space lit by dormer roof windows. When four main rooms were insufficient, the terraces were a double version with four rooms on each floor—a front and back room each side of the central passage.

By 1840 there was a sufficient number of buildings in the new flat style to cause local apologists to point with pride to the change of character that was coming over Sydney. While some rued the passing of the eminently practical Colonial verandahs, they nevertheless felt that, in the balance, the change was undoubtedly for the better. Rows of two-storeyed buildings, their unshaded walls of real or plaster imitation stone, spoke more of a civilized metropolis of the future and less of a rude precarious past that was self-flattering and appropriate to their ideas of what should and would be.

The new buildings appeared to retain much of the quality of Regency buildings. But it was largely facade architecture. Because other buildings would soon be built hard against them at the sides and nobody but the owners would see the backs, care and trouble were given only to the design of the street front. The windowless boundary walls were built crudely in brick or poor quality, quarry-faced or rough-dressed uncoursed stone. The rear wall was treated little better and often retained the lean-to verandahs characteristic of Colonial architecture.

A house and shop in Queen Street, Campbelltown, New South Wales: about 1840

But the street walls were strictly composed and built with well-fitting, good quality squared stone with accurately picked, scrabbled or smooth-dressed faces laid in courses. Sometimes the rougher finished stones had smooth-dressed margins to emphasize their stoneness. The street walls were not all they seemed, however. The dressed stonework was essentially veneer built in two six inch leaves with a cavity twelve inches or more wide between them. The cavity was roughly filled with loose stone rubble crudely set in a poor quality mud-like mortar. The windows and doorways were consistently rectangular. The large panes of glass became more readily available although still comparatively expensive as the cylinder manufacturing technique became standard. Better buildings could afford the larger frames and ground floor windows increased in size without increasing the number of panes. Consistent with the current tenets of good design, the upper windows were the same width but less high than those on the ground. The reduction in size was usually achieved by eliminating one horizontal row of panes. Arched fanlights, with their curving woven glazing bars, had no place in this Australian Regency style and main doorways were flat-headed. Where they were important enough to warrant sidelights and a fanlight, these also were rectangular, broken by straight glazing bars into a smaller pattern of rectangles. The joinery work became heavier. The glazing bars of the windows and doorways in particular were thick and heavy, losing much of the delicacy and subtlety that had marked the work of the twenties and thirties.

The general simplification and coarsening of the joinery work was a result of several factors. The change from penal camp to colony that had taken place over the previous quarter century was finally recognized and the last vestiges of the past shed when the transportation of convicts to New South Wales ceased in 1840. Part of the price for this respectability was the drying up of this important source of cheap skilled labour. At the same time the prosperity of the thriving community and the welling tide of migrants created a lively demand for building. These two circumstances made quantity a more saleable commodity than quality. There was more money to be made from two quickly finished buildings than from one painstakingly crafted. Opportunists with little knowledge of, and less inclination to produce, good building jumped in to fill the vacuum between availability and demand and standards dropped further. In addition, there was no time to waste training apprentices and the skills which had been acquired so carefully in England were not being passed on or developed in Australia. Moreover, clients were not educated to demand perfection. Lowered demands and lack of numbers in the ranks of the true master-craftsmen, whether convict or free, allowed lesser work to be accepted. The rising tempo of building activity made it unavoidable that speed rather than quality made money for builders and tradesmen alike. The sum total of all these things was a dropping away from the time- and skill-consuming workmanship of the 1830s.

The same circumstances were reflected in the masonry. Window dressings were left plain as bands of smooth faced frames, string courses at the first floor or upper window sill levels were simple, uncarved projections. Cornices were the same and parapets were a mere continuation of the wall, sometimes broken in silhouette for relief by stepping an additional course in lengths around its perimeter

The Prince of Wales Hotel, formerly at Battery Point, Tasmania, now demolished: 1843

over the doorway, the corners or other important parts. But always the stone was worked in a way that was quick and required only rudimentary skill. Intricate mouldings and carvings were non-existent. The effect was not unpleasant. It was spartan and direct and this alone was immeasurably valuable compared with what was to come.

Where the building was on a corner the facade treatment carried around both street faces. As often as not these sites were occupied by pubs. The Hero of Waterloo Hotel, built in 1844 in Sydney's Rocks area, had its bar entrance in the splayed corner angle of the building and is a fine and typical example of the architecture of the times. The Custom House Hotel, built on the corner of Murray and Morrison Streets in Hobart in 1846, is another. Unlike the Hero of Waterloo it has a rounded corner. Many corner-sited buildings, both in Sydney and Hobart, adopted this way of handling their transition problem. In the curve there was invariably a doorway on the ground floor and a window on the upper floor. The curve of the wall was carried into both the doors and the windows. The frames, the sashes and the doors themselves were all built as arcs on plan with the same radial centre as the wall. It was a fairly tricky piece of joinery, certainly not in the same category as the work of the thirties, but as skilful as any that was done in the forties. The evidence of old pictures shows that numbers of buildings with these corners existed in Sydney but they have now all vanished. But in Hobart there are still several used as banks and hotels. The Prince of Wales Hotel built in 1843 on Battery Point, demolished in 1967, is one of them.

Unlike the majority of buildings of the time the brick-built Prince of Wales Hotel was left naked and unashamed without the usual coating of stone-imitating plaster. But even it was not typical of the few buildings which frankly displayed their bricks. Generally brick buildings were in the forefront of a growing architectural fashion consciousness. In conformity with the latest and smartest dictates of that fashion, these buildings were decked out in a bagful of Classical paraphernalia. Windows and doorways were surrounded with Classically moulded

The Lord Nelson Hotel, Kent and Argyle Streets, Sydney: 1834-43

plaster trims, painted stone colour, and crowned with triangular or arched pediments deeply moulded and painted. The size and elaboration of the dressings descended in order with their distance from the main entrance or the corner which became the focal point of the display. On private buildings this Classical school of decoration was restricted to one or two ambitious hotels such as Skinner's in Sydney. In the private field it was an overflow from the public buildings where it was to take hold most strongly.

Classical scholasticism was rooted in the academic controversies that developed in the salons of England in the latter part of the eighteenth century. In these hot-houses of refinement the virility of thought of the century after the Restoration had finally expended itself. Debilitated and carping, its remaining energy was dissipated into fragmenting discussions on the relative merits of the architecture of Greece and Rome against those of mediaeval times.

The Dilettanti Society, founded in 1736, had sent an expedition to measure and record the buildings of Greece. The society beat a loud drum for Classic architecture as the repository of all worthwhile architectural knowledge. In 1762, it helped publish James Stuart and Nicholas Revett's *Antiquities of Athens* which was to be a major influence on architectural thinking. From 1769 it published numbers of its own works, and in 1821 Taylor and Cresy's *Architectural Antiquities of Rome* furthered the Classic gospel. During the same time the Society of Arts, crusading 'against carelessness and callousness in aesthetic culture', ran a successful series of exhibitions which further prepared the way for a return to Classic art.

The antagonists of the Classic Revivalists were a romantically minded group who, deploring the cerebral primacy of Classic building, saw the emotion-laden cathedrals produced in a rustic, religious England as closer to English hearts. The interest in Gothic building was but one facet of a general revival of interest in mediaeval times that fascinated a large number of art lovers and architects from the mid-eighteenth century. Sir Walter Scott made the subject fashionable in literature and Horace Walpole helped to take it into architecture when he built Strawberry Hill in the third quarter of the century. The Gothicists countered the publications of the Classicists with a spate of books of their own. John Britton brought out *Architectural Antiquities of Great Britain* in 1807 but his was only one of dozens of learned and meticulous analyses of English mediaeval buildings. The works of the two Pugins were the outstanding literary contributions to the Gothic protagonists' way of thought.

The champions of each school had fought the main Battle of the Styles in England; the heat of controversy had ebbed and the main issues were settled by the time its consequences arrived in Australia. Except for Greenway, who was essentially a traditionalist architecturally, there were few architects among the settlers and convicts until the general upsurge in migration of the 1830s. Most of those of the early years who had some architectural skill and were given the chance to exercise it—people such as Watts and Archer—had done so secondarily or even fortuitously. Their engineering or military backgrounds and their services to hard-headed military governors or private merchants did not encourage anything but straightforward matter-of-fact designing. But the wave of newcomers of the thirties included a small number of people who had been trained in the fashion-conscious architectural circles of the early nineteenth century. They came seeking opportunities to practise their craft in the growing field of private enterprise in New South Wales. With them they brought the ideas, the ideals and the philosophies of a new profession that thought academically. And this thought had formulated a stylistic truce in which it had been decided ecclesiastical buildings should wear the Gothic dress of religion-centred mediaeval ages while government and public buildings were appropriately garbed in the garments of

St Peter's Church of
England at St Peter's,
New South Wales: 1839.
Architect, Thomas Bird

a rational Greece and Rome. Domestic buildings, being minor and inferior things in themselves, were generally considered too unimportant and unsuitable to be concerned with the heady monumentalism that lay behind the main argument. Consequently, only a few self-consciously important houses, such as Lindesay, built as a Gothic style-setter at Darling Point in the late thirties, were affected. It was not until after the mid-century that houses displaying details that had a Gothic genesis made any real impact on the domestic scene. And when they did it was a very impure brand of trivia applied to a standard form that carried the name Gothic.

The Classic and Gothic schools of design were impressed most indelibly on Australia by Mortimer Lewis who, after twenty years' experience as a surveyor and architect in England, arrived in Sydney in 1830. By the middle 1830s he had been appointed Colonial Architect at a time when the Government, acutely aware of Macquarie's unhappy experience, was ready to move back carefully and timorously into erecting public buildings. Like most ordinary architects of the time, Lewis was completely schizophrenic architecturally. In him the division between the appropriateness of the Classic and Gothic styles was clear and unquestioned. By designing his numerous churches consistently and uncompromisingly in Early English Gothic and his many court houses as Classic edifices, Lewis strongly influenced, almost imposed, a rigid categorization of architecture that everywhere marked Australian architecture for nearly a century and a quarter. Until the mid-twentieth century only a few individual non-conformist congregations, mainly the Baptists and the Jews, have stepped out of line by building Classic or, in the the case of the Jews, Egyptian places of worship. In the field of public buildings none defied the formula even after the strict requirements of Revival dogmas were abandoned.

Lewis' Classicism in itself was often a hybrid affair of Greek and Roman with at times hefty doses of the national domestic idiom. The amount of Classicism varied inversely to the distance of the building from Sydney or its public impressiveness. Its high point was the scrupulously correct but ponderous and inordinately dull sandstone Greek Doric courthouse built at Darlinghurst. It was more than Lewis' masterpiece. It is, in fact, the pinnacle of Greek Revival architecture in Australia. Elsewhere, at Parramatta, at Hartley, at Berrima, at Newcastle and at Raymond Terrace, Lewis designed and caused to be erected courthouses on which he planted simple Greek facades. Lewis was an architect of limited capacity whose taste lay largely in books and rules rather than innately in his heart. When he was able to give close supervision to his buildings, as at the Darlinghurst courthouse, the result was unimaginative and leaden; when the job was further afield and his supervision was scanty or non-existent the result was usually crude, rustic and often faintly comical.

By the forties many of the new buildings were intensely Classical. Banks, a museum, a post office, a Wesleyan church, a Congregational church and a library were displaying Renaissance or Classical faces to Sydney's streets. The results ranged from the amusingly naive to the pleasantly correct. Built of local sandstone they contrived, whether functionally necessary or not, to be, or at least appear to be, two and a half or three storeys high. Giant Orders of double-storey-high, free-standing columns or pilaster strips were somehow worked into the entrance or up the walls. In some of them such as Henry Ginn's Renaissance Australian Library building and John Bibb's unorthodox but quaint Grecian Union Bank, the lower portion of the building was formed as a rusticated base in accordance with the rules of the day. But whereas in England the base would have been a lofty ground floor fifteen to twenty feet high, in these buildings it was a mere six to eight feet with grilled openings cut into a semi-sunken basement or, if a normal occupiable floor, a low ten feet. The rest of the building was proportioned

St Mark's Church of
England at Darling Point,
New South Wales: 1848.
Architect, Edmund
T. Blacket

to the base. The result was a small scale, almost miniature, replica of the English prototype. Irrespective of the correctness, whimsicality or just plain ignorance of these first pretentious public buildings they were all marked by this doll's-house scale, imposing enough amongst their contemporaries but odd in later years.

They were expensive buildings and absorbed the best resources of the colony. Glass up to three feet by one foot six inches was used in the large windows. Easily worked but durable sandstone was painstakingly carved into elaborate mouldings. Until Lewis introduced a little Ionic decoration on Gladesville Asylum in the 1830s the Tuscan or Doric orders had been the only ones employed anywhere. The big buildings of ten years later made liberal use of intricate Corinthian and Composite capitals or acanthus-shaped acroteria and antefixae. The public buildings commanded the best of materials and skill that were available on a seller's market. Consequently, they were inordinately expensive by earlier standards but better built. While joiners' skill had coarsened, that of the stonemasons had lost none of its touch and, in fact, in quantity available it had increased—for those who could afford it.

At the same time that Sydney was being adorned by consciously stylistic buildings, the island of Van Diemen's Land was determinedly keeping step with the mother colony. Trinity Church in Hobart was crowned by a truly lovely brick and stone Renaissance tower that is without peer in Australia; St Andrew's Church at Evandale was a modified Roman Doric temple whose departures from the strictly correct, including its elegant little bell tower, were charmingly successful. The purest piece of Revival building on the island was erected in 1843 under the sponsorship of the Governor's lady. In the orchard lands of Newtown, Lady Franklin caused a solid little Greek temple to be faithfully reproduced and to serve as a museum and cultural centre. In its excellence of craftsmanship it reflects the high standard of stonemasons' skill which Tasmania had in such abundance in its early years. The fact that the vision proved abortive and the building lay abandoned and eventually found a use as an apple shed reflects the dichotomy of breathtaking natural beauty and incredible human ugliness that afflicted the island colony for so long.

The architects and craftsmen who built in Tasmania were mainly convicts or ex-convicts. Tasmania was still overwhelmingly convict in character in the thirties and forties so the free-settling private architects who came to Australia during this period headed for Sydney. Consequently, time was of no great moment to the Tasmanian builders. As a result their buildings were erected solidly and carefully and with greater attention to soundness of construction and correctness of architectural detail than those in Sydney. Convict architect James Blackburn, who was later to build several of the better churches in Melbourne and to become the father of Melbourne's water supply, erected and designed Romanesque churches at Newtown and Glenorchy and a small gem of a church at Pontville in the same style. In the same years Launceston was graced with the slender white beauty of a Regency St John's Church.

The yearning to create another England in the antipodes lay strongly in the hearts of all those whom England had cast out. The climate of Tasmania allowed it. The native trees were cut out. Rolling fields of the greenest grass were sprinkled with clumps of oaks, elms, beeches and pines, the roads were lined with poplars and hawthorns and small nests of houses clustered around solid little Early English Gothic parish churches. And along the main road linking Hobart to Launceston a series of large substantial coaching inns were set up a half-day's journey apart. Architecturally they are best described as being Classically disposed, in imitation of English country houses. Some of them, such as Ellis' Tap at Kempton, were larger and grander than anything of the same sort built in New South Wales. And, withdrawn from the main roads, over the hill and out of the

Above St Mark's Church of England at Pontville, Tasmania: about 1840. Architect, James Blackburn
Right St George's Church of England at Battery Point, Tasmania: 1838. Architect, John Lee Archer; tower in 1840 by James Blackburn, portico later

The Presbyterian Church at Glenorchy, Tasmania: 1841. Architect, James Blackburn

Gala Kirk at Cranbrook, Tasmania: 1845

sight of wayfarers, large private Georgian mansions, the homesteads of the rising local gentry, were the centre of a cluster of elaborate self-sufficient farm buildings. Because the large country houses in Tasmania were not beset by the violence done by building regulations, the transition from the Colonial to the Victorian was a gradual development with constant overlappings as reactionary-minded owners stretched past ideas into a time when others were well committed to Classic. The transition from Georgian to Victorian is still well preserved in the Tasmanian countryside architecture. Westfield, a transition building, and Hagley House (both built in the late 1850s) were Georgian only slightly modified by simplified Classic porches at a time when the rigidly Classic Panshanger and Lake House were fifteen years or more old. In the geographically tight little island of Tasmania with its closely knit and inbred landed gentry class the difference is more significant than it might seem.

Meanwhile, at Port Phillip the town of Melbourne was thrusting forward with tremendous speed. Unencumbered by the drag of military government or convicts, it missed the slow retarded early stages that marked all the other future capitals. With an exploding population composed entirely of free men dedicated to the virtues of individual enterprise and self-reliance, it hastened to recreate the standards of living its members were used to. Consequently, the Colonial phase and style of building was not seen in Melbourne as, after the first spate of the ubiquitous primitive structures, it hurriedly dressed itself in plastered and parapeted fashion. A few bricks were imported from Sydney or even England but most buildings were built of 'samel' bricks, wood-fired at pits near the banks of the Yarra. The first bricks came from a pit in what is now Little Collins Street,

Franklin House at Franklin Village, Tasmania: about 1839

then from a pit near the site of the present CTA building in Flinders Street. By the middle forties the main pits were on the south bank of the river near Prince's Bridge and on the low lying ground south-west of Spencer Street. Melbourne's site was clayey and rockless. When stone was discovered a few miles out of town to the north and the west, it was a hard dark grey basalt. When used in buildings the sombre colour killed shadows even in bright sunlight and the hardness precluded fine carving or moulding. A rough squaring and a simple margin were the most that was done to block stones. When, as occasionally happened, bluestone was used for window and doorway sills and surrounds the surface was plane finished. Normally it was used with a quarry-face finish and laid randomly or even as rubble. In some of the churches and the better buildings sandstone was imported from Van Diemen's Land for dressings. The contrasting colours of the stones gave Melbourne buildings a distinctive expression of extreme solidity and heaviness.

Within ten years of Melbourne's founding many imposing buildings equal to those in Sydney and Hobart were rising. As early as 1839 Robert Russell had designed and commenced the large stone St James' Church. It was modelled on

Lake House at Cressy, Tasmania: before 1842. Architect, Robert Corney

its Regency namesake built by Greenway in Sydney and was intended to rival it in both style and size. In fact, in its comparative crudeness, it reflected the differences between the two in economy, materials and the skill of the architects and the change that had come over architecture and building standards in twenty years. From the early forties numbers of churches were erected in religion-conscious Melbourne, each trying to outdo the others. They were all frankly stylistic. The larger and better ones were consistently Gothic. Samuel Jackson's Scots' Church and St Francis' Church were orthodoxly Gothic as were Charles Laing's John Knox Church and St Peter's Church and Robert Rogers' Independent Church in Lonsdale Street. But the Classic school also was represented to a lesser degree in Laing's Jewish Synagogue in Bourke Street and John Gill's Baptist Church in Collins Street.

The stylistic ideas of the academically inclined designers, rude though they were, fell on fertile soil in Melbourne. Very early in its life the town acquired

Macquarie Fields House at Macquarie Fields, New South Wales: about 1843

and determinedly developed a reputation for being culture-conscious. On 8 September 1847 at the Mechanics Institute, Redmond Barry, a gay, gallant and polished young barrister, delivered the town's first lecture on architecture to Melbourne's citizens—a thing that had never happened in Sydney. It was a flowery, pedantic talk full of learned myths, Latin verse and Classic quotations. Barry castigated Palladio and all his ilk as the *bêtes noires* of Classical purists. As a warning to his audience, he listed twelve major architectural sins that could be laid at Palladio's door. The Gothicists were dismissed as of no consequence and their works as abominations. Barry appealed for beauty and elegance in Melbourne's buildings, virtues which, in his dogmatic view, were to be found only in Greece and Rome. As a judge and first Chancellor of the University of Melbourne, Barry was a man of tremendous influence and, in later years, his views were a powerful factor behind Melbourne erecting in the mid-Victorian period the finest Classical public buildings in Australia.

Most of Melbourne's better buildings were architect designed. Architects swarmed into the free-enterprise town to take advantage of the opportunities they saw growing daily before their very eyes. Samuel Jackson, a builder by trade and an architect by ambition, had come from Van Diemen's Land with Fawkner's settlement party. He was followed across Bass Strait by John Jones Peers in 1837, two brothers James and Charles Webb in 1841 and James Blackburn in 1848. Robert Russell had arrived from Sydney early in the town's history as a surveyor with Captain William Lonsdale's government party when Melbourne was a hamlet of twelve buildings. Henry Ginn had left his Garrison Church in Sydney half finished to emigrate to Port Phillip in September 1846. Charles Laing in 1840 and Robert Rogers in 1845 came directly from England. By the mid-century there was a host of people in the town calling themselves architects. Some such as Laing and Rogers were architects by training and profession, some such as Jackson and Peers were primarily builders, and others were architects, neither by training nor experience, and were no more than opportunists.

In the jostling and scramble for work, shady practices developed and unskilled work such as collapsing walls and splintering roof trusses brought the whole profession of architecture into disrepute. In an attempt to protect both their reputations and their pockets a few self-proclaimed respectable architects met on 12 May 1851 to form the first but short-lived professional group of architects in Australia. Formulating its objectives as 'the formation of a Library of Standard Architectural Works, the promotion of Architecture in all its branches and the fixing from time to time of a scale of professional charges; also the upholding of Architecture in this colony in its proper rank as one of the polite professions', the group elected Henry Ginn as president of their Victorian Architects Association —the forerunner of the present national Royal Australian Institute of Architects. It is an exemplar of all the differences that existed between Melbourne and Sydney that this first step into corporate professionalism should have been taken nineteen years earlier in the former.

While the better country buildings of Tasmania, the inns and the homesteads, clung to a strong English flavour, either Georgian or Renaissance, those in the settled parts of New South Wales outside Sydney remained generally Colonial. Apart from a few which threw off the verandah and adopted the upper class fashions of plastered Regency, the wide spreading eaves and the embracing shading verandah were everywhere. In the slack building conditions that prevailed in England, many architects attempted to keep their hands in and their stomachs full by dreaming up fancies for the colonies. Numerous books of house designs became available in the bookshops. Some of them were prepared by architects eminent in their field—John Soane for instance. But to all of them Australia and its conditions were as unknown as Mars or, at best, were conceived as being something akin to India. For a few shillings their ideas on anything from a mansion to a labourer's cottage in a variety of styles—Greek, Egyptian, Chinese, Indian or Gothic—were to be readily had. But the benefits of this enlightenment were spurned by the benighted colonists. Country architecture in particular was little affected by the dictates of fashion and preferred to retain the practical advantages of a style which was well adapted to the hot dry conditions of the inland. On the roads leading out of Sydney to Goulburn, to Bathurst and to Newcastle and in the countryside around, many inns and homes were built but always in the unaffected idiom that had prevailed before the 1837 Building Act and the advent of the professional architects.

Further out, on the fringes of expanding development, the settlers faced the same problems that had faced all the pioneers. With a saw, an axe, a hammer and a spade on his cart and possibly one of the useful little books on construction written especially for him by builders who had been hard hit by conditions at Home

in his pocket, he had to do the best he could with the materials that were to hand
wherever he stopped. Helped a little by his book, a fair amount by advice and
precedent and a great deal by ingenuity and native wit, the settlers developed
a surprising number of variations on standard constructional materials and
techniques. Usually, and wherever possible, the first rude huts followed the
technique used in the first days at Sydney Cove—walls of grooved posts filled
between with tongued saplings and plastered with mud, roofs of bark laid green
and tied down with cross saplings to prevent curling as it dried, leather hinged
doors and shutters, one mud-lined fireplace and chimney and an earthen floor.
Slab buildings were on the very lowest rung of the building ladder. The next
step upwards was a wattle-and-daub hut, leaving slabs for the barns, the wool-
sheds, the stables and the general run of lesser farm outbuildings. In the usual
wattle-and-daub structure of the forties wattles, ranging in diameter from

Top The Prince of Wales Hotel (Mahogany Creek Inn) at
Mahogany Creek, Western Australia: 1843. *Bottom* A farmhouse
on the Perth-Albany Road. Western Australia: about 1840

one-half to two and one-half inches and taken from three branches or young saplings, were nailed directly and horizontally to the outside face of the normal squared timber posts and spaced from three to eight inches apart. The nailed fixing was quicker and cheaper than the earlier technique of slipping the wattles into grooves between the posts and was made practicable by a readier availability of nails. The whole wall structure, wattles and posts, was encased in mud and whitewashed. In a common variation of the technique wattles were fixed to both the inner and outer faces of the posts and the space between them packed with mud, leaving the wattles partly embedded and partly exposed on the faces of the wall.

But while the settlers' houses of the forties were the same rural form of the first huts, they invariably had the low roof carried outwards and supported on untrimmed tree trunks as a verandah. In areas where aborigines were troublesome, walls often stopped a foot short of the eaves to leave a gap for firing rifles through and, incidentally, providing excellent ventilation. The verandahs were narrow because of the steep roof pitch commonly used and were as much a protection against spears being thrown through the aperture as a sun-protection device. Improvements usually followed fast after the first anxious months. Ceilings and walls were lined with sailcloth making an ideal refuge for birds and snakes. Collapsing ceilings as perished sailcloth gave way under the weight of accumulated dirt, twigs and straw were one of the accepted banes of frontier life.

Where trees were scarce, walls were made of pisé, a mud mixed with the toughest grass available. Where they were plentiful, various ways of utilizing them with the minimum expenditure of labour were developed. Along the Murray River, where small diameter but straight-grained Murray Pine grew abundantly, shafts of the timber were set upright in the ground like a palisade or used vertically in short lengths to fill a frame broken into four feet square with longer material and then completely encased in mud. It was not uncommon when a certain degree of permanence and stability had been achieved and the farmhouse was enlarged in the same material for an almost pathetic gesture to be made to civilization by working a moulding or two around the door and windows and by marking out the mud plaster in stone joints and colouring it brown.

Only occasionally was the log cabin technique, of logs halved into each other at the corners, of North America used even in well timbered areas. One or two barns were built in this technique in Tasmania as were the sturdy lock-ups erected in the Victorian towns of Bright, Omeo and Harrow. The solidness of the construction is well demonstrated by these comparative rarities being still in sound condition whilst most of their flimsier contemporaries have long passed away. The first areas to be settled were along the rivers and the native timbers that grow in these places are usually twisted and branch close to the ground. Such trees yield only short lengths of timber. But even where long timber was available it was too hard and difficult to work to warrant the laborious adzing and squaring needed in this otherwise admirable building technique.

Many homesteads burnt their own bricks with clay and wood from the property. With weatherboards pit-sawn or split from suitable and handy trees, the tried and proven timber-veneer construction was often used for better, more substantial houses. Lime concrete had been tried for footing strips but it was unsuccessful. The lime was either washed out or it was found that after several weeks in the ground the mixture had turned to jelly. Footings were built in brick. Dampness in the walls was a continual problem with the wood-burnt bricks. Where limestone was to hand and lime could be obtained from burning it, solid brick houses were built but, except in the driest places, were plagued by the normal shortcomings of porous bricks. Time and cost of cartage put lead out of the question for dampcourses. Planks of wood, dry-set courses of stonework and even beds of straw were used to do the same job—usually unsuccessfully.

In the forties in at least one instance a settler near Maitland had a bright idea which eventually, in the eighties, developed into a practice that became first a standard Australian building practice and then a world-wide one. He built double-leafed stone walls in his home and omitted the usual rubble core. It was one of the few contributions to construction to have originated in Australia. Unfortunately, he filled sections of the cavity with mud and straw and its water-proofing potential lay undiscovered. Also, in the welter of ideas that the settlers tried in the years just before the upheavals that came after 1851, there was discovered another technique that was destined to become both Australia- and world-wide—brick veneer.

In this technique—the reverse of the older timber veneer method—a protecting sheath of brickwork is placed around an inner structural timber building. In the earliest examples the brick was erected indiscriminately around wattle-and-daub, pisé or any type of building at all. Gradually it evolved into a standard system. After the introduction of light timber-framed buildings from North America by the diggers who came from California after the gold strikes of 1851 brick veneer slowly came to mean a brick skin tied with wire to an inner structural timber frame. The method had the practical advantages of effectiveness, cheap initial cost and low maintenance combined with the appearance of brick—a socially important factor where bricks reflect money and hence status while timber is cheap, inferior and shameful.

What has been claimed to be the first brick veneer building in Australia, and hence in the world, was erected near Swan Hill in 1850 when Peter Beveridge burnt a kiln of bricks and used them to put a brick skin around his pine cabin. With his brother Andrew he had been the first settler in the area in 1846 when he staked claim to 300 square miles of land running from Major Mitchell's camp-fire site on the Murray River thirty miles downstream and extending ten miles into the scrub from the south bank of the river. The brothers chose their land wisely. In 1854 it was purchased by John Holloway. Under his management and that of

Balala, a slab homestead near Uralla, New South Wales: 1840-70 his descendants it developed into Tyntyndyer, one of the finest stations in Victoria. Today the original 1846 log hut with its brick skin of 1850 serves as the breakfast room of the present Tyntyndyer homestead.

The life of Tyntyndyer has been typical of numbers of its colleagues. Many of the early settlers' homes perished, either by abandonment for more stately homes as fortunes flourished or by abandonment for other fields when they did not or by the ravages of time, flood or bushfire. But numbers of them became the nucleus onto which later additions were rather haphazardly tacked. As times improved and needs increased, the one or two room shacks gathered an accretion of bedroom wings, refinements of living such as drawing-rooms, music-rooms, dining-rooms, box-rooms and the necessities of a successful station homestead, a gun room, a lamp room, an office and, later, bathrooms. Odd holes were filled with disjointed lengths of verandah. As the extensions were usually made expediently, the result was a rambling broken but characterful conglomeration. The effect was heightened by a collection of adjacent buildings from one, two or three hole latrines to a service block housing the large kitchen with its colonial oven and baking oven in the end wall, the pantry, scullery, dairy and meat house. Workmen's living and sleeping quarters, wash house and stables, blacksmith's shop, stack, barns, and underground cellar, sometimes separate and sometimes under the kitchen or men's quarters, a traveller's hut and, not infrequently, an overseer's house, a house for guests and a schoolhouse for the station children with quarters for a governess and even a chapel for everybody on Sunday were added. The mud hut turned into a mediaeval village.

Back in the cities, just before the half century, significant changes were taking place in domestic architecture. The changes were not overtly clear at the time but they were seeds which held the making of future history. The stylism that everywhere was accepted as normal for public buildings started to spill over into those' houses which it had previously left unaffected. By the middle thirties the banner of the Gothicists was carried into the domestic field when, in 1835, James Hume designed Lindesay at Darling Point which was then the country-harbourside retreat of Sydney's élite. Lindesay was essentially a symmetrical Georgian box wrapped in a smooth plastered shroud, imitating stone, of steep false gables and Tudor chimney clusters. In 1836 Major Thomas Mitchell, the Surveyor-General, erected his own house, Carthona, a castellated pile of bombast, in the same area.

In 1838 Mortimer Lewis began supervising the erection of the military-Gothic Government House designed inappropriately by Edward Blore in England. However, these and several other examples of the heavily castellated Gothic idiom, with its manifestly thick stone walls, its diamond-leadlighted windows and forbidding pseudo-military overtones, were restricted to official residences and the self-important mansions of the nabobs of the colony's society. It was not until the late 1840s that the carpenter's version of a Gothic villa came on the scene. In 1846 Edmund Blacket had given a slight Gothic flavour to Greenoaks Cottage, a large two-storeyed house in Darling Point. This building was secluded and well away from public view but not so the even more Gothic house Mortimer Lewis built for himself in full view of everybody.

In 1849 Lewis erected, on land overlooking the Domain, the two-storeyed stone Richmond Villa as a home for himself. In its plan and verandahed box form it was essentially a Colonial house. But Lewis dressed it up with a number of visual tricks that were to develop into a strong stream of house building known as 'domestic', 'timber', or 'carpenter's' Gothic. The ground floor was asymmetrical with a prominent bow window on one side and a lesser bay window on the other. Solid stone piers formed the angles of the bow window which was filled with pairs of tall narrow glazed lights each ending in a straight-sided, pointed head. The

Carthona, Carthona Avenue. Darling Point, New South Wales: 1844

Richmond Villa in Hospital Road, Sydney: 1849. Architect. Mortimer W. Lewis

bay window had a wide Tudor-flavoured window consisting of a bank of five lights with the same pointed heads. The upper floor windows, while evenly spaced, were of two sizes arranged alternately—the larger being made of two of the smaller ones placed side by side. Over each double window the roof eaves broke into a steep little decorative gable edged with spiky fretted timber bargeboards having, in silhouette, something of the shape of a mediaeval hammer-beam roof truss. At the bottom of the gables and at the corners, the fascia was similarly fretted into holed pendant bosses. The verandah had an open lattice-like valence made of light straight timbers running zig-zag between two light rails. The pointiness of the valence was repeated in straight wooden bracket-pieces sloping shallowly upwards from the posts to meet at the mid-span. As a result the verandah, made of light straight timbers, reflected the pointed quality of the ground floor windows and had the Gothic character of a pointed arched colonnade. These characteristics —the asymmetrical front, the pointed window frames and the verandah arcade, the varying sized windows, the decorative gables with their frilly bargeboards— became the hallmarks, in fact, the sum total of the timber Gothic house.

The example of Richmond Villa was not to have serious consequences for another ten years; but another event that was to affect strongly the appearance of Australian architecture up to the beginning of the twentieth century was already starting to modify the appearance of buildings. This was the introduction in the forties of a product of the industrial revolution—cast iron. A series of technical discoveries in England during the eighteenth century had improved the methods of obtaining and working iron that had traditionally been employed by the early smiths. By the 1830s the industrialization of the manufacture of iron made cast iron widely available and at a reasonable price. By the forties it had reached Australia. Cast iron stoves and fireplace grates found their way into the kitchens and drawing-rooms. When it first came to building it was not as a structural material but as one whose decorativeness was its main attraction. Outside panels of ironwork were bolted together to form a guard along dangerous verandahs and balconies, themselves supported on cast iron brackets. By the middle 1840s cast iron columns were being used structurally internally to support balconies in churches, in theatres such as the Theatre Royal and in hotels such as the Royal Hotel, the monster John Terry Hughes designed himself—both of them in George Street, Sydney. The first locally made cast iron was cast at Richard Dawson's Australian Foundry in George Street in 1845 when he cast a set of bronze-finished Corinthian style columns as supports for the balcony being installed by John Bibb in the Congregational Church in Pitt Street.

The iron was almost wholly imported from England. Iron ore had been discovered by Surveyor Jacques at Nattai near Mittagong during the cutting of a knoll for roadworks in 1833. In the same year the first iron forge and foundry, the Australian Iron and Brass Foundry, was set up in Sydney but it used imported pig iron in its work which consisted largely of making agricultural implements, fire grates and sub-floor ventilators. It was not until 1848 that five men under the leadership of John Thomas Neale combined to develop the Nattai ore under the management of a Mr Povey. Using locally found limestone as a flux, charcoal made from trees cut on the nearby hills and ore obtained by open cut mining, Povey managed to turn out the first local pig iron from his Fitz Roy mine. At the end of 1848 specimens of products made from locally produced iron—a stove and some spades—were displayed in Sydney.

The first cast iron panels that came to Australia were the same mass-produced products that adorned London terrace houses of the same time. They were of light and delicate design, often incorporating Greek motifs and still strongly influenced by the characteristics and working techniques of malleable wrought iron. The bars were fine and either straight or smooth, freely flowing with a preponderance

The Settlers Arms Inn at St Albans, New South Wales: 1842

of void in their total design. They depended for their effect on the pattern of the work against space rather than on any modelling of the surface of the material itself. They lacked the sharp precision of edges inherent in wrought iron but whether used as a fence of parallel vertical lines or a swirling flowing line-drawing of Greek acanthus form they had not yet shed the influence of the older material or realized the potential of the new. The local founders who started to cast panels by the late forties used the imported designs for their own work. Unworried by copyright laws, they did not bother to make their own patterns but pressed an actual imported panel into their moulds of sand and fine clay into whose graphited faces they poured molten pig iron. Consequently, the timid cast iron that shyly appeared on upper floor balconies—the balustrades, the brackets and even the grated floor—of the forties was very different from the heavy overpowering masses of the same material of the seventies.

Also in the forties, that ugly handmaiden of cast iron, sheet iron, made a quiet entry into the Australian scene. It was made from the metal that had been used for centuries to make wrought iron, in which pig iron was melted and puddled with slag into a malleable form. It was a slow process and the quantities produced by the method were limited. The technique of mill-rolling puddled iron had been invented in England in 1784 by Henry Cort. The ironworks of Payne and Hanbury was the first firm to produce the new material. Improvements and variations to their machine put thin sheets of iron on the building market. While still soft the billets were pressed between a succession of shaped heavy rollers to form flat sheets which were fixed to the roof in three feet wide strips with upstanding two inch rolled edge side-laps. The result was a smooth-sheeted roof marked out in bold semi-circular ridges running directly up the roof slope. Morton Herman in his *Early Australian Architects and Their Work* has recorded that at least one building in Kent Street, Sydney, had a verandah roof of iron as early as 1837. But until changes in production technique lowered its price, and machines were developed to corrugate the sheets, and galvanizing gave it a longer life and sheer necessity forced its use, it made little headway towards displacing the traditional shingles.

At first corrugated iron was used mainly to form quickly constructed verandah awnings stretched out over footpaths. A light timber frame was supported between the face of the building and widely-spaced timber posts at the kerbside. These verandahs had a somewhat chequered story. The Sydney Building regulations of 1833 and their Act which had been primarily concerned with protecting the public from hazards and dangerous obstructions, had made specific mention of street awnings and allowed their erection in front of shops and houses provided they were at least seven feet high and the posts placed close to the outer edge of the footway. This would indicate that they were a part of the building scene at that time but, to judge from contemporary pictures of Sydney, they were rare. The Building Act of 1837 strictly prohibited any projections in front of the building line other than cornices and necessary brackets. Under this restriction footpath verandahs ceased to be erected and under another clause of the same Act those already erected were demolished when they became decrepit. This prohibition was one of the causes of the angry discontent with that Act. The amendments of Snodgrass' investigation committee had re-allowed verandahs under certain conditions but it did not permit the re-introduction of verandahs across footpaths. It was not until 1845 that a further amending Act made it clear that the 1833 Act was not to be superseded, but supplemented, by the 1837 one. Street awnings were again allowed.

In the other future capitals the situation was always more clear cut. Adelaide's first building ordinance of 1849 included the duplicate of the clause of the 1833 Act in Sydney. Brisbane's Act was the same. The Melbourne Building Act of 1849 also gave specific approval to them in that proud city but, unlike the others, it allowed them on all buildings and laid down details of their sizes and materials. Melbourne's shade was to come from uniform verandahs that had to be twelve feet wide, at least ten feet high and made of masonry brick, metal or hardwood. It is not clear what control existed in Hobart or Perth but footpath verandahs were common in those cities as well by the late forties.

In the country towns, where little or no control existed over building and local government was non-existent, street verandahs were everywhere. In fact, they had found their way to the main towns by way of the small country towns, many of which had sprung up around isolated rural houses and inns where the virtues of verandahs had been long appreciated. As first one shopkeeper and then another spread a verandah across the footpath in front of his business, the streets became spotted with pools of welcoming shade. When a half-dozen adjacent ones did it a worthwhile stretch of protected footway resulted that drew custom and benefited all. By the fifties, Sydney in particular was a very different town from the flat-faced one that it had been when the decade began, and along the main shopping streets of the towns, large or embryonic, patches of timber posts with their shingled or iron awnings were sprouting.

As the half-way mark of the nineteenth century came around, Australian architecture ranged from the crude blunt frontier shacks of the inland pioneers to a sophisticated titillating concern for the latest building fashions in the cities. It was an innocent society that was just beginning to feel the changes that the products of the industrial revolution brought to architecture everywhere, a society that had almost managed to step out of the shadow of its convict origins and a society whose stability and future seemed clearly discernible. But even as finer and better buildings were being erected in Melbourne to challenge those of Sydney, and while in June 1851 the population of the new colony of Victoria celebrated its freedom from an oppressive mother with bonfires, roasted oxen and blazing tar barrels, men whose digging was to unleash an earthquake were quietly scratching in the hills out of Bathurst and at Ballarat.

Australian architecture left its innocence behind when gold was officially discovered in May 1851. For several years there had been disquieting rumours but it was not until Edward Hargraves panned some glittering dust at Lewis Ponds near Bathurst on 12 February 1851 that the Government was forced to acknowledge what it had known but had tried to ignore for fear of the consequences. And its fears were well founded. Almost before Hargraves had finished addressing a specially invited audience at Bathurst on his find, men were heading for Lewis Ponds. Gold-fever raged through the town and swept back to Sydney. The facts were distorted and amplified by exaggerated rumours of fabulous nuggets and breathtaking strikes.

6

As people deserted their jobs to chase the end of the rainbow, the economy trembled. Prices soared and essential work was left undone. When, in August, the newly-created colony of Victoria announced bigger and better gold strikes, first at Ballarat and then at Bendigo, the trembling became an earthquake. The stability of the economy, which had jolted along from crest to crest of small boom to small boom separated by periods of depression or stagnation caused by drought, change of government and apprehension, was shattered. The society, nicely ordered on traditional lines into an upper landed-gentry class and a mass of illiterate workers, was at first levelled and then upturned in the sudden revolution.

The immediate effect of the turmoil on architecture was negative. Building virtually stopped. As labourers and craftsmen dropped their tools and joined the floods of wild-eyed dreamers streaming west out of Sydney and north and west out of Melbourne, partly finished buildings stood gaunt and abandoned. In Sydney, where the strikes were further away and less rich, the town was more fully developed and more able to absorb the disruption, building slowed down, prices rose but work did not stall. In Melbourne, which was almost emptied of certain classes of men, particularly of building labourers and craftsmen, the only important building under construction on which work continued in a desultory sort of way was the new diocesan cathedral of St Paul on the north-east corner of Swanston and Flinders Streets. By threats, cajolery and hard cash the contractor managed to retain a carpenter and a couple of stonemasons to keep his job limping along.

By the end of the year for most of the starry-eyed the wonderful chimera had evaporated in the dusty realities of the fields. Those who lacked stoutness of heart or who awoke to the fact that the real wealth coming out of the ground was not to be found in the diggings but in the opportunities opening in trade and commerce drifted back to the cities and the towns. The more perspicacious and cunning found their own real goldmines in selling equipment to those setting out for Eldorado, satisfying the hedonists with the venal delights of wine, women and song or providing, at a rich profit, the material extravagances demanded by the lucky ones whose pockets were filled with gold which had been easily won and was just as easily spent. It was in these conditions that many of the substantial business firms of today were founded.

Within twelve months of the first findings of gold immigrants, intoxicated with heady stories, began to arrive in droves. The inrush of migrant gold-seekers started in full spate and continued for a decade. In that period the population of Australia trebled to 1,200,000. The greatest increase occurred in Victoria, the richest of the gold centres. Between March 1851 and December 1861 the population of the golden colony rose from 76,000 to 540,000 souls. All of them entered through the Port of Melbourne where they paused to equip themselves with hats, boots, picks, pots, cradles, lamps, tents and the paraphernalia needed for the fields and waited impatiently for a seat on the thriving coach runs. And to Melbourne they returned either disillusioned or with their dreams fulfilled— to spend or to earn.

The effects of gold reached into every nook and cranny of the country. The total fabric of society was twisted, changed and altered as the gold flowed out. Politics saw the flowering of new liberal and radical philosophies, the abolition of property qualifications for members of the Assembly and manhood suffrage. The northern part of New South Wales was established as the separate self-governing colony of Queensland in 1859. The old class order disintegrated. The selfish throttlehold of the powerful landed gentry was broken. The squat-tocracy was replaced by a new bourgeoisie having its strength in commerce. And its background, its tastes, its values and its standards were new and different.

The sum total of all these happenings was devastating to the whole society including building and architecture. When the goldfields at first sucked the heart out of Melbourne, building was paralysed. But when, within a few months, life pulsed again the throbbing came back stronger and more powerful than ever. The demand for all types of buildings shot up.

There was real money, and in quantity, waiting to be spent in the cities. And there were people demanding to have buildings to work in, hotels to drink in, halls to meet in, churches to worship in and houses to shelter in. The newly-rich men-of-means wanting large and substantial warehouses and offices; town councils wanting magnificent city halls befitting their new-found place in the sun; the churches with coffers filled by affluent respectability-seeking parishioners wanting larger and proper Gothic edifices; the publicans wanting imposing palaces in which to milk a sybaritic clientele; and tens of thousands of people just wanting a home—all of them made demands that created a splendiferous boom for the building fraternity.

The building industry is a sensitive barometer of economic conditions. In building the ups and downs of the economy in general are exaggerated and magnified far beyond the average. Minor general changes cause the building pendulum to swing wildly and the whole industry wobbles unnervingly. When the swing is caused by over-demand invariably there is a search for quicker and cheaper ways of meeting it. Short cuts are adopted. Labour-consuming methods are discarded and with them the high standards and techniques which have been built up in periods when quality, not quantity, made money. The situation is saved by the inescapable cycle which decrees that sooner or later the pendulum swings back and once again quality becomes the saleable commodity. The conditions of the 1850s created an over-demand to an extreme degree.

The primary and most important demand was for housing. On the south side of the Yarra River at Emerald Hill tens of thousands of people huddled uncomfort-ably in a sea of tents called Canvas Town. Many solutions were tried and most of them abandoned in an attempt to meet the ever-rising call for houses. Some of them were old and some were new. Ingenuity brought forth canvas, hessian, mud, grass and, the oldest of the emergency answers, prefabrication. Buildings of various sizes suitable for houses, halls or churches were cut and worked where both materials and labour were readily to hand and shipped in a dismantled

A prefabricated iron cottage in Patterson Place, South Melbourne: about 1853

condition to Australia. Pre-cut timber buildings came from Singapore and America. Their individual parts, identified by a code of numbers and letters, were put together with a hammer in one hand and book of simple instructions in the other. Iron ones—walls, roofs, windows and doors fixed to a timber frame—came from the smoking industrial towns of the English midlands.

'Iron Pot' churches were erected by the non-conformist denominations in both Sydney and Melbourne. Some of them, such as the one erected by the Presbyterians in Macquarie Street and now re-erected at Lidcombe, are still in use although not on their original sites nor for their original purposes. An 'Iron Pot' school was built in Sydney and a number of prefabricated iron houses, imported for £25 complete and sold for £70, were erected and still stand, rather dilapidately, in South Melbourne and Port Melbourne. George Coppin, the titan of Australian Theatre at the mid-century, erected an imported 'Iron Pot' on the corner of Stephen (Exhibition) and Lonsdale Streets in Melbourne and conducted it as Coppin's Olympic Theatre. An 'Iron Pot' became part of the White Horse Hotel in George Street, Sydney, and was later used as a boxing academy where the publican Larry Foley trained such people as Bob Fitzsimmons, Peter Jackson, Young Griffo and other champions of the bare knuckle days. A large prefabricated iron house erected in Woolloomooloo became the headquarters of, and gave its name to, one of the most feared pushes to roam the jungles around Woolloomooloo .and Paddington—The Iron House Mob. J. M. Oxley, the son of Lieutenant John Oxley of Blue Mountains fame, ordered a large iron mansion from England in 1853 for his property at Bowral in New South Wales. A series of set-backs including transport from Sydney and a shortage of labour delayed its erection until 1857 by which time, with conditions returning to normal, it proved to be more expensive than a conventional home. The house, a plain spreading single-storeyed box, still stands and is in excellent condition. Pretentious, out of scale cast iron urns teeter on an abruptly finished parapet which screens the low roof. A framed timber verandah with cast iron brackets and a sheet iron roof have been attached on three sides to protect the corrugated iron walls but even this on-site modification has done little to lessen the house's basic and faintly quaint and ridiculous inappropriateness to the site and climate. The name of the house is Wingecarribee.

The most outstanding example of the cast iron buildings is Corio Villa which stands on the corner of Fitzroy Street and Victoria Parade, Eastern Beach, Geelong. In 1855 a strange assortment of cast iron wall and roofing sheets, columns, urns and fancy barge, porch and pelmet trims was landed on the Cunningham Pier at Geelong to which it had been sent from Glasgow. The migrant consignee proving untraceable, the pieces were eventually bought by Mr Alfred Douglass and hauled to the top of a high point overlooking Corio Bay. It was then discovered that the foundry which had cast the pieces had been destroyed by fire soon after shipping them and the local builders were faced with trying to assemble the jig-saw of parts without any plan to guide them. In 1856 they had completed their task and the house became Douglass' home. It is an extraordinary and fascinating achievement. The walls are made of $\frac{1}{2}''$ thick boiler plate cast in three feet sections welded together; the cast iron window sashes slide into wall cavities; the original broad corrugated roofing iron and the heavy cast iron roof gutters are still completely serviceable; verandah and porch posts support arched filigrees of amazingly intricate guilloche decoration while a similarly intricate cast iron decoration embellishes the roof barges. Roses of England and thistles of Scotland form the main motifs in the filigree and the iron coat of arms which surmounts the main entrance porch, while the lion's head of England is repeated in the arch keystones. A series of Classic vases complements the general fecund floridity of the assemblage whose elaborate intricacy is without peer in cast iron buildings in Australia.

The iron buildings were stiflingly hot affairs. They were designed and made in England with little thought for the climatic conditions of Australia. Most of them were simple boxes with a hipped roof, close-cropped eaves and bare unshaded walls. The inside walls and ceilings of the buildings were usually lined with a canvas scrim which was sometimes papered. Size was the only real difference between the cheap little houses of South Melbourne and the large barn-like theatre erected by Coppin. A certain degree of architectural stylism was given to the churches which came with cupola-topped towers, Gothic windows and, where there was a balcony, spindly Classic columns. Attempts were made to insulate some of the better buildings such as the churches by lining the inside walls and the ceiling with a natural or artificial boarding covered with hessian or canvas, and in the country, covering the ceiling with bark, but the results were unsatisfactory.

Neither the timber nor the iron prefabricated building was any more than a helpful expedient. The quantities available were far too limited, the eventual cost was too great and the results were too unsatisfactory for prefabrication to be other than a transient phase in a time of pressing emergency.

Opposite Corio Villa, a prefabricated iron house at Eastern Beach, Geelong, Victoria: 1856

A country cottage on
Main Road, north of
Berrima, New South
Wales: about 1860

Bridal Cottage in Henry
Street, Richmond,
Tasmania: about 1860

Out of the conditions of shortage which called for experiment and novelty in building there eventually evolved a type of cheap, quick and reasonably satisfactory building which was to become a mainstay wherever similar conditions prevailed. It was the timber-framed, weatherboarded and iron-roofed building which, eventually, was to be carried the length and breadth of the country. In varying degrees from utter crudeness to high sophistication and from tiny sheds to huge palaces, usually ugly but occasionally beautiful, it was carried on the drays of the settlers throughout the whole of Australia. It made Tasmania and Queensland into timber states and, outside the main cities, the other states as well. Large areas of what are now Melbourne suburbs were painted with the wooden brush. Because of the spectre of the horrible effects of white ants Sydney, a brick town, escaped the ubiquitous timber house until the end of the Second World War but, after 1945, under conditions similar to those of ninety years before, it came to the new suburbs of that city too. By that time Melbourne had long discovered the virtues—particularly the social ones—of brick veneer construction and was shedding weatherboards as fast as possible.

The tin and timber building was the result of the confluence of a number of factors. The social and economic conditions gave rise to the need while the technical and industrial conditions provided the means. The idea of a frame of widely spaced light timbers was brought from America by the gold seekers who crossed the Pacific when the Californian fields started to wane at the time when the strikes in Victoria became known. The system had been invented by George W. Snow and had been used first on a Chicago church in 1833. It was derided by the old craftsmen and scornfully dubbed a 'balloon frame'. It was still a youngster when it came to Australia but its virtues had already been proven in conditions almost parallel to those that awaited it.

Australian builders modified the balloon frame in a number of ways. They discarded the rough timber sheathing used for bracing in America. The frame was made even lighter, less greedy of timber and made stable by slim wooden braces checked flush into the frame at the corners. The local builders, with a growing knowledge of structural principles, also developed the technique of using the ceiling joists to tie the feet of rafters and so form a simple but effective truss. The timbers used were easily worked softwoods imported in the quaint quantities of 'bundles' from the west coast of America, the Pacific Islands and from the Far East or, when necessary, straight lengths of ash from Tasmania. The increased availability of timber and its cheapness was a consequence of industrial advances. Newly developed mechanical saws driven by steam engines ripped through logs in a twentieth of the time taken by the old pit saw and the adze.

The balloon frame used a further benefit of the industrial revolution to hold this fragile skeleton of sticks together. In the factories of England machines spewed forth millions of cut and, later, wire nails at the rate of over 100,000 nails per machine a day. They were regular in size, reliable in quality and cost a fraction of their hand-forged predecessors. From being an expensive item needing to be carefully conserved, nails could be dropped and lost, bent and thrown away and used lavishly by the barrel-full. No longer was it necessary to rely on a system of accurately worked mortice and tenon joints, wedges and pegs. The timbers could be quickly knocked together with rough butting, a minimum of skill and a handful of nails.

Over the years further developments in the technique were evolved. The heavy square corner posts which were part of the American balloon frame became redundant when a refinement was made to the joining of the corners so that whole lengths of wall frame could be cut and nailed together conveniently and quickly on the ground and then levered upright into position. At first the frame was set on timber blocks fixed to a continuous timber plate buried an inch or two below ground level; but this practice later gave way to separate square timber stumps with a timber sole nailed to the bottom to spread the weight and sunk eighteen inches or more deep. Rot-resisting hardwoods such as redgum were used in these vulnerable positions and were often painted with creosote to increase their durability.

In areas where white ants roamed and brick or stone were available the frame was set on outside base walls and inner piers of masonry. Such was the practice around Sydney, but in Queensland where these materials were hard to come by the white ants were combatted by raising the whole building well above ground on hefty tree trunks so that the mud tunnels of the light-fearing depredators could be seen and destroyed. This method of coping with the white ant had been accidentally discovered as early as 1839 when four of the prefabricated buildings taken to the new settlement at Port Essington were erected on eight feet high piles. Other non-prefabricated buildings were erected on short dwarf stumps and yet others were built directly on the ground. A short time later three of the prefabricated buildings were walled in with stone or brick below the floor line to provide additional accommodation. Within months all the low level buildings were devastated by white ants and the Commandant, Captain John McArthur, reported to Earl Grey that the 'temporary method of piling in order to raise the buildings has proved very useful. Had they been fixed to the ground in the usual manner they must have been destroyed long since . . .'[1] Later when three of the

Como in Como Avenue, South Yarra, Victoria: 1847-55

raised prefabricated buildings were also attacked Earl Grey replied to the Commandant, 'I have to add that it appears to me very doubtful whether the destruction of these buildings by the white ants may not have been a good deal accelerated by closing in the open space originally left beneath them. While they were raised on piles leaving a free circulation of air beneath, it must have been much easier to observe and check the attacks of these destructive insects than it can be now that for the sake of giving additional accommodation, the space below has been closed in and converted into a ground floor.[2]

The Port Essington settlement was abandoned in 1848 and it is unlikely that this fortuitous discovery had any direct influence on other Queensland architecture. But because the problem faced by nearly all Queensland settlers was the same as that at Port Essington the same solution was eventually found. A few houses raised high off the ground appeared in the country by the late 1870s but it was not until nearly the turn of the century that it became an almost state-wide Queensland trade mark. White ants were no real problem in the other populated areas but as the country developed pockets were found in places, such as around Melbourne, which previously had been considered free of them. A system of continuous downward bent iron caps was developed and fixed to the tops of the footings to effectively forestall them.

There were other refinements in the constructional technique of timber framed buildings brought about by peculiar regional conditions and differences. In New South Wales where the weather is reasonably reliable it became the practice to construct and fix the stumps, the bearers, the joists and the flooring-boards before the walls or roof were erected in order to obtain a flat free-working area as quickly as possible. In Victoria with its prolonged wet spells of wind-driven rain, wet floor-boards became badly stained around nail holes so the frame was erected, the walls sheeted and the roof covered before any flooring was laid. In Queensland, where the rain when it comes is a deluge that falls straight down, the practice was to erect the frame, cover the roof, lay the flooring and lastly sheet the walls.

Whatever the differences of detail adopted they were all aimed at speeding up what was from the beginning a fast and effective system which required little real skill. Two hard-working men could put in the footings and erect the frame of a four-roomed house in two days.

The covering-in of the frame was equally quick. In the hasty times of the 1850s iron sheeting came into its own. It was used for both walls and roof. Ship after ship landed ton after ton of bundles of corrugated iron onto the wharves at Melbourne. And it was now better, cheaper and more durable than before. The process of galvanizing in which the thin sheets of corrugated puddled steel were protected by a skin of non-rusting zinc had been patented in England in 1837. The sheets of iron that came to Australia in the fifties were nearly all galvanized. It was a highly utilitarian material, easily transported, easily worked, quickly fixed and there was little waste. Within a few years it blanketed Melbourne and splashed out over the whole country. Shingled roofs which, shrinking in the sun and expanding in the rain, had a tendency to leak badly when rain came after a sunny period were covered with the new ubiquitous panacea. Usually it was placed directly on top of the shingles which were left in place as heat insulation. The problem of heat beating through roofs also gave rise to the practice of coating the underside of slate roofs, which were fixed to battens rather than to close-boarding, with a thick layer of lime plaster as an insulating barrier. From the middle fifties, except in the roughest pioneer outback shanties where bark and shingle roofs still lingered and in the two main cities, roofs were iron. In Sydney and Melbourne they were either iron or slate—and the type of roof covering was an unmistakable signal of the building's pretensions.

The main functional drawback of iron sheeting was its hot-box properties. It was possible to cope with the problem created by an iron roof in various ways. Straw thatching could be laid as an insulation before fixing the iron sheets; the bulk of the roof space could be augmented by increasing the pitch, thus giving a larger volume of insulating air; the hot air in it could be kept moving out in numerous ways—ventilators in the gables, perforations or inlets in the eaves lining, outlets near the ridge or, best of all, a combination of eaves inlet and small ventilating gables at the apex of hipped roofs. The walls, however, were a different matter. The amount of air trapped between the outer iron wall covering and the inner wall lining—either iron, hessian, or lathe and plaster—was poor insulation in itself. To keep it moving was a difficult problem as any holes that would let new air in also let mice into the frame where they could not be reached. And, finally, the main problem arose from radiation. Attempts to solve the problem by making the inner wall facing a heat barrier by lining it with vertical timber boarding were only partially successful.

As soon, then, as the bubbling of the times began to subside and society settled into a new pattern, iron dropped from the walls of houses to be replaced by timber weatherboards which, like the framing itself, were accurately cut and dressed by machines—quickly and relatively cheaply. Only on the most utilitarian of buildings—sheds, out-houses, stores and the secondary buildings on the country properties—did the iron walls remain.

And so it was for these reasons and in this way that the framed weatherboarded iron-roofed house, which was to form the bulk of outer suburban houses of the cities and all those of the country towns and homesteads, was spawned in the turbulent house-hungry conditions of an exploding Melbourne in the years immediately following the discovery of gold. It is a derivative building, to be sure—its basic idea, and for many years its materials, were imported. But its constructional evolution is Australian.

The rivalry, amounting to resentment, which existed between Melbourne and Sydney was spurred as the wealth of the gold fields flowed back to the cities. Both Sydney and Melbourne had been incorporated as cities with authority and powers to manage their own domestic affairs at the same time in 1842; but the equality was illusory. Melbourne, for all its progress, had remained much smaller than Sydney and was jealous of the older town which continued patronizingly superior to the southern upstart. Separation and self-government for that part of New South Wales south of the Murray River as the colony of Victoria in June 1851 had helped the self-pride of the area. But it was the greater richness of its gold deposits that enabled Melbourne to outstrip Sydney and become, for the next fifty years, the largest city in Australia.

With their new-found wealth both towns were able to indulge their longing for primacy by taking on its trappings. Sydney still held the lead when it opened its University to the first students in October 1852. Hard on its heels Melbourne University enrolled its first students the next year. But Melbourne was accelerating much faster. In 1854 the first town hall in Australia was opened on the north-east corner of Collins and Swanston Streets, a full twenty-one years before the first part of Sydney's first town hall was completed. Geelong, second only to Melbourne in having its fortunes propelled forward by gold, started building its town hall in April 1855. The building is still in use—the oldest town hall in Australia.

Melbourne's first town hall was an almost exact replica of one of the classics of English Renaissance architecture—Inigo Jones' Banqueting Hall at Whitehall. The main bulk of the box—the plinth-base together with the back and the ends away from public view—was crudely worked local bluestone; but the whole of the main facade, the balustered parapet and the pilaster piers which striped its

The Town Hall, Geelong,
Victoria: 1855 (section
left of portico only).
Architect, Joseph Reed

The Melbourne Club in
Collins Street, Melbourne:
1858. Architect,
Leonard Terry

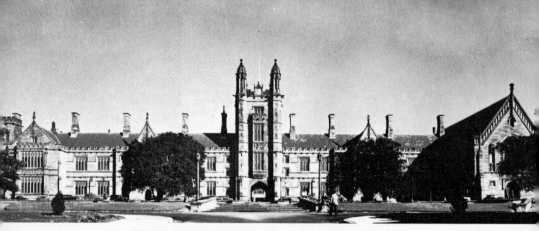

The University of Sydney at Darlington, New South Wales:
1857. Architect, Edmund T. Blacket

bluestone ends and back were finely worked sandstone brought from Tasmania and Sydney. Separated from the main building was a free-standing square Romanesque bell-tower. Without a carillon the tower had no purpose other than to highlight the building and to impress. As such it typified the change of outlook to building that marked the fifty years following gold.

Robert Louis Stevenson, writing at the height of the Victorian period, gave succinct form to its essence. 'Man is a creature who lives . . . principally by catchwords, a form of sustenance to which the half-educated are peculiarly addicted.' After 1850 catchwords became the staple of architecture. Stylism, appealing to the tastes and the pockets of the community, first took hold, quickly became rampant and eventually finished in wild uncontrol. Architecture became a profession concerned with the theatrical dressing up of buildings in a kind of make-believe. Fundamentally simple forms were dissembled in the clothes of every nation of every time. Looking back on this unbelievable fifty years which started in extravagance, hastened into opulence and finished in bulbous ostentation, Robin Dods, a pioneer of a return to sanity in the 1920s, said it was difficult to believe that such buildings could have been done seriously; that it was kinder to believe they were the result of a sense of humour—tongue-in-cheek buildings erected for the amusement of future generations. Forty years after Dods wrote his remarks his tolerance may not seem so necessary. His views were part of the inevitable cycle of reaction to an extreme. The virtues of Victorian building, and it had many, were not so apparent in 1920 as they are when a further generation or two gives a deeper perspective and a sharper edge to its outlines. It was a unique period which will never be repeated and the buildings, despite Dods' somewhat patronizing view, were deadly serious—serious, grave, pompous and self-important as only the Victorians could be. They reflected the ideas, standards and conditions of a unique age in which the British Empire was the means used by an omnipresent, omnipotent and omniscient Almighty to govern the universe.

The period started simply enough by continuing along the clean-cut lines already accepted—Gothic for ecclesiastical work and schools, Classical for public buildings and a frivolous impure dress of either for houses. The architects who worked the lode disparaged all that had been done before as not even building let alone architecture. Colonial architecture was 'a semi-military mannerism' at the best, said one of them; while another, a little later, considered that the number of Macquarie's buildings 'was only equalled by their ugliness of design'.

In Sydney, Edmund Blacket, the son of a London cloth merchant, ruled unchallenged in the architecture world. He had arrived at the age of twenty-five in November 1842. He brought with him letters of introduction to influential people in Sydney but little, if any, architectural experience. By January 1843 he had designed his first Australian building—All Saints Church at Singleton. He quickly consolidated his entry into the Sydney building world by being accepted by Bishop Broughton, the first and only Anglican Bishop of Australia, as the chief architect for his diocese. In 1849 he left his thriving practice to succeed Mortimer Lewis as Government Architect but, five years later, on being asked to undertake the design of the buildings for the new university, re-entered private practice. Before 1863, when he was joined by Horbury Hunt, he carried out a large number of fine ecclesiastical, commercial and domestic buildings.

Like all architects of the time Blacket adopted the current stylistic conventions. His churches, such as St Philip's on Church Hill, St Paul's at Redfern, St Mark's at Darling Point and Christ Church St Laurence, together with others at Ashfield, Greendale, Picton, Berrima and Wollombi were nearly all strictly Gothic, sensitive and correct. Occasionally, as at St Silas', Waterloo, he strayed into Romanesque, but that was all. Blacket was most at home with Gothic and his best work was all in that style. Naturally enough it was Gothic which he chose for his work at Sydney University, including the magnificent Great Hall which is generally considered to be the finest Gothic Revival building in Australia. It was considered to be even greater than that when it was finished in 1857 and a not easily pleased critic remarked that 'there is no other place in Australia at all comparable to it'. Blacket's commercial work—banks, offices, hotels and insurance buildings—were conventionally Classical but neither his heart nor his ability was in tune with it. In his domestic work, where the conventions allowed him a choice of style, he accepted the Colonial form with his head but chose its dress from his heart. His

The Bank of Australasia, George and Jamison Streets, Sydney: 1857. Architect, Edmund T. Blacket

The Treasury Building in Spring Street, Melbourne: 1862. Architect, J. J. Clark

Parliament House in Spring Street, Melbourne: 1856. Architects, Kerr and Knight

choice and his influence did much to further the popularity of domestic Gothic which had been implanted by his predecessor Mortimer Lewis. Nor was his influence limited to New South Wales. Blacket's ecclesiastical connections took his particular touch of Gothic throughout Australia from Geelong to Brisbane. When he died in 1883 leaving a tremendous legacy of building, both in quantity and quality, he was working on the Anglican Cathedral for Perth.

The opportunities that faced Blacket and the Sydney architects were nothing compared to those enjoyed by those in Melbourne. Not only was Melbourne richer than Sydney but her needs were vaster. Sydney, already more than sixty years old, was already well supplied with a number of adequate if not particularly desirable buildings. Melbourne, a youthful sixteen years of age, was composed of buildings which were still largely pioneer, ill-built and totally inadequate for the needs of its bloated population. These factors made it necessary for Sydney to expand what it had but allowed Melbourne to demolish exuberantly and start afresh.

In these conditions the early pre-gold guard of Melbourne architects found themselves joined by a deluge of colleagues from overseas. Amongst them were some thoroughly trained and extremely able practitioners who came well and worthily recommended. People such as Clark, Purchas and Knight were to enrich the city with the finest Classical public buildings in Australia including the Victorian Treasury Building and Parliament House. William Wardell was another and greater one. He left England because of ill-health in 1858 bearing impressive testimonials from thirteen influential people including Lord Petrie, Sir John Simeon and the High Sheriffs of London and Norfolk. He was then a Fellow of the Royal Institute of Architects and an Associate of the Institution of Civil Engineers. When he came to Australia he was already 'one of the foremost architects in England highly regarded for his theoretical and practical knowledge, his taste, talent and judgement and the highest personal qualities of integrity and honour', according to one of his referees.

Wardell had started his working life as a railway surveyor. His work gave him the opportunity to study old buildings. After he had met Pugin he turned his attention to measuring and studying the many Gothic buildings near his railway work. In 1843, having come under the influence of the Oxford Movement and the future Cardinal Newman, he became a member of the Roman Catholic Church. The move greatly affected his whole life. As a result of it, he lost many friends and an inheritance but gained new and important friends and a host of church building opportunities. He built his first church on the Thames in 1846. During the next twelve years, before he left for Australia, he built at least thirty churches.

Wardell's first Melbourne commission was for the huge St Patrick's Cathedral. The earlier cathedral had been designed by Samuel Jackson in 1850 and was only partly finished when gold was found and work came to a halt. Wardell arrived just as the church authorities had decided that Jackson's design may have been sufficient for a provincial town but was 'entirely inadequate . . . as a cathedral in the most thriving city of Australia'. The cathedral they got from Wardell was the largest and most imposing in the country.

The Victorian Government grabbed Wardell as its Government Architect in 1859 and gave him the right of private practice. Like Blacket, Wardell carried out a vast amount of work during his life and left an indelible impression and influence wherever he went. And he went far. He carried out flood control work in low-lying areas around Melbourne, harbour works at Warrnambool in Victoria, at Fremantle in Western Australia and at Auckland in New Zealand, and defence works at Newcastle, New South Wales. He built a bridge over Darling Harbour at Sydney and a graving dock in New Zealand.

Despite a wide-ranging involvement in engineering works, Wardell's major effort was architectural. His churches were consistently Gothic, generally in the mode

St Patrick's Cathedral at Eastern
Hill, Melbourne: 1858-1937. The
original architect was William
Wardell

of the Decorated period. They tended to squatness, heaviness and dullness and, except for St Patrick's Cathedral, none of them approached Blacket's Great Hall. Much of his practice was in Sydney where he turned out St Mary's Cathedral in 1865 as an unsuccessful challenge to St Patrick's.

In Victoria, in 1877, there was a sordid affair of greed and corruption in high places which centred around the Governor, Sir George Bowen. In the aftermath 'every man who wore a clean shirt was booted out of his job', according to *The Bulletin* in its own typical language. Wardell was one of them and was dismissed from his post of Victorian Government Architect. He immediately set out on a journey of architectural study and sketching to Europe where he concentrated on the buildings around the Mediterranean. On his return he settled in Sydney, restricted his practice to non-ecclesiastical works and spent the latter part of his years indulging his newly discovered love for Italianate, Palladian and Venetian design on such buildings as the Union Club, the New South Wales Club and the English, Scottish and Australian Bank.

Great though the work and influence of both Blacket and Wardell were, neither of them was as important as the man who stepped off a boat at Melbourne one day in 1852 or 1853. Joseph Reed was not only the best architect of the three but his work and influence, both directly and indirectly, were to prove far more important, effective and lasting.

The great volume of work done by both Blacket and Wardell had been dissipated widely throughout Australia and New Zealand; though Blacket's work had tended to concentrate in New South Wales, and Sydney in particular, while more than half of Wardell's work had been given in the same area—an area already strongly proscribed by seventy years of development. Reed, on the other hand, just as prodigious in his output as his two contemporaries, worked almost exclusively in Melbourne and only occasionally strayed into a Victorian country town or to Tasmania. Working in an almost virgin field at a time when it was being transformed from a rough, pioneer town to a polished metropolis bigger than any other in the continent, Reed's vast number of large and important buildings virtually determined Melbourne's architectural character of solid Victorian respectability which subsequent waves of change have scarcely touched. The mood of the town was set on acquiring and displaying all the Victorian virtues—respectability, culture and materialism—and Reed gave it architectural expression.

Reed's influence on Australian architecture did not stop at creating Melbourne. The practice which he founded has continued uninterrupted under various changes of name and combinations of partners. Now as the architectural firm of Bates, Smart and McCutcheon it is the oldest and one of the two largest practices in Australia. When the conditions of the 1850s and 1860s were repeated a hundred years later after the Second World War and Melbourne and Sydney launched out on a re-building programme that radically changed their faces it was the architectural lineal descendants of Joseph Reed who carried out the first and most important works whose impact and direction very largely influenced those who followed and shared in the re-creation.

Reed entered the Melbourne architectural field directly at the top and having proved his ability, there he stayed. He did no small work. Except for an odd parsonage or two, which he accepted from obligation, he hardly touched a house. The one house which he is known to have designed, Rippon Lea for F. G. Sargood in 1868, was more a mansion than a house even by the standards of a hundred years ago when huge homes were boringly common.

This extraordinary practice commenced when, in January 1854 and only a few months after his arrival, the thirty-year-old architect won a competition for the Melbourne Public Library which was to be set on the top of the hill at the northern end of Swanston Street overlooking the town. It was an ambitious scheme by any standards and Reed and the heirs to his practice worked for the next sixty years on his magnificent Classical design with its imposing portico of giant ordered Corinthian columns. The next year, 1855, he was engaged to design the town hall for Geelong. Thereafter followed a succession of buildings which constitutes a catalogue of almost every important building in Melbourne before the Second World War—over twenty ecclesiastical buildings of all denominations including the central city churches for the Baptists, Methodists, Presbyterians and Congregationalists, a dozen large buildings at Melbourne University including Ormond College and the old Wilson Hall, ten banks including the Banks of Australasia in Collins Street and Elizabeth Street and the old Bank of New South Wales in Collins Street whose facade now sits incongruously on one face of a 1940 Commerce Building at Melbourne University, the Town Hall, the Weather Bureau, the Trades Hall, the Victoria Arcade, Menzies Hotel, the Exhibition Building, the Masonic Homes at Prahran and a number of others, such as the Bijou Theatre and the Eastern Markets, which have now been demolished but which in their day were part and parcel of Melbourne's character.

Reed was a Cornishman with all the hard-headed business ability combined with the fey temperamentality of his Celtic ancestors. He became the unofficial but acknowledged leader of his profession almost from the day of his arrival. He was the first member elected to the Victorian Institute of Architects on its foundation on 11 September 1856. Like its forerunner the Victorian Architects Association of 1851, which had expired in the hubbub following gold, the venture waned; but when it was re-established in 1871 Reed was its first president. Five years later, in a huff, he abruptly severed his connection with the organization which he had done so much to found and foster. Reed's power made him the object of jealousies with his professional colleagues and his mercurial temperament led him into constant conflict with committees, clients and employees. But his tremendous abilities enabled him to grow from strength to strength and to impress his stamp indelibly on a city which more than any other was moulded by one man. Melbourne, even today, is Joseph Reed's city.

Rippon Lea in Hotham Street, Elsternwick, Victoria: 1868-76. Architect, Joseph Reed

Above the Melbourne
Public Library in
Swanston Street,
Melbourne: 1854-1913.
The original architect
was Joseph Reed

Below The Royal Society
of Victoria building
(Weather Bureau),
Victoria Parade and
Exhibition Street,
Melbourne: 1858.
Architect, Joseph Reed

Royal Terrace in Nicholson
Street, Fitzroy, Victoria: 1858

Bank of Australasia,
Port Fairy, Victoria: 1856.
Altered 1890. Architect
(alterations), Anketell
Henderson

Reed, Blacket and Wardell were the three giants of Australian architecture in their time. They set the standards that the host of lesser but still able colleagues followed. Their work consisted largely of public buildings. In the fifties they remained fairly strictly within the Classic–Gothic dichotomy, designing correctly and rigidly according to the appropriate classification and building soundly with the best of materials. Massive stone walls, meticulously carved stone columns and dressings, slate or lead roofs, large windows with finely made cast iron frames; and imported polished marble and well-wrought cedar finishes inside were the norm in these lavish and expensive buildings.

Further down the line where the minor architects and the builder-designers operated, things were different. While the same deep-set belief in stylism permeated all levels of building, the desperate shortage of housing and minor buildings such as small shops and public houses created a speculative builder's paradise. In the city itself the main streets burst forth into dense rows of three- or four-storeyed business houses with shops on the ground floor and offices for the new trading class above. The upper masonry walls were carried across the shop fronts on stout wrought iron bressummers (breastsummers). The unexpected sight of two or three floors of massive walls apparently being supported on long bands of flimsy glazed sashes or large sheets of plate glass brought protests from the staid and reactionary who were disturbed by an effect so contrary to all natural laws. The separate rickety old Colonial structures were torn down to make way for long continuous hedges of bland plaster facades.

Further out, on the best sites on the hills surrounding the town, a few lone blocks of stately terraces were erected to house the rising merchant princes. Architecturally restrained and dignified at first, their Classical severity was soon replaced by the ubiquitous plasterwork as they swayed with the winds of fashion. But the Gothic idiom with its plethora of steep decorated gables and asymmetrical form was inherently unsuited to the long repetitive form of the terrace. Consequently, the style almost never appeared on the terrace houses. And on the fringes of Sydney and Melbourne, in areas that are now the inner suburbs, future slums were tossed together. Row upon row of narrow-fronted terraces appeared. They were rude, crude and cheap. Ill-lit and roughly constructed with poor materials, they were dark, dank and unhealthy from the beginning. At Surry Hills, Redfern, Waterloo and Paddington in New South Wales and at Carlton, Collingwood, Fitzroy and South Melbourne in Victoria acres of crowded one- or two-storeyed hovels jammed hard against each other found ready buyers and made a quick profit for their builders.

Building societies appeared in Australia in the late 1840s. One of the first really successful ones, the Metropolitan Permanent Building Society, was registered in Melbourne in 1854. Its aim was to erect well built workers' cottages and make them available to artisans on reasonable terms. The society bought broad acres in areas such as Collingwood and Richmond, subdivided the land into small blocks and erected soundly constructed, if pedestrianly designed, red-brick houses which were sold on £10 deposit and low weekly payments. For thirty-seven years the society prospered exceedingly and did a splendid job for the working-class until, its directors becoming caught up in the greed of the land boom of the eighties, it was destroyed in a smother of bankruptcy in 1894.

The main change in the planning of houses of 1860 was that the kitchen, having crept closer and closer to the main building, now became attached to it. It formed one end of the rear verandah while a similar room at the other end was used as a bathroom housing a cast- or sheet-metal bath and a shelf with a hand basin. The water-closet and the wash house with a pine wash-trough and a bricked-in copper were left in a separate building at the back of the site as far away as possible. The reasons for the development were the disappearance of just those causes which had given rise to the separation in the first place. Servants were no longer convicts but free individuals. They were, therefore, more acceptable socially and more expensive to employ. Consequently, the proportion of homes that could afford servants was much less than before. In the majority of homes the housework was done entirely by the housewife. The convenience of an attached kitchen was a functionally labour-saving move. In a large proportion of the homes which did employ servants—the upper- and middle-class homes—the arrangement was often on a daily or even a once-a-week basis. Domestics lived in their own homes and living-quarters for them were unnecessary. In those upper-class homes which still employed live-in servants it was necessary to give some consideration to the comfort and convenience of their working and living conditions if their services, given to the highest bidder, were to be retained in a booming market.

While all these buildings differed in size and seemingly in quality, they were all tarred with the same brush of superficiality and poor construction underneath. In better quality work the external walls were at least fourteen inches thick and the inner walls nine inches thick. In the tawdry standards that came with the speculative fifties, sheltered external walls were sometimes made nine inches thick even in supposedly good work. In cheap work all the walls were nine inches thick. They were built of stone or brick which in the fashion of the time was coated, at least in those parts that could be seen, with a thick plastering of stucco marked and painted to imitate dressed stone and with Classical mouldings. Decoration was embraced ardently and was more blatant than before. Even the conservative buildings, which kept an overall effect of simplicity, boldened the mouldings around the windows by deeper cutting and added elaborated doorways. Indented Classical motifs were tentatively impressed into or scooped out of the thick plaster on the corbelled tops of the protruding and dividing fire walls.

But the real fashion-setters—some of the shops, the pubs and the more pushing of the speculative terrace houses—treated their facades as frankly aggressive eye-catching displays. They attempted to disguise the building's shortcomings in quality by distracting the eye with an assortment of fanciful frippery. Cornices, doorways and windows were embellished with a mass of busy plaster details. Doorways were encrusted with an ecstatic pot-pourri of mixed Classic details, window-heads arced upwards again and their trims became elongated fasces crowned by curved label moulds which broke sharply downwards at the corners to dangle a boss of grapes, a swirl of leaves, a rose or a miniature head. Cornices, like the doorways, became ponderously heavy, deeply cut and a jumble of Classical miscellanea marked at the extremities with cast-plaster urns having fluted or scalloped sides and a bunch of grapes at the top. Over the main doorway of the building the cornice jumped up in a free-standing pediment on the panel of which was stuck a bigger urn or a draped garland. The main bulk of the walls was still left bare. In these buildings, the progenitors of the coming fashion, stone colouring was shunned. They were uniformly and smartly grey.

The conditions of the time, the materials, the workmanship and the fashions formed a cycle of interrelating causes that lead to the worst of gimcrack construction. With the knowledge that the walls were to be plastered the bricks or stone were thrown together almost haphazardly and held apart by weak lime mortars often no better than a sandy mud. The excuse was made that stucco required a good key and necessitated coarse and crude walling. In fact it was quicker and cheaper to build thus and the stucco was necessary to help true-up misaligned piles of rubble. The stucco was supposed to protect the walls from dampness but it was also of such poor quality that it had to be painted to achieve this desirable state. If it were left bare it was found to be more like a damp blanket perpetually soaking the wall. Another result of the practice of stuccoing was to encourage the manufacture of poor quality bricks. With no call for good quality

The Court House at Ipswich, Queensland: 1859. Architect, Charles Tiffen

The Treasury Buildings in Victoria Square, Adelaide: 1860.
Architect, Edward Angus Hamilton

bricks any advances in brickmaking were delayed and the plastered walls which pervaded all but the very best public buildings of mid-Victorian work were made more inevitable.

In order to further combat the problem of damp walls whose only preventative lay in a thin skin of paint, efforts were turned to devising a new type of construction. These efforts, ineffective though they were at the time, were the genesis that led in the 1880s, when good quality machine-made bricks became available, to another Australian contribution to world building technique—the cavity wall. The first steps in designing what were known as 'hollow walls' were taken in the very early fifties. By 1854 two methods had been imported from England and were in limited use. 'Dearn's' walling was a system producing a nine inch thick wall in which, in each alternate stretcher course, the bricks were set on edge leaving a cavity between them. The bricks in the other course were set as headers running from the outer to the inner faces of the wall. The arrangement allowed both faces to be plastered directly and saved material but because of the tie course it was far from waterproof. The other system was known as 'Loudon' walling and resulted in an eleven inch wall. In this system all the bricks were laid on the flat in English bond of alternating courses of headers and stretchers. In Loudon walling the stretcher bricks on the inner face were corbelled two inches leaving a gap between them and their outside neighbour. To enable the inside face of the wall to be plastered battens were fixed to the corbelled bricks and onto these were nailed close-spaced thin oregon lathes to form a key for the plaster. Thus, while there

Terrace houses in Merriman Street, West Rocks, Sydney: about 1860

Cast iron verandahs on
Above Linden, 26 Acland
Street, St Kilda, Victoria:
1870. *Left* Terrace
houses in Windsor
Street, Paddington, New
South Wales: about
1870

was no direct path for water to pass between the outer face and the plaster there still remained an indirect connection. Loudon walls were better than solid walls—but not a lot. The problem remained and 'hollow walls' were never widely used. But the idea lingered, nascent, until the time was right for it to bear fruit.

The buildings of the post-gold years made increasing use of the products of the industrial revolution—from brass brackets to support the gas mantles which, introduced as public street lighting in the forties, started to cast a steady lambent flame over building interiors in the fifties, and the cast pipes which brought the water of newly completed water reservoirs at Yan Yean and Prospect to the cast brass taps in the back-yard, to the iron on the roof and the cast iron grate in the fireplace.

No material played a greater part in changing the face of domestic architecture than did cast iron. It was a material which was perfectly attuned to the age. It was cheap, it was plentiful, it was reliable. Being factory-made it required little on-site time and skill to use and the eye-catching forms in which it came chimed with the rising taste for decoration and effect. In spindly attenuated columns and in a variety of panels needing only to be assembled with the simplest tools it spread across the faces of the houses. Painted brown or green it was pulled taut between the columns to form a balustrade, sprouted in fans from the top of the columns and hung in dainty frills from the eaves of verandahs. It was an un-classconscious material which was used equally freely on the meanest one-storeyed terrace and the elaborate mansion. The ironwork itself was still largely imported from England. In Sydney locally cast panels found a ready sale. In Melbourne the firm of Scott,

The Corio Hotel at Goolwa, South Australia: about 1858

Clow and Prebble opened that town's first foundry at Richmond in 1856 to supply gas lamp standards in competition with the imported standards which had been soundly derided for their design. By 1859 the Richmond Foundry, as it was called, had turned to skimming some of the cream that was brought by the increasing popularity of decorative cast iron and was supplying part of Melbourne's insatiable building demand.

The verandahs on which the iron was displayed climbed the full height of the building whether it had one storey or four. Wide, cool and inviting, they were used firstly for utility but as they gained popularity as a highly decorative and inexpensive feature in themselves they appeared in the most non-utilitarian of conditions. They faced wildly across narrow laneways where neither view, air nor privacy was to be had; they faced bravely into bleak southerly winds lashing in from the sea and, in the hot areas, turned blindly into a burning western sun. But by the end of the fifties fashion had such a stranglehold on architecture that utilitarian carping, if it had been given a thought, was of no consequence at all. Cast iron verandahs were the very height of the latest fashion and were racing on towards a heyday in the next two decades.

As the fifties came to a close and things began to steady and settle down, the Australian way of life in its two pace-setting colonies was a radically different one from that which had seemed so stable when the decade began. The economy was different, the structure of society was different and the buildings were different. The innocent days were far behind and the stage was set for a surging thrust into the excesses of the true Victorian period.

[1] Letter dated 16 October 1847 of Captain John McArthur to ————————, in *Historical Records of Australia*, Series 1, Vol. 26, p. 374.

[2] Letter dated 14 April 1848 of Earl Grey to Sir Charles Fitz Roy, in *Historical Records of Australia*, Series 1, Vol. 26, p. 373.

7

By the beginning of the sixties the mood of Melbourne, the vital heart of the country, was changing. The erratic boom-town frame of mind that had prevailed since the discovery of gold, when men looked to Lady Luck and their own sharp wits to bring them a quick and cheaply earned fortune, was gradually replaced by a sober awareness that industry and sound business-planning would yield a slower but more solid substance than the get-rich-quick tactics of the previous decade.

Before 1830 the few Australian coastal ports had been little more than clearing-houses through which rum was poured into the interior and out of which wool was taken to the hungry mills of England. Few people believed the country itself had any real future and fewer still had any affection for it. Between 1830 and 1850 the increased flow of free settlers and the coming of age of second or third generation native-born Australians had given rise to a certain degree of permanence and visions of future nationhood. Just prior to the discovery of gold Melbourne, for instance, was considering the appointment of a London town-planner to create a plan better than the unimaginative gardenless chequer-board which it had. A grid-pattern of streets may have been sufficient for a temporary town but a city-of-the-future should, it was said, have a plan suited to its site with large public squares, fine public buildings, wide boulevards and public gardens encircling the town and separating the suburbs. This was not the talk of an ephemeral town.

The discovery of gold had overwhelmed this budding nationalism in a flood of happy-go-lucky adventurers. The mood of the early years had returned. Australia became, for them, a country to be milked of its riches as quickly as possible in order that one might return to enjoy the civilized comforts of Home. Ten years later, the dust had settled, the fire and the wildness had been almost quenched. They were replaced by an adherence to the virtues of sobriety, hard work and a belief in the future.

The change was reflected in the type of migrant who stepped off the ships. In the early fifties they had been a rag-tag lot of illiterate and unskilled opportunists drawn from the lower social strata of America, China and the United Kingdom. From the end of the fifties a high proportion was from the middle classes—doctors, lawyers, architects and semi-professional businessmen. They brought with them a background of culture, education and skill. An even greater number of them were tradesmen and artisans with at least a certain degree of education and an array of skills. Their influx greatly strengthened the local bourgeoisie which was rising out of the debris of the turmoil that followed gold. Together these two streams combined to establish the middle class as the ideal and, eventually, the dominant feature, of Australian society.

The tone of the thirty years that began in the 1860s was set by the Queen, to whom respectability and formality were the very corner-stones of civilization and order. As the greatest empire the world had ever known spread its blessings of unchallenged greatness and peace around the earth, success became physically measurable. The wealth of the whole world flowed to England to be manufactured into even greater wealth. Materialism reigned. By their nature these three things— respectability, formality and materialism—could only find fulfilment when they were known by others. Appearances became all important. The external, the superficial and the apparent rode high. Such an attitude inevitably bred hypocrisy— in behaviour and in building.

Typical in every way of the central Victorian period was the matter of religion. There was an upsurge in church-going. The energetic activities of numbers of evangelical non-conformist preachers had a lot to do with it. But when imposed on the general outlook of the times the result of their work was mainly an increase in religiosity rather than a higher moral consciousness or true religiousness. The Queen herself went regularly to church each Sunday and it became a mark of dutiful imitation for her faithful subjects to do likewise. Dressed in the finest quality clothes to display the success and substance of Father, the mother and children trooped submissively and obediently to church, an act which in itself was more a public show of family rectitude and respectability than an act of worship. They may not have been over-fearful of God but they certainly feared the disapprobation of their social equals.

To house the willing flock a spate of churches was built. The picture general to most of the colonies was to be seen at its sharpest in Victoria. In May 1851 there were thirty-nine churches and chapels of all sorts in that colony; in December 1871 there were 2,602 of which nearly two-thirds had been built in the second decade at a completion rate of over three a week. For the next five years an average of five new churches a week were opened for divine service in Queen Victoria's Victoria. It was not only the swelling total of church-goers that gave rise to the large number of churches erected. A further important factor was the divisions and disruptions that existed within the major denominations and the implanting in Australia of a number of fringe sects. Except for the Church of Rome which maintained a monolithic unity, all the other denominations were split into antipathetic and often fiercely antagonistic groups. While the majority of Church of England congregations followed evangelical and Low Church principles the more socially appealing ideas of the High Church found a limited following amongst the pretentiously inclined of the newly rich class. Rival groups of Methodists gathered separately as Bible Christians, Wesleyans, Primitive Methodists and United Free Methodists.

News of 'The Disruption of the Kirk' which happened in Scotland in 1843 arrived in Australia in 1844 and by 1850 the Presbyterians in Australia were listening to sermons preached under the banners of the Established Church of Scotland, the Free Presbyterian Church of Scotland and the United Presbyterian Church (a combining of the Secession and Relief Churches in Scotland). The Baptists had General, Strict or Particular congregations, the Churches of Christ had two rival subdivisions as did the Jews and the Lutherans; while the Independents had an unnecessary fragmentation built into their very fundamental concept. The plethora of groups that the major denominations spawned was augmented by a large number of minor sects including the Unitarians, Quakers, Plymouth Brethren, Christian Israelites, Moravians and Welsh Calvinists. And each sub-denomination and each sect wanted its own church building. None of them was an Established Church in the sense that such was known in the United Kingdom but many of the overt arguments and covert politics of the time revolved around this touchy question and helped to aggravate and increase the fragmentation. The root causes of the divisions may have been variously doctrinal or ritual but their manifestations were often largely political. And in Australia the hottest and most violent political fire involved the question of state aid to religion.

State aid to churches took the form of both grants of land and direct fiscal gifts. To help establish religion in the Australian colonies the British Parliament

Above St Peter's Presbyterian Church and manse, Blue Street and Blues Point Road, North Sydney: church 1866, manse 1871

Right Launceston Wesleyan Chapel, Launceston, Tasmania: about 1878

Scots Church in North Terrace, Adelaide: 1851, spire 1856. Architect, Thomas English

The Bible Christian Church in High Street, Willunga, South Australia: about 1860

passed the Church Building Act on 29 July 1836. The Act provided assistance to the Church of England and the Roman Catholic Church but after agitation by the Reverend John Dunmore Lang and the Colonial Committee of the Church of Scotland help was extended first to the Presbyterians and then to all denominations. As a result of the Act any congregation could obtain a grant of land by depositing £300 as a bona fide of its intention to build a church. Sites were granted on an annual quit rent of a farthing a year. The Treasury also made £1000 available towards the cost of the building on a pound for pound basis as well as an annual grant of up to £200 towards a ministerial stipend.

It was not everybody who was grateful for the State's benevolence. At first there were two schools of thought on the subject. The Anglicans, Roman Catholics, the Established Presbyterians and the Jews found state aid fully acceptable. At the other extreme were the Baptists, the Primitive Methodists, the Bible Christians, the Free Presbyterians, the United Presbyterians, the Independents and nearly all the minor non-conformist sects to whom state aid meant nothing other than state interference in their hard-won religious freedom and raised the spectre of the control of the spiritual by the temporal. They were voluntaries and to them state aid in any form was anathema. By the fifties a third, compromise, school appeared. The Baptists, the Free Presbyterians and the Independents (who had never been wholehearted in their stand on voluntaryism anyway) had modified their views to enable them to accept land grants but still to look on direct financial assistance with abhorrence. The architectural quality of the churches that each school built reflected its stand on the burning issue of state aid with remarkable precision. While the Primitive Methodists and their kind gathered in plain thatched roofed weatherboards or shingle roofed brick boxes on the outskirts of the settlements, the Anglicans and Roman Catholics trooped into well-sited magnificent stone or brick edifices and the Baptists and Independents had substantial but simpler buildings on some of the best available sites.

For these three reasons then—the rise in social religiosity, the increase in the number of religious subdivisions and the availability of state aid—during the sixties and seventies a tremendous number of churches arose and a large part of the practice of any successful architect consisted of churches, church halls, church schools and rectories, manses, presbyteries and parsonages. The practices of the big three—Reed, Blacket and Wardell—were more than half ecclesiastical work of one sort or another, as it was, also, with the lesser men. The architectural style was normally Gothic but the Early English idiom, which had sufficed before, was discarded for elaborated Perpendicular and, where the congregation was really affluent, Decorated Gothic piles. Size as well as decoration was impressive and the churches were far bigger as well as more magnificently finished with gleaming stained-glass, leadlighted windows, carved cedar, polished brass and marble. Even the smaller, humbler and more puritanical sects gave way before the pressure of fashion and, when their teachings frowned on spectacle inside the church, they had no hesitation in contributing their mite outside.

While Gothic continued as the only proper church form in most people's minds, its impact was becoming blunted by over-use. The need for something different and even more imposing was felt. The small congregation of the Zion Particular Baptists planted a black and white painted baroque front of arced pediments, scrolled buttresses and heavy rusticated trims onto the front of its tiny plain brick box in Lonsdale Street, Melbourne, in about 1860. Many of the pre-gold churches had of necessity been extended in the fifties. Some had been torn down and rebuilt. Whether extended or rebuilt nearly all had been given a stone Gothic screen of tower, spire and porch across their fronts. The Lonsdale Street Baptists were somewhat tardy in covering their nakedness but when they eventually did the clothes they wore were in the very forefront of fashion—a full

The Independent Church
in Collins Street,
Melbourne: 1868.
Architects, Reed and
Barnes

Scots Church in Collins
Street, Melbourne: 1874.
Architects, Reed and
Barnes

twenty years ahead of the rest of the town.

When Joseph Reed toured Europe in 1864 he brought back with him fresh ideas on architectural fashions. Accordingly, when he was commissioned in 1867 to erect a church for the Independents on the very highest hill overlooking Melbourne, he outshone the recently improved Gothic Scots Church across the road by building a red brick pile with a lofty tower in a two-toned Sienese style.

Reed's choice was symptomatic of the proliferation of architectural styles that came in the sixties. A building need no longer be restricted to Gothic or Classic, no matter how debased it may become in the hands of inepts striving for variety. Suddenly a whole rackful of architectural dresses was in fashion— French chateaux, Viennese palaces, Chinese, Indian and Moorish spices were waiting. Not to use them was to be crassly reactionary. Nor should one feel hampered by any need to strive for 'purity' by staying consistently with an inspiration. A mixture of styles added a tang to the final dish.

It was still considered right and proper that town halls, museums, art galleries, post offices and the other symbols of culture and worthiness should remain massively dignified. For such buildings the Classic style was the only fit and proper one, but it was solely the Classic style of Rome that could provide sufficient ornateness. Greek-inspired architecture was passed by as being too plain and too simple for the Victorians. With the Roman buildings as a starting point it was the fussiest versions—the Ionic, the Composite and the Corinthian—that were most popular; and even these were elaborated beyond anything the Romans knew.

Most public buildings and churches were still built of stone whose finish was determined by the type of stone and the money available. Because of fashion after the forties and deterioration in quality and workmanship during the fifties exposed brickwork had disappeared completely for any self-respecting building. By the middle of the 1860s an interest in brickwork was reviving. It was brought about by the widening of the gamut of architectural styles to include some which were essentially brick and by an improvement in brickmaking and bricklaying. When Joseph Reed began work on his self-respecting Independent Church in Melbourne in 1867 it was the first important building to be erected on the road back to brickwork.

While Reed was re-introducing brickwork to Melbourne, Blacket, possibly under the influence of his employee Horbury Hunt, was doing the same for Sydney. In one or two of his surburban churches, such as St Silas' at Waterloo in 1866, he carried out his Romanesque design in brick and embellished it with diaper work—contrasting coloured header bricks set in an interlacing diamond pattern. It was an old thirteenth century Hanseatic brick technique but in Sydney of the 1870s both it and the brickwork were as fresh as tomorrow. Blacket's lead was followed by Thomas Backhouse when he designed his All Saints' Church at Petersham in 1870, and gradually by the other architects who were bent on keeping abreast with the latest and smartest fashions.

Reed took his bricks from the kilns of John Glew. Glew, whose firm had turned out bricks for Melbourne from 1849, had been hard hit by the swing away from good brickwork. To establish the quality of his product he sent samples to England. Testimonials from the brickmakers and architects there supported Glew's contention that his bricks were of high quality. This verification came at the same time that Reed, having returned from Europe with new ideas of architectural style, began to think about the Independent Church. At the same time there were heard the first mutterings against the uniform greyness of the stuccoed buildings. A few voices began to urge for more colour in buildings. Reed obliged and by doing so foreshadowed general developments by fifteen years.

Glew's bricks, like most others in the colonies, were hand-made. They were top with what was called a frog. In 1852 a steam-powered machine capable of turning out 10,000 bricks a day began operating at Parramatta. It was followed by others of even higher capacity.

Then, in 1870, the Hoffman Patent Steam Brick Co. Ltd was established in Melbourne to produce bricks by the first wholly mechanized and continuous process. One set of machines was capable of turning out up to 240,000 bricks a week. Naturally there were problems and shortcomings at first. There was a high proportion of underburnt and overburnt bricks and a great deal of distortion in the shape of the bricks. For these reasons, other mechanical methods continued to be tried out for many years. They all had problems and the old hand method continued for at least another thirty years before it eventually succumbed to the improvements that were at last made to mechanically-produced bricks.

The introduction of the Hoffman process and its eventual triumph had two important long-term effects. Because of its quantity production it caused a fall in the cost of bricks. In 1880 the cost of burning hand-made bricks was 8/6 a thousand while that of Hoffman bricks was 2/- a thousand. The difference was reflected in the final cost and became a considerable factor in the revival of popularity of brickwork in the nineties. The second important result was due to the fact that the Hoffman machines came from Germany and consequently made German sized bricks—$9'' \times 4\frac{1}{2}'' \times 3''$.

The early Australian bricks had been the normal English size though the necessity to fashion tools on the spot had quickly lead to varying sizes of bricks. Restorations carried out in 1967 at Old Government House, Parramatta, unearthed part of the foundations of Phillip's original building of 1790. The bricks, soft and porous and set in the purest mud, measure $9\frac{1}{4}'' \times 4\frac{1}{2}'' \times 2\frac{3}{4}''$. The same restoration brought to light bricks of Governor Hunter's later Government House of 1800 and Governor Macquarie's additions of 1815. The former bricks, set in a mortar of mud, sand and lime made of partly calcined shells, measure $8\frac{7}{8}'' \times 4'' \times 2\frac{3}{8}''$ and the latter, set in a good quality mortar of clean sand and well-burnt shell lime, conform to the English legal standard. In Greenway's time bricks were a uniform $8\frac{3}{4}'' \times 4\frac{1}{4}'' \times 2\frac{1}{2}''$ but after that time variations had crept in. When mechanical presses had arrived in the forties they were of mixed origins—English, German, American and local—and increased the number of sizes made. Until nearly the turn of the century mechanical bricks ranged from the old English size to the Hoffman size of $9'' \times 4\frac{1}{2}'' \times 3''$ and even, at Merrylands in Sydney, up to $11'' \times 11'' \times 11''$. But after 1900, by which time the German process was triumphant, Australia saw no more of the elegantly proportioned bricks of England and the heavier, cruder German blocks became the standard.

In commercial and domestic architecture of the 1860s the aim was to impress the passer-by, not by ponderous dignity but by aggressive display, with the affluence and material success of the owner. While the underlying form of the buildings remained box-like and simple the plastered walls became an inviting canvas for moulded relief decorations. Italian plasterers, the most skilled in the world, were brought in to carry out the intricate work demanded. Inevitably they introduced flourishes and modes that were more highly developed than anything previously seen. As a result, the plaster work took on even greater elaborateness. Plaster decoration spread discreetly at first from the doorways, windows and parapet to include the previously plain wall surfaces as well— a bunch of grapes here, a garland there, a cluster of rosettes elsewhere. The parapet became a fence of round bottle-shaped balusters supporting a serried array of urns and bric-a-brac. Window reveals became wider and were often

Two rather different buildings of the seventies —
Above Mount Pleasant at Launceston, Tasmania: about 1870
Below The Royal Hotel at Hill End, New South Wales: 1872

Toorak, 21 St George's Road, Toorak, Victoria: 1850-54

flattened, especially when they broke downwards at the shallow-arched springing line. At the same time real or false plaster keystones were made more robust and prominent. Label moulds over the window heads became heavier and fancier while the windows themselves were double lights set in twin round-headed wooden frames within one large sash. The same motif often appeared on the front door as well.

The concern with Italian influence spread beyond mere applied decoration. Italianate buildings with a block-like main bulk, shady arcades and loggias and a tall square lookout tower topped by a flag pole became the popular form for mansions. The style was launched when the highest social accolade when the newly-founded and newly-rich colony of Victoria leased wealthy merchant James Jackson's spacious mansion named Toorak as a vice-regal residence at a rental of £10,000 a year. A further £29,000 was spent on alterations and additions to make it a fitting home for the Governor of 'one of the wealthiest colonies of Her Majesty'. When Sir Charles Hotham and his lady drove up the 3,000 yards of new carriageway on 22 June 1854 Toorak's Italianate style and its square tower glittered in extravagant welcome. Having received such an imprimatur the style quickly became a vogue amongst the *nouveaux riches*. It spread rapidly to lesser houses until by the seventies excrescences of fake square towers were appearing on any home whose owner nursed social delusions or ambitions. For the next forty years only the meanest of working-class house was immune to the square tower fashion.

The taste for ever more decorative plastering was given a boost by a fall in costs below the high rates that had prevailed during the fifties. In 1864 bricks, which had cost up to £26 a thousand in the shortages of the fifties, had dropped to 45/- a thousand, lime and sand mortar was 1/4 a cubic foot, hair mortar 1/6 a cubic foot, shell lime 1/4 a bushel, sand 4/- a cubic yard and a skilled tradesman, a bricklayer, a carpenter or a plasterer was paid 1/3 an hour. While Portland cement was available by the 1860s, it was used almost solely for making concrete pipes. It was seldom, if ever, used for mortar or plastering and never constructionally before the 1870s when concrete was first used for block footings. Until the nineties concrete was kept below the ground.

Inside the buildings as well the simplicity of Colonial times was left far behind. Ceiling heights were lifted to a light and airy twelve or even fourteen feet. The old plastering materials of lime, sand and hair were gradually abandoned in favour of plaster of paris imported in barrels from America. The material, which had received its common name from the large deposits of the natural material obtained from Montmartre, a suburb of Paris, was produced by calcinating gypsum, and had been used as a mortar from time immemorial. Although it had been in common use for the intricate ceilings of European houses from over two hundred years it was not until the 1860s that it came into common use in Australia. It allowed interior surfaces to be finished glass smooth and, in skilled hands, to be decorated with precise and finely finished mouldings run in situ. Ceilings were the usual lathes thickly plastered with a heavy rough-finished coat of sand, lime and gypsum. A second thinner coat trued it up and finally a thin float coat of pure gypsum produced an extremely flat and smooth finish. A similar finish was produced on the walls by plastering directly onto the brick. Where wall met ceiling the different expansion properties of the two produced cracks and heavy, deeply moulded undercut cornices disguised it and pleased the aesthetic tastes of the day. Colour came inside with the new smooth finishes. White or sometimes cream had been the only colours used when tallow candles were the only light source but with the new strong gas-lighting reflective surfaces were not so important. Walls and ceilings were tinted with pale, contrasting pastels.

At the same time cast iron proliferated. The patterns were heavier, less sensitive

Domestic Gothic —
Above Roslyndale, 38
Roslyndale Avenue,
Woollahra, New South
Wales: about 1856.
Below House at 157
Hotham Street, East
Melbourne, Victoria:
1861. Architect, Joseph
Reed (?)

and sometimes elaborated to the point of obscurity. Instead of the valence running as a neat band from post to post it fell deeper and hung in tassels and scalloped edges like a paper doily. Cast iron patterns became registerable and protected by copyright in 1870. As local manufacturers were forced to rely on their own resources, crudity in both design and workmanship became evident. The bars were heavier, the edges were round and rough thick plate bosses were used. The surfaces of the bars were patterned with mouldings and the bosses with bas-relief pictures. The debasement of the cast iron work was effective mainly in Victoria and New South Wales where the locally made work was exclusively produced. Most of the local cast iron work was used in the producing colonies but some of it found its way to the other eastern colonies—Queensland and Tasmania— to mix with imported iron. As a result there was much in common between the the cast iron work of the four eastern colonies. Nevertheless even in this largely fashionable material the effect of the climate was discernible. In Tasmania the iron work tended to be neater, smaller in extent, tighter and purely decorative. But in travelling northwards it was built up into fuller and richer drapes which answered a functional need, until it reached Queensland where deep curtains of shading iron work are commonly to be found.

Western Australia and South Australia were still dependent on supplies from England and the ironwork from there was still much lighter, trimmer and more refined, without the excesses of the local work. English ironwork was more geometric and open in its patterns of straight lines or circles and lighter in section than the heavy florid swirls that came from the Sydney and Melbourne foundries. Local designers often turned to the Australian native birds and plants for their ideas. They incorporated parrots, cockatoos, ferns and lyrebirds whose tails lent themselves to swirling design. Consequently, cast iron is seen at its most extravagant in New South Wales and Victoria.

In the middle fifties curved corrugated iron, both imported and local, became available. The curved sheets could span their length without side or intermediate structural support and still remain strong. By the seventies verandahs were covered with arced, bell-cast or bull-nosed roofs whose curving forms appealed strongly to people to whom a straight line had become anathema.

Side by side with the Classically-derived plaster and cast iron houses, the Gothic domestic stream had flourished; but by the late seventies it was waning. Nevertheless, with their steeply pitched gabled slate-covered roofs edged with intricately fretted bargeboards (usually wooden but sometimes of cast iron), fancy brick chimneys and narrow slot windows filled by casement sashes, their asymmetrical plans and their abhorrence of verandahs, these Gothic houses carried safely through the sixties and seventies the essential features that were to become modified into the typical house of the nineties.

Until the middle fifties the towns had clustered tightly around their centres. As long as the horse was the speediest mode of transport and most town-dwellers had to rely on their own legs to go about their day's business, people could not live far from their work. These circumstances had given rise to the proliferation of dense terrace housing no more than a half-hour's walk from the town. Only the few leisured families could afford to live an hour's drive or more out in the country. Consequently, the towns were compact and defined. Beyond the edge of the town, where land became suddenly rural and cheap, a few stately homes, invariably placed on the brow or the crown of a hill with an eye to the view (but none for orientation), sat in fifty to one thousand acres of their own spacious grounds. There was no gradual merging of the town into the country and the transition between the two was abrupt and complete.

The sixties saw the creation of the suburbs and the pattern of row upon row of individual houses each on its own quarter-acre allotment. The endless sprawl of the former has become the universal characteristic of all Australian cities and towns and the ownership of one of the latter the universal goal of every good Australian.

The change was due to the introduction of the railway. It was a general development, but its most extreme example was Melbourne. The first train in Australia ran from Port Melbourne to Melbourne on 13 September 1854. Twelve months later, on 26 September, New South Wales rejoiced when its first train puffed its way between Sydney and Parramatta. Over the next five years private companies built lines from the cities to the closer settlements. By 1860 Williamstown, St Kilda, Prahran, Brighton, Hawthorn and Essendon were joined to Melbourne by iron roads. With these developments a man could live in one of these previously rural towns and still travel to his work in the city in the same time that he could walk from Carlton. And in the country the land was cheap. The new suburbs centred on the railway stations.

There was little control over the subdivisions that were made. Local government was weak or non-existent. The over-riding concern was to obtain the greatest number of building allotments in the simplest way. The layout of the subdivisions was limited only by the one or two existing tracks which linked the settlements and whose line had been determined by the easiest grades for bullock waggons and horses. Paying no heed to the form of the land, often without a surveyor ever seeing it let alone taking levels, a rectangular grid of streets was mindlessly drawn

Tay Creggan, 30 Yarra Street, Hawthorn, Victoria: 1898

up with T-square and set-square. With a few strokes of a pencil the blocks formed by the streets were divided into rows of back-to-back pairs of allotments with forty feet frontages—five or six to an acre. The long straight streets began at nothing and ended at nothing. They took no notice of the pattern of adjacent subdivisions, achieved no related continuity with them and only where it was convenient was any use made of neighbouring streets.

Landowners divided their parcels of land to the money-making maximum. They made no attempt to provide parklands or open spaces, or to preserve natural features for the public's good, or to protect buyers from unsuitable allotments, or to provide drainage. The soggy undrained low-lying swamp and the foreshore were equally grist for the mill. Only very occasionally were shopping centres provided. In the settlements these were already established by usage. New ones coagulated wherever a station was placed in open country; others were left to develop eventually around corner stores opportunely built and conducted on some promising but unintended spot in the standard subdivision. And so, for £20, those who for the first time in the history of their class would be able to be king of their own little domain, were able to own their own land.

The houses which were built were as cheap as the land. For as little as £120 each four-roomed, timber-framed houses with weatherboard walls and iron roofs were built in long lines twenty feet back from the street and three feet from each side boundary. The front garden was formally laid out with beds of geraniums, hollyhocks and roses, the back garden was a vegetable plot spotted with fruit trees, and the six feet between the houses was a wind tunnel in which only moss or fuchsias would grow. The house was a miniature version of those homes that the owners and their fathers had seen but had never hoped to own. It was far from being self-sufficient, in fact, but by owning it a man gained respectability, position and pride. The cheapest of the houses were plain in the extreme but always there was a verandah along the front. The fashion tricks of their betters were sprinkled over them. Little bits of cast iron trimmed the verandah or a simplified Gothic bargeboard hung from the gables of those whose tastes lay in that direction.

The rows of identical single-storeyed homes were spottily punctuated by an occasional more pretentious two-storeyed place where the architectural fashions were given greater scope and to which the lesser lights paid due deference. And over all gazed the older country homes, aloof and detached in their secluding acres.

In this way over the years, as public transport spread out like a fungus, the cities spread patchwork suburban skirts of individual homes, and the towns and the country came together and merged with each other. With the rise of the suburbs the distinction between urban and rural life was blurred. At some indistinct point the urban became the suburban and at an even less recognizable boundary the suburban trickled off into the rural. And where until the sixties there had been two classes of houses—town or country—there was now a third, the suburban house, which eventually was to form the great majority of Australian homes.

Gold and its aftermath had made Melbourne the centre of Australian growth. The same causes had made it the leader of architectural trends. And just as the other colonies were affected to a greater or lesser extent by Victoria's prosperity so was their architecture similarly influenced by what happened in the main colony. The developments outlined spread to all the other centres. Architectural fashion, with its spectacular paraphernalia of plaster and iron adornments, grew vigorously in Sydney, in Hobart and in Adelaide, bravely in a less affluent Brisbane and weakly in a still-poor Perth. Irrespective of climatic or other local variations, buildings identical except for size were to be found in any of the well-established cities and towns of all the colonies.

The Town Hall,
South Brisbane: 1862.
Architects, John Hall
and Sons

The Town Hall, Launceston,
Tasmania: 1864.
Architect, Peter Mills

The Derwent & Tamar
Assurance Co. Ltd Building,
Murray and Macquarie
Streets, Hobart, Tasmania:
1876. Architect,
Henry Hunter

In the flow of migrants from England not all the architects had chosen to reap in the obvious fields of Melbourne and Sydney. In South Australia, Henry Stuckey had built one of the finest Gothic buildings in Australia, St Peter's College, by the mid-century. Edmund William Wright, a London-trained architect who had worked in Europe and America, arrived in Adelaide in 1850 and set up practice. In a smaller way he did for William Light's city what Joseph Reed did for Melbourne with a series of banks, churches and the town hall. Throughout the seventies William McMinn, a native-born currency lad who had spent his early years as a surveyor in the Northern Territory and as an inspector on the Overland Telegraph, helped to create the character of North Terrace with a series of fine terrace houses and left the Supreme Court and a number of fancy hotels such as the Crown and Sceptre.

In Tasmania, Henry Hunter bestrode the local architectural scene. Having tried gold-digging, unsuccessfully, in Victoria, he commenced practice in Hobart in 1855. From then until his removal to Brisbane in 1888 when architects first started to flock to that city, this enthusiastic devotee of Gothic architecture designed dozens of churches—thirty-one in Hobart alone—and practically all the major commercial and civic buildings throughout the island. The Hobart Town Hall, the Tasmanian Museum, the Derwent and Tamar Assurance Building, the Hobart Masonic Hall, St Mary's Cathedral and a host of banks which form the the core of Tasmanian Victorian architecture came from him.

Before the 1880s Queensland was a struggling colony and architecture remained correspondingly weak. F. D. G. Stanley, an Edinburgh-trained architect, was appointed Government Architect in 1862. In this position he was able to implant a certain amount of architectural stylism on Brisbane in his work on the Classically derived Parliament House, the Brisbane Hospital and court houses and post offices throughout Queensland. In 1881 he left his official position to set up in private practice which he developed into a huge business. As a private architect he designed, in 1887, the Queensland National Bank Building in Brisbane which was claimed, then and for a long time to come, to be the finest bank building in Australia. In 1864 Richard Gailey, a Donegal-born architect who had practised in Londonderry, arrived in Melbourne as a visitor. Within a few weeks he had decided to stay in the colonies and before the year was out had hung up his shingle in Brisbane. From that time until the eighties he led building in that city in the way that Hunter did in Tasmania.

The situation in which an individual could so completely dominate architecture in his area was a unique aspect of Victorian times. Reed, Blacket, Wardell, Hunter, McMinn and Gailey ruled their domains with the unchallengeable authoritarianism with which Victorian fathers ruled their families. And all of them were architects utterly dedicated to the rightness of the tenets of scholastic architecture. Questions or doubts about them were as unthinkable as they would have been about the Empire itself.

It was the same mental climate and outlook that showed itself in the successful organization of the architectural profession and the establishment of architectural education in Australia. After two abortive attempts to form professional associations in 1851 and 1856 in Victoria the architects of that colony re-formed the Victorian Institute of Architects in 1871 and their colleagues in the mother colony followed with their own institute in 1874. Both have continued uninterruptedly— presently as chapters of the Royal Australian Institute of Architects— to the present day. Until 1865, trained architects had been imported. Local youths who felt the urge to be Christopher Wrens had to pick up what they could how they could. In that year a class in mechanical drawing was started in Sydney's Mechanics' School of Arts for such people. By 1878 and as a part of the Technical or Working Men's College the drawing classes were being supplemented by 'a course of lectures on architecture and building instruction'. For an outlay of sixpence a lesson for seniors and threepence a lesson for juniors the City Architect, Mr Sapsford, aided by Mr Elphinstone, Mr Kirkpatrick, Mr Cyril Blacket 'and other professional gentlemen' laid bare the secrets and mysteries of their craft. It was the first professional course of architecture in Australia and, after nearly ninety years of growth, expansion and various changes of names, still continues as the nation's largest school of architecture at the University of New South Wales. In the middle of the mid-Victorian times the formation of professional institutes and the establishment of formal courses exemplified the growing power of the architects and the strength on which their influence rested.

It was not that the architecture and the blind enslavement to fashion were without their critics but rather that the critics were powerless against the combined will of the architects and the tastes of the community. Firstly, there were those who questioned the sensitivity and skill exhibited by the designer in his chosen style. One critic, skating close to the libel laws, let go a broadside at Blacket's St Andrew's Cathedral in Sydney. It was 'stiff . . . hard . . . the architect aiming

The Queensland National Bank, Queen Street, Brisbane:
1887. Architect, F. D. G. Stanley

at severity has succeeded in producing an epitome of all that is commonplace . . .
uninteresting . . . ungraceful . . . hideous . . . unfeeling . . . harshness . . . seldom
has so dull an inanity been produced at such a cost . . . a noble opportunity has
been employed to create the stiffest the coldest the deadest erection . . . a series
of gas pipes . . . unvarying stupidity . . . the least interesting cathedral in the
world.' Having exhausted his vocabulary he dismissed Wardell's St Mary's
Cathedral as being even worse.

Amongst the crossfire and the protests some unexpectedly enlightened and
fundamental views were expressed. A small minority, alarmed at the way things
were going, propounded ideas which would eventually be forced upon architecture
as it struggled to extricate itself from the sticky honey that was then settling over it.
There were those who, disturbed at the growing excesses, demanded a return to
an architecture based on 'practical utility'. 'The character of the building should
be expressed on its face and the face should be designed to suit its particular aspect
and construction of fit materials . . . rather a wall left perfectly plain than burden
it with useless weight, which is of no utility, and therefore can contain no
beauty; and which above all costs a great deal of money,' wrote one critic in 1865—
anticipating by some fifty years the rest of his profession. However, most of those
who inveighed against the heavy corniced plaster surfaces as a 'worthless vulgar
dirty sham' as they called them were usually engaged in carrying on a sputtering
Battle of the Styles and for all their logical arguments were found, in fact, to be
carrying a torch for Gothic in all its forms and everywhere.

There were those who, believing in the need for a native style of architecture
but being still tightly entwined in the web of stylism, noted that Australia's climate
approximated to that of the Mediterranean and advocated the adoption of Spanish
architecture as a sound starting-point for its development. Again the idea
anticipated by more than half a century a movement that had a brief life in the
twentieth century. Others advocated the compulsory use on all buildings of
'practical and extremely ornamental verandahs'; while others even more forward-
looking put forward the idea of the breezeway which became one of the symbols
of progressive domestic architecture in the 1950s.

Modern town-planning also had its embryonic basis voiced. In 1857 William
Bland said he hoped that in the not too distant future 'the nature and condition
of the ground plot of our towns and cities will be held of infinitely more importance
than even the grandeur and beauty of the buildings'. And, in 1867, when the
number of horses and carts in the streets led some to imagine the cities had a
traffic problem a seer, writing in *The Colonial Monthly*, showed astonishing
foresight.

> Suppose it were required to lay out a new street in a city like Sydney or
> Melbourne the best plan would appear to be to disconnect as much as possible
> the horse traffic from that of the footpassengers; and like the ancient city
> of Chester, to have the dwellings raised some feet above the roadway;
> and if the inhabitants could be persuaded to remove their shops to the first
> floor a much pleasanter promenade would be provided . . . together with an
> atmosphere cooler and more free from the dust of the streets. Cleaner lighter
> and more elegant shops would thus be provided, and the street would in fact
> be duplicated, the ground floors serving for the purposes of stowage of heavy
> cases of goods and the street itself devoted chiefly to the horse traffic. There
> could be no difficulty in arranging such terraced streets as the upper floor
> for the footpassengers could be carried on iron columns which . . . would
> be about twelve feet high.[1]

In 1963, when the horses were made of tin and had wheels instead of legs and the problem had increased a hundredfold, the Buchanan Committee in England put forward an identical proposal to cope with London's traffic ills. Enthusiasts hailed it as new and brilliantly inspired.

But the voices of the prophets, the protestors and the pleaders for sanity were ignored. By the end of the seventies the love for showiness and opulence in building was everywhere triumphant. Plaster adornment and cast iron lace came thicker and richer as Australian architecture raced unbridled towards the frenetic climax of the 1880s.

[1] Article, 'On Colonial Architecture' by F.S.P. in *The Colonial Monthly*, Vol. 1, No. 4, December 1867, p. 319.

8   In 1878 a short, sharp recession jolted the economy. Building hesitated for twelve months but then, as the cloud passed, slipped back smoothly into full power. The recession had been no more than a missed beat in the steady powerful drive that had started thirty years before.

The decade which began in 1880 saw tremendous changes, developments and growth. Under their influence the six separate colonies were forced closer together and established a political climate which twenty years later gave birth to a federated nation. Melbourne and Adelaide had been linked by electric telegraph in 1858 and by 1877 the metal thread was carrying its chattering message to all the capital cities and to Darwin. In 1883 the last spike was driven in the railway joining Melbourne to Sydney. Five years later the iron roads ran continuously from Queensland to South Australia.

In 1870 the native-born population outnumbered, for the first time, those who had immigrated. By 1880 two-thirds of the population were Australian-born. For this society the Sydney *Bulletin* printed the stories and poems, heavily spiced with Australianism, of Henry Lawson and Banjo Patterson, preached a vehement nationalism and blasted all who fawned on England. Men such as the self-made, vulgar and sensual Henry Parkes with his insatiable taste for women, the flamboyant, coarse, uncouth and licentious George Reid and the high-minded, prim and gifted Alfred Deakin strutted and postured on the political stage grandiosely declaring Australia's worldly glory and her right to a place in the sun. Despite the varying standards of their private lives which were hidden behind public masks of upright respectability they were, one and all, extremely talented men with a grand breadth of vision and astute and lively minds.

Government and private enterprise expanded recklessly and secondary industries, with mounting exports, began to contribute appreciably to the national income. Nationalists winced under the jibe that colonial goods were second-rate and shoddy, and the quality improved. Under the unfettered conditions of competitive individualism the working-classes were faced with the need to band together for their own survival. Trade unionism, which was soon to issue into a major political party, was born. In 1880 this turbulent time of ferment, faction and flamboyance was beginning.

The pumped-up prosperity based on over-extended borrowing which was to envelop the whole of eastern Australia during the eighties was to reach its hysterical climax in Melbourne. In that town financial caution was to be thrown to the winds; crazy ventures were to be launched with loans over-subscribed within an hour or two of opening and with people fighting for the opportunity to invest their money; clever unprincipled financiers, many of them penniless when the decade began, were to float dozens of finance companies and building societies and, by the peak year of 1888, create an artificial and frantic land boom which was to be the prelude to the greatest and most terrible of depressions in Australia's history.

The stage was to be set for Victoria's madness by a government Protectionist policy which by 1890 was to give the colony 3,000 large factories, 215 brickworks, 165 large sawmills and 74 breweries and distilleries. To accommodate the workers of these industries, thousands of cottages were to be speculatively built with money borrowed from the bottomless coffers of the building societies and, in the process, Melbourne was to be transformed as its suburbs flowed out over the rolling countryside. The spread of the city was to be stimulated by the undercover influence of the land speculators on the government. In 1880 the Victorian Parliament was to authorize the construction of 475 miles of new railway line for their benefit. Four years later it was to pass the 'Octopus Act' authorizing a further sixty-five new lines totalling 1,170 miles of track and to cost forty-four million pounds for the same reason. New stations were to be built on existing lines and the rural villages which had clustered around the first stations were to become linked to each other in a continuous ribbon of workers' homes.

Private companies were to open up for subdivision the near-city land which had been left untouched by the railways by building horse and cable tramways to all points of the compass. Between November 1885 and 1891 cable trams were to clatter to Fitzroy, Clifton Hill, Brunswick, Carlton, Brighton, North Melbourne, West Melbourne, South Melbourne, Port Melbourne, Windsor, St Kilda, Kew, Hawthorn and Toorak. Where they went suburbs of workers' cottages were to swallow the countryside and the land boomers were to make fortunes.

On the picked positions at the end of the railway and tramway lines, clever speculators and merchant princes were to erect palatial mansions costing up to £80,000 (about $800,000 in 1968's values), plus another £10,000 to furnish, as memorials to their success as much as for homes. Mark Moss, a Jewish money-lender, was to build Norwood, a 'fantastic castle' at Brighton, and Sir William Clarke was to build the huge squat bulk of Cliveden at East Melbourne—both grotesque reminders of the tastes of their owners. Better testimonies were to be built by Albert Miller at Toorak (Whernside), W. K. Thomson at Brighton (Kamesburgh) and Henry Ricketson at Caulfield (Glen Eira). Like many others Ricketson was to be forced to sell his glorious home (to F. G. Sargood) to pay his debts when the crash came. The house was to become eventually the Caulfield Military Hospital and finally to fall under the wrecker's hammer in 1964 when new economic circumstances were to cause many of the old stately homes to give way to a new wave of subdivision pressures. The florid Italianate style was to flourish and Hawthorn, Kew and Brighton were to be graced with stuccoed wedding cakes whose embossed names such as 'Villa Callantina', 'Villa Alba', and 'Villa Maria' were to commemorate the origins of both their style and their builders.

Two International Exhibitions mirrored the conditions as the eighties began. In 1879 a timber and glass pavilion, covering five acres of Sydney's Botanic Gardens and topped by a one hundred feet diameter dome, housed a display of the industrial wonders of the modern world. In 1880 an even larger timber and plaster structure brought a more ambitious fair to delight the senses and tickle the pockets of the citizens of Melbourne. The populations of both towns were headed towards the half-million mark and they were cities by any standards. And the world brought its goods to them.

The Exhibitions were significant for architecture for two reasons: firstly, because of the goods they introduced, and secondly, because of the extravagant style of decoration which they made even more fashionable in architecture.

The first passenger lift to be seen in Australia was displayed by the Whittier Machine Company of America at the Sydney Exhibition. When the Exhibition closed it was installed in Toohey's Brewery. With the introduction of mechanical passenger lifts Australian buildings were freed from the bonds that had limited them to the three, or possibly four, floors that could be ascended comfortably by leg power.

Right Benvenuta,
48 Drummond Street,
Carlton, Victoria
about 1890

Below Stonnington,
336 Glenferrie Road,
Malvern, Victoria,
about 1892

Above Astolat,
122 Riversdale Road,
Camberwell, Victoria: 1882

Right Kamesburgh,
North Road, Brighton,
Victoria: 1884.
Architect, Lloyd Taylor

Above The Exhibition
Building, Melbourne:
1880. Architects,
Reed and Barnes

Right Iroquois,
258 Mowbray Street,
Chatswood, New South
Wales: 1888

In Australia, until 1855, a hand-powered system of pulleys called 'crab' or 'grab' winches had been the only mechanical means of lifting goods to upper floor levels in warehouses. In that year mechanically powered 'sack tackles' or 'American hoists', which had been developed in New York and Boston about 1840, were introduced into Sydney flour mills. They were a big advance on the grab winches and could raise and lower a man as well as goods. Powered by wind or steam they consisted of an open platform hauled up and down by a rope turning around a barrel and controlled by a hand rope moving a friction belt-and-pulley arrangement. Such a primitive contraption was not only unsuitable but far too dangerous for passenger travel. When one prominent Sydney building installed a platform with sides a few novice employees tried to save their legs but 'it was generally noticed that experienced persons took to the stairs in preference'.

Safe passenger lifts were developed by Elisha Graves Otis of New York and installed at the Crystal Palace Exposition of New York in 1853. They were a development of the American hoists brought to Sydney in 1855 and incorporated spur-gear and safety-rails in case of the lifting-rope breaking.

The Whittier lift installed in Toohey's Brewery was powered by steam operating a worm-gear and screw-shaft which sank into a pit in the ground and on top of which was supported the passenger cage. The first passenger lift using the Otis principle of a suspending cable was installed in Farmer's store in 1881. Within a year lifts were being installed widely in new and old buildings. Three types were used—mechanical, direct hydraulic and indirect hydraulic. Hydraulic lifts were the most favoured but they had the disadvantages of being wasteful of water, limited in the height to which they could operate and, where loads were variable, expensive and uneconomic. The first hydraulic lifts were installed in the Pyrmont Sugar Works by the English firm of Sir William Armstrong. At first the driving power, whether water or steam, had to be provided within the lift-owner's building by tanks on the roof and engine and pumps in the basement in the case of hydraulic lifts, and machinery and boilers in the basement in the case of mechanical lifts. When the special hydraulic companies were formed to provide lift power as a public utility to raise lifts at a rate of four hundred feet to five hundred feet a minute hydraulic lifts won the day and mechanical lifts disappeared until the 1920s. For

Strathroy, Hobart Road, near Launceston,
Tasmania: about 1888

the first few years arguments raged on the best method of support for passenger cages. The protagonists of screw supports pushed hard for its high degree of safety. 'It is a well-known fact that there have been dozens of accidents in Sydney and Melbourne, some resulting in death, with suspended lifts,' said Sydney's leading lift consultant in 1894. But direct-acting screw shafts were noisy and disconcerted the passengers with their wild vibrations despite attempts to achieve smooth running with barrels of emery lubricant. They travelled slowly, shafts corroded from seepage water in the deep wells and some lifts collapsed from rotted metal. Eventually the suspended cage, as developed by Otis, ousted the shaft but many accidents lay ahead during the next forty years.

The effect of the lifts was soon evident. Buildings shot upwards to take advantage of the new invention, land values rose and buildings soared even higher as a consequence. In December 1882 E. W. Cracknell addressed the Engineering Association of New South Wales: 'In consequence of the great strides which have been made in commerce together with increased facilities for quick communications the value of our City property has increased to such an extent that many of our warehouses, public buildings and hotels must be increased in height.'[1]

By means of the lifts, buildings were enabled to meet the mounting pressures for more building on less land. They climbed up to six or even seven storeys. There were, of course, the Jeremiahs. The *Australian Sketcher* said that 'it has yet to be proved that people will ascend to such heights to transact their ordinary business.' But no one took any notice. Then, in 1885, Prell's Building in Queen Street, Melbourne, speared ten storeys up into the sky. It had been designed by the architectural firm of F. M. White and Son and had cost £60,000. Conservatives were distressed at the violence done to the familiar scale of the city and protested that 'elevators will be the bane of the artistic side of architecture'. In Sydney, George Allen Mansfield installed two lifts which travelled 104 feet in his new Australia Hotel in 1889.

In July 1889 the Melbourne Hydraulic Power Company commenced operations by providing power for lifts as a public utility. In January 1891 the Sydney Hydraulic Power Company offered the same service to Sydney. Freed from the need to provide their own power at considerable cost in money, space and manpower, buildings rushed to couple up a single pipe to the Companies' mains. Tall buildings were given a further shot in the arm.

By 1892 there were several buildings reaching ten or even twelve storeys high in both Melbourne and Sydney. The Assistant Government Architect of Victoria, E. W. Dobbs, described them as 'box-like . . . gigantic . . . hideous . . . grotesque . . . gruesome . . . ugly . . . [and] monumental without being sublime.'[2] He voiced the views of many of his contemporaries who were scandalized by the fact that in many cases 'each floor is similar in detail'. The Romans had only five Orders and with ten or twelve storeys there were not enough of them to conform to the established tenets of allotting a more complicated Order to each surmounting floor.

The tall buildings posed new constructional problems for the architects. They not only went higher but they also went deeper. Two or even three of their floors were sunk below the ground. The main structure was still built in brickwork. The load was carried downwards on ever-thickening walls until by the time they reached the basements they were four or even six feet thick. As long as buildings continued to be built of load-bearing brickwork this necessary increase of wall thickness imposed an economic limit to the height to which they could rise. While hydraulic lifts could have gone higher the loss of floor area at the ground and lower levels as well as the initial cost imposed a practical limit of around one hundred feet. But even with the structures remaining brick, concrete began to find a place in building. Cast iron columns had normally been used to carry light loads such as verandahs or balconies in theatres or sometimes as intermediate supports carrying

Above The A.N.Z. Bank,
59 King William Street,
Adelaide: 1875-78.
Architects, E. W. Wright
and Lloyd Tayler.

Right The Commercial
Banking Co. of Sydney Ltd.
Queen and Prince
Alfred Streets, Berry, New
South Wales: 1889

one or two floors. As buildings went higher they were used as storey posts three, four or more floors high. This imposed a load far beyond anything for which the columns had been used previously. To add strength the practice was developed of filling the hollow posts with concrete. It was the first tentative use of concrete for structural purposes. Its other uses were restricted to non-structural conditions. Deep basements often went well below the water table or opened cracks in the rock or struck springs. Water seepage was a new problem. Brick structural walls were coated with Portland cement mortar or even thick concrete. Richard Gailey, for instance, used concrete in these structural and waterproofing ways on the Courier Mail Building in Brisbane in 1887.

Gailey also used concrete on this same building to provide fireproofing. He placed curved sheets of corrugated galvanized iron below the timber floors and covered the iron with a two inches thick layer of concrete. The technique also proved to be a most efficient sound-insulating barrier. If Gailey did not actually invent the idea he certainly seems to have been the first to have used it in Australia. When a large part of Sydney north of Moore Street and opposite the rising Australia Hotel went up in flames in 1890, the manager Edwin Moore pointed out to his architect, Cyril Blacket, his fears of the results of a similar unhappy occurrence in his own hotel. Blacket immediately incorporated Gailey's fireproofing in the new building.

Fire loomed large amongst the new problems facing the architects of the tall buildings. While they continued to install timber floors they discarded oregon and the other softwoods in favour of ironbark, a local hardwood which in a fire charred on the surface. This, in turn, acted as an insulator by excluding air from the inner wood which remained unimpaired. The big buildings also complicated planning. Additional fire stairs were needed. The normal fire-fighting services of the insurance companies had equipment, ladders and water pumps that would reach two floors up. Consequently, the tall buildings had to provide their own. Normally this consisted of axes and buckets of sand and water placed at strategic points. Some hotels, where the danger was most acute, particularly at night, installed electric bells reinforced by watchmen armed with whistles and whirling rattles who constantly patrolled the dimly lit corridors.

Just as the sixties and seventies had been a period of churches and church schools erected for the good of the soul and the mind, so the eighties belonged to secular buildings catering to money-making materialism and worldly pleasures made available by shrewd financial investment, canny land deals and handsome business profits—banks, insurance offices, town halls, theatres and grand hotels.

The Australia Hotel was the biggest and most sumptuous hotel in Sydney when it was completed. But it was only one of several which were but a little less ambitious. The same situation prevailed in Melbourne where a number of grand hotels such as the Federal, built in 1888 to glorify the virtues of abstinence, were erected. In its cause, size and magnificence the grand hotel caught the essence of all the changes that were taking place.

Bulking high on the skyline with 200 to 600 bedrooms stacked in tiers above a ground floor of dining-rooms, coffee-rooms, ballroom and kitchen and with billiard-rooms, stores, cellars, new-fangled refrigeration cool-rooms, lift and hot-water service rooms and electricity generators below ground, they were monuments to the benefits of technology, the affluent materialism of society and the vulgarity of its tastes.

The need for such piles of bedrooms was a direct result of the railways. With the rise of industrialism family businesses were replaced by public corporations with connections throughout the country. A constant stream of businessmen passed to and fro between the future capital cities. Before the coming of the inter-colony railways they had travelled by coastal ships but now they could go faster and more

The Bank of New South Wales,
King and George Streets, Sydney:
1886. Architects, E. C. H. Blackmann
and (1889) John Sulman

The Mutual Life Assurance
Building, George and Wynyard
Streets, Sydney: 1891. Architects,
Sulman and Power

The Sydney Permanent Freehold
Land and Building Society offices,
Macquarie and King Streets, Sydney
1889. Architect, Varney Parkes

The Federal Hotel, King and
Collins Streets, Melbourne:
1888. Architects, Ellerker and
Kilburn with William Pitt

safely by train. Commercial travellers fanned out into the country towns for a week of collecting orders for goods which, in turn, would be despatched to their destination by rail. In its turn the increase in wealth, which was largely due to the trains, made it possible for country people to travel quickly and comfortably to the cities for a short holiday and a shopping spree in the big stores which were replacing the small private shops.

The possibilities for profit opened by the new accessibility to the cities that the trains gave to country people drew new attractions especially created to please them. These, in turn, enhanced the magnetism of the cities. For one reason or another traffic generated by the railways increased the movement of people tremendously. At the junctions and at the termini large hotels with many bedrooms were built to handle the traffic. And the greatest concentration was, naturally enough, at the city terminals. At Spencer Street Station in Melbourne and Central Station in Sydney, train after train disgorged 400 to 500 soot-begrimed people at a time. Half of them wanted a hotel room.

As a result the grand hotels came. Their great size was dressed in a way that took its cue from the domed buildings erected for the great Exhibitions in 1879 and 1880. Bulbous, bloated and fat-bellied, they were given a thick cosmetic of rampant decoration. The buildings of the preceding twenty years had been exuberantly opulent. The buildings, particularly the grand hotels, of the eighties were pompously ostentatious.

Their method of construction limited their height but above their six to ten floors they sprouted a tall imposing tower invariably capped with a splendid dome. The main part of the tower was masonry but the upper part and the dome were erected on a frame, often prefabricated in iron. The tower began as a separate unit behind the parapet and was capped with a shallow ogee dome covered in double curved iron. It quickly moved to the wall face and had part of its circumference made by extending the wall upwards. The pitch of its covering dome was increased and formed by a reversed ogee. It became spiky instead of flat. Quickly it moved outwards beyond the face of the wall and bulged as a hexagonal or octagonal oriel tower over the footpath below. High above the pavement the tower petered out in a thin flag pole from which the symbol of the country's satisfaction with its achievements could be floated with puffing pride. The walls were richly encrusted with the exotica of the world translated into plaster by the skilful hands of the Italians. A bare space of wall was considered to be something almost obscene needing to be covered and disguised from lewd eyes. Garlands, grapes, shells, volutes, scrolls, medallions, vases and Orders, both known and invented, hung thickly over the buildings. Bands of flora and statues of fauna were set on string courses, cornices and parapets. Pediments were piled one on top of each other.

The full-blown and gaudy buildings afforded one of the few available outlets for display of wealth. The sombre and almost Puritanical code which emanated from Windsor Castle after the death of the Prince Consort and which permeated throughout the whole of the Anglo-Saxon world frowned on personal adornment. Lavish and expensive dressing which probably would have eventuated in less forbidding conditions was not tolerated. The successful man could not adorn his wife, let alone himself, with jewels, furs and brightly coloured silks when a touch of grey or muted lavender colour was the only relief permitted to the universal and gloomy black or brown suits and dresses. He found the answer to his frustration by dressing his buildings in a way which in other times he would have dressed his wife.

The inordinate pride in success showed itself in innumerable small ways as well. Keystones were made in the form of portraits of well-known people— politicians, public figures, the owner himself and, of course, the Queen. The client had his name or that of his firm and the date of the erection of his triumph

Above Cast iron rotunda
in Elder Park,
Adelaide: 1885

Right House at 16 Robe
Terrace Medindie, South
Australia: about 1890

moulded into the plaster at the visual centre of the building as a record of his belief in the permanence of the existing order and as a reminder to posterity of his own importance.

There had been increasing dissatisfaction with the monotonous overall greyness of the sixties and seventies. Demands for colour on buildings were insistently raised. 'Polychrome' became the architectural catch-cry of the eighties. The idea suited the mood to perfection as architects looked frantically for new ways of making their buildings proclaim their clients' greatness. They found one way in colour. Their plastered extravanganzas broke out in a rainbow of reds and purples with the detailed decoration picked out in white and gold and practically every hue in the palette.

Inside the grand hotels the same ornate richness prevailed. Costly materials were used in the most prodigal way. Expansive entrances were paved with intricate Italian mosaic tiles. Massive cedar or marble staircases, with thick bulbous turned balusters and carved newels topped by bronzes of heroic knights and romantic nymphs bearing gas or electric lights, led to the upper floors. Walls were embellished with plasterwork and either painted or, more likely, covered with rich wall papers (another new material of the times) printed in patterns of red, green or blue and gold. Dining-rooms and ballrooms were lined on two adjacent walls with large plate glass mirrors set in extravagant frames which quadrupled their apparent size. Coffered ceilings were riotous and magnificent displays of the plasterer's art with deep undercut mouldings and all the paraphernalia of the outside transferred inside with the form of each rose, each grape and each ribboned basket highlighted and enhanced by individual hand painting. Cut-glass crystal chandeliers supported electric lights and sparkled like festoons of diamonds. Columns were sheathed in green, brown, russet, white or black marble. Door furniture—the pulls, the pushes, the handles, the plates and the hinges—were polished, embossed or engraved brass; while public doors, their upper sections of thick plate glass with bevelled edges and incised lettering picked out in gold leaf, glittered like diamonds as they swung. Carpets were deep and luxuriant and furniture and joinery were rich red and brown mahogany and walnut.

The grand hotels were havens of sumptuousness but they were no more than a concentration of the ideas and ideals that pervaded all architecture of the High Victorian period. The theatres were another similar manifestation of the times. The unpretentious playhouses whose austere finishes could satisfactorily withstand the brawling and bawling that were likely to ignite at any time in the rough and tumble days following gold were insufficient for the sybarites of the eighties. Voluptuous domed temples encrusted with all the plaster cosmetic, the colour and the materials of the grand hotels were erected for them. The inside glowed with red plush and mahogany, plate glass and gilt, coloured marbles and thick red carpet. There were wide ample staircases, velvet curtains with gold tassels and tiers of balconies supported on cast iron columns. Private boxes looked on to a vast proscenium surrounded by giant Orders, dancing plaster putti and gambolling gods and goddesses and flanked by a pair of huge alabaster urns. In Melbourne in 1887, architect William Pitt built, or more strictly redesigned, the Princess Theatre to be the largest and grandest theatre in the land. In it Pitt gave Melbourne the world's first opening roof and ceiling which could be rolled back on balmy nights to give the patrons entertainment under the stars. Sydney got Her Majesty's Theatre in the same spirit at the same time while lesser towns such as Hobart and Brisbane and large provincial towns built theatres for themselves that were different in size but identical in spirit and usually in name.

Architecture in the country towns was inevitably influenced by the fashions in the cities, but particular circumstances and limitations just as inevitably prevented exact reproduction. While they mimicked the superficialities that were all the rage in Melbourne and Sydney, the available materials were more restricted and less luxurious, the same degree of skill was not available and the more severe climatic conditions all imposed modifications. The smaller the town the greater was the gap. Plasterwork was simplified, decoration was both cruder and less extensive, and roofs were always iron. Features which had some shading possibilities were often distended to make them more so. By this means, window trims sometimes became beetling hoods of bullnose iron. And, with the exception of shire halls, the storeyed verandah retained a strong hold on practically all country town buildings. While the banks, the shops and particularly the hotels wore the fabrics and the jewellery of their city betters, they were too close to the reality of a burning sun to discard the cool brims of the verandah.

In the eighties, except for a few cases, public buildings forsook their rigorous adherence to strictly Classical models. There had been an increasing growth of local government during the sixties, seventies and eighties. In New South Wales, for instance, the Municipality Acts created thirty-five new councils in 1867 and each of them had its heart set on acquiring an appropriately impressive symbol of civic pride as soon as possible. For a time statutory limitations on the power of councils to levy rates or borrow money kept their ambitions in check but in 1880 these were relaxed. The result was a proliferation, in the cities and large country towns, of town halls—all of them particularly prone to the pompous grand hotel brand of showiness. Within the space of a few years at the peak of the boom

The Princess Theatre in Spring Street, Melbourne: 1887. Architect. William Pitt

Melbourne dressed up some of its larger buildings to suit the times. A new front was built across Parliament House, the Public Library facade was completed, the Town Hall was given a new portico, the Post Office received its long-promised third floor. The railways built a viaduct to link the old Spencer Street Station with a new giant Flinders Street Station built on the site of the old Fish Markets. Large theatres, hotels, coffee palaces, banks and insurance offices were erected throughout the town. But Melbourne's architectural character had been already largely determined in the years following gold and the new buildings heightened rather than destroyed it.

Sydney embarked on erecting or completing many of the buildings which its precocious daughter, Melbourne, had been able to afford twenty years before. The older town had made a start on several ambitious public buildings during the sixties and seventies but political intrigue had stopped many of them on the drawing board or at a rudimentary stage. Museums, public libraries, art galleries and town halls had been Melbourne's lot in the sixties and seventies. In the eighties and nineties it was Sydney's turn. The difference in the architecture of the two periods accounts for much of the difference of character of the two towns. The Queen Victoria Building (1893–98) in Sydney supported a cloud of billowing domes and cupolas; the Lands Department Building (1876–90) shot a stream of stone topped by a wonderful onion-shaped verdigris copper fantasy 150 feet into the air; and the General Post Office begun by Colonial Architect James Barnet in 1866 was extended in 1886 and crowned with a skyscraping clock tower with a result that its critics likened it to an upright T-square. When, in 1867, Melbourne had replaced its thirteen-year-old Town Hall with a bigger and better one by Joseph Reed, it had still chosen to do so Classically. When it added the present main portico in 1887, the addition while attempting to follow Reed's footsteps was big, fat and gross. Sydney got the first part of its Town Hall between 1866–75 and the second, and visually significant, part in 1883–88, just in time to warrant the name of 'The Centennial Hall'. With its tall ornate clock tower, its extreme ornamentality, the lollipop building is the epitome of the sugared town halls of the Victorians. At Camberwell, at South Brisbane and in many of the provincial cities such as Goulburn the wedding-cake halls reared up to dominate their area and fix their character for three-quarters of a century or more.

The highly modelled and decorative plasterwork which was so much a feature of all the buildings of the eighties was the result of a new trade which had developed during the preceding decade—the architectural modeller. He was a plasterer who was distinguished from the 'solid plasterer' working entirely in situ and limited accordingly, because he worked in a factory where he cast ornaments for both inside and outside use. The rise of the practice of precasting plaster ornament simplified the work of the solid plasterer. No longer need he run elaborate mouldings in the living work and his job henceforth required that he be able to do little more than plaster a flat surface. He could choose his cornices and bric-a-brac from a tremendous variety available from the merchants' shelves. The mass production of the separate parts for plaster decoration resulted in a drop in price which, in turn, enabled it to be used more widely and in all classes of building from the richest to the poorest. It was largely due to the development of plaster modelling that the tastes of the Victorians could be indulged so lavishly and that plasterwork reached the extremes that it did.

The ornaments made from plaster of Paris for internal work were able to develop in the way they did not only because of precasting but also by the introduction of a technique which had originally been discovered and patented in Germany in 1837. In this a framework of lathes was formed roughly in the shape required and covered with hessian which was then covered with wet plaster and

Two High Victorian city buildings — *Above* The
Queen Victoria Building in York Street, Sydney:
1893-98. Architect, George McRae *Right* The
Lands Department Building, Loftus-Bent-
Gresham Streets, Sydney: 1876-90.
Architect, James Barnet

placed in the main plastered mould as a reinforcement. This 'rag and stick' method as it was called enabled deeper, stronger, yet lighter, forms to be cast. Instead of being limited to thin flat plates shallowly moulded, rag and stick shell castings could be deeply three-dimensional and much larger. Massive cornices, ceiling pendants and coffers became cheap and easy to fix. By this method also, flat panels up to six feet square were produced and fixed by screws to the ceiling joists. They were the forerunner of fibrous plaster sheets.

During the late eighties when cast gypsum plaster was reaching its peak another ceiling material, stamped metal sheeting, came on the market. It was not as decorative as plasterwork and was inherently and essentially flat. For a while it was combined with deeper plaster features but as it was even cheaper than plaster and its overall low-relief patterning was simpler it gradually replaced plasterwork when, surfeited with an over-rich diet, public taste found such qualities once again desirable.

The first stamped metal work to come to Australia was pressed zinc windows imported into Sydney in 1885 by Ernest Wunderlich, an English-born migrant who arrived in that year. The windows were installed in houses at Rushcutters Bay. The windows were followed by pressed zinc ornamental roofing finishes— frilled and fence-like ridge-capping which was installed in a number of important buildings such as the Colonial Secretary's Office in Sydney and on banks and insurance offices in Melbourne and Brisbane.

Then, in 1888, when the Sydney Town Hall was nearing completion, the thought was cannily expressed by Wunderlich, an accomplished amateur musician, that the plaster ceiling planned for that noble edifice might not withstand the vibrations set up by the huge pipe organ being installed. Having raised the doubt in the minds of the architect, the organist and the city fathers, Wunderlich suggested that a pressed metal ceiling would run no such risks. His suggestion was accepted with relief and, needless to say, Wunderlich was able to arrange quickly for a supply of English sheets to be sent out in a hurry. Consequently, when the Town Hall reverberated to the thunder of its mighty organ for the first time, its 2,500 square yards of ceiling magnificently resisted the attack. It was the first metal ceiling in the country. Its performance allayed all doubts. When, in 1890, Wunderlich commenced to press his own metal sheets using the new mild steel sheets in place of zinc, it was the beginning of a thirty year reign for the material.

It was in the eighties that building took a definite turn away from being a work of craft lovingly created by hand on the site to being a process of assembling units made elsewhere by machines. Plasterwork, pressed metal sheets, window sashes and frames, doors and their frames, skirtings and architraves, together with fittings such as hinges, baths, pipes, basins, were all available off the shelf. The builder put them together and the highly skilled craftsman languished and soon perished. Even the parts for staircases were available in the same way. The skilled joiner was one of the first to go. The new machine lathes were already turning out voluptuous balusters like sausages and would soon be large enough to be turned to producing shaped verandah posts. As the craftsmen faded their special skills went with them. Wreathing a stair handrail, for instance, the most demanding of the joiners' achievements, almost disappeared to be replaced by simpler and cruder techniques.

A further feature of the buildings of the eighties was the return of the

Opposite The Town Hall, Sydney: 1866-88. Architects. J. H. Wilson and others. Tower by T. and E. Bradbridge

semi-circular arch. It had been a commonplace on main doorways until the 1820s when it had given way in the thirties to elliptical and three-centred arches. The late forties and fifties had seen it disappear altogether when all wall openings became flat headed. In the next twenty years door and window heads had gradually curved upwards becoming more rounded as the years went by. In the eighties the semi-circular arch returned. It was used both in doorways and windows but most importantly it was used in arcades. It was the arcade, in fact, which was new and wanted. Consequently, the character of doorways and windows was not that of a hole in a wall but rather that of one section of an arcade. They were surrounded with heavy, often rusticated, dressings such as massive piers and arches rather than thin frames. Often windows were, grouped in pairs or threes to emphasize their arcuated quality.

The use of arcades was advocated by many of the architectural big guns of the times. John Sulman, for instance, wanted to make it compulsory for buildings along certain sections of streets to erect stone arcaded verandahs over footpaths. Having migrated to Australia in 1885 after twenty years of travel, training and practice in Victorian England, he found the flimsiness of thin cast iron posts and corrugated iron roofs which abounded in Australia a shoddy abomination, but he recognized their climatic usefulness. Looking for a way in which the qualities of good architecture, as he saw it, could take cognizance of local conditions and thereby meld the two into a native style, he advocated not only that arcades should be made of substantial material (by which he meant stone) but also that as they were a public amenity their location, their height and their design should be determined by government authorities. In Sulman's scheme the cost of the arcades would be carried by the owner of the building in front of which they were erected. The building would have to harmonize with the arcade if the owner wished them to be complementary but not the other way around. In this way, Sydney would, he maintained, achieve a homogeneity of design at eye level such as a proud city should have.

In an age which valued unfettered private enterprise and individual rights above all else, Sulman's suggestion was received with bleak indifference; but the virtues of stone arcades registered. A series of solid stone stumps marching around a building had qualities of strength, permanence, irresistibility as well as a certain ponderous self-importance that found favour. The true arcade was particularly suitable where large numbers of people moved in and out of a building. It was used with great success on the General Post Offices in Sydney and Melbourne and hotels such as the Largs Pier Hotel outside Adelaide and the Grand Hotel in Brisbane. Even where the opportunity for continuous arcades was not so great, small lengths of three or five arches, repeated in tiers if possible, were somehow worked in; and the round-headed arch, even as a single unit in a cumbrous portico, became the visible symbol of permanence and respectability. And so the stone arcade, the round-headed doorways and windows with massive trims, the towers and the domes came together with the clusters of columns and the smother of highly coloured plaster ornament to delight the eye of the late Victorians. And what they saw happening on their town halls, their hotels, their civic buildings and their theatres they liked so much that they did the same thing on their shopping stores, their offices and their homes.

There were exceptions to the general fashion for extravagance. For practical reasons warehouses—big, bulky and solid in fact as well as appearance—were left comparatively plain with only the name of the firm chiselled out of their stone walls in bold letters painted gold for decoration. For economic reasons the crop of government-run schools which came in the eighties and nineties were also simply dressed. Compulsory education was introduced into Victoria in 1872 and into all the other colonies by 1885. As the nation's children were herded reluctantly towards the classroom, schools were hastily built to receive them. Some of the early ones were given a tentative treatment of polychromatic brickwork and steep gabled roofs but by the nineties even these concessions, which were always in a simplified form, were being pared off. The schools were well planned, simple and direct. Their designers were forced to rely on basic form, colour, texture, proportions, light and shade for their quality. In numbers of cases they succeeded and to later generations were seen to hold the seeds of future thought. In New South Wales in particular, the architect of the Department of Public Instruction, William Kemp, managed, by means of a functional form and a fine sense of proportion, to imbue many of his schools of the nineties with a Doric strength that his contemporaries found devoid of beauty or any other architectural merit but which are now admired.

The homes of the eighties were decorated with the same rich hand that smothered the larger buildings. Cast iron reached extreme heights of elaboration. The iron work—fuller, more intricate and showy than ever—festooned in great curtains across the face of houses and was used along the eaves, up the barges, around the doorways and over every possible place to add its richness to an underskin of equally lush polychrome walling. In symmetrically fronted houses the centre focus of the facade was emphasized by breaking the verandah roof into a gabled pediment or parapeted porch at the mid-point. In some houses this accent was reinforced and backed by repeating the same type of treatment in a one-, two- or even three-tiered pediment complete with urns, shells and fruit at the wall line.

Domestic Gothic finally expired under the weight of Classic paraphernalia in the eighties. However, its influence was left in the basic form of the typical house of the period which became a blend of both Classic and Gothic, the two styles which had run parallel with each other during the preceding thirty years. The symmetrical plan, which had lingered from the very first huts erected nearly a hundred years before and which had formed the essence of Colonial and Classic architecture, was finally abandoned. The asymmetrical Gothic plan, in which a bow window projected forward, had been exaggerated until a whole room, usually a sitting-room, stuck out past the line of any verandah to form an L-shaped front. This Gothic form was modified with a low pitched hipped Classic roof as the gables were snipped off and bestrewn with Classic jewellery. The corners of the projecting room were chamfered to become a bow again. The windows were glazed with large single sheets of glass, produced by the recently invented mechanical cylinder blowing machines, and trimmed with ornate plaster mouldings. A popular window consisted of three round-headed double-hung sashes with the centre one wider and higher than the two narrow flanking lights. Broad box mullions were fronted by elongated spirally-moulded columns supporting the brickwork at the springing. Topped with miniature Corinthian capitals and standing on fanciful bases their skinny barley sugar shape was satisfyingly elaborate. But the window's crowning glory was the label mould. As it followed the shape of the window head its continuously arced line lost all pretence at functional justification. Had rain ever been able to reach it as the window nestled deep behind a verandah, it would have been unerringly guided to the weak-link mullions.

A verandah, stretched along the recessed part of the L, was trimmed with cast iron and had a bullnose iron roof. The cast iron was deeper and thicker than ever. The brackets became larger and sprang from the posts at head height to sweep continuously up and down to the next post and form an arch. The verandahs thus became cast iron arcades echoing, more lightly, those of stone. Each room had a fireplace placed back to back in adjoining rooms and chimneys, sprouting into joined pairs of flues, were elaborate fantasies of complicated brickwork. Where the roof was slate, and it usually was, galvanized iron or pressed metal

Some typical urban houses of the seventies and
eighties — *Opposite above* House at 16 Yarra Street,
Hawthorn, Victoria, about 1870 *Opposite below*
Fitzroy Cottage, 2 Tebbut Street, Windsor, New South
Wales, 1879 *Above* Guernsey House, 232 The
Esplanade East, Port Melbourne, 1886.
Architect, J. B. Grut

The asymmetrical plan —
Above one-storeyed in a
house in Alma Road, North
Caulfield, Victoria. *Below*
Two-storeyed in a house in
North Terrace, Adelaide.
Both buildings were built
about 1880

cappings marked out the ridges while at the eaves the overhang was supported on small decorative scroll brackets often arranged in pairs for mutual support.

The front door and its sidelights were glazed with rolled, figured and brightly coloured glass in brilliant reds, blues and greens. A tight entrance hall narrowed down even further to a passage running through the middle of the house. The transition was marked by a semi-circular arch. The passage debouched into a back verandah. The individual house on its own block of land was now standard so that each room could be lit by a window on an outside wall. Only the requirements of the owner limited their number. The kitchen had come inside from the end of the back verandah and was now included under the main roof as the backmost room on one side of the passage with a maid's room opposite. Where the family area finished and the kitchen and servant area began, the passage again marked the distinction with another round-headed arch.

Inside the house the love of ornament concentrated. The fireplaces cradled cast iron grates. The windows were shaded with dark green venetian blinds and doorways and archways were draped with glass bead curtains. Antimacassars protected the rich plush covering of voluptuously stuffed chairs and a highly polished table displayed a bowl of waxed fruit in a glass case. Every available nook and cranny was jammed with tables, stands, aspidistras and fussy ornaments. The mantel shelf, backed by a Landseer painting, was packed with silver-framed photographs of members of a respectable family, candlesticks, a tribe of diminishing ebony elephants and a centrally placed ormolu clock. A gloomy light was shed by an electric bulb hidden beneath a domed shade of rich dark silk with scalloped edge from which dangled a deep bead fringe. The surrounds of the fireplace held a trim of brightly coloured Persian-inspired tiles and were made of turned and moulded timber with double mantel shelves supported on small Classic columns. Hearths were of tiles, either mass-produced glazed vitreous squares painted in gaudy patterns which were repetitive and could be assembled in an infinite number of arrangements, or Italian mosaics which had the same advantages. The ceilings were riots of pattern. Some were pressed metal but generally in the eighties because of the scarcity and newness of that material they remained plaster. It was here that the work of the architectural modellers came to full flower. Cast plaster cornices, extremely elaborate, deeply moulded and heavy, stepped out from the wall to meet the ceiling a foot or even two feet further in. The ceiling itself was embellished with further cast plaster ornaments ranging from demure rosettes to whole three feet square panels of the popular leaves, grapes, figures and lattice work. But the proud focus of the ceiling was the cast plaster ventilator which, in a tremendous variety of intricate patterns, was stuck to the middle of the ceiling. It was round, oval or square and, measuring from two to five feet across, was chosen, like many of the materials in the building, directly from the merchant's shelf.

High Victorian architecture reached its most opulent in booming Melbourne where buildings of both the highest and lowest degree shared in and were imbued with the excessive love of voluptuousness. The architectural wings of the other colonies were clipped in proportion to their economic fortunes but the frame of mind paralleled that in Victoria. Only in South Australia was there a significant local development at variance with the general trend. South Australian architecture of the eighties was comparatively direct and simple, largely avoided sham and was strongly regional in its expression. In Adelaide readily-to-hand 'bluestone', which ranged in colour from light buff through browns to a dark blue-black, had been used for building from the earliest days of the settlement. The stone split easily and fairly smoothly on its bedding plane but across the grain it shattered unpredictably and uncontrollably. The resultant randomly shaped stones were necessarily bedded in thick mortar which was smoothed to the approximate

House at 18 Sandergrove Road, Strathalbyn,
South Australia: about 1880

face of the stone. The final wall with its inconsistent and smeared joints was always rugged and sometimes had something of the appearance of a plum pudding. As with Melbourne's lifeless grey-black bluestone buildings which used Sydney or Tasmanian sandstone for dressings to the wall openings, Adelaide builders used bricks to form the surrounds to windows and doors and often for quoins at the corners to give a sharp true line. By the eighties the bluestone was practically worked out and extensive quarries of a soft, easily worked sandstone had been developed. This light-coloured cream and pink sandstone was used with bright red brick trims to create a vast number of buildings which, because of the lack of smoke from heavy industries and the inherent qualities of the materials, have retained a pristine freshness to the present day. The settlement of Adelaide had been conceived as a high-minded if impracticable venture offering a life of opportunity to the sober, upright and industrious. For the first five years the South Australian colony blossomed in an artificial hot-house climate of make-believe. A paper prosperity came from the money brought in by immigrants and by land speculation. An elegant Transylvanian society evolved with the pace being set by Governor Gawler and his musical-comedy court. It was more important to walk the non-existent streets in paper-thin leather shoes and Bond Street clothes or to ride insouciantly in an expensive equipage than to clear and develop the land. Apparent wealth was accumulated by the pale-handed Cockney colonists gambling in town land rather than by the rude toil and sweat that had developed New South Wales. Most of the people stayed in the settlement. Fine homes, almost mansions, were built and energy was lackadaisically squandered in clearing the surrounding parkland to provide the Governor's firewood in preference to going out into the rugged countryside. In 1841 when the flow of immigrants stopped the bubble burst and the colonists, disillusioned with the colonizing theories of Edward Gibbon Wakefield, finally settled down to hard work and a realistic attitude to the Australian wilderness. From the beginning the South Australian venture had included families of industrious Lutheran Germans. Such people left a legacy of tidiness, cleanliness and order which permeates the state to the present day. The buildings of South Australia of the eighties reflected that character. They were simply planned, functionally finished and solidly built. The typical home was a single-storeyed cream stone rectangular box with brick dressings to the openings and corners, a symmetrical arrangement of doors, windows and chimneys, and with a wide neat cast iron verandah stretched across the long street face. Cast iron ventilators inserted in the wall between the verandah and the roof eaves were a minor but distinctive and unique hallmark of this refreshing and sparkling architecture of South Australia. At North Adelaide, Goolwa and, most particularly, Strathalbyn as well as, to a lesser extent, Willunga, Mount Barker and Gawler, this type of architecture indelibly marked the churches, the shops and the houses with the character and qualities of the state's forefathers.

While the majority of buildings of the eighties were either massively stone or riots of plaster, the revival of exposed brickwork, begun twenty years before, gained strength. As usual there was no one cause for it. It was the consequence of a simultaneous confluence of factors—material, constructional and aesthetic. As we have seen, the cry of the day was for polychrome buildings. Painted plaster and wall papers were so temporary as to verge on the tawdry. Unlike their successors, the Victorians knew that strong colours did not come only from a pot of paint. They preferred to achieve their ends with stone, marble, brass, gilt and tiles. But these were expensive and were beyond the means of any but public buildings and a few rare private palaces.

Then, in the late eighties, it was found that with the new mechanized brick-making processes it was possible to turn out bricks with a range of colours from the same pug by varying the pressing and the burning. Amongst the numerous brick-making methods being tried was the 'dry process'. It could be used in both the hand-made and the mechanized systems. In this process the material for making the brick was mixed, not into a clayey pug, but as varying-sized ground granules using only

House at 286 Ward Street,
North Adelaide: about 1880

enough water to dampen them slightly. When placed in the form the material was subjected to heavy pressing to pack the particles tightly together. The moulds were then subjected to a bath of pressurized steam which penetrated through the particles. Sometimes a further heavy pressing and another steam bath followed. They were then fired in the normal way.

The process had a number of advantages. It eliminated the long preliminary drying time that was necessary with the usual process and thereby saved space and a deal of handling. Both factors meant money. The double pressing resulted in dense and accurate faces. The lack of excess water meant less distortion of the brick during burning. The bricks were extremely hard—almost metallic. And, finally, as a great deal of the bricks' physical properties came from the pressing and steaming the amount of firing could be varied considerably without too much loss of strength. By manipulating the firing time bricks could be produced which ranged in colour from cream through reds to dark brown. And this suited the Victorians of the eighties.

The process also had limitations. Because of the high pressing it was difficult for the steam to penetrate evenly through the brick and many, probably a great majority, of the bricks were vitrified or case-hardened with an exceptionally tough half-inch thick skin surrounding a still friable and crumbly core. The strength of the bricks was more apparent than real. When cut, a much more difficult task than with ordinary bricks, the centre could sometimes be scratched out like sugar. Attempts to overcome the problem by excessive steaming merely turned the outer skin to slush before it could be burnt. It was these shortcomings which eventually led to the dry process being superseded when other mechanical processes, such as that of Hoffman, overcame their own particular problems.

The first steam or dry process brickworks was started at St Peters in Sydney by W. G. Collins and Company in 1878. Six years later there were a dozen such brickyards in Sydney and seven in Melbourne. Other manufacturers, using both hand-made and continuous systems, adopted the technique of double pressing to produce face bricks and varied the colour by varying the firing. The result here however meant, as everybody knew it would, a wide variety of quality. The light cream bricks were underburnt doughboys, soft, easily damaged in handling and weathered poorly, while the dark colours were clinkers, metal-hard and extremely difficult to work with. There were many other experiments with the mixes to vary the brick colours. The Hoffman Brick Company, for instance, mixed iron filings with the clay. When fired the iron speckled the brick with dark grey-blue patches. Others mixed fine organic matter, such as sawdust, which left dark charcoal coloured splotches but unfortunately also left cavities where it burnt away. One way or another, the late eighties found itself able to choose from a colour range of bricks which started from cream and descended through buffs and browns to very dark metallic greys.

At the same time the true cavity wall came into common use. Cavity brick walls were used around Southampton in England as early as 1804 but they had not been widely adopted. Just who made this most important of all Australian technical advances, and when, is not known. We have seen that cavity stone walls were built in the 1830s but their waterproofing potentiality was missed, and how the 'hollow walls' of the fifties had been a conscious attempt to build a waterproof brick wall. It was probably an evolutionary development of these two moves combined with the well-known lessons of the brick veneer wall that eventually produced the cavity wall. At any rate, by 1885 at the latest some Australian builders were encasing their brick buildings with a non-structural brick skin, leaving a gap of a couple of inches and tying the two leaves together with cast iron ties laid in alternate courses and staggered. The system meant that the porosity of the bricks and the mortar, which had been the main cause of trouble, was no longer of much

The Anglican Cathedral
at Armidale, New
South Wales: 1875.
Architect, Horbury Hunt

consequence. The outer leaf could become saturated with rain and water could run down its inner face but the inner structural wall remained dry and unaffected. It was used tentatively at first but within a few years its perfection was acknowledged. By 1895, when all buildings were brick, the cavity wall was standard practice. And from Australia it spread to the rest of the world—a genuine Australian contribution to world building practice.

The cavity wall enabled buildings to come out from under their plaster shrouds. And gradually they did. In response to the call for more colour architects stretched their ingenuity to imagine speckled, striped and patched multi-coloured brickwork versions of the elaborate architectural dresses that were the height of fashion. In houses, walls were relieved by contrasting bricks in imitation of stonework quoins at the corners and similar brick patterning around the windows and doorways. At the same time, the slate roofs sprouted fins, spikes and lace work of pressed art metal work along the ridges. Numbers of them, both large and small, used a French Second Empire style and somehow managed to incorporate a tower with a fence of the same art metal work around its top observation platform. More often than not the tower and its platform were an expensive piece of purely visual ostentation without access to either of them.

One of the main crusaders for a return to brickwork was John Horbury Hunt who, with a single-minded passion, had preached against stylistic pretence since the seventies. Hunt, the son of a builder, had been born in 1838 at St John's, New Brunswick, and brought up in Boston, U.S.A. At the age of seventeen years he began articled training under E. C. Cabot, with whom he worked for the next ten years. At the beginning of the American Civil War, Hunt set out in 1862 to live in India. His ship put in at Sydney and James Barnet, the Colonial Architect, persuaded him to stay in the colony. Hunt agreed but instead of working with Barnet he joined Edmund Blacket as an assistant until in 1869 he set up his own practice.

Hunt was not opposed to borrowing architectural themes but was an ardent believer in 'original variations developed within the severe discipline of a personal idiom', sound construction, professional competence, and enlightened civic design. A conceited man given to strange mannerisms and quaint dress (his suits were a labyrinth of pockets in which he kept a host of drawing instruments and papers which practically made him a walking architect's office), and with an utter disdain for money, Hunt made many enemies within and without the profession because of his outspoken criticisms of Sydney's architecture. But he was a gifted designer with a passionate hatred of sham. Among his pet ideas, honest brickwork was foremost. It was probably Hunt's influence that induced Blacket to build St Silas' Church in diaper brickwork and his example in his own work, such as St Peter's Cathedral at Armidale and his Cloncorrick house at Darling Point, became one of his most important contributions to local architecture. In his houses and churches Hunt built as he exhorted. By the 1880s his message was being understood.

Multi-coloured brickwork came to the stores and office buildings as well. In the Rialto and Olderfleet Buildings in Collins Street, the architect William Pitt let his head go in a riot of coloured brick and fanciful form which he himself described as 'free Italian Gothic'. Gradually he was aided and abetted by others of the same stripe so that by 1892 the coloured plaster rainbows of the late eighties were already *passé* and everything was coming out brick.

At first the new brickwork was used in the same spirit and with the same ideals in mind that lay behind the plaster spectacle which came to its explosive climax as brickwork re-emerged. One of the influential architects of Melbourne in the late eighties stated the basic philosophy to which most of his colleagues adhered when he said that one of the canons of good architecture was that it should be

The Rialto Building in Collins Street,
Melbourne: 1890. Architect, William Pitt.

'imitative combined with active effort after novelty and aggressive eclecticism'. The only proviso he laid down was that the effort should not result in fiasco.

But even while architecture reached out towards more and more extravagant effects another material was introduced into Australia which, combined with the re-emerging brickwork, the frantic searching for new styles and a wave of romanticism, spawned a style of architecture that was to be the only and triumphant one of the nineties and early nineteen hundreds. The romanticism that gripped the English-speaking world in the eighties had its roots in a discontent with, and reaction to, the changed tempo, standards and qualities brought by the industrial revolution. In the middle of the nineteenth century it took the form of a desire to recapture the spirit by reproducing the art and craft conditions of pre-industrial England. Headed by William Morris a group of malcontents preached a return to native craftsmanship and materials and extolled the satisfaction these gave to the soul. It was a recurrence of the same deeply grounded human trait that had led to the Gothic Revival a hundred years before and which went back in history at least as far as the story of the Fall in the Garden of Eden. Now, led by Philip Webb, it focussed on the architecture of Queen Anne's time—a period which was seen in retrospect to combine all the desirable qualities which had since passed away.

It was not really a new material but rather an old material in a new form which gave the Australian Queen Anne style its crowning glory. It was the terracotta Marseilles pattern roof tile. Despite the general satisfactoriness of galvanized iron and slate the search for other and better roof materials had not stopped. Asphalted felts and impregnated papers had been tried in Melbourne in the

Police Station in George Street North, Sydney: 1882. Architect. James Barnet

pressing conditions of the early gold-rush years, but had been unsuccessful. In 1859, a Joseph Curet had patented a design for a terracotta tile in Melbourne. It was claimed to be 'light, cool, durable indestructible by fire, and pretty in effect'. Curet's tile was produced by the Patent Tile Company after 1860 but heavy production costs, the cost of additional roof-framing to carry the extra weight, sheer conservatism and a design that was not particularly waterproof doomed Curet's tiles to a short life. Another terracotta tile was patented in New South Wales in 1860 but it also failed. Pressed zinc tiles made brief appearances but until 1886 Australian roofs in general remained doggedly iron or slate.

Marseilles tiles with their ridgy tops, interlocking end lips and overlapping sides were a traditional roof covering for the cheapest and flimsiest of rural buildings around the south of France. A few had been imported to Melbourne and Sydney during the 1850s when every sort of material flooded into the building-starved colonies. But they were too expensive to compete with iron and when grey was the vogue too different in colour to compete with the highly popular slates.

By 1886, a new generation with different tastes and much experience of the sweltering conditions beneath iron or close-boarded slate roofs was ready to try Marseilles tiles. The firm of Roche and Company imported the first of the new batch into Melbourne in 1886. In the same year Walter Lamb brought a small shipment into Sydney. As soon as the first bright orange-red spots glowed amongst the sea of grey they were overwhelmingly popular. In addition to their colour, which was considered a perfect foil to the grey-green of the Australian landscape, the loose fit of the tiles with their many chinks and gaps allowed good ventilation of the roof space and their mass made them good heat absorbers. It was noticed with approval that the rooms underneath were appreciably cooler. And withal the tiles were permanent, maintenance-free and completely waterproof. Supplies were very limited and demand was so great that builders took delivery directly from the shipside. People were grateful if they could obtain sufficient of the special ridge and apex tiles to decorate their otherwise slate roofs and replace the iron capping that had been their weakest point. Slate roofs outlined in orange-red were the next best thing to a fully tiled roof.

The French tiles were used on all styles of buildings during their first few years. The Queen Anne style was then only one of the many fashions in use. At first Marseilles tiles were not used exclusively in that style but merely as another touch of colour to be added to polychrome architecture in general. One architect of 1890 was so impressed with the tiles that he was moved to predict, with uncommon foresight, that in future all Australian buildings would be roofed with them. It was a remarkably accurate statement but before it happened the tiles had to become the catalyst that enabled Australian domestic architecture to throw off its coat of many colours and settle for one standard style—Queen Anne. And before that could happen Australia and its architecture had to weather and be purged in the trials and tribulations of a great depression.

At the beginning of the nineties architecture was still swimming exultantly in a welter of stylism. As the wave reached ever more dizzily upwards many adulatory voices were raised in self-satisfaction—and a few cautionary ones in warning called for a return to fundamentals and pleaded for architects to re-think their philosophies and work. E. W. Dobbs, an archpriest of stylism who considered all Colonial buildings and the Macquarie buildings in particular as being 'without any pretensions to Architecture . . . hardly even buildings . . . [because] prison labour and military ethics had very little of the aesthetic about them', championed the architectural work being done in the late eighties. It had, he said 'led the Art life of the nation to a higher and nobler destiny'. Architecture, in Dobbs' opinion, had commenced in the reign of Queen Victoria and his own period was its glorious flowering. Another of like mind was Alex North, a Tasmanian architect, who described the age of George III as 'the reign of ugliness whose miles of bald unlovely buildings with their never ending straight lines, square window and door slits and monotonous tinge we would not now tolerate'. North lauded the colour, the complexity and the ornamentation which he found altogether delightful in 1890. (Five years later, however, he had a change of heart and wrote contritely, 'If a building violates no principle of construction, participates in no imposture, is decorous and truly serves the purpose for which it was erected it can scarcely fail to achieve some artistic merit.') The cheers came from any place stylism touched. Queensland had a remarkable period of prosperity during the eighties and architects swarmed into Brisbane. The author of the *Jubilee History of Queensland* wrote proudly in 1889, 'The advent of each new man introduces to the community new styles in architecture, resulting in a variety that gives to Brisbane a quality that no other city in the colonies possesses.' Brisbane carries the stamp of the spree they had to the present day.

Amidst the hysterically uncritical approval that came from the main bulk of the community some people, such as J. B. de Libra, knew something was wrong and were destructively critical. 'A few feet of plain wall surface seem to be regarded by our architects much as a red rag to a bull. The height of some ambitions must surely be to besmatter a facade with so-called ornament much as a perverted

The Mitchell Building, University of Adelaide, North Terrace, Adelaide: 1879. Architect, E. J. Woods

ingenuity does that direst of human perpetrations—the bride-cake,' he wrote in 1886. 'No one,' he went on, 'seems able to strike out as is being done in India, a style of architecture really suited to our climate and requirements.' Horbury Hunt, always crusading against popular taste, spoke fearlessly of the 'vile . . . false . . . reckless piles [which are] revolting to the cultured taste and demoralizing to the public mind.' In 1889 Howard Joseland, a leading Sydney architect, preached against the insincerity of the current fashions. He reiterated, as something new, the age old principles that had been forgotten by calling for honesty in the use and expression of materials, attention to climate and the elimination of extraneous decoration in everything from the art metal roof apex to the cast iron grate. But Hunt, de Libra and Joseland were almost lone voices when they spoke. Most thought with Dobbs and North but, like the latter, were to come around to the loners' point of view before another decade was out.

A financial crash in Argentina, a centre of world speculative finance, took place in the middle of 1890. Its waves sped across the Atlantic to crash against the shores of England. London banks trembled and one of them failed. To support the tottering economy English funds were hastily withdrawn from Australian financial institutions. As the underpinning was sucked away the boom that had gripped the country subsided. It was no crash; but at first slowly and then faster and faster as it gathered momentum the towering curler of sham prosperity ebbed into a deep and catastrophic depression. Phonily puffed-up speculative finance institutions, including all of the building societies, collapsed in droves, taking with them their sound colleagues and the savings of thousands of small wage-earners who, tempted and snared, had been hypnotized with the prospect of sharing in the flood of boom riches. Stories of financial fraud and scandals broke every day. Dozens of financial titans, whose shady machinations had made them paper millionaires during the late eighties, went bankrupt or made secret compositions with their creditors and paid as little as nothing in the pound, went to gaol or bolted overseas or committed suicide in a variety of flamboyant ways. Building stopped dead. Architects, contractors and tradesmen were thrown out of work. They were soon to be joined by a flock of clerks as one bank after another closed its doors. As the tide of unemployment rose groups gathered in the streets to mutter, to plan and to plot. By 1893 the foggy cloud of depression lay thickly and darkly over the whole of the eastern two-thirds of the continent. It was a cloud that suffocated High Victorian architecture, which was never to revive.

Looking back on the period that started in exuberance in 1880 and finished in despair in the vast depression of the early nineties, one can see an extraordinarily interesting and startling picture. It had been a period with an inordinate love of display and ritual which had given rise to both the colourful Anglo-Catholicism and the High Church in religion. The worldly found an outlet for the same impulse in erecting gaudy and meretricious buildings. It had been a period which held a peculiar philosophy that identified the apparent with the real which, in turn, led to blatant sham and accepted hypocrisy and deception. The vast differences between the public utterances and private behaviour of its citizens have become legendary. Its politicians could lead private lives of the utmost licentiousness and, provided it was well shielded by a mask of public respectability, still retain the regard and esteem of their fellows. The same attitude approved the falseness of disguised plastered buildings, the fake lookout towers which did not even have an entrance, and gave rise to the practice of tuck-pointing which had no other purpose than to give a misleading impression of the quality of the brickwork. It had been a period which paid deference to eclecticism in architecture by gathering and turning to its own purposes the exotic architectural mannerisms of the world in the same way that the Empire, of which it was a part, acquired and used lands and their

The Customs House
at Rockhampton, Queensland: 1900

peoples. It had been a period in which pride in that Empire reached its apogee. The Queen's subjects swelled with satisfaction as bands in the well-cared-for parks played Elgar's 'Pomp and Circumstance' on Sunday afternoons. The buildings preserved in plaster and fat materials the same pompous mood and repeated, a little erratically, the sonorous measured beat of the bass drum.

But more significant than the truthful reflection of the characteristics of a unique period were the changes that had come during the same period. Foremost among them was the drastic change to the scale of the cities that resulted from the introduction of lifts. The familiar one, two or three storeys that had been the maximum since the beginning of civilization and with which people felt safe and comfortable was displaced by a height three times as great. The result was a matter for pride but it was also disturbing in its unfamiliarity and a little frightening.

The most significant change of all, however, was that which had happened to the activity of building itself. Hand-crafting had been replaced by machine technology. The cornucopia that was the factory began to pour forth its flood of new articles and new materials. The architect had become a selector and the builder an assembler. The trends that were first evident in the eighties have diversified and grown with head-spinning acceleration and are still increasing. The architecture and building of 1879 were still basically mediaeval; the mechanics of architecture and building of 1890 were to all intents and purposes of the twentieth century. In that lies the unique and tremendous significance of the period.

[1] Cracknell, E. W.: *Passenger and Warehouse Lifts*, a paper read to the Engineering Association of New South Wales, December 1882, F. Cunningham & Co., 146 Pitt Street, Sydney, 1882, p. 3.

[2] Dobbs, E. Wilson: *Rise and Growth of Australasian Architecture*. Reprinted by Australasian Builders and Contractors News Office, 1892, p. 13.

9 For over sixty years the settlement centred on the Swan River had struggled to maintain a precarious livelihood. The gold strikes which had been responsible for propelling New South Wales, Victoria and Queensland along the road to well-being and whose effects had spilled over into South Australia and Tasmania, did not have enough momentum to cross the 1,400 miles of arid desert between Adelaide and Perth. Unaffected by the general prosperity, Western Australia had remained an undernourished Cinderella while its sister colonies in the east waxed and grew fat.

In 1892 their fortunes were reversed. As the eastern colonies, their economies ruthlessly bled to a standstill, lay prostrate in torpor, the gods at last smiled on the south-western corner of the continent. In September of that year two wandering prospectors, Arthur Bailey and William Ford, found the gleam of gold in the rainless red scrub country 350 miles east of Perth. The township which sprang up as miners flocked in was named Coolgardie. In June the next year three Irish goldseekers named Hannan, Flanagan and Shea made another strike twenty miles further east. The spot became Australia's richest gold producer—the Golden Mile—at Kalgoorlie. The experiences of Victoria forty years before were repeated as fortune hunters, streaming through Perth, headed towards the fields. They came from the United Kingdom, India and the moribund eastern colonies. Within two years the West was transformed. Building boomed. In Coolgardie and Kalgoorlie iron sheeted buildings sprang up. Within months these rude structures were giving way to more substantial brick buildings decorated with the best of cast iron and plaster finery. The materials were extraordinarily expensive. All of them were imported. Even bricks had to be shipped from Melbourne or Adelaide to Perth and carted out to the fields. But expense was no real object where the earth was so prodigal and wealth so easily won.

While some of the riches of the mines were re-invested in the two gold-towns in the form of showy buildings, most if it flowed back to the capital. In the ten years or so following Bailey and Ford's find Perth got so much building and its character was so overpowering that subsequent changes have hardly touched it. Led by the firm of Porter and Thomas, the architects who followed their fortunes to the west indulged themselves in a veritable banquet of turgid, lavish decadence that only a depression had put a stop to in the east. There was no gradual evolvement of style over a period. In 1892, Perth had been a primitive frontier town with all the rawness and lack of style of a pioneer settlement. By 1900, it had been dipped bodily into a bucket of pure Victoriana and taken out, dripping plaster and spiked with towers and cupolas in a bewildering variety of shapes, to dry. The His Majesty's Theatre surpasses any other in Australia for the lavishness of its ornamentation. The Palace Hotel is smaller but was, in its day, as sumptuous a hostelry as any in Melbourne or Sydney. But numbers of others in both Fremantle and Perth easily surpassed it in external showiness.

Perth, Fremantle, Coolgardie and Kalgoorlie blossomed with towers, domes, thumping arcades and twenty feet wide iron lace verandahs. The highly charged atmosphere that goes with gold is always touched with madness and folly. Late Victorian architecture tended to be touched the same way. Consequently the buildings erected in the West while the rest of the colonies struggled to throw off the blight of depression have resulted in a concentration of High Victorian building which is a unique and marvellous treasury of the style.

By 1895, the worst of the depression was past. It had been a sobering experience. Many fortunes had been lost, many old families and businesses had been ruined and much grandiose thinking had been swept away. The wind had been knocked out of the ebullient self-confidence that had prevailed during the eighties when the wildest speculations and the craziest schemes appeared astute and courageous. Before the community could catch its breath it was hit by a series of crippling strikes and a severe drought. Consequently when building hesitantly started again it was restricted in scope and ambition. Most of it was housing. Not until the last two or three years before the century ended were any commercial buildings undertaken and, except for schools, it was even longer before public building recommenced.

When housing emerged after the hiatus many of the aberrations had been shaken out of it. Many of the factors which had been only incipiently important before the depression had now become actually so. The economic conditions of the time precluded extravagant and expensive work; certain classes of skilled labour had drifted into other fields. The Italian plasterers, for instance, had taken to market gardening and green-grocering almost in a body. However, the tradesmen who remained were glad to have work at any price and their time was cheap. A first-class bricklayer, for instance, was normally paid 4/6 for a nine hour day. The quality of the bricks was improving under the spur of a buyer's market and the nagging of the engineers and architects. The cavity wall had proved itself and was everywhere used in brick building; and similarly the Marseilles terracotta tile had proved functionally superior and aesthetically popular.

The brickmakers had been hit particularly badly by the depression. During the halcyon days from the fifties through to the eighties they had been able to sell practically any sort of rubbish. But in the middle nineties their products had to be good to find a buyer. Good quality common bricks could be bought at the kilns for 14/- per thousand in 1896 and when the Melbourne and Metropolitan Board of Works required 2,000,000 selected face bricks for the construction of a sewer a tender of 21/- per thousand delivered was received. The cost of production of these same bricks was 33/- per thousand, the Victorian Parliament was told.

Only good quality bricks could be sold at all. The cream doughboys that had been so popular before the depression had been produced by excessive pressing and underburning. It had been found that the light colours were prone to discolouration by both chemical and organic action and for this reason they dropped from favour. The various continuous mechanical processes were still plagued by a high proportion of clinkers, doughboys and distorted bricks. During the depths of the depression, in 1893, George Fischer deplored the fact that brickmakers still showed no interest in turning out better bricks or taking outsiders into their confidence. In 1894, James Nangle said that the hand-made brickyards were 'turning out much better bricks than those from the patent kilns'. Two years later the same architect was pleased to note that the patent kilns had got the message and that good quality bricks, reliable in size, shape and hardness, were available. In the take-it-or-leave-it conditions before the depression bricks were made in one shape only. By 1896 a wide range of shaped bricks of high quality was available. Using them an architect could give his client all the mouldings to plinths, cornices and around windows and doorways he could want. If, by any

Opposite His Majesty's Hotel and Theatre,
Hay and King Streets, Perth: 1904. Architect, William Wolff

Two uses of cast iron —
Above on Brent Terrace
in King's Cross, New
South Wales: 1895
Below on Buchanan's
Hotel in Townsville,
Queensland: about 1890

chance, the architect's design called for a shaped brick that was not readily procurable the brickmakers were only too pleased to make special moulds and run a batch to order.

When the Marseilles tile was first imported it had sold for £14 per thousand. By 1895, the same imported tiles were available for £10 per thousand. Imported tiles could not meet the demand being made for them as they became the only acceptable roof material. Local manufacturers stepped in to take advantage of the opening. They were encouraged by the authoritative pronouncements of James Nangle, the panjandrum of Sydney architecture, who saw them as an excellent answer to the requirements of the time provided they were properly burnt and hard. The condition was important and was not often met. Local techniques were poor. Materials were badly ground and to achieve the essential red-orange colour the tiles were often underburnt. They fretted away within months. Attempts were made to overcome the problem by increasing the thickness from the 7/16″ of the French tile to 11/16″ in the local product. This not only failed to make a better tile but increased the roof load by nearly fifty per cent. Consequently, local tiles were shunned until about 1910 when the local product had become as good as those from France. Up to 1914, 75,000,000 French tiles were brought into Sydney alone by Wunderlich Ltd, who had entered into the business in 1892 when a shipment had been sent to a Sydney importer who, because of the depression, was unable to take delivery. On the urging of the Belgian Consul the art metal work firm took them over and the largest terracotta tile firm in Australia was launched.

From all these conditions the standard house that emerged in the middle 1890s wore the dress of Queen Anne's buildings. The deeply-rooted and genuinely held romanticism that gave it life and potent appeal in Victorian England was not present in Australia where history was short and what there was of it people preferred to forget. After crossing half a world Queen Anne architecture arrived in Australia as, at first, no more than another fashion—the latest one and rather picturesque. In the early eighties Horbury Hunt had built several of his houses, such as Tivoli at Rose Bay and Cloncorrick at Darling Point, both in Sydney, in the style. Hunt's red-brick buildings had all the hallmarks of Queen Anne architecture with their irregular massing, broken gabled roofs showing exposed trusses and latticed strutting, polygonal bay windows, turned timber verandah posts and cowled chimneys. Architectural thinking about stylism had not changed in the least during the depression. Rather was it that conditions were such that only this one style was both economical and acceptable. The essential qualities of the style which was now unanimously chosen were its overall brick-red colour, its emphasis on the roof shape and the use of painted timber instead of cast iron.

The redness of the walls was achieved in a number of ways. In some fortunate areas the clay produced the right coloured bricks. In others the natural colour of well-burnt bricks went into the buffs and browns. Where the clay normally produced a buff brick attempts were made to colour the pug artificially with chemicals and salts before firing. The darker bricks left no alternative but to use them as they were or to paint them. To emphasize the colour, tuck-pointing, which had been used in the eighties to disguise bad brickwork, became more or less standard. The joints were raked out while the mortar was still green. It was then filled with other mortar coloured to match the bricks. A narrow groove was ironed into the coloured mortar and filled with a white mortar. The result was apparently very tight, over-accurate jointing, highly contrasted with the bricks and altogether artificial. Like many of the practices of Queen Anne building it was a time-consuming business but, with skilled wages at sixpence an hour, not unduly expensive.

The red walls sat discordantly with the orange tile roofs. The roof became

House in Prince Albert Street, Mosman,
New South Wales: about 1905

The Church of England Rectory, Pacific Highway,
Wahroonga, New South Wales: about 1905

the focus of the building as it broke out in a romantic profusion of gables and spires intended to display the tiles to the utmost. The rough texture which the tiles gave to the roof was carried into the upstanding frilled tiles which capped the ridges. The tiles came to a climax at the apex of the gables where ornamental finials were proudly placed. The Queen Anne roofs were most advanced in Melbourne. In Sydney the finials were standard and prosaic in the form of plain crockets or simple pillars and balls. The ridge tiles were also limited to a couple of standard forms available from the Marseilles Tile Trading Company in France. In Melbourne there was a predilection for individuality in the decorative tiles. The silhouette of the ridge tiles became elaborated into a wide range of fanciful shapes, some of them much more delicate and lacelike than the thick, solid scales that projected from the spine of Sydney roofs. But it was the apex decorations which were the greatest glory of Melbourne roofs. They came in the shape of great bunches of leaves and flowers, of winged dragons and other mythological beasts and of Grecian acanthus. Rectangular terracotta panels, displaying a wide palette of patterns and pictorial decoration, were built into the gable walls of Queen Anne houses. The local manufacturers added to the range by turning out gable panels and apex pieces in the form of waratahs, gum nuts and gum leaves, lyrebirds, kangaroos and kookaburras.

Many of the roof shapes had no functional justification. Gables were built for no better reason than that the style called for them. Corner towers, inherited from the Italianate period, were no longer lookout platforms but merely an excuse to introduce a steep cone or pyramid of tiles. Sometimes they covered an alcove in a room below but usually even this tenuous justification was not given. However, the plan of the house did change to justify at least the two main gables. The asymmetrical plan of the boom period was made more so by projecting another

House at 104 Riversdale Road, Camberwell, Victoria: about 1900

room at right angles to the front room. The two projecting rooms, each in the form
of a bay, were diagonally opposite to each other on plan so that one of them was
on a front corner of the building and the other on the side towards the back.
A verandah, broken with a gable at the front door, linked the two projecting rooms
by running along the front and down the side. At the corner where it turned mid-
way between the gables covering the two rooms the cone-capped tower was
placed.

The verandah was a timber structure. The Italian mosaic floor tiles and the cast
iron posts, balustrade and valence gave way to wooden posts (turned on power-
driven lathes which could handle a ten foot length of timber with ease), timber
floors and timber balustrade, valence-board and brackets. The round posts and
balusters, swelled and tapered, were deeply gouged to form a series of three or
four balls two-thirds of the way up the height. All the pieces of which the posts
and the balusters were made were turned and shaped on machines and, like the
roof tiles, needed only to be cut and slipped into place to achieve a satisfactorily
complicated effect.

Timber also came to the gables. Boxed eaves disappeared with the disappearance
of the hipped roof, and eaves were lined either on the under or top side of the
rafters with timber boarding to follow the line of the roof. When the lining was
placed to expose the rafters their ends were frequently shaped with curves and
nicks into round knobbly silhouettes. Bargeboards were simple planks of timber
left unmoulded but the triangular part of the wall in the gable was decorated with
timbers to simulate, in a derivative but not accurate way, a truss or other roof
construction. In small, cheap houses this part of the wall was in fact framed up
in timber, sheeted in plaster or pressed metal and then decorated. In New South
Wales and Queensland by the end of the century the timber gable decoration had

Shops in Military Road, Mosman, New South Wales: about 1905

broken clear of the wall and was strung between the bargeboards. Using tiny turned spindles or wide flat planks to form imitation trusses, fans and sunbursts, the bargeboards supported filigreed timber cages and spiderwebs. Frequently windows were protected by sun hoods. Supported on large intricately worked timber brackets echoing the gable filigree, they added a satisfying complication to the general roof complexity. In the other states but most particularly in Victoria and South Australia, the gables and the eaves soffits were festooned with curtains of wooden jigsaws in which the turned pendant drops were the dominating and ever-present motif.

Terracotta tiles and, to a lesser extent bricks, were largely restricted to Sydney and Melbourne. In Queensland, Tasmania and in the country generally people had to make do with timber and iron. The timber of the verandahs and the gables remained much the same as did the plan and the complexity of the roof form. But in these areas the Queen Anne style was translated into weatherboard walls and iron roofs painted red. The red paint became standard for iron roofs everywhere.

By 1897, a few banks and commercial businesses were ready to resume the erection of buildings in the cities. Regulations prevented the use of timber which was such an important feature of domestic Queen Anne. In its commercial version the discord of red walls and orange roofs was emulated in piles of red face-brick mixed with banks of rough dressed sandstone or, where this was not available, banks of cream painted plaster. Its main feature was the Classic mouldings entirely executed in brick. In the buildings of the original Queen Anne, carved brickwork had given rise to a highly skilled craft and some very clever and lovely effects. In its nineteenth century successor carved bricks were replaced by moulded ones. The undercutting necessary in Ionic or Corinthian decoration which was used in much of the original was not possible in moulding. Consequently, the commercial Queen Anne had to be content with reproducing Doric details. For reasons of economy window and door heads were once again flat and were bridged by mild steel angles, another product of technology which was becoming readily available. Arcades, derived from Italian work, had no place in a style that was as English as any Classically inspired style ever was. Arches, where there were any, were restricted to one bold sweep of semi-circular brickwork over the opening leading to the entrance porch which, in turn, became incorporated into the body of the building without breaking the flush line of the outside wall. With the highly reliable and accurately finished double-pressed face-bricks and an imaginative selection from the wide range of shapes available, commercial buildings were arrayed in Classical dresses made at the kilns. Some of them had terracotta tiled roofs but they were hidden out of sight behind compulsory parapets. However, the terracotta tile manufacturers were producing the material in the form of a hollow $9'' \times 9'' \times 4\frac{1}{2}''$ brick by the mid-nineties. It was used for lightweight floors and internal partition walls by 1894. The innovation spread and was so successful that when the various Building Acts were amended the practice, or something like it, became mandatory.

During the fifty years of the second half of the nineteenth century the timber-framed iron-roofed building was taken by the settlers, the squatters and the selectors into the dry hot outback. Unconcerned with architectural fashions, they built practical buildings designed to combat the harsh, all-pervading sun. Wide verandahs spread their protecting shade over the walls of small shanties, rambling homesteads or the stacked storeys of hotels. Where a blacksmith, a few stores and houses clustered around an hotel to form a tiny town, the verandah stretched out over the footpath giving unbroken lengths of darkness. They were unpretentious and pragmatic structures making the maximum use of scarce materials which had to be carried from the cities and put together by the settler himself, and giving the most effective protection from heat, dust and wind.

Over the years changes and modifications were made to the early techniques. In the northern part of New South Wales and the country areas of Queensland a distinctive type of building was evolved. By the nineties it was fully developed and had become the standard building of a vast inland area. In that area by the late sixties the practice had developed of fixing the weatherboards to the inner face of the stud frame and leaving the outer face of the frame uncovered. Timber rot was no problem in country which was normally parched. By making the one lot of boarding serve for both external sheeting and internal lining, a great saving in material and time was achieved. By the seventies refinements had been made to give a more attractive finish. Advantage was taken of the exposed framework to make an attractive pattern. The timbers were dressed. The vertical, widely-spaced studs and horizontal noggings were uniformly arranged around the perimeter. The bracing timbers were equally carefully placed to form a diamond pattern of diagonals. The whole arrangement was both functional and decorative. In many cases the timbers were quirked and chamfered to add a further decorative touch to the overall pattern of the framework. When the normal one inch thick butt- or slip-tongue-jointed flooring gave way to machine-produced tongue and grooved boarding in the seventies, it was used in thinner form and with a further decorating bead-joint for lining the building. In its more refined form the framework became a sophisticated product requiring both time and skill but it took no longer and was still cheaper in material and far more attractive than the usual method of sheeting both sides of the framework. By the beginning of the eighties, when decoration was rampant in the cities, the same quality which was inherent in the exposed timber frame made it universally popular in the outback. But there was an essential difference. The city-bred decoration was false, disguising and dishonest while that of the country was revealing, entrancing and, growing naturally out of the structure, completely honest. The exposed timber frame was used for homesteads, shops, churches and hotels. There are very many fine examples to be seen in the countryside of Queensland and New South Wales. One of the oldest extant examples of the advanced type is St George's Church of England built at Beenleigh, Queensland, in 1876.

Economic and material conditions gave rise to the exposed timber frame. Climatic conditions gave rise to other important changes with which it was combined. The framework was lifted one foot six inches above the ground on timber stumps to produce better ventilation below the floor and thereby help to cool the building. As had been accidentally found by the Port Essington settlers it was also the best answer to the depredations of white ants. With this discovery Queensland buildings became stilted on thick whole tree-trunk columns. Gradually the height was increased. By the turn of the century it was six to nine feet and had percolated into the city where the Brisbane Queen Anne houses sat high on stilts and used the undercroft for a variety of secondary but useful purposes from drying clothes to play areas for noisy children.

The verandah became increasingly a living area. A small box of rooms was surrounded by ever broader verandahs on which, for most of the year, a large part of the normal activities of a country home took place—eating, talking, sewing and reading became out-door activities as people moved out of the stifling conditions indoors. To protect the verandah from the sun, especially in the late afternoon, but to allow the passage of cooling air, screens of open wattling were fixed between the posts. From the late seventies these first rudimentary efforts were replaced with lattice or trellis work of the thin oregon battens used in the south by the plasterers. The screens at first appeared on the western side but by the time battened screens were used they were hung continuously around all four sides like a skirt. Their continuity and uniformity became an embracing black and white

St George's Church of England at Beenleigh, Queensland: 1876

A typical Queensland country house —
The Roman Catholic Presbytery at Richmond, North Queensland

chequered pattern giving an extraordinary unity and compactness to the building.

To make use of the air in the roof space as a heat insulator, the roof became steep and bulky. Large gabled ventilators were built into the apex of hipped roofs to keep the hottest air moving out, and resulted in a broken and distinctive gambrel silhouette. For the same reason, rooms were arranged in a square so that a large pyramid roof topped by a ventilating cap at the apex could be achieved. Such a roof has no pockets in which hot air can be trapped and is the most effective roof form for quick ventilation. The development was so effective that many of the early Colonial period buildings in New South Wales, when replacing their old wooden shingles with galvanized corrugated iron, extended the outer roof slope of their old M-form roofs upwards to enclose the valley to form a single ridge or pyramid roof. The slope of the extension was often made at a lower pitch than that of the original roof so that the resultant form was a type of mansard roof. The different pitch was caused by the formation of a six inch or so gap between the lap of the new and old roof as a continuous ventilator half way up the roof. There are many examples of these unusual roofs to be seen in the areas in New South Wales which had been well settled before the mid-century. Throsby House near Bowral is one of the best.

By the nineties, then, there had been developed in parts of New South Wales and particularly in Queensland a type of building which was usually square in plan, was raised high off the ground on heavy tree-trunk stumps, was a tight box of rooms whose timber bones showed, surrounded by wide verandahs laced into a band of deep trellis work and topped by a pyramid iron roof. Growing logically out of physical causes, it had a distinctive character that was the closest that Australia has ever come to producing an indigenous style. But, because it was cheap and rural, and mostly because it was indigenous and not imported, it stayed out in the country to die in the desiccating heat of the inland when, in the mid-twentieth century, city stylism came to the outback.

10 The coming of Federation in 1901 put joy into the hearts and strength into the minds and bodies of all Australians. The creation of a new nation was a highly-charged emotional affair which had been long dreamed of. At the same time, the old sombre Queen, who was the only ruler most people had ever known and whose presence had seemed as permanent as that of the Empire itself, died. The new King was gay, pleasure-loving and escorted by a beautiful woman full of life. And also, at the same time, the desolatory effects of depression, strikes and droughts lifted and once again the economy was set fair. For Australia more than any other country in the world the new century dawned full of hope, enthusiasm and good omens.

The new confidence showed itself in a steadily increasing tempo in building rather than any drastic changes in style. The stake which the lower and middle classes had in their new nation was reflected in the types of buildings that were erected. There were practically no really large buildings, normally financed by overseas money. Instead a host of medium-sized buildings—city stores, shops, meeting halls, breweries, hotels and schools—all to cater for middle and lower class demands—blossomed in the city and suburban centres and were wrapped in a vast swaddling of new housing. The style was still Queen Anne but, because of economic changes, the classes for whom they were erected, and slowly evolving fashions, the style underwent variation and change as well. The trade unions, for instance, which had 'fair and reasonable' wages as one of their main aims, had succeeded in obtaining better working conditions and agreed minimum wages for their members. In 1903, the Commonwealth Parliament established the Commonwealth Court of Conciliation and Arbitration which, in 1906, established a basic wage for all workers. Largely for this reason but also because of the increasing prosperity, costs rose. To combat them building finishes were cheapened.

The new breed of hotels, stores, shops, halls and schools retained the overall colouring of Queen Anne. As well as using stone and specially shaped bricks for the better standard buildings, the ordinary Queen Anne building of Edwardian times was carried out in common red bricks, plaster and paint. And the bulk of Edwardian buildings fell into the 'ordinary' category. The main body of the walls was brick while the plinth, the window and door dressings, the broad bands at each floor level, the cornice and parapet were plastered in flat planes and painted cream. Moulding of the plaster was reduced to a minimum. Only at the top of the brick pilasters was there a bulbous blob of scrawled moulding. Gradually the amount of plastering increased. The pilasters were next to become cream painted, a medallion was introduced high in the wall over the centre entrance on the corner and the band at the cornice was given a pattern of repetitive moulding. By 1905, commercial buildings were a bold grid of cream paint with rectangular panels of red brickwork in between. They were chunky buildings—solid and compact. Verandahs, light, airy and porous, were discarded to reveal the blockiness of the building. Extraneous whimsy and fussiness were rigorously eschewed.

The Edwardian buildings turned against cast iron in all its forms. The old cast iron awning posts at the footpath's edge had been thrown out. By the late nineties the street awning roof, still bull-nosed, was being fixed to a light framework of rolled steel angles supported directly from the wall on large wrought iron brackets. The smartest Edwardian buildings went further. They hid the iron roof covering out of sight by making the roof a flat awning projected horizontally from the face of the building and suspending it on steel tension rods angled back into the brickwork. The suspension ties were wrought iron bars twisted, convoluted and dressed in curlicued wrought iron bows at their ends and half way along their length. By 1915 nearly all street canopies were built this way but the square wrought iron bars had become round machine-produced mild steel rods, shorn of frills, fixed with a flat boss plate to the brickwork anchorage and adjusted by a plain turnbuckle. The canopy itself was framed in light riveted steel angles built up to a thick outer edge in timber and drained back to the building face instead of spilling into the gutter. Galvanized iron covered the roof and pressed metal sheeting lined its underside.

In 1908 the first of the cantilevered awnings appeared. By using heavy steel sections embedded well back into the brickwork they did away with all visible means of support. To unaccustomed eyes the flat edges projecting twelve feet straight out from a building was a disturbing thing. J. Barlow wrote in 1909 that the one or two he had seen looked 'like the legendary coffin of Mahomet as it lay suspended between earth and sky'. He much preferred to be satisfied rather than mystified. He personally found greater satisfaction in seeing the supports and therefore favoured bracketed awnings. However, he predicted that suspended awnings would win out in the long run. The cantilevered awnings were aesthetically worrying and economically expensive. It was, in fact, the high cost of imported steel, the major sort available, that held back cantilevered awnings until after the First World War when locally made steel became plentiful and cheap. The awnings cut the buildings in two. In later years, when the building became old fashioned and out of style, they were a godsend. A facelift could be carried out below the awning line to create an up-to-the-minute look for a minimum outlay while the original face was left to float undisturbed on top.

About 1910 the walls below the awning were covered to a height of six feet in glazed vitreous six by three inch tiles in dark reds with cream strip tiles as a frame near the edge. Tiles had been used to face a few buildings when the cry for polychromatic buildings was at its highest during the eighties. But they had discoloured, collected dirt and been prone to falling unexpectedly. For these reasons, they had never become popular. Used as a band near ground level the highly glazed tiles were easily cleaned, never dangerous if they fell and provided a much more permanent coloured and rugged finish than easily scuffed and chipped painted plaster.

By 1905 a new type of decoration was being given to buildings. It was called Art Nouveau. It had come to Australia from its place of origin in Belgium, where it had first found expression in the nineties, by way of England where an ultra-precious coterie of artists, publishers, poets, writers, critics and architects orbited in enamelled sensuality around such people as the magnificent illustrator, Aubrey Beardsley. They proclaimed themselves to be decadents and had as their credo Oscar Wilde's dictum: 'The first duty of life is to be as artificial as possible.' In building, Art Nouveau had started as a fundamental theorizing about the relationship between architecture and the conditions of an industrialized society. Discontented with the sterile constricting thinking that looked backwards to historical styles, it sought to create an architecture appropriate to its times which

would be a launching platform into the future. In its home Art Nouveau had attempted to make materials, structure and decoration integrated parts of a whole with each aspect revealing, reinforcing and enhancing the other. Instead of disguising and falsifying an underlying form by cloaking it in marshmallow as the Victorians had done, the proponents of Art Nouveau held that decoration should grow out of the physical properties of materials, the techniques of working them and their structural potential. Where these were all different from previous ages it followed that their form should also be different and independent of the past. Mild steel was the important new material and from this and their philosophy the leaders of the Art Nouveau produced forms which were light and delicate, marked by writhing sinuous lines, tendrils, gracious curves and simplified limpid shapes abstracted from nature. The straight line was abhorred.

By the time Art Nouveau had arrived third-hand in the Antipodes, its underlying philosophy had become clouded and almost lost. It had become emasculated into little more than another new and romantically-flavoured style whose astringency and novelty of form appealed strongly at a time when the heart was thoroughly sick of sugary sweetness and costs were high. It had been reduced to a handful of decorative cliches. The few who appreciated it as something other than a new fashion could see it as going no deeper than a call for unprecedented decoration, sparse and full of movement, divorced from the past.

Art Nouveau made its first appearance in Australia in 1902 when it appeared on a couple of brewery-built hotels in Sydney. Despite this the only place in which it gained any sort of real strength was Melbourne, where Robert Haddon was its sympathetic champion and most influential exponent. Art Nouveau decoration ran wild over Melbourne's buildings for a few brief years. Mostly in a spotty or patchy way it was applied to the most sedate bank, a robust warehouse, a gay shop, a vulgar hotel or fretted into verandah valences and brackets on frivolous suburban homes. In his own home Anselm, built in 1906 in Glenferrie Street, Caulfield, Haddon produced a doll-scale house in which the Art Nouveau idiom was applied to a basically Queen Anne house. Using red bricks and terracotta panels decorated with sinuous patterns of his own design externally and white plaster and dark wood internally, Haddon created a minor gem of the new school of thought. When the prevailing taste was for red Haddon's favourite colour was green, and he managed to use it in most of his work both on his city buildings such as the Fourth Victoria Building in Collins Street, where two large green terracotta lions heads dribbled green streaks down the clean rendered facade, as well as in his domestic work. In his own home Haddon used green glazed tiles to make the fireplace fenders and in the form of sea-waves in the tiles of the bathroom. He delighted in designing and making by hand the most minute parts of his buildings; roof gutter brackets, door hinges, handles and locks were hand-made and ingenious in their simple effectiveness and individuality. His diamond patterned lead-lighted windows, glazed with obscure glass, had a secret framed portion of the diamonds which opened to reveal clear glass which acted as a spy-hole on door knockers. With this sort of trick he anticipated the gadget-conscious homes of several well-known architects who came to prominence a decade or more later.

Haddon had a sincerity and depth of understanding of what he and the style were about but in the hands of his followers and imitators Art Nouveau was sterilized into utter superficiality. It was applied cosmetically to the basic Edwardian buildings of the time with little change in their real form. The projecting corner towers of city offices, hotels and houses became round, the roofs shallow, bulging or dripping cones. Spidery Art Nouveau tendrils grew on the bands of wall allotted to them. As they twisted and flowed upwards they diminished in thickness and came to rest with an abstracted leaf in the shape of a heart. The

Anselm, 4 Glenferrie Street,
Caulfield, Victoria; 1906
Architect. Robert Haddon

Art nouveau house at 1258
High Street, Glen Iris,
Victoria: about 1908

Two Edwardian style hotels — *Above* The Metropolitan Hotel in George Street, Sydney, 1910 *Below* The Broadway Hotel in Balaclava Street, South Brisbane, 1906

diminishing tendril and the heart became the hallmark of the style. They appeared in isolated shyness high on cornices, were worked, green and red, into stained glass windows, pressed into metal ceilings and scattered over verandahs. In the houses particularly, the geometrically patterned timber verandah of the standard Queen Anne style gave way to looping, swirling fretwork of unwonted shapes in which posts and valence swept unbrokenly into each other in a turbulent mass of detail. The same busy bag of worms went inside and draped itself as a lopsided timber screen around the sitting room fireplace.

A few innovators tried to give Art Nouveau an Australian bias. The tenuous openness of the original was transmogrified into concentrated clusters of native flora and fauna in which gumnuts mixed with the hearts and kangaroos sodomized with sheep. The sparseness was translated into spottiness as these concentrated packages were cut as capitals on heavy bare stone-shafted columns on insurance buildings in Melbourne or strung as a dado around warehouses in Hobart.

Iconoclastic Art Nouveau was an amusing and refreshing interlude after the voluptuous pomposity which preceded it and beside the blobby Edwardian that ran concurrently with it. But because it was an exclusive movement essentially mannered, narcissistic and, in its popular form, shallow and concerned only with different decoration for its own sake, it withered quickly. By 1910, even in Melbourne where it had thrived best, it had died. Only the upwards twisting diminishing tendrils and the heart shaped leaves carried on. Its main motif became debased into a stiff tapered stalk topped by an inverted heart like an arrowhead to be fretted into the balusters of wooden verandahs in the dying days of the Queen Anne style.

After 1910 the timber verandah and gables, having outgrown their happy spindled youth and voluptuous middle age, settled into a stodgy old age. Turned timber gave way to planed surfaces. Posts were thick and square with large flat angels' wings sprouting from the top third. Balustrades became almost solid fences with a narrow gap left between their wide flat board balusters. The handrail was heavy and plain. The winglike brackets and the balusters titivated with a little sinuous fretting carried the last vestiges of the Art Nouveau influence. These ponderous structures graced the footpaths of country towns and the gardens of suburban villas in the years immediately preceding World War I.

By the time Art Nouveau ceased to be a force the buildings which had eschewed its fragile other-worldliness had developed new mannerisms. The standard cream and red Edwardian buildings broke loose at the skyline. The parapet jumped up and down in an agitated series of steps, loops, curves and slopes. Dutch gables, triangles of jerky scrolls, scoops and steps appeared. The outline of parapets and gables was marked in the inevitable cream band of flat plaster while at the corners and on the horizontal sections squatted smooth spheres, the remnants of a past fashion which could not be quite abandoned.

At the same time the first of the modern architecture came across the Pacific. In 1909 there was practically none of it. In 1910 it was going up everywhere. It was a style that had originated in Chicago with Louis Sullivan, who in the 1880s had decided architecture need spring-cleaning—by him. The style was clean, it was shorn of plaster and it was frank. Its marks were straight clean cornices with brick walls and giant semi-circular brick arches fused into one unit. Arthur Blacket had made a most successful essay in the style when he designed a brick warehouse at Pyrmont in 1893. But the depression had stopped any further follow-up and development. The semi-circular arch had marked the entrance five years before. Generally, the large semi-circular arch had been used in the nineties as part of the popular Romanesque style and it had lingered into the early part of the new century for use as main doorways in some of the Queen Anne buildings. But despite the wildest aberrations of the architect it had always remained within the

John Taylor Warehouse in Pyrmont Bridge Road, Pyrmont, New South Wales: 1893. Architect, Arthur Blacket

Warehouse at 441 Kent Street, Sydney: about 1897

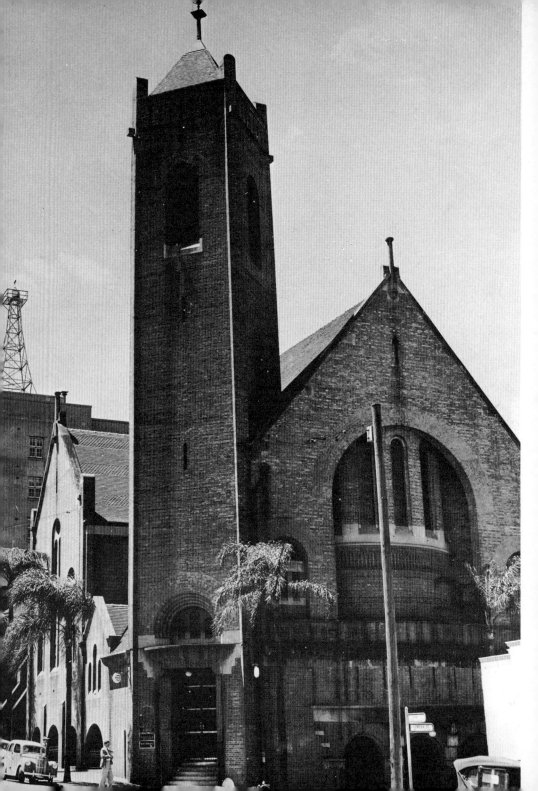

accepted limits of its scale to the whole building and retained at least the appearance of structural justification. Now it returned. But it was used in a new way. It was huge in scale and used decoratively and quite independently of any structural needs. Usually it was independent of any vertical support at the corners or, if it were not, the support was so squat and stocky as to appear as an extension of the great sweep of the arch. Large semi-circles of recessed brickwork were sunk in the faces of walls. Sometimes they were left blank leaving the arch form without competing elements; sometimes they were thrown over a bank of three or so rectangular windows placed close together. The big brick arches, always with their brick infill panels, sprang across the tops of pilaster strips at the top of multi-storey brick office buildings and took giant strides down the faces of single-storeyed warehouses. Wherever they were used, which means on practically every new office building, church or factory in every city in the nation, their huge scale stood in extreme contrast to the complicated fussiness of the High Victorian confections which surrounded them.

Possibly one of the finest examples of the early modern architecture of sheer, uncluttered, precisely-cut, brick planes and clean-cut arches was erected by G. D. Payne for the St Andrew's Presbyterian Congregation in Brisbane in 1910, the nascent year. In the hands of the inept who could not entirely rid themselves of the notion that their naked buildings needed Classical mouldings, garlands and medallions the style became ponderous, heavy and debased. Many of the banks and hotels around Oxford Street and Taylor Square in Sydney which were rebuilt at this time are exceedingly thudding. In the hands of an adept it was dramatic architecture. St Andrew's, despite its unfortunate site halfway down a hill and at the bottom of a gully, is a dramatic building. Set high on a hill it would have been superbly so.

The timber-framed house had come from America and now, in 1910, the first of the modern architecture had come from the same place. After Federation, Australian eyes increasingly turned eastward for example in all fields. Australians saw their country as similar in size and potential to the burgeoning republic whose origins, background and history were so like their own. It was particularly so with architecture, where new ideas rooted in the increasing tempo of technology were flourishing. And one of the impressive advances that they saw on the far horizons in 1910 was skyscrapers. In America they were steel-framed and it was the steel which made them logical and possible. Steel of the quality and sizes required was not available in Australia but the thought of streaking upwards even in a more modest way was too enticing to resist. In 1912, it happened. In Castlereagh and King Streets, Sydney, the firm of Spain and Cosh erected in solid brick Culwalla House, 170 feet high. Immediately there were cries of protest as the city's skyline was shattered. People shuddered at the effect on Sydney's narrow streets should they become lined with such monsters. Deep sunless chasms of dust, dirt and damp were not inviting prospects. It was pointed out that Sydney's fire services could not possibly handle a fire in such a building. Neither the eighty feet ladders, the longest available, nor the steam-pumped water-pressure could cope. Unless a halt were called the city would be a potential incinerator. The city fathers were both frightened and convinced. It was hastily enacted that, for Sydney, 150 feet was the highest limit that would be allowed. In Melbourne as early as 1888, Oakden, Addison and Kemp had designed the Australian Building to be 150 feet high. A shocked Melbourne City Council forced a reduction of two floors

Opposite St Andrew's Presbyterian
Church, Brisbane: 1910.
Architect, G. D. Payne

in the height. The Council was saved from similar predicaments by the depression but by 1910 it was obliged to recognize the imminent introduction of tall concrete and steel framed buildings. It clamped a limit height on that city. The height varied according to the street onto which the building faced. The limit was rationalized at one and one-third times the width of the street. With a maximum street width of ninety-nine feet, the height limit automatically became 132 feet. Only decorative unoccupiable towers and flagpoles could go higher. Although there was no immediate spur in the other capitals they gradually followed suit during the 1920s.

The limit height imposed on buildings was but one aspect of a more general problem. The question of fire in the tall buildings was seen to create a completely new set of dangers. The revisions of the building laws that took place were cast to take account of them. The Acts also made it compulsory for city buildings to have flat roofs to serve as working platforms for fire fighters. Pitched roofs and the terracotta tiles which swamped the suburbs were banished from the heart of the towns. The Acts also laid down requirements for the fire-resisting properties of the parts of the building. Fire-ratings enforced the provision of at least one fireproof stairway and the encasement of steelwork in concrete or terracotta and virtually made the use of reinforced concrete in floors mandatory for most city buildings.

Concrete came into Australian buildings as a structural material about 1905. As we have seen, it had been used to help strengthen cast iron columns, to make water pipes, to form a level bed for brick foundations and for fireproofing for some twenty years before then. Cement mortars had been commonly used for waterproofing and exterior plastering for some time. But from the beginning concrete had been considered an unsightly material to be buried in the ground or hidden in columns and ceilings. It was not particularly suitable for building structure as it needed to be used in mass form. Its full structural potential did not come until the practice of reinforcing it by embedding mild steel bars at the tension planes was developed.

Reinforced concrete was a development that had been discovered in 1868 in France by a gardener named Monnier [sic]. Annoyed by breakages to his cast concrete tubs, he had the idea of making them stronger by reinforcing them with chicken wire. By the early 1890s this elementary idea had been developed in France by F. Hennebique and in America by E. L. Ransome to such a stage that it was being used in large-scale engineering work. In 1895 the first reinforced concrete structure was erected in Australia. Under the direction of the Engineer in Chief of the Public Works Department in New South Wales, C. W. Darley, two test arches were erected at Forest Lodge in September. The trials, carried out in connection with the Sydney Sewerage Scheme, showed these two arches to be twice as strong as similar brick or mass concrete arches. As a result of these satisfactory tests two permanent arches using the 'Monier System', as it was called, were built to carry part of the new Sydney Sewerage Scheme reticulation across Johnston's Creek and White's Creek which empty into Iron Cove at Sydney. The larger of the arches spans seventy-five feet, rises seven feet six inches and has a thickness of fourteen inches at the springing and twelve inches at the crown. Both of them still exist and serve their original purpose.

After a most satisfactory introduction the use of reinforced concrete quickly gathered momentum. However, it was restricted to civil engineering work and kept out of building. In Melbourne one of the first people into the new field was John Monash, already regarded as one of Australia's most competent engineers. In 1899 he designed the Anderson Street bridge across the Yarra River to link South Yarra with Richmond. In 1900 a German, Gumnow, and an Australian, Forrest, formed the first firm in Sydney to design and erect reinforced concrete structures. Throughout the ten years after the two Forest Lodge arches were built reinforced concrete bridges, dams and country water tanks were erected with the material. A reinforced concrete water tank holding one hundred thousand gallons and measuring twenty-eight feet seven inches in diameter, five inches thick and supported fifty-five feet above the flat plain on twenty-two feet diameter columns was erected by Monash at Mildura to provide good pressure for the town's water supply. In 1909, two and one-half chains of experimental fencing using reinforced concrete posts and strainers were erected at the Cowra Experiment Farm and proved highly successful.

The advantages of reinforced concrete were too strong to be denied. But, at a time when Queen Anne red was all the rage, the visual offensiveness of its cold grey crudity restricted it to places where appearances did not matter—out in the country or in rugged engineering works. When eventually its advantages forced it into buildings, the same attitude held. Until the 1960s its inherent finish was always covered with a coat of cement-based plaster, bricks, tiles, stone or some other acceptable material, or hidden well out of sight.

The first use of reinforced concrete in building may well have been in the main floor slab of the new railway station building erected at Central in Sydney. The design was commenced by the Public Works Department in 1903 and the building opened to the public in September 1906. Once reinforced concrete had breached the ramparts of resistance it became accepted quickly for large buildings. In 1912 the architectural firm of Bates, Peebles and Smart, successors to the practice of Joseph Reed, erected a 114 feet diameter shallow reinforced concrete dome—the largest in the world and the first of its kind in Australia—over the main reading room of the Melbourne Public Library. In the same year John Monash, in addressing the Victorian Institute of Engineers, was able to report that reinforced concrete buildings, using the material in columns, beams and floors, were common in Melbourne. Monash was a strong advocate for reinforced concrete, both as an engineer and as a businessman, and in the same year had contractor George Higgins build a house for him at Beaumaris in Victoria. The house had its foundations, floors, walls and roof made entirely of reinforced concrete. The form was simple—a plain two-storeyed box covered by a low pitched roof of shallowly dished concrete sections four feet wide. The building was cement-rendered inside and out to give a smooth plain finish. The first floor slab and the underside of the raking roof slab were plastered and left as the ceilings. It was not the first but it was the most important experiment in use of the material for housing. Numbers of succeeding attempts have been made but, except for a highly specialized pre-cast system suitable only for factory production and large-scale repetitive work developed by the Victorian Housing Commission, it has never been of much consequence in domestic work.

The smooth plastering that was done directly to the concrete surfaces on the house at Beaumaris was another way of achieving the cleaned-down look that started to make itself felt on the outside of the big arched buildings and the inside of houses after 1910. The taste for comparative simplicity was a natural reaction to the confections of the preceding half-century. The trend was helped by the arrival of another new material—fibrous plaster.

The use of large factory-cast sheets of gypsum plaster reinforced with fibre and fixed to the timber framework of ceilings and walls with clouts was, and still is, an almost exclusively Australasian practice. In New Zealand its use is still geographically restricted but in Australia it is the universal method of obtaining a flush plaster surface on a timber frame quickly and cheaply. It was introduced into Australia just prior to World War I. The war retarded its use because of slackness in the building industry and shortage of materials. But when conditions returned to normal by 1920, fibrous plastering rapidly swept away the pressed metal ceilings and the traditional lathe and plaster method. Its advantages of low weight, fire resistance, strength, smooth finish and low cost made it particularly suitable at a time when low-cost timber housing was the major field of building activity. By 1930 the older techniques had perished.

The 'rag and stick' method had been used to cast decorated panels up to six feet square in the eighties. Fibrous plaster sheeting, as it is now used, was invented in New Zealand in 1910 by Robert Wardrop. He was a woodcarver who had emigrated from Victoria in 1900 because of the building recession. In New Zealand he joined forces with a German named Schafer to form the Carrara Ceiling Company in Dunedin. The firm later expanded to Wellington. Schafer introduced a German method of casting plaster called 'Stuccolin' in which the plaster was mixed with cotton wool. However, it proved too costly and was abandoned. In 1908, sheets reinforced by tow obtained from old mattresses was tried and was reasonably satisfactory. Then, in 1910, the Carrara Ceiling Company hit upon the idea of reinforcing their sheets with New Zealand flax. It was completely successful. The idea may have come from Sydney. As early as 1905 the firm of Grant and Cocks was using hemp to reinforce plaster, but only for decorations, not for sheets. At any rate, fibrous plaster had been born. With this step plaster sheets could be produced in unlimited size, stock-piled and bought off the shelf. It meant that the only trades left to be pushed into the factory were plumbing and painting.

The first sheets of fibrous plaster were imported into Melbourne from New Zealand in 1912. In the same year the Lottoid Company in Richmond, Melbourne, imported its own flax from across the Tasman Sea and began manufacturing locally. Melbourne became the main centre of manufacture in Australia as a result. The gypsum at first came from America but after overseas supplies were cut off during World War I the extensive fields in South Australia were developed and have ever since been the main source of plaster of Paris. Attempts had been made to produce plaster of Paris from the deposits of gypsum at Tub's Lake on York Peninsula in 1883 but, because of the presence of salt, they had failed. It was not until 1910 that the first successful Australian production of plaster of Paris was made from the South Australian fields. In 1916, fibrous plaster sheeting was introduced into New South Wales and in the early twenties into the other states.

After World War I flax from Java was used instead of that from New Zealand. It was not until 1928 that cornices ceased to be reinforced with battens and used fibre instead. At first the sheets were used for ceilings only but by 1930 thicker sheets were being made and fixed to the walls as well. Those who regarded this sheeting as too flimsy to withstand the buffetings it would be subjected to on a wall provided a stout backing by sheeting the wall in rough boarding first. Some conservative financing authorities, such as the Queensland Housing Authority, insisted on it. By the mid-thirties, however, it had proved itself even in this vulnerable position and was being fixed, like the ceilings, to battens or even, in the cheapest cases, directly to the studs of the frame themselves.

The new fibrous plasterer tradesmen came into conflict with the solid plasterers and the carpenters. The carpenters' union, ever jealous of its members' interests and its own powers, scrapped about who should cut and nail the battens and drive the clouts. The solid plasterers claimed that stopping the clout holes was their job. Fibrous plasterers should be limited to measuring and cutting the sheets, it was claimed. Eventually, the new trade was recognized as legitimate and fibrous plasterers were allowed to carry out all those parts of the work provided that they used a plasterer's hammer and never a carpenter's claw hammer. But it was agreed carpenters would continue to fix skirtings, architraves and any timber cornices—a division of labour which still persists.

Fibrous plaster came at a time when cheap housing was becoming a major field of building activity. Within a couple of years either side of 1910 every state government established a scheme to fulfil every Australian's dream of owning his own home on his own block of land. Working either directly through commissions or trusts or indirectly through state-owned banks, the state governments set out to provide low-cost houses on low-cost land on terms within the means of the poorest paid worker. The Workers' Homes Board of Queensland was typical. Money was made available for thirty year terms. Interest was charged at six per cent. Repayments were a standard two shillings and sixpence a week for each £100 borrowed. The authorities supplied both the land and house, with house prices ranging from £330 to £550. Speculation was prohibited. After World War I, the activities of the various authorities were taken over by War Service Homes on a national basis.

To provide homes and land under these conditions the Boards and the banks acquired broad acres on the fringes of the cities and on them erected cheap little four-roomed villas. Under their influence, a rush to the suburbs began in earnest from 1910. After the trains spawned suburbia in the 1860s further extensions of the lines had drawn the threads of houses further out into the country. But development had stayed within a mile or so of the stations. With the low-cost Workers Homes the areas further away began to fill up with weatherboard Queen Anne villas. The green countryside started to be a sea of orange-tiled or red-painted iron roofs. The Australian city passed out of its embryonic form and acquired the character that has grown stronger with time.

The growth of the suburbs came at a time when town planning in general had undergone major changes. Until the depression of 1892, town planning thinking had been restricted to considering the ideal town of the future which was seen in Renaissance terms of a rectangular grid of wide streets with appropriate squares, symmetrical vistas and formal parklands.

During the lean years of the nineties, architects, engineers and surveyors had little work and plenty of time. In the age-old manner of their kind, they turned to producing ideas for the time when things recovered. Numbers of them gave their attention to town planning as a nicely general and innocuous sort of subject which leant itself to dreaming.

Having new concepts to consider, town planning, like science, often has to invent or borrow words to suit its thinking. Many of the words die quietly as their need subsides, others become a jargon that has a brief and overworked life, others, more inspired and useful, pass into the general language. Jargon words at the turn of the century were 'citadel' for the city-centre and 'emporium' for a suburban shopping centre. Both have died but a word of the same time that has passed into common usage is 'neighbourhood', which was used by surveyor J. Keily in 1889 to describe his idea of a number of separate two square mile suburbs clustered around a four square mile citadel.[1]

In the nineties planners began to advocate abandoning the grid street pattern for new towns and subdivisions. Some of them talked of the desirability of allowing the contours of the land to be the determinant of street alignments. When it was proposed to develop a model suburb on the watershed area of the old Botany Bay swamps, which had been Sydney's water supply before the Prospect Reservoir came into operation, a competition was held. The winning scheme, submitted by Vernon, Joseland, Oxley and Mocatta, was hung around a two chain wide loop road whose alignment had been fixed by the contours from both sewerage levels and aesthetic considerations.

John Sulman, in 1891, hoped that the day was not too far distant when a General Planning Council would be set up to control all town planning matters within New South Wales.[2] The day was in fact seventy-two years distant. The

The Methodist Church
at Narooma, New
South Wales: 1915

state-wide New South Wales State Planning Authority, the first of its kind in Australia, was established in 1963. Sulman also was one of the most forceful opponents of the grid pattern. New towns, he declared categorically, should be sited and laid out from considerations of 'convenience utility and beauty', not because the land was cheap and the brainwork required minimal. 'The town,' he said, 'should be like that marvel of ingenuity—the spider's web.'

The two concepts, the importance of the natural land form and the interest and practical advantages of a radial road-pattern, simmered and gained adherents. They eventually found concrete form in 1912 when a young American architect, Walter Burley Griffin, won a competition for a new national capital—Canberra. The opportunity of designing a large city on a virgin site was a rare one in history and Griffin had not fumbled it. With a great empathy for nature that had been nurtured and developed in the nature-conscious atmosphere of the Chicago School of Architecture, Griffin created a highly imaginative blend of formality and informality that was outstanding. Using three natural features as apexes of a triangle and the hubs of three interlocked, spider-web series of wide roads and the valley between them as a meandering lake, he achieved a remarkably successful marriage between the land and a controlled geometry of radial streets. It was a complete break with traditional Australian town planning. But, because of two world wars, a major depression and virulent professional jealousies, it was fifty years before the child of Griffin's genius ceased to be merely an exciting vision and started to take recognizable shape under the guiding hand of the National Capital Development Commission.

While the Canberra plan of 1912 unexpectedly and successfully embodied the previously disparate ideas that had been put forward by town planners for some twenty years, the very uniqueness of its opportunity and its success precluded it from being of great significance to the broad picture of Australian town planning. In addition, it was in fact no more than another phase in the old occupation of designing a town of the future. This had been a subject that had received a lot of attention for a long time. Griffin's answer was a different and more imaginative answer than had been found before. For these reasons, it was of great interest to, but had little influence upon, Australian town planning.

A less spectacular and interesting development that came to town planning after 1900, but one that was far more important in its consequences than Canberra, was the change that involved a fundamental reappraisal of the real sphere of interest of town planning. The change of thought regarding town planning was indicated by the introduction of another new word into the language—slum. It became part of Australian town planning jargon during the discourses of the quiescence in the late nineties.

Many of the crowded terrace buildings which had been built speculatively during the 1840s and 1850s had deteriorated into squalid hovels by the 1890s. Erected when unrestricted private enterprise rode roughshod over any consideration but profit, many of them faced onto lanes eight feet wide or even, in some extreme /cases, two feet six inches wide. They had been thrown together in the skimpiest way using the poorest materials, their inadequacies hidden under a smother of plaster. Fifty years later they were damp, ill-lit, unhealthy hovels infested with rats and disease, and were a breeding ground for vice. They had become dilapidated, rickety piles of rubbish, their wavy walls shored up with baulks of timber propped across narrow alleys and with sagging ceilings, rotted woodwork and peeling plaster. In 1896, Archdeacon F. B. Boyce said Sydney's slums were equal in dirt, vice and crime to anything in London. Boyce advocated clearing out the near-city slums and erecting in their place large blocks of multi-storeyed homes for the workers. At the same time, he urged local councils to encourage the lower classes to move to the suburbs by making it easier to obtain land in the outer areas. He predicted that if something were not done about the slums a catastrophe in health or crime or both would force Sydney to come to its senses.

Nothing, except talk, was done and as Boyce had foreseen so it happened. In 1900, bubonic plague, carried by the innumerable rats that came ashore from the ships, swept through the jungle of the Rocks area. In May 1901, the Rocks Resumption Board was hastily set up to assist in cleaning up and replanning the area. In the wash-up a large portion of the area was swept clean of most of the filthy characterful mess that had built up over eighty years. It was the first instance of Australian town planning being redeveloped. Under the urging of people like Bishop Boyce and with the example of the Rocks Redevelopment Scheme to demonstrate the possibilities, planners were quick to realize that their field was much wider than merely theorizing about hypothetical new towns and that redevelopment had become a vast problem that offered a much more real challenge to their energies. When the first national conference of town planners was held in Adelaide in 1917 redevelopment of blighted areas occupied practically the whole of the agenda. It was not an accident that Adelaide was the venue for such a meeting as the town was the most lively centre of town planning thinking in the nation. In 1916 the South Australian House of Assembly passed the first Town Planning and Housing Bill in Australia and appointed Mr Charles C. Reade as its first Government Town Planner. His energies, in practice, were almost entirely taken up by redevelopment work.

The years 1901–16 were a time of incipient change for Australian architecture. Philosophically they saw the introduction of the first modern thinking. Technologically they saw the introduction of new materials such as reinforced concrete and fibrous plaster. They saw the suburbs become a sea of red tile roofs. Finally, the same years saw new dimensions added to the concept of town planning.

As the effects of the First World War took hold, building slowed down. Materials were in short supply. Men were in the Middle East or France or occupied with essential work directly related to the war effort. By 1917, building had almost stopped and the emerging changes of the pre-war years were dampened until the carnage on the other side of the world ceased.

---

[1] Keily, Captain J.: A paper read before the Victorian Institute of Surveyors, 7 Sept 1889, entitled *Study on Unity of Design in Planning New Towns and New Suburbs*, in *Victorian Institute of Surveyors Transactions and Proceedings*, Vol. III, 1885-1891, pp. 88-104.

[2] Sulman, John: Presidential address 'The Architecture of Towns' in *Report of the Third Meeting of the Australasian Association for the Advancement of Science held at Christchurch New Zealand in January 1891*, published by the Association 1891, pp. 424-33.

The depression of the 1890s was the first of a series of alternating depressions and wars which plagued the world during the succeeding half-century. As each broke over Australia it acted like a 'Stop' sign on the progress of building and architecture. During the blackout of building that came with each blow the need for more building did not cease. It was merely that the continuing need was not met. The delays resulted in a build-up of pressure which, as soon as the cause was removed and the community's progress slowly regained momentum, caused a regular pattern of building priorities. As the number of people reaching marriageable age had not dropped and the number of new families had increased steadily during the period of darkness, the most pressing need, because it was most personal, was always housing. Consequently, after a set-back, architects, builders and the whole building industry are exclusively occupied for some time in the housing field. Only after this pressure has been lowered and business generally has recovered its strength are, firstly, industrial and then commercial and, finally, peripheral and luxury buildings erected. It was the pattern which had followed the depression of the nineties, it was the pattern which followed the First World War and was to follow the depression of the 1930s and the Second World War.

The rush to the suburbs which had started about 1910 resumed even more strongly as the clouds of war lifted in 1919. The movement was aided by the activities of the War Service Homes Scheme which was charged with repaying society's debt to its heroes by giving them Australia's dream as quickly as possible. It was made a practical proposition by the internal combustion engine—not placed in a motor car but in a motor-bus. The war had changed petrol engines from play-things of the rich to reliable essentials of modern society. The bus had matured and been proved in the rugged conditions of Flanders and the Western Front. Now in peace-time Australia it was turned to filling the vacant country between the train lines. Not being tied to run on a fixed and expensively provided track, its flexibility made it admirably suited to form cross links of public transport between the railway stations or even to open direct routes from outlying areas to the city along already existing roadways.

The houses that grew up in the areas opened by the omnibus had undergone a change. Apart from the red roofs which they still wore, they were very different from the Queen Anne villas of the Edwardian period. In about 1911 a new style had come across the Pacific from its home in California. It was a result of the search which had been gathering strength for fifty years for a type of architecture appropriate to Australian conditions and which the more optimistic believed could be a starting point for the evolution of a true native style. The climatic and social conditions of the American Far West were closely parallel to those in Australia. It followed, then, that its houses should transplant well. They did. Of all the exotic importations to Australian architecture the Californian bungalow was by far the most successful.

The general bungalow style was introduced to normal domestic building by

11

Sydney architect Jeffreson Jackson in 1900, when he grafted some of its features in a timorous and far from successful way on to what were basically and mainly Queen Anne houses. In that year he began erection of a house for the Chief Justice of New South Wales, Sir William Portus Cullen. The house, Tregoyd, in Raglan Street, Mosman, with its octagonal pyramid topped tower, was still strongly a Queen Anne house; but with its bold gable roof, natural colouring and brooding verandah Jackson had brought the concept of the bungalow to Australia. The idea of the bungalow was taken up and found its first popular use as a cheap light summer camp or week-end house. In the first decade of the century numbers of unlined, low-pitched malthoid roofed, wide verandahed week-enders with their weatherboard walls and exposed roof framing dark-stained with oil and their window and door trims painted white, appeared on the harbourside hills of Balmoral in Sydney and Frankston in Port Phillip. In 1911 the first clearly Pasadena type of American Bungalow, as the style was first called, was completed in Toorak Road, Melbourne, for Mr Harry Martin to the design of Oakden and Ballantyne. Over the next year or two, and pushed along by architectural enthusiasm and building magazines, other scattered examples of the trans-Pacific style appeared; but for one reason or another the virile strength and directness of the American originals were tempered, hybridized and partly emasculated by modification brought about by timidity, lack of understanding or wary and reticent clients.

In 1915 a Sydney estate agent, Richard Stanton, imported a prefabricated timber bungalow from California. The project was intended to test the acceptability of both timber building and the Californian (Pasadena) style of bungalow

Redwood, an imported prefabricated
bungalow at 252 Gardener's Road,
Rosebery, New South Wales: 1916

in Sydney. It was erected as the first and exhibition house on a large new subdivision being developed as a model working class suburb in what was to become Rosebery. The experiment was not a success on the first count but the house itself was vastly important and influential because by introducing a full-blown, genuine and undiluted example of the Californian bungalow to the Australian scene, it acted as stimulus, catalyst and model. The large prefabricated wall and roof units were assembled and set on on-site brick footings and supplemented by a rough-cast brick chimney. In every way the house was typical of its kind—the large-spanning, low-pitched gable roof covered with wooden shingles; the spreading three feet six inches roof overhang at the eaves and gables which were supported on solid eight inches square projecting purlins (fake); the low spreading verandah carried on sturdy battened verandah pylons; the natural finished cedar panelling on the inside walls and the same materials used for the built-in cupboards and joinery; the dark oil-stained weatherboard exterior and the banks of white-painted casement windows—all were essential and typical parts of the style. Even the name it bore, Redwood, was aggressively in character. By 1917 the type of domestic architecture that Redwood epitomized, and was largely responsible for spreading, was being everywhere accepted and enthusiastically embraced.

The Californian bungalow stood in extreme contrast to its predecessors. Instead of the hot redness it was dark greys and browns; instead of the romantic jumble of broken roof peaks and wooden gable draperies it was one simple, unadorned, low-pitched gable over the main house with one other bold gable at right angles facing the street; instead of the open asymmetrical plan it was a compact rectangular block; instead of the wide airy peripheral verandah of turned or fretted woodwork painted red or white it had a heavy cavern-like spreading verandah with massive pillars, a solid balustrade and a low eaves line; instead of large double-hung windows sometimes reaching from floor to ceiling it had poky little casements; instead of fancy ridge tiles and even fancier apex tiles its roof was planar, plain and bare.

The plan of the Californian bungalow was different from anything that had gone before. Through all the changes of outward form that had taken place over the years the passage had always run straight as an arrow from the front door to the back. From the single-celled hut at Sydney Cove through the Colonial period, the terraces, the Gothic, the High Victorian to the Queen Anne, the direct passage had remained unviolated. Now, after starting as a square entrance hall, it shot off sideways at right angles. The plan of the outer walls of the bungalow was a squat L. The shallow projecting room was the main bedroom on one side of the entrance hall. On the other, double plate glass doors opened into a living-room running along the front of the house. The passage ran behind the living-room. On the other side of it and along the rear of the house were bedrooms, a bathroom and, finally, a kitchen and dining-room which frequently joined to the living-room with another pair of double doors. With this arrangement the house sat across the block of land instead of running down its length and its size was thereby restricted. Where it was necessary to build on an old forty feet wide block the bungalow was turned to run lengthwise down the site. In these cases the front to the street showed two gables offset to each other—one over the main house and the standard one over the projecting room and entrance.

The whole Californian bungalow style was suitable only for a small single-storeyed two- or three-bedroomed house. It broke down, both functionally and aesthetically, if it became two-storeyed or was not placed across the block. For this reason it was restricted to lower and lower-middle class areas but such areas were in the majority anyway. Even in these it forced subdividers to broaden their allotments. Whereas forty feet had been a good frontage and fifty feet an exceedingly generous one before, the Californian bungalow required fifty feet and preferably sixty feet. At the same time during the 1920s the motor car also began to

House at 11 Cranbrook
Avenue, Mosman, New
South Wales: 1918.
Architects, Esplin
and Mould

House at 20 Ormond
Grove, Toorak Gardens,
South Australia:
about 1920

House at 323 Portrush
Road, Marriotville, South
Australia: about 1920

add to the width of building allotments. To allow access to a garage sited in a back corner of the site an eight to ten feet wide driveway was needed down one side of the house. The bungalow was the first and more influential of the two but between them the bungalow and the motor car increased the normal width of a building block to sixty feet. As there was no reduction in the depth of the allotments to compensate for the additional width the two influences, taking twenty-five to fifty per cent more land for each house, accelerated the physical spread of the suburbs.

The Californian bungalow was plain, direct and close to nature. Using dark oiled timbers, rough stonework or smooth river-washed pebbles and boulders and rough-cast finishes it was a retreat and shelter from an antagonistic nature. It recognized its environment in a negative way—by excluding it. Set low and close to the ground, it was a fortress within which a man could feel secure and safe from a nature which was superior to him and which was continually trying to prove it. The parts of the building tended to extremes. The roof, a weighty mass of heavy tiles pressing down to the earth, threw an impregnable protection over the walls. The pillars of the verandah were chunky and solid tapering masses of brick or stone, widely spaced. They supported a hefty over-sized beam of solid wood which carried the low-sweeping, beetling roof. The masonry balustrade to the verandah was low and solid and made to appear even thicker and heavier by a broad capping of stone or brick. The verandah floor was set one low step above the ground and the house floor a few inches higher. The chimney was placed as a separate mass on the side of the building and was often tapered like the verandah pillars. In these buildings the outside was kept there. The windows were small— even light was not welcome inside. The interior walls were panelled to a height of six feet in timber stained brown and varnished. Being small and low-priced buildings the panelling was usually carried out in another new and cheap material— plywood, its joints covered by flat two inch wooden strips. Above the panelling the walls and the ceiling were plain plaster and painted with white calsomine. Though the interior was dark and a little gloomy it was also restful.

While the general character of the bungalow was constant the means of achieving it varied with different localities. In Sydney it was a brick building usually a dark purple-brown. The gable section of the wall was often given a bell-cast and sheeted vertically with sawn shingles stained brown. Sometimes a panel of the same form and material was placed beneath a bank of small casement windows or used to close in the verandah balustrade. The verandah pillars were usually vertical blocks of brickwork or quarry-faced sandstone and the balustrade was flat topped. In Melbourne much more use was made of rough-cast on the pillars while the walls were frequently weatherboard stained and oiled dark brown with the exposed timber trims painted dark green. In Adelaide the bungalows were built of rough local bluestone or the sawn pale buff-coloured stone materials which distinctively characterize that city at any period but which were particularly appropriate and suitable to the new style. In Queensland and Tasmania where stone and brick were in short supply the pillars were made of a closely gathered cluster of three or four timber posts and the paint colours were chocolate and green.

After the 1920s, variations began to creep in as a reaction to the extreme introversion of the early bungalows took place. Principally they affected the verandah, whose logical simplicity was lost in the process. To lighten the lowering effect of the verandah the pillars were stopped a foot or two below the eaves line and continued up as one or two timber posts. The balustrade, starting off with a short straight run, dipped in a long loop in the middle. The pillars dropped away from the verandah quickly until by the time that the 1930 depression hit they had been reduced to no more than squat stumps a mere three feet high. Another

Pibrac, Pibrac Avenue, Warrawee, New South Wales: 1890. Architect, Horbury Hunt

deviation from the simple prototype came when the single wide offset gable was elaborated as fancy dictated into a play of two or even three staggered or asymmetrically arranged gables.

The Californian bungalow was ideally suited to the lower-class servantless households for whom it was built. Because by its very nature the style required a single-storeyed compact form, it was unsuited to large upper-class houses. In these a two-storeyed home became almost a social necessity to proclaim that the owner was a man of means independent of government assistance. Their two storeys gained additional height by pulling the roof upwards into a tall peak. The roof swept steeply downwards close to the ground, often forming a series of garret rooms on the upper floor. As it came near the ground the roof was supported on a large sweeping arch over the front entrance and possibly a heavy arcaded verandah around the front and side. The walls were usually rough-cast and painted off-white, and wooden trims were stained dark brown. Although it had many features in common with the bungalow—the large roof mass and the dark woodwork, for instance—it was a style that had been derived from England and the work of C.F.A. Voysey. In the 1890s Horbury Hunt had hinted at the style when he built two timber-framed homes, Highlands and Pibrac, in the bushlands of Wahroonga north of Sydney. Hunt had used steep gabled roofs, tall chimneys gashing up through the walls which, like the roof, were entirely sheeted with timber shingles, and deep recessed verandahs supported on over-sized thick square and plain timber posts. Hunt's houses, built for moneyed merchants, set a new style for the whole of that social class—a style which came to fruition around the time of the First World War. It was essentially a romantic style that took to leadlighted windows, weathervanes and clay shingled roofs. The black and white of its outside was repeated inside with oak stained plywood panelling topped by plate shelves at doorhead height and smooth white dados and ceiling. The romanticism was expressed internally by wide, open fireplaces with firedogs instead of a cramped grate, and cosy low-ceilinged inglenooks. Despite the many similarities between it and the bungalow its constant backward glance and, in Australia, superficiality, were fundamentally at variance with its time and place. In the spacious grounds in the better-class suburbs the Picturesque style, as it is known, was highly fashionable; but in the larger picture of the national story it is without any great significance.

During the early 1920s Australian architects continued to look even more anxiously towards America for inspiration. In 1920 Hardy Wilson, a confirmed romanticist who believed architects should be artistic geniuses above and beyond all practical constrictions and responsibilities, wrote. 'In the United States of America is being born architecture which I venture to say is approaching and may surpass the flower of the Fifteenth Century.'[1]

One of the things the architects saw as they looked eastwards was the charming whitewashed terracotta-roofed mission building left in California and Mexico by the Spaniards. In 1918, Leslie Wilkinson arrived from England to take up his duties as the first Professor of Architecture in an Australian university, in Sydney. Wilkinson was a man of taste, dignity and elegance. To his discerning eyes the white, textured walls pierced by round-headed arches, arcaded loggias and their thin strip of low pitched rounded mission-tiles was a most appropriate style for a new home he built for himself at Vaucluse. Judged as decorative stylism, it was a far more appropriate manner of building than was the English-based Picturesque style. As the only Professor of Architecture in the nation, Wilkinson was in a position of awe and authority with both the practising profession and the future profession in the form of his students. When this was reinforced by a commanding personality, great fluency of speech and sound knowledge, his edicts carried tremendous weight and influence. With the successful example of his own home to demonstrate his point he advocated Spanish Mission for the better-class home of Australians. In capable hands the style produced a number of eminently compatible and pleasant houses. Because it could be equally satisfactory in one or two storeys it was more versatile then either the Bungalow or Picturesque styles which were rigidly tied to one and two floors respectively. Almost single-handedly Wilkinson was responsible for making the Spanish Mission style popular in all the eastern states of Australia.

In Western Australia at the same time the Spanish style was introduced by another, and much more deeply-grounded in the style, architect. In the East it had been, even at its best, another style. It had all the superficiality and eventually the debasement that is inherent in such an approach. In the West, however, it came from a man who had lived and worked for several years in the

Highlands, Highlands Road, Waitara, New South Wales: 1891. Architect, Horbury Hunt

Bahamas where it was the traditional and only style.

John Cyril Hawes' architecture was a highly personal and emotional one. Because he was a loner who worked in the lonely places, he did not greatly influence the overall picture in Western Australia. But, because his work was so powerful and interesting, no outline of Spanish Mission architecture would be complete without mentioning him. Hawes was English-born and had received his architectural training in the 1890s under Edmerton and Gabriel, William Lethaby (a disciple of Ruskin), and John D. Sedding, a revolutionary church architect of the times. Concurrently he had taken up carving in wood and stone at the London County Council Arts and Crafts School. This experience had bred in him a sympathy with, and a love for, hand-crafting in general and the nature of these two materials in particular. He was a man to whom life was a deep running river of pure emotion. In it he immersed himself closely and lovingly.

Between 1897 and 1908 Hawes worked on a number of Anglican churches in England. In 1909 he moved to live in the Bahamas where he erected several more Anglican churches. Attracted by the emotional beauty and ritualism of Roman Catholicism he became a convert in 1912 and was accepted into the Franciscan Order as a student priest. In 1915 he arrived in Australia as a missionary on the Western Australian goldfields. His training as an architect and his love of the wilderness were put to good use by his local bishop who, while not always sympathetic to his work, nevertheless gave him ample opportunity. Between 1915–39 Hawes designed and often erected with his own hands a number of cathedrals,

St Francis Xavier Cathedral at Geraldton, Western Australia:
1916. Architect, Cyril Hawes (Friar Jerome)

churches, convents and presbyteries at Mullewa, Geraldton and Northhampton.

Hawes' architectural style was strongly eclectic. It mixed Gothic plan forms, Romanesque columns with Spanish arcades, and gables and crosses with Byzantine domes, roofs, tiles and colouring. With materials gathered from the district Hawes, as Friar Jerome, cut and carved stone, hewed and worked wood, moulded clay across his thigh to form tapered pan-tiles, assembled them all into buildings of tremendous power and painted highly coloured murals on their walls. Where he could he got others to build for him or to learn from him. Where he could not he did it himself. Shunning rectangles and straight lines, his buildings have a rough hand-made quality to them. His aim, he said, was to follow nature not to coerce it. He denied strongly that he was following a dilettante craze for the picturesque. He was, however, self-confessedly romantic. ' I rebel against the trumpeted march of progress,' he said. 'I won't be a slave to convenience.'[2] For a man who gave up a promising career as a professional architect to find happy fulfilment working close to nature in the harsh conditions of the Western Australian countryside it was a perfectly rational remark. When he returned to the Bahamas in 1940 to live as a hermit until his death in 1956 he left Western Australia architecturally richer by the Church of St Lawrence the Martyr at Geraldton, the Churches of Our Lady of Mount Carmel and St Peter and St Paul at Mullewa, and, his masterpiece of crafting, the Cathedral of St Francis Xavier at Geraldton.

The Californian Bungalow, the Picturesque and the Spanish Mission styles which held sway in domestic architecture during the 1920s were basically no different in approach to the problem of Australian architecture than any of the other stylistic attitudes that had been adopted for the previous eighty years. They were essentially concerned with finding, in other places, a style suited to Australia. While the emphasis had changed from a style chosen purely for its visual effect to one which was functionally more appropriate, it was still a matter of style selection. In attempting to find climatic and social parallels to Australian conditions and thence extracting a ready-made solution, prime concern inevitably remained with the effect rather than the cause. Until Australian architects began to consider their own causes, their work remained shallow and of the nineteenth century.

The real spirit of the twentieth century came to Australian architecture with the domestic work of a quartet of practitioners after the First World War. Between them they encompassed all the virtues and the vices, the strengths and the weaknesses which have marked the last fifty years. The only thing they had in common was a conviction that architectural thinking had to start at a more basic level than anything that had been known for a hundred years. If any worthwhile architecture were to be produced, it must throw off its obsession with style as a starting point and concern itself with fundamental causes out of which a style would come as an effect. A building, they were agreed, should be a response to a set of human, geographical and social conditions. And the tortuous path that led from the initial causes and conditions to the final result and effect was one that each had to discover and travel alone. There were no ready-made rules, no existing sign posts, no preconceived answers on this lonely journey of discovery. When each had to write his own creed it inevitably followed that there should be as many creeds as there were messiahs. And this led inevitably to the individualism and fragmentation of architecture which has plagued it ever since.

The trail blazers went deeper and broader in their thinking than architects had gone before. They encompassed philosophy and the nature of ideas and things, psychology and the nature of people, sociology and the nature of society. In all these fields they were the rawest of amateurs and much of their thinking made the point manifestly clear. In struggling to free architecture from the suffocating embalmment of style they led it into a clogging mire of ignorance. Because the foundations on which they attempted to erect a new architecture were so shaky the result was temporary. But it lasted long enough to indicate a method to those who followed. Unfortunately the followers have had no sounder a grounding in the broad bases. Amateurism has continued. The pace of fragmentation has increased. Where the pre-World War I architectural world may have been empty and superficial, it at least had at any particular time a commonly accepted set of rules which gave the work of any period a cohesion—degenerate though it may have been in other ways. While the architectural world after World War I has seen sounder quality in a few rare cases, it has offset its gains by the equally disturbing qualities of callowness and diversity.

The group of thinking-architects responsible for ushering in the twentieth century were Hardy Wilson, Robin Dods, Harold Desbrowe-Annear and Walter Burley Griffin. They worked in different places and they worked individually, each following his own lights and his own path to redemption. They were different in temperament, different in their philosophies and approach and they produced different architecture. But between them they covered most of the ideas and attitudes that followed. Because, with the exception of Griffin, they worked almost exclusively on houses, their effect was strongest on domestic work. The same depth of thought and changes which they brought to homes did not begin to percolate into other types of building, which merely acquired from them the vices of individualism to compound their blatant stylism, for another forty years.

None of the quartet was a young and starry-eyed revolutionary when his work began to influence architecture in 1920. Each was a mature architect whose ideas had been tested and tempered for ten years or more. Theirs was not a firebrand theorizing but tried, proven and demonstrated practice. Theorizers there had been in plenty ever since the architectural slump began in the 1840s. But the

Purulia, Fox Valley Road, Wahroonga, New South Wales: 1914. Architect, Hardy Wilson

theorizing, impressive though it had seemed in its initial arguments, had been distorted to arrive not at a logical conclusion but to justify a particular architectural style of which the propounder was already enamoured.

Early in the twentieth century, Robert Haddon, himself a dyed-in-the-wool stylist, had advised his students of the Melbourne Technical College to think out their buildings 'not in plan, nor in section, nor in elevation, but as a whole, a single entity.' The idea of an integrated building needed restatement after the preceding sixty years. He also advised them to search out the nature of the materials and to ensure that these qualities were expressed in the way they were used. Wilson, Annear, Dods and Griffin went further than this. They went further than the plea for simplicity which was preached during the 1920s by Professor Wilkinson.

Hardy Wilson had been born in Sydney in 1881. His search for architectural truth, a deep love and appreciation of beauty, an interest in history and an abiding faith in the concept of the artist-architect led him to strive for the pre-Victorian virtues. But his was not mere copyism. Sensitive to the underlying qualities of Colonial architecture, he sought to apply their timeless principles to his own work. In 1912 he built, after years of thought, his own home, Purulia, at Wahroonga, a suburb to the north of Sydney. Designed for servantless living, the house was a simple rectangle in plan with plain plastered walls painted white, a low-pitched hipped roof covered in multi-coloured shingle tiles and with boxed eaves. The windows, simple rectangles with Georgian sashes and louvered shutters, were protected by striped canvas awnings. At a time when Queen Anne was riding high and in an area with pretensions to being the élite suburb of Sydney, its barrenness brought a deputation from outraged neighbours who claimed the values of their

Tamrookum Church at Beaudesert, Queensland:
about 1918. Architect, Robin Dods

properties would be undermined. Wilson could not be stopped. When it was finished he had created a home of honesty, simplicity, sincerity and integrity. Wilson claimed it was not a masterpiece. But it was his. He never produced anything better and its influence was widespread. It became a prototype for all North Shore homes and, to the next generation, the epitome of respectability.

Robin Dods was Brisbane-born. His training had been in that city and in Europe and Scotland. After a series of comings and goings between his home town and overseas he eventually settled down to practise in Brisbane in 1894 at the age of thirty-five. He built a number of offices and several churches. He was very much a conventionalist as far as current styles were concerned; but in buildings such as his Tamrookum Chapel at Beaudesert he displayed a fine sense for materials and an ability to impress even a style with individuality and strength. Just prior to the First World War he erected a number of houses in which the traditional Queensland house, perched high on its stumps and dressed in a Queen Anne style was turned, by a penetrating study of the climate and the environment, into a highly practical, positive and personal solution. Dods' houses at New Farm for himself and H. Robertson and at Clayfield for Mrs J. Reid are massive shading shelters visually firm to the ground with great hipped roofs and wide verandahs. Every part of the buildings, from the verandah post brackets to the chimneys, from the high overscaled timber balustrades flanking the entrance steps to the roof, is bold, positive and sure, designed to fit in with and control a vast landscape. Although Dods dismissed Brisbane's climate as being so mild that almost any shelter would do, he spent long hours and meticulous thought on answering its problems. By means of the bulky roof and a number of ingenious devices and arrangements for ventilating it, by means of wooden shutters around the verandah and french doors, by means of planting and screens and overhangs, he established his own distinctive personality in his buildings and made architecture aware of the aesthetic benefits to be had from a determined and original assault on the climatic peculiarities of Australia. In 1913 he moved to Sydney, where with Hardy Wilson as a supporter he was attempting, successfully, to find a peculiar answer to that city's climate, when he died in 1920. But the example he set was not lost. After the Second World War Dods was rediscovered as one of the genuine pioneers whose work a new generation of dissatisfied architects studied with respect and admiration.

Desbrowe-Annear was the first pure Functionalist. Australia has a functional tradition in building going back to the First Fleet. It was developing strongly during the Colonial period of architecture until it was abruptly pruned by the implementation of the 1837 Sydney Building Act and the coming of the fashionable architects in the forties. From that time architecture had had little practical place for functional considerations and functionalism was permitted to work only on those buildings which were well out of sight or which nobody regarded as architectural anyway. So it was only in the back lanes, the outer fringes of the towns and the country where it could continue. But unnoticed and ignored it did—to provide outstanding examples of its soundness to the eyes of a generation which was looking desperately for an answer to its troubles. In the 1920s those who looked could see splendid functional statements in the early stone bridges at Richmond in Tasmania and at Lapstone in New South Wales; and in the water mills and water wheels, the windmills and post mills. There were superb oast houses on the hop fields of Tasmania, and Fort Denison on Sydney Harbour. There were warehouses in every capital which taught the same lesson and carried the tradition from the early days up to the turn of the century. There were sheep shearing sheds in the country which did the same. Also in the country there were large simple concrete water towers standing dramatically in the landscape and highly sculptural banks of cylindrical wheat silos with their inevitable cluster

Early functional buildings — *Above* Fort Denison in Sydney
Harbour: 1855-57. Designing engineer, W. Coles *Below* Outbuildings
at Clarendon, near Evandale, Tasmania: about 1833

Country functional
buildings — *Above*
Oast house at Valley
Field, near New Norfolk,
Tasmania *Below* Nant mill
at Bothwell, Tasmania
Opposite Mill at
Mountford, near Longford,
Tasmania

Old and new functional
buildings — *Left* A windmill near
Mount Barker, South Australia
Right Typical wheat silos

of parched gum trees and railway trucks at their base to carry the tradition right to their 1920 present. And there were many others; the smoke stacks of industry, the storage tanks of petrol and gas, and the water dams of power stations—even the first concrete arches for Sydney's sewerage system at Forest Lodge. But there was precious little to be seen in architecture as it was understood and in this Desbrowe-Annear, in common with other Functionalists, saw that the troubles plaguing architecture lay. Practising in Melbourne during the latter part of the nineteenth century and the early part of the twentieth, he had paddled without distinction in the pool of stylism until he heard of the radical Functionalist doctrine. Its precepts fitted Annear's ideas like a glove. He was, by nature and conviction, opposed to taste and distrustful of all emotional theories. Being a man with a limber intelligence he had an inventive turn of mind and a belief in the supremacy of reason. To Annear every building was a bundle of new challenges to his ingenuity. He had invented a counter-balanced sliding window that disappeared into the wall cavity and dragged a fly screen after it as it went. He had designed chimneys which helped to ventilate the room with side flues and which had a stepped form as a result. He had designed and used a flush faced door with ledges fully dovetailed into the back of a series of vertical butted boards. He was a ready-made Functionalist—a native pragmatist who needed no conversion to its rationalist philosophy.

In 1918, guided by his new-found star, Annear built Broceliande for Mr R. D. Elliot in Toorak in Melbourne. It was a plain box of a building with a low-pitched wide-eaved roof and groups of windows making long slots in its unrelieved slabs of whitewashed rough-cast walls. It was an austere building whose every part, even to the position of its windows and doors, was determined by utilitarian purpose. Nothing was added, nothing was adjusted or changed because it would look better. To work better was the only criterion. The angle of a wall or the size of a balcony were determined by their functioning alone.

Having found his *metier*, Annear continued to erect houses large and small in the same manner in the suburbs and seaside resorts of Melbourne. Annear's contribution to architecture did not stop at a plain Functionalist exterior. His inventiveness had long found the standard house plan with its few variations a challenge. Using fireplaces and cupboards instead of walls to define his areas, he had introduced open planning with one area moving smoothly into another even before he erected Broceliande. When he died in 1933 at the age of sixty-seven the fluid open plan and the simple logical common sense of Annear's later houses were still twenty years away from being generally accepted.

During the years 1914–34 another highly individual architect designed a number of houses in and around Sydney. Alexander Stewart Jolly, the son of a timber merchant and furniture maker, was born at Mearsham Vale near Lismore in 1887. After two years of working and training in the furniture trade he went to Sydney about 1909 where for three years he trained as an architect in the office he set up practice doing a few houses and a block of shops in the town and a church at nearby Alstonville. By 1917 he had returned to Sydney to establish a practice concerned with houses which displayed amazing divergency of approach.

Jolly was a dreamer with a restless mind. His homes were never a mere parroting of current popular trends. He tried a radical idea in a house only to discard it at the next attempt for one almost diametrically different. He turned functional, romantic, pedestrain, rustic and sophisticated with the speed of a catherine wheel. Jolly never left Australia and while many of his designs may have been launched from ideas assimilated from abroad they were quickly changed, added to and interpreted to make them distinctively his own and wholly the work of a highly creative mind. His houses bristled with gadgets—a dining-room table

running on rails from the kitchen through a wall opening to the dining-room and a six feet high rotating cupboard between the kitchen and dining-room to enable a full meal to be prepared or cleared away from one of the rooms only were just two of many labour-saving devices he used. At the same time he could design and build largely with his own hands a rustic Hans Andersen fairy tale house in which the windows had glazing bars of intertwined twigs carefully grooved by hand to take the glass. As might be expected of such a man his work was uneven not to say erratic. He produced some horrible failures but some outstanding successes. One of the two most successful is a house in Cranbrook Avenue, Cremorne, built in 1919 when the Californian Bungalow was thriving. Jolly's version, using the usual trade mark of the style, was an eloquent sculptural statement of massive dark timbers, sheer planes of clear white rough-cast and low sheltering eaves that anticipated later domestic work by nearly half a century.

In the late 1920s Jolly abandoned architecture to engage in land speculation. His architectural work was resumed in a desultory and short-lived way in the early 1930s. When he died at Wollstonecraft in 1957, after a life of professional loneliness because of the speculative ventures in which he had twice been declared bankrupt, he left not only a highly solvent estate to his heirs but, to posterity, several houses whose advanced thought had virtually been ignored during his life but whose merit was to be rediscovered in the middle sixties.

Wilson, Dods and Annear, operating in Sydney, Brisbane and Melbourne respectively, were colleagues with a sympathy and respect for the road which each was following. They supported each other in word and deed. Walter Burley Griffin, on the other hand, was a professional outcast—the object of jealousy, spite and obstruction. Having won the competition for the design of Canberra, Griffin arrived in Australia in 1913 as consultant town planner for the nation's capital. Even before he arrived his success had aroused the animosity of those with whom he would have to work. His appointment carried the right of private practice. With his wife, the co-author of the prize-winning design, he set up a practice in association with established architectural firms in Sydney. His town planning enemies were joined by a phalanx of private practising opponents. Professional ostracism and personal intrigue ran them out of town within a year. The Griffins moved to Melbourne where for the next ten years they disseminated a type of architecture they had learnt from the giants of the Chicago School in general and Frank Lloyd Wright in particular.

Griffin's houses, breathing a previously unknown headiness, set the profession in Melbourne talking. When his atmospheric hexagons of Newman College and the crystalline ceiling of the Capitol Theatre were completed, he set the whole town talking. His many houses, churches and halls were carefully scrutinized, discussed and loved, lampooned or denigrated. By scheming, insinuation and machinations, and helped by the effects of the war, Griffin's enemies gradually wrapped his Canberra dream in a cocoon of red-tape. Finally they succeeded in bringing about a Royal Commission to discredit him. At the end of it they were successful. In 1921 Griffin severed his connection with Canberra and entered full private practice. In 1924 he returned to Sydney where for the next twelve years he engaged in the speculative designing and building of municipal incinerators around Sydney and at Ipswich in Queensland, and a hospital and houses on a subdivision he laid out

Opposite above Two houses by Harold Desbrowe-Annear —
Top House at 28 The Eyrie, Eaglemont, Victoria: 1903
Middle Broceliande (Troon), formerly in Orrong Road, Toorak, Victoria, now demolished: 1918
Opposite below House at 7 Cranbrook Avenue, Cremorne, New South Wales: 1919. Architect, Alexander Stuart Jolly

on a bushland promontory in Sydney's Middle Harbour—Castlecrag.

Griffin's architecture was fervently organic. He loved nature and the bounty she provided; he loved her lines and her everchanging moods; he loved her power and her timelessness and he loved her wisdom and her inspiration. By working with rather than against her a man could build in such a way as to give comfort to his body and satisfaction to his soul. Using natural materials, preferably those close at hand, eschewing rectilinear and embracing natural forms, he built close to nature. Even his most unlikely buildings were heavy with it. To go inside the sophisticated cinema, the Capitol Theatre, was to enter an Aladdin's Cave of wonderment. His highly functional incinerators reared high on a craggy cliff or dribbled and jutted down the rugged side of a hill as though they were sculptured from a part of the living rock. His houses, tall, roofy and timber in Melbourne, squat, solid and stony in Sydney, with their diamond-shaped cement tiled roofs which he designed and made himself, were agelessly mature and at home with their environment from the day they were finished.

Despite Griffin's command of form, his understanding of materials and his sensitivity to environment, his greatest strength did not lie in them. Even less did it lie in his interest and experimentation in constructional techniques. For, while he believed in questioning traditional methods and tried to evolve his own from first principles, his knowledge in these was not as good as the combined experience of all the human race and his constructional efforts were often lamentably unsuccessful.

It was in his handling of space that Griffin came close to greatness. To him space was a material to be moulded, worked and shaped, and one which skilfully used could evoke depths and subtleties of feeling far beyond those of bricks and mortar. His forms and shapes were no more than boundaries shaping space for him. Griffin's space was a living three-dimensional thing—sculpted and created by walls, floors and ceilings pulsating in and out, up and down. It danced, slithered, skipped and darted in, out and about the Capitol Theatre, rising to an airy climax in the ceiling. At Newman College it swept and soared or paced sedately. In his Castlecrag homes it embraced, contracted, led, expanded and enfolded.

When Griffin left Australia in 1936 to die in India the next year his work was reviled and sneered at by his lesser colleagues who were glad to have driven him out. A post-World War II generation of young architects, having lived through five years of dehumanized hell, rediscovered in his work the values and warmth for life which they had not known had ever existed. To them and to every student generation since, Griffin assumed the proportions of a deity.

These four men each brought, in his own way, the twentieth century to Australian architecture. Hardy Wilson, an awareness of the aesthetic beauty of controlled simplicity; Robin Dods, an awareness of the potential of climate and environment to mould even the most prosaic style into building of power and character; Desbrowe-Annear, an awareness of the interest, purity and beauty that lay in an unswerving and exclusive fidelity to function; and Walter Burley Griffin, the beauty of nature and an awareness of the humanity of space. All of them in one way or another, pointed out the virtues of honesty, integrity and common sense.

When, in 1923, conditions had settled sufficiently to allow non-domestic building to be resumed, it picked up exactly where it had left off in 1917. There had been

Opposite Two buildings by Walter Burley Griffin —
Above House at 21 Glenard Drive, Heidelberg, Victoria: 1923
Below Newman College at Melbourne University, Parkville, Victoria: 1918

Willoughby Municipal
Incinerator, Small Street,
Willoughby, New South
Wales: 1934. Architect,
Walter Burley Griffin

no radical style changes equivalent to the Californian Bungalow. Even less had there been any introduction of radical new thinking parallel to that brought by Wilson, Dods, Annear and Griffin to domestic work. Even the cleaned-down big-arched buildings had died in the interval. The next crop of city building was still red brick and cream plaster Edwardian with small windows in flush faces. The main change was that a new style of lettering—round, fat, thick and distorted—was used for the names and dates stuck on the buildings.

Underneath their conventional skins, however, changes were taking place. Electric lifts were introduced in 1923 when the first of them was installed in the new railway building at Spencer Street in Melbourne. The fascinating, highly decorative and intricately designed iron and brass cages which did a sprightly and exciting dance up open stair wells were replaced by panelled and glazed boxes adorned with a crystal vase of flowers. By 1930 the smoothly and swiftly moving electric lifts were being enclosed in solid walled fireproof wells in an attempt to minimize the effect of movement and 'that sinking feeling'. A ride in a lift was emasculated and dull. Also by the early twenties a framework of reinforced concrete or steel was being used as a structural skeleton before being hidden beneath brick or plaster. In 1926, architectural terracotta tiles in a variety of baked-on ceramic colours, and shaped and moulded to order, became available. They were used for the first time on the Government Savings Bank in Sydney. Both developments—the electric lift and the framed building—enabled the big buildings in the centre of the cities to bump their head regularly against the height limit ceilings.

The steel-framed building was made possible largely as a consequence of the war which had caused the local steel industry to prosper. There had been numerous attempts to establish iron production after the discovery of ore at Mittagong in 1833. Victoria, South Australia and Tasmania had each tried during the 1860s and 1870s. Temporary success came to the British and Tasmanian Iron and Charcoal Company with its works at Beaconsfield on the banks of the Tamar River. Inadequate iron resources had caused each to fail. The only successful iron production of the nineteenth century was at Lithgow where the Eskbank Ironworks Company began operations in 1876. Generally the local foundries and the rolling mills were dependent on imported pig iron for their material. Enoch Hughes, who established Australia's first rolling mill in Melbourne in 1860, had used scrap iron to produce his rolled iron rails and bars. In 1900 steel was produced for the first time in Australia in a small open hearth furnace.

The structural use of steel had developed slowly. It had been held back by technical problems of production and manufacture. Cast iron had moved from the use of columns for supporting lightweight balconies during the forties to their use as internal storey posts filled with concrete for extra strength during the eighties. As rolling techniques were developed and improved, puddled iron had been turned out as flat sheets, then corrugated sheets and finally shaped sheets. But they had little structural application. After the seventies and along with the train rails, bars and light steel sections came out of the rolling mills to be used in shop front bressummers, awnings and to support the heads of wall openings.

In Sydney in 1890 Edward E. Raht, an American architect of Austrian birth, designed a nine-storeyed office block for the Equitable Life Assurance Society of the United States on the corner of George Street and Angel Place. It was a massive pile of sandstone masonry in a grandiose American Renaissance style with a heavily rusticated face, a wide overhanging cornice and a huge semi-circular main entrance. Beneath the petrified exterior there lurked a steel frame. A large part of the total load was carried on the massive external walls and similar heavy walls which formed the main central and transive passages. But an appreciable part of the load was carried on steel columns and beams built up from smaller plates of rolled steel bolted together and reaching up eight floors. It was essentially a light load-bearing conception however as all the stability was provided by the mass of the masonry walls. In Melbourne in 1892 the same architect designed, and David Mitchell, Dame Nellie Melba's father, built for the same client a similar building on the north-west corner of Collins and Elizabeth Streets using the same mixture of steel framing supported by thick masonry walls. In the Melbourne Equitable Life Assurance Building the stone was grey granite from Harcourt with a base of red granite from Wollamai and dressed to a finer polished finish than the one in Sydney. In both buildings Raht used hollow terracotta blocks for a lightweight floor to which the floorboards were stuck with a cement grout. And he finished them with the most expensive of marble, glass, brass and cedar, all carried out at a superb standard of craftsmanship.

The first self-supporting fully steel-framed building in Australia was Nelson House erected in Clarence Street, Sydney, in 1910 at a cost of £12,758. The architect, Louis Spier Robertson, a carpenter and joiner by training, was the son of a New South Wales Government Architect. Having set up practice as an architect in Rockhampton, Queensland, in 1896, he returned to Sydney in 1904. The site Robertson was given for Nelson House was a mere twenty feet wide. On it he raised a nine-storeyed building. The cladding was brick decked out with Art Nouveau squiggles but the visibly thin side walls which did not increase in thickness as they neared the ground and the window strips running up the street facade and terminating in two large arches below the cornice line revealed that it was no brick load-bearing structure. Robertson used a framework, both joists and

The Life Assurance
Society of the United
States building in George
Street, Sydney: 1890
Architect, Edward Raht

columns, to carry the load of his building directly down to the stone foundation. There were no guide-lines to follow in the mechanics of such a system and the local building regulations dealt only with masonry load-bearing walls. Consequently, when the Sydney City Council considered the plans on 12 April 1910 it covered its ignorance and passed the buck of responsibility by endorsing them as 'approved subject to the steelwork being of sufficient strength'.

Steel became a potent factor in local building when the previously separate activities of the production of pig iron and the production of steel were combined into one operation to produce mild steel and a company financially strong enough to embark on the expensive business of mass production on a sufficiently large scale could be formed. It happened in 1915 when Broken Hill Proprietary, whose wealth had been made from the silver mines of western New South Wales, blew in its first blast furnace at Newcastle. In May the first mass-produced steel was produced. With the tide of conditions running strongly in its favour the company soon became a giant turning out high quality steel cheaply. When the war ended its product found a hungry market awaiting.

As a consequence when tall buildings—banks and insurance offices—started to grow in Sydney in the mid-1920s they were held up by strong bones of mild steel columns and beams riveted together and encased in concrete. The buildings which were built this way still appeared to be masonry and load-bearing. The frame was thoroughly enshrouded in ceramic terracotta tiles or stone and the dress was invariably a distended and stretched Classical dream topped by lift towers in the form of small Greek temples.

In 1929, as a result of the crash of the financial world in Wall Street, New York, wool and wheat prices fell and English capital was withdrawn from Australia. The Australian national income dropped by more than fifty per cent. A depression wider, deeper and darker than anything that had happened before plunged the country, with much of the rest of the world, into the blackest of nights. Unemployment skyrocketed and once again building ceased completely.

In the decade or so after the end of the war and before it was abruptly halted, architecture had seen some significant stirrings and veerings in direction. Most of the changes were related to the house. It had seen the increased spread of the suburbs and the adoption and increased acceptance of an eminently suitable style of domestic architecture in the Californian Bungalow. It had seen the first examples of the Functional and Organic philosophies. Most important of all, it had seen the planting of the seeds of future controversy, disintegration and division which came from the questioning of fundamentals and the broadening of the basis of architectural philosophy.

[1] Wilson, William Hardy: *Domestic Architecture in Australia*, Angus and Robertson, Sydney 1919, pp. 13-14.

[2] Anson, Peter F.: *The Hermit of Cat Island*, Burns & Oates Ltd, London 1958, p. 69.

12   Between 1921 and 1929 every state except Queensland had passed Acts of Parliament requiring architects to be registered and to meet specified minimum standards before being able to be so. The banner of registration had been flown by certain members of the profession as early as the 1890s. The objective was twofold: to stop the activities of certain disreputable charlatans whose practices often besmirched the profession as a whole and, on the other side of the same coin, to raise the social status and exclusiveness of respectable practitioners. Architects had barely had time to taste the delights of legalized professionalism when the great depression threw them down from their pedestals.

By 1933, along with a third of the rest of the bread-winners of the community, many of the architects had joined the ranks of the 'sussos', barrowing earth to make the Yarra Boulevard, hawking small cases of soap, ties and bootlaces from door to suburban door or standing in line for a handout of a bowl of soup at the Salvation Army kitchens. To keep their professional egos bolstered they formed, in August 1930, again after many years of discussion, a national federation called the Royal Australian Institute of Architects. To keep their architectural souls nourished they met to discuss, talk and argue.

And how they talked! Not for them the petty quibbles that had seemed important to their predecessors—the 'rightness' or otherwise of an entablature or the 'correctness' of placing a storey of the Corinthian Order on top of a Doric ground floor without an Ionic Order between. They looked at the big questions, the fundamental questions. They philosophized on Man, on Truth and on Reality, all spelled with capitals. They tore the various theories which had been introduced fifteen years before into little bits, inspected them this way and that. They rejected, accepted and reassembled. They tested the variants of the same theories which were seeping through via returning colleagues and the architectural magazines. Many of the older men could not understand what all the dust and heat was about. Only some could grasp the essentials of the controversies and fewer still could contribute and lead them forward. But all could enjoy the fun and, at a time when the arguments were as close as most of them were getting to real architecture, it was exhilarating and heady stuff. For five years or more they talked. At the end of it, hardly having lifted a T-square or moved a pencil, they had changed the face of Australian architecture. To the many who had not understood, the new architecture was just another and novel style—a cosmetic like any other. To the some who could follow the essentials, it was the opening of a new window on architecture. To the few who really understood, it was a transcendental way of life that offered hope for all the ills which had racked architecture for nigh on a hundred years.

Some of the thinking-architects reserved their own special interpretations and formed their own sound bases, and built their houses and flats accordingly. But the general ideology that gained acceptance, at first in the profession and then by the public, was a compound of bits and pieces from the main contending schools in Europe and America. It was partly Dudok, partly Wright and partly Le Corbusier. It was constructivist, organic and mechanical, all at the same time. Because its adherents so little understood in any depth the tenets of what were mutually exclusive philosophies, it succeeded only in being crassly superficial—more so than any other style had ever been. It was quick and it was slick. It was also new. To show just how new, it was proudly but naively labelled 'Modern'.

The new type of architecture which crept onto the scene from 1934 when building slowly revived was a world away from that which was being built in 1929. It was by no means a simple architecture of the type that had been advocated in the twenties. To be sure it was plain and made up of simple individual elements. But the plainness and the simple elements were put together in an austerely cerebral way. It was a highly directional architecture full of violent and positive movement, assertive forms and spectacular gymnastics. It was mechanical, hard and austere but extraordinarily confident. Applied decoration was shunned. The complication of the combination of the individual parts was considered to be purely decorative in itself. Heavy banks of brickwork were supported, apparently invisibly, on large areas of glass. It was overpoweringly horizontal with windows tied together in long stretches, their heads and sills emphasized into a sort of string course and vertical mullions reduced to nothing. Corners were rounded to strengthen the horizontality by eliminating the vertical line which marked the change of direction of a wall. Roofs were flat or appeared to be so as they sank below unbroken parapets with their horizontal line of capping. Amidst all the horizontality one strong contrast was introduced. It may have been a projecting stairwell, a series of bulls-eye windows, a chimney or a plaster fin which gushed upwards from the parapet, dribbled down the face of the building only to be sucked inside again somewhere above the ground. Metal-framed windows made the window openings appear as blank gashes in the walls. The colours were light. Bricks were buff or pale cream in Sydney, salmon or cream in Melbourne and cream or painted plaster in the other cities. Horizontal lines were picked out in cream or green.

It was a glib formula which could be applied to any situation. The streamlined look appeared on bus shelters and office blocks, on factories and cinemas, breweries and churches, hotels and houses. On each of them horizontal lines raced around corners, waterfalls gushed down walls as chimneys on houses and blades of undulating plaster on hotels, bands of bricks alternated with glass strips in a stack of solids and voids on an insurance office. A facile architecture to be sure.

An exception to the general run of debasement was to be found in the hospitals. Huge cathedrals of the twentieth century religion, science, they were forced by eagle-eyed governments to justify every penny of their cost. There was little money available to chase commercial gimmickry. While they had to be of excellent quality they were, at the same time, forced to be pared down to essentials. The results were bold, clear statements of all that was best in the theories of the time. The sheer brick walls of a tall, clean-cut service tower provided a most satisfactory vertical foil to strongly horizontal slabs of wards which were again a stack of alternating solid and void. Long uninterrupted balconies provided sitting-out areas for patients and, at the same time, acted as sunshades for the glass walls of the rooms. The brickwork was cream or salmon and the balconies were white. The service block, the wards and the balconies were clean-cut with the precision of a machine. Held back from the temptation to titivate, they were, aesthetically, exercises in massing and, because the principles were sound, they were highly successful.

Side by side with the horizontal Modern which permeated and affected every type of building there grew a rather esoteric vertical Modern. The underlying philosophies were the same in both cases but the latter emphasized the vertical

The Myer Emporium in
Bourke Street, Melbourne:
1937. Architect, Harry
Tompkins

lines of a building. Tall, narrow windows and between-floor spandrels were recessed between closely spaced columns which were projected forward in a series of uninterrupted vertical angular fins. The annihilation of the wall and window and the protrusion of the columns were reinforced at the skyline where the columns shot up past the parapet as double-chamfered jagged pinnacles. By reason of its starting point the vertical approach was suitable only for tall buildings. Hence it was restricted to city buildings. Statutory height limits precluded the essential and basic form from being built. Deprived of this fundamental start the idiom sat uneasily on the stunted, basically contrary buildings such as the Myer Emporium in Melbourne.

While a number of houses used the whole box of horizontal Modern tricks most of them baulked at flat roofs. The terracotta tile had proved itself such an outstanding functional covering, and flat roofs were so notoriously prone to trouble, that all but the most adventurous or determinedly up-to-date preferred to stay with the tried and true. The normal house therefore still had a tiled roof. It was usually hipped and always its eaves were boxed. Where the roof was gabled the boxed eaves caused many headaches where they came to the end wall. Sometimes the wall was corbelled out in a series of short steps to form a screening wing in which case the roof tiles finished flush with the wall. Sometimes the gutter was returned around the end to do the same job. In Sydney the gable itself was constructed in timber and also boxed out from the wall to enable the flat soffit of eaves to run continuously around the house. The gable was sheeted with fibrous cement or weatherboards and painted white to contrast with the bricks. The effect was cumbrously heavy and ugly but it became a unique trade-mark of Sydney domestic architecture from the late thirties until the present time. The roof tiles themselves were being produced in colours other than the old even orange-red. By salting and burning, variations of mottled browns, creams and reds were produced. Mottled roofs were the height of fashion.

The plan of the house became an elongated L with one bold gable thrust out at the street. The verandah shrank to a tight little portico in the re-entrant angle of the L where the front entrance door crouched. The portico had a flat slab of concrete for its roof which was supported on a precast concrete column and a solid fence of brick around its hand-ground terrazzo floor. Metal windows tore gashes out of the brickwork at the corners of the protruding wing. The upper brickwork appeared to hover in space. With its heavy gable above, it was a disturbing phenomenon.

Inside the houses were lined, ceilings and walls, with fibrous plaster flat smooth and flush. The sitting-room had a broad fanciful cornice of dentils or egg and dart moulding but the other rooms had a simple two inch scotia moulding around the top. A timber picture-rail at doorhead height hid the joint where the thicker dado sheet met the thinner sheet of the ceiling and drop. The ceiling and drop were calsomined cream, while below the picture-rail the walls were a pale pastel green or pink. The doors, flush faced with plywood, were, like the plain narrow skirtings and the architraves, yellow varnished. The rooms were furnished with fat overstuffed chairs, floral carpets in autumn colours and festooned satin curtains. The furniture was plywood with rounded corners in the usual waterfall idiom and varnished dark brown. In the kitchen a bank of built-in cupboards had rebated doors and butterfly hinges, the kitchen sink was stainless steel and the colour scheme, including the linoleum, was cream and green.

In many of its underlying ideas Modern architecture had much to commend it—at least as a starting point for the construction of a new type of architecture. In its insistence on a functional justification for anything it did, in its simplification of lines, planes, masses and voids and its rejection of applied decoration, in the value it placed on the decorative quality of a functional form for its own sake and in its attempt to capture the machine- and speed-dominated character of the times, and in its visual aesthetic which emphasized the harmony and repose of emphatic horizontality opposed by a minor but abrupt vertical contrast, it incorporated much of the ideas of Wilson, Annear, Griffin and the overseas schools. It learnt little from Dods. In the hands of those who understood, reasonably good work was produced. In its popular form, called Moderne by the magazines and the real estate agents, however, one of the essential qualities for success—honesty—was lost. On the one hand, parapets, used to force a cut off or flat-roofed look, or vertical fins, arbitrarily stuck on without justification, produced buildings as spiritually stultified as any had ever been. On the other hand, there were rabid disciples of one particular outlook whose fervour was not matched by understanding. With them sound tenets were misinterpreted or even inverted. There was the classic case of the large building on a city corner of Melbourne where one wall was an unplanned tangle of plumbing and sewerage pipes. Because it worked as a system it had to be beautiful, reasoned its Functionalist architect, who promptly had each pipe painted a colour in violent contrast to the brickwork backdrop.

At least the Modern style was the result of attempts to grapple with basic principles. Although the Moderne results were often contorted or debased it had much that was sound. But, side by side with it, there was a style which was unsurpassed for superficiality. This Jazz style was the result of the cinema and

pure mindlessness. It was essentially an interior style whose initial samples were displayed in the celluloid fantasies that came from Hollywood. Films produced to take their audience out of the drab world of a depression, with its cold sausages and potatoes, frayed trouser cuffs and a drawer full of unpaid accounts, showed a sophisticated glittering sugary world of make-believe where everything was carefree, brittly gay and where everybody always wore evening clothes as to the manner born. The shadow world on the screen had its own equally unreal settings. Because the stories were invariably set in night clubs and sumptuous penthouses the designs produced were essentially interior. The same glamorous character was repeated in the cinemas in which the films were shown. Again, it was entirely an interior style to be seen by people inside the building. For these reasons, the Jazz Style which was the effect of the films of the thirties was also interior in character and wholly applied. Its marks were shiny black vitreous glass, chrome-plated bars and cast plaster grilles in hard geometric patterns of circles, slashed by diagonals of sunbursts and lightning zig-zags. Generally it stayed inside, in mirrors, light fittings and on walls. But it also moved outside to pattern chimneys and front doors of houses. The intricate plaster grille work, needed in the cinemas to hide the large ventilating openings, moved as pure decoration to the facades of city buildings. And, finally, it affected shop fronts. Below the awnings which, with the abundance of steel and the passage of time, were now universally cantilevered, black vitreous glass replaced the tiles—red, brown and yellow in the

Far left The Bank of New South Wales in George Street, Sydney: 1932. Architects, Robertson & Marks

Centre The E.S. & A. Bank in Collins Street, Melbourne: 1939-41. Architects, Stephenson and Turner

Near left The Bank of New South Wales in King William Street, Adelaide: 1940. Architects, Claridge, Hassell & McConnell with Louis Laybourne-Smith

The Hotel Clare in Broadway, Sydney: 1941. Architect, S. Warden

teens and cream and green in the twenties—which had been the fashion before. As the interior ground floor spaces of old buildings were rejuvenated as smart shops, they brought people face to face with an anaemic materialization of the celluloid dreams they saw on the cinema screens.

The Modern and the Jazz idioms were popular fare. The great bulk of the architectural profession was more than willing to pander to a taste that would allow them at least to earn a living. The distasteful architectural drought was too vividly close and existence still too precarious to take high-minded talk about fundamentals too seriously.

But there were some who carried the torch of honesty and sincerity during the thirties. Most of them were young Turks and most of them were idealists convinced of the rightness of directness and the importance of climate and the environment. They built houses with open pergolas and verandahs on which the only decoration was the dappled play of tree shadows on cool cream painted brickwork. Low pitched or flat roofs projected protectingly several feet beyond bagged walls to cast shade during the hot part of the day. Generally they were cantilevered, but where they sailed out without a break to form a verandah, they were supported on square posts painted white. One and all they were sensible and logical. For the first time they gave greater weight to aspect and prospect than to public effect. They did not face the street but a view or an orientation. The roofs projected where they needed to, to give sun protection. Where the sun was no problem they stayed close to the walls. They rediscovered that the Australian climate is conducive to outdoor living and built cantilevered balconies or paved terraces covered by shadow-casting pergolas or verandahs outside the living room. They almost dissolved the wall between the two by means of a transparent net consisting of a series of glazed doors placed next to each other.

House in Killeaton Street, St Ives, New South Wales: about 1950. Architect, Sydney Ancher

House in Maytone Avenue. Killara, New South Wales: 1945. Architect, Sydney Ancher

The linking of the outside with the inside was part of the overall approach to the controlling of space. Internal doors between dining room, living room and entrance became broad openings across which folding glass doors could be drawn if needed but which visually linked each area with the next. While each area was confined and contained, it was no longer a self-contained or isolated box but part of a larger pattern in which the parts were related to and dependent upon each other. The walls were flush finished and mouldings were reduced to a minimum. Architraves, skirtings and cornices were trimmed down to fine lines.

These buildings were designed by people like Gerard McDonell, Sydney Ancher and Walter Bunning in Sydney and by Roy Grounds and Geoffrey Mewton in Melbourne. They gave paramount consideration to the convenience and pleasure of the occupants, they were a conscious relationship of areas, they rediscovered the colonial virtues of sunlight and shadow, they strove to fit their environment and to do it all with directness and logical simplicity. They were a small but vitally important spark in Australian architecture before World War II. These aspects were all concepts which had not been there before and it was to be left to a post-war world to realize how important they were and make them widely used.

The bombs that rained down when Hitler's war began blasted not only the cities of Europe. They also, more mercifully, shattered the slightly crazy fads which made up most of Australian architecture at the time. This phase had only started after 1934. It was just beginning to get a grip by 1939. For a couple more years it continued, gradually losing thrust as the effects of war seeped over the community. In 1941, after Pearl Harbour, the war suddenly became real. All the resources of architecture and building were turned to rushing up army camps. The somewhat zany popular architecture of the thirties was snuffed out.

13

It was a transformed world that, in 1945, stepped out of the dust and debris of a war that had engulfed it for six years. It was a world which, having seen accepted standards and old values vaporized in a ball of fire over Hiroshima, looked to the future with as much fear as hope. In the new world everything was altered— politically, economically, technologically, morally and spiritually.

In Australia the peace was to bring important changes to the established order. After years of enforced saving, businesses and individuals had money to spend but there was little to buy. As people clamoured to get necessities which had been denied them, costs rose. Both labour and material were insufficient to meet the demand. The cost of both leapt up and wages followed. In 1948, a forty-hour working week became statutory. It brought not more leisure but more overtime, fatter pay packets and higher prices. In a seller's market inflation shook its menacing head. After 1949, several years of record wool prices enabled the country to enjoy an insecure prosperity and increased the speed of the inflationary merry-go-round. Not until 1953, when wool prices dropped slightly and a mild recession put a brake on things, did Australia settle down to earning its prosperity soberly and with industry. True prosperity flooded over Australia and affected everybody and everything.

Before the war only the well-to-do owned a motor car. Now, on the average, every family had one. People who had never been away from their home town drove to work each day and toured over their country in the weekends and vacations. Overseas travel, once the preserve of the rich and old, became commonplace for the young as well. Jet air travel shrank the world to a couple of days circumference. Television obliterated national boundaries. Australia was no longer an isolated paradise. She was unavoidably involved in the whole human family and affected by its conditions, progress and thoughts.

As the exhausted British Empire deflated, Australia became more closely tied to the United States of America. Not only from political expediency and for ethnical reasons but financially. American finance poured into Australia to establish huge industries and by doing so provided further power for expansion and prosperity. The consequence was a hastening of the Americanization of Australian tastes and ideals.

Australian insularity was broken down further by the policy of all the post-war Federal governments of encouraging and assisting migration. Between 1947 and 1965 an average of over 87,000 arrived each year to make Australia their new home. In the peak years of 1949 and 1950 over 150,000 migrants landed annually. Two-thirds of them came from the United Kingdom. The rest came principally from Europe, particularly from around the Mediterranean. To a certain degree this diluted the uniform Anglo-Saxon culture that had existed hitherto, resulted in new living habits, new tastes in food, clothes, and motor cars and helped to rejuvenate some of the derelict near-city terrace areas.

A somewhat less but still significant post-war influence on broadening Australian cultural horizons was the influx of overseas students. Coming from Malaya, Singapore, Thailand, India, Ceylon, Indonesia, Hong Kong, Japan, Taiwan and even (a few) from Africa, they adapted themselves largely to Australian customs. But, inevitably, there was a certain amount of cross fertilization. Many Australians, to whom Asia had been a vague over-populated amorphous area 'up north', became aware of the history- and culture-rich civilizations who were their next door neighbours. From Chinese food to Japanese houses they were seen to have lessons worth learning.

For these reasons, then, the Australia which developed after 1946 was less British and more American, less insular and more international, less gauche and a little more sophisticated than it had been. The high wall of parochial self-satisfaction and myopic delusions which had been built over a century and a half was breached. Gradually it began to crumble and a little healthy light and air seeped in.

As usual, when the clouds lifted, the most urgent need was housing. The war had swallowed up the few building materials that were produced as soon as they became available. There was no stockpile of materials ready to be released to a hungry civilian market. Only gradually, as demobilized soldiers returned to the factories, the brickyards and the bush, did even basic materials become available to the public. The shortage of framing timber, weatherboards, bricks, tiles, glass, fibrous plaster, piping, roof guttering and fittings remained chronic for five years. And what was available, being rushed out, was usually shoddy. Bricks were badly burnt, moved roughly about they were chipped and broken, and available only in the one standard size. Special shapes or face bricks were unavailable. Scantling timber was so green that the sap clogged and jammed carpenters' saws. Frames erected with it warped and pulled apart almost before the eyes. Joinery timber had been so poorly seasoned that it twisted and moved long after it was painted to leave gaps and reveal unpainted strips. Flooring, which had been firmly cramped, shrank to leave wide gaps between the boards. Fibrous plaster came from the works so green that it could not be painted for weeks and when it was it showed insidious dark oily stains from the copra being used expediently as fibre. Even some of the paint, instead of using linseed oil, was made with cheap fish oil which caused it to contract into a crocodile pattern within a couple of months.

Tradesmanship was not much better. With so much work to do and high wages being offered on all sides, employed tradesmen were assured of a fat living for a minimum return of quality and quantity. If the contractor objected to either there were plenty of others ready to snap up their services. A bricklayer who before the war laid at least 900 bricks a day now felt he had done a day's work when he had laid 500 or even less. Individual or small groups of tradesmen took to sub-contracting for the work of their trade. They worked quickly but not cheaply. With their own time being money they did the work quickly and roughly. Working seven days a week they made three or four times their award trade wage.

With the rise in costs generally, the gratuities and considerations that had to be paid to obtain materials, the reduced output for a fixed wage and the reasonable work output for a high wage, building costs sky-rocketed. An average brick veneer house of 1,200 square feet had cost £1,000 in 1940. In 1946 the same house cost £1,500, by 1950 it cost £4,500 and by 1955 the cost had reached £6,000. Over the same period general living costs had risen only half as much.

The problem of ever-increasing costs had a number of results. In a piecemeal attack on the trouble, there was much talk about, and a couple of abortive attempts at, prefabrication; new and cheaper materials were produced; new techniques were developed; houses were pared down to essentials in an attempt to wring as much house as possible out of the money available. Many people turned to building all or part of their houses with their own hands.

The talk about factory prefabrication hung on the sensibleness of using facilities built in wartime to produce aircraft and equipment for the fighting services to turn out three or four standard models of mass-produced houses. Logically they would be better finished and cheaper because of their method of production. The Hawker-Siddeley Group of aircraft manufacturers in England did produce three or four standard house-types of pressed aluminium framing walls and roofing. A number were imported but after the cost of transport and duties were added they were not any cheaper than houses produced in other ways and, being metal and not insulated, were infernally hot. The wartime Labor government in Canberra made plans to turn its aircraft production factory to making a cheap 'Beaufort' house. A private company, the Commonwealth Aircraft Corporation, decided to do the same with its 'Myer' house. Both schemes were dependent on government support and goodwill. When an anti-socialist Liberal government was elected to office in 1948 it was bound to discourage government interference in what was considered a legitimate area for private enterprise. It killed both schemes dead. As overseas prefabricated houses, designed without due awareness of Australian conditions and economic factors, were unsuitable and there were no other industries in Australia large enough or equipped properly to undertake large-scale factory production of houses the idea of prefabrication came to nothing more than a few odd prototypes.

Secondary industries had been given a boost by World War I. The period between 1939–1945 stimulated the swing even more and turned Australia from a mainly primary producing country to a secondary producing one. After the Second World War Australia was classed as an industrialized nation. From industry there came a number of new materials to feed a building industry famished for materials. The new products were not, in the main, aimed at finding really new materials but rather satisfactory substitutes for old ones which were in scarce supply.

A number of different types of building-boards made from sawdust, waste timber or sugar cane were produced in Queensland and Tasmania to fill the gap caused by a shortage of plywood and fibrous plaster. Some of them were thin and hard, others were thick and soft. Their physical properties, particularly their reactions to temperature and humidity changes, were very different from the almost inert fibrous plaster and plywood and led to some unhappy results before partially satisfactory techniques for using them were developed. Some of them were produced with patterns simulating the finish of other traditional materials such as tiles, timber and fabrics. They could be purchased already painted and needing only to be fixed in position for a finished job. But none of them had all the good qualities of fibrous plaster. This material, however, was suffering from a shortage of suitable fibre. A plaster board made of an unreinforced half-inch core of plaster of Paris sheeted and strengthened each side with thick paper came on the market in an endeavour to meet the demand for plaster lining.

To cover their cheap materials and rough workmanship the post-war houses made fortunes for the paint and putty manufacturers who, nothing loth, stimulated the trend to paint for all they were worth. They flooded the magazines and newspapers with articles and advice on new daring colour schemes. They established advisory centres to hand out bundles of paint colour cards to young couples on the last lap of making their new home and to old couples refurbishing a home which had been denied any maintenance during the war years. They experimented in their laboratories and produced a rapid succession of new types of paint, each claimed to be a miracle of the chemists' skill and a heaven-sent foolproof gift to bungling amateur painters. Because paint was both cheap and needed, and egged on by high-powered publicity, the buildings of the ten years after the war were strident rainbows of solid, garish colour.

Terracotta roof tiles and bricks were in particularly short supply for many years. Substitutes were found in cement products of similar shape. Cement roof tiles, using a simplified Marseilles pattern, were produced with a wide variety of coloured finishes. Because of their casting process of manufacture, they were much more accurate and regular in size than burnt terracotta tiles. For this reason, they fitted more closely and as a result were more water-tight. At first they were used in the same way as terracotta tiles but, when it was found that they were more waterproof, they were fixed to roofs of a lower and lower pitch. When low-pitched roofs came into architectural favour, cement tiles were found to have an advantage which made a serious dent in the supremacy of terracotta tiles. By the 1960s, this advantage together with the introduction of unfadeable colours had made such inroads into the market previously enjoyed by terracotta tiles that the manufacturers of the latter were forced to subsidize considerable research into their products and undertake wide publicity campaigns to extol their virtues— neither of which they would once have dreamed necessary.

Like the tiles, the silicon-cement bricks were predictably accurate. Their low cost and colour range made them popular with home owners. The same quality of regularity of size made them unpopular with bricklayers who were forced to build accurately with them. Poor workmanship with the cement bricks was obvious to even a most undiscerning eye. Bricklayers much preferred to have the leeway given by uneven irregular clay bricks. Before the war, bricks were laid regularly to give thirteen and one-half inches for each four courses. The size of the post-war bricks was so uneven that even a conscientious bricklayer worked to thirteen and three-quarter inches for four courses and most of them even more. In these circumstances, architects could not work to predetermined dimensions but had to wait and see the dimensions the bricklayers could achieve with the bricks on the job before finalizing their drawings. Bricklayers made all sorts of excuses to avoid using silicon-cement bricks. The sharp arrises ripped their hands, the bricks dried out their mortar and turned it to dust before it set properly and the materials of the bricks dried and cracked their hands causing discomfort, pain or even sores. For one reason or another, the bricklayers found they had to increase their rates for laying so that the cost of a silicon brick wall eventually was more than a clay brick one. On top of this, it was found that the uniformity of the bricks without any of the enlivening variations of colour or texture made the walls look dead and lifeless. Eventually architects and even clients turned against them. It was not until they were evolved into large concrete blocks in the middle 1950s that they gained any real, but limited, popularity.

The practice of self-help which had a heyday for the decade after the end of the war had a number of variations. It was aided by the introduction of a number of factory-made items which could be installed by any handyman. Glazed louvered windows, for instance, required no more than a drill and a screw-driver to fix their pressed metal frames into position. The frames came in four separate pieces and with the pre-cut glass blades they could be bought from practically any suburban hardware store. They were cheap and so easily fitted that they spread like a rash over the suburbs as verandahs were enclosed to make additional living space in houses where newly-married couples moved in to live with their in-laws, where young families grew in size or owners on fixed incomes divided their houses into flats to make additional money to cope with the rising cost of living. As a flood of servicemen returned to civilian life and married, the number of families needing a home increased much beyond the rate of new buildings. Temporarily they were fitted into existing houses. Additions and alterations were necessary and more often than not they were done by amateurs.

The amateurs did not restrict themselves to extensions. Some of them lived for two or three years in a garage on their block of land while they gave every possible minute before work, after work and at weekends to building the whole of their home themselves. Even the plumbing and sewerage and the electrical wiring which, by statute, had to be carried out by qualified and licensed tradesmen they did themselves and illegally paid a fee to a tradesman to have him shoulder the responsibility. Others had part of the house built by firms specializing in partial erection—to any stage from the frame to everything but the painting— before moving in and completing the job themselves.

One other factor which had an important effect on the privately built houses of the first six or seven years after the end of the war grew out of the interaction of two different sets of regulations. Various lending institutions placed a ceiling on the amount they would lend. Private sources, such as insurance companies and some banks, generally worked to sixty per cent of their valuation of the land and building or twice the annual income of the borrower whichever was the less. Government authorities, such as the Federal War Service Homes Division, lent up to eighty-five per cent of the value of both the land and building or £1,250, again whichever was less. In 1950, the Federal War Service Homes Division raised its ceiling to ninety-five per cent or £1,500. Being essentially related to the cost of living these ceilings were considerably below the cost of building which was rising at double the rate of normal living costs. In addition, lending institutions tended to be conservative and to value properties considerably below their market value. All of which meant that, in practice, the amount which could be borrowed was fifty per cent or less of the actual cost. As a result, there was a strong tendency to reduce the size of houses as financial conditions forced them to become smaller and smaller. By 1950, conditions were adjusted to take account of the realities of the situation but costs were rising so fast that the changes did little more than maintain the position. Groups of prospective building owners tried to find an influential voice in their own welfare and obtain more realistic financial conditions by forming co-operative building societies which would lend up to ninety per cent. However, like all lending groups, they were careful to protect themselves from a collapse in costs by considerably undervaluing properties and, in addition, the sums available for lending in such schemes were inevitably limited.

Working counter to these financial effects were the local councils which all had regulations which laid down the least amount of accommodation they would approve, the minimum sizes of rooms and usually a minimum overall area requirement. The latter varied from about 400 square feet at a seaside resort to 1,600 square feet in a high-class residential suburb. In the sort of working-class to middle-class area where most of the new houses were being built the minimum area was usually around 1,200 square feet.

Squeezed in a vice of two opposing forces—financial conditions causing houses to shrink and local governments preventing them going below 1,200 square feet— the vast majority of houses built between 1946–1950 was a standard twelve to thirteen squares. In areas which had higher minimum limits councils were forced to accept the situation. They did so reluctantly and guarded their standards by permitting the erection of smaller houses under the proviso that they would be increased to their stipulated minimum when conditions improved.

Other changes in the post-war society tended to bring about an even greater levelling of conditions and imposed a strait-jacket of similarity upon housing of all classes. The years of shortages and the industries which sprang up to meet the demands for all types of goods created a severe labour shortage. Women were wooed by soft-spoken managements and enticed by regular hours, attractive conditions and high wages to sit all day at a factory bench. In the 1930s when people were grateful to hold any kind of a job a country girl was prepared to put up with a shrewish mistress, unreasonable demands, a fourteen-hour working day with only a half-day a week to herself, and do any work from making beds to gardening, from cooking to washing babies or laundry for her bed and board and fifteen shillings a week. All upper-class and most middle-class homes had domestics. Those which did not at least had a laundress and a charwoman to do the heaviest of the housework for two shillings and sixpence a half-day. Only the working-class housewife had to do all her own work. After 1946, domestics were a vanished race. The few families which were able to offer wages, hours and conditions comparable to those of the factories could not obliterate the stigma of servitude. Nothing would entice women to be domestics and the wife of even the most affluent family had to look after the house by herself. The result was that for the first time houses were planned with great care and thought for their working convenience.

The actual working of the house, what was used how, when and where, what was done and the effort involved by each member of the family, but particularly the housewife, became of prime consideration. Scientific ergonomic studies were made and the esoteric results published in architectural journals or, translated into everyday English, in magazines and newspapers. Architects or people designing their own houses with the aid of the scores of popular home magazines which sprang up to help them, ideas culled from their friends' homes, the builder and a sheet of graph paper thought either logically or intuitively about this major problem of efficiency even before they thought of comfort and the impression that would be made on neighbours.

During the process, the kitchen, which had started in Colonial days as a detached outcast and had gradually crept closer until it became attached to and then incorporated into the main house, became the very heart of the house. It was the centre in which the housewife spent more of her daylight hours than any other and which, consequently, warranted the best prospect and a cool aspect. Ideally, it needed to allow her to do the cooking or dish washing and, at the same time, to watch the children playing and be convenient to both the main door for visitors and the secondary entrance for tradesmen. It was planned with meticulous thought for working in. From the entry and storage of food, through their preparation, cooking and serving to the disposal of rubbish, it was considered as a miniature factory to achieve a logical sequence of movement. It was ranged with walls of cupboards below working benches and at head-height, with a refrigerator, a pressed stainless steel sink and a gas or electric stove. Every article had its special place—brooms, cutlery, crockery, large cereal packets, bottles, tins and jars of factory-produced foodstuffs had their own niches. There were cool-cupboards ventilated from floor to roof space, ventilated vegetable bins and air-sealed bread boxes. The surfaces, the cupboard doors, the benches, the walls and the floors were smooth and flush and easy to keep clean. Re-entrant angles between the bench tops and between the floor and walls or cupboards were coved for the same reason. Bench tops were covered with linoleum or plastic laminate while glazed tiles or wall board marked to look like them formed a wall backing to the benches, the sink and the window sill. The conservatives stayed with green and cream as a colour scheme but the most popular colour combination became bright daffodil yellow and pale grey. By the 1950s this, in turn, became the mark of the conservative as charcoal grey and flame pink splashed into the kitchens of the *avant garde*.

In their most developed form some of these kitchens were masterpieces of comfort and functional designing. In an area ten feet by eight feet, the minimum size allowed by law, it was often possible for a housewife to work without ever having to move her feet more than a couple of steps. For all their logical efficiency, however, they were often highly unsatisfactory. Factors which are not easily foreseen became manifest shortcomings in practice. Perhaps it may have been that when the kitchen was being so carefully thought out there were no children around or their idiosyncrasies may have been overlooked. Certainly it was not appreciated that young children demand, rather capriciously, to be physically near their mothers. It soon became clear that a child playing with a pot lid on the kitchen floor was a hazard to life and limb of both mother and child. In addition, the unforeseen intrusion of a child completely wrecked the carefully organized system of work and the kitchen became extremely awkward to work in. Other unpredictable minor human frailities became huge spanners in the works as well. Few people are as methodical in their actions or in keeping articles in their right-and-only place as these kitchens required. With no spare space ('waste space' it was thought when it was being designed), they were inflexible creations which demanded constant thought and awareness to keep operating properly. This itself created mental stresses and frayed tempers. Their tightness often led to feelings of claustrophobia and the psychological consequences of spending long hours without talking to anybody in an area which did not force one to move out and about were considerable. The highly functional kitchen was found not to be so at all in the larger picture. It was both inefficient and unpleasant. By the early 1950s they were expanding, becoming looser in their arrangements and more workable.

For ease of working the kitchen was connected to the dining area with a wide servery. Sometimes, especially in homes where dinner-parties were given, the division between the two became a broad serving bench so that the hostess could take part in the pre-dinner conversations while continuing to prepare the meal. However, it was a short-lived and not widely popular innovation. While the pre-dinner smells may have been tantalizing, the same ones after dinner were nauseating and the sight of used plates, pots and dishes was embarrassing and depressing. By the 1960s the kitchen and the dining area had become physically separated again by a wall with a servery and door.

Under the twin effects of economics and functionalism the fireplace was eliminated or reduced to a blank gaping hole in a bare wall. Without its mantel piece and surrounds it was no longer the strong focal point which it had traditionally been. To fill the vacuum cheaply and easily, and at the urging of the paint manufacturers, the practice developed of painting one wall of the living-room a different and usually strongly contrasting colour, and adorning it with a special picture, a beaten copper plaque, a Chinese silk print or a small tapestry. It was called the 'feature wall' in the jargon of the time. By the 1960s the 'feature wall' had spread to all types of houses and became lush and extravagant. It was built of stone or covered with expensive Japanese or French wall papers or a tile mural.

The houses of the first five years after the war ended were minimal houses in all ways. Ceilings were reduced to the lowest allowed by regulation and strong pressure developed to have the normal requirement of nine feet reduced to eight feet. In searching for ways to reduce unnecessary expense, building regulations were subjected to close scrutiny. Under the microscope, many of them were found to be ambiguous or capable of being manipulated in such a way as to be met in the letter but not in the spirit. Different municipal councils interpreted and enforced the same regulations in different ways. It became necessary to know not only the regulations but also the stand taken by various councils and even the quirks of individuals within the same council. To submit plans to a council for approval became a nerve-racking experience full of suspense, apprehension and often a deal of argument.

Where the building regulations allowed, or could be interpreted to allow, a separate laundry was often eliminated and a washing machine was installed in the bathroom or the kitchen. The close grouping of kitchen, bathroom and

laundry to cut down on expensive plumbing and drainage costs became so widely
accepted that many people imagined it was mandatory. Secondary rooms, such
as bedrooms, were pared down to the minimum allowed. Where councils calculated
the clear floor area and excluded the area occupied by built-in cupboards,
it became an accepted, but not acknowledged, practice to install the cupboards after
its clearance by the council's building inspector. Careful thought reduced passage-
ways to an essential minimum or occasionally expanded them into multi-purpose
utility areas useful for children to play in, for sewing, for ironing, for sunning
or for reading as well as for moving from one room to another. Entrance halls were
squeezed down tighter and tighter until they often disappeared altogether. This
collection of little boxes was compressed into a rectangular or L-shaped plan.
For all the ingenuity of thought that went into them they remained scaled down
versions of pre-war houses.

Externally the same paring and compression took place. Verandahs or pergolas
were unknown, the entrance porch became a thin slab of concrete cantilevered
in the re-entrant angle of the L or supported on a thin two inch pipe column over
a concrete slab floor. Balustrades were discarded. The chimney was a rectangular
block. Most houses had a hipped roof covered with lively dark brown terracotta
tiles or highly coloured cement tiles in green, grey, blue or yellow, often arranged
in diagonal or spotted patterns.

With all this pruning and saving the average standard house of the immediate
post-war years was an unlovely thing. It was simple but because it was handled
insensitively it was utterly sterile. Because of this the uniformity to which it
was reduced resulted in an awful monotony rather than a gracious harmony.
Restricted by circumstance from having the individuality in his home, which
is so important to the average Australian, he resorted to cheaply obtained effects
to achieve it. Nobody but the owner was aware of them but to him they were
desperately important. The pattern of the roof tiles, the colour of the front door

A typical house of the immediate post-war years
in Park Avenue, Roseville, New South Wales

House at Turramurra, New South Wales: 1950.
Architect, Harry Seidler

or the weird shape of the letter box were immensely important individual
distinctions to the owner but in their eye-assaulting stridency they were minor
but repellent prickles in a sea of sterility.

The architects' houses of the period were different. Having doodled grand
ideas in his tent for five years, the architect came back to his profession to find
conditions far less free than he had imagined they would be. For the first few years,
his only jobs were small houses and his problems were the same as those of
everybody else. He worked hard to meet the challenge. Generally speaking, by
imagination and courage he succeeded. Where an architect managed to get a finger
in the pie, his plan was a rectangle and his chimney a plain rectangular block,
perhaps wider than was strictly necessary. The architects experimented with the
roofs. In trying to cut costs and to create a low-lying form in harmony with the
land, so they said, they depressed the roofs. Their houses had low-pitched gabled
roofs covered with corrugated asbestos cement sheets and wide eaves. When
this material had been made of the same configuration as iron it had been
unpopular but a new, large, bold corrugation that was produced after the war
did away with this stigma and it became acceptable. To save on roof plumbing
and drainage they experimented with single pitched skillion roofs and double
pitched inverted butterfly roofs. To lower wall heights and save money and also
to achieve a lower profile but still abide by the regulations by producing an average
ceiling height that conformed to requirements they eliminated ceiling joists and
lined the underside of the roof rafters.

Most of all the architects tried to overcome the cramped effect of compressed interiors by creating a feeling of spaciousness. Wherever possible areas were joined by wide openings rather than separated by walls. Floors and ceilings were seen to pass under or over screens suspended clear of both and walls moved out of sight behind a corner, all with the object of hinting that the area went further. The dining area was no longer a room but an extension of a lengthened lounge or a small area joined to it by a wide opening, or separated from it by a free-standing stone, copper or brick fireplace. The entrance hall was eliminated and the front door gave directly into the lounge. A suspended coat cupboard or a screen gave visual privacy without lessening the usable area and, at the same time, heightened the effect of spaciousness. In the same way the kitchen was linked by a large opening to the dining area. In the lounge the windows became a whole glazed wall with a door opening on to a paved terrace as they attempted to open the inside of the house and link it to the outside. The answers which they found to the new conditions were ridiculed at the time but ten years later many of them had passed into the ordinary idiom of domestic building.

When the 1950s began building was still crippled with restrictions on materials, shortage of labour, shoddy workmanship, and official delays. Architects were afflicted with frustration and the public with apathy. When towards the end of 1951 Dr John Burchard, Dean of Humanities and Social Sciences at Massachusetts Institute of Technology, toured Australia to give stimulating and fascinating glimpses of the new fields of structure and space being constantly explored in a vital United States and revealed to astonished eyes that bare unpainted brickwork properly handled was the latest thing for the offices of even the highest paid executives in the States, he drew a comment that captured all the disillusion and frustration of the Australian architectural profession when one member said, 'Frankly, Doctor, we wouldn't be snobbish about a brick wall either if we could find enough bricks to build one.'

Much of the architects' trouble was psychological. In 1951 they were shaken to be shown that the sort of architecture that was happening in America and which they thought local conditions withheld from them could be produced in Australia. It came from only one small house designed by a young migrant architect, Harry Seidler, and erected at Turramurra, a bush suburb of Sydney; but the effect on Australian architecture was tremendous. Seidler, Viennese-born, had studied architecture and town planning before winning a scholarship to take a postgraduate course at Harvard under Walter Gropius. With his family he arrived in Australia from New York in 1947. The home which he designed for his parents at Turramurra was a highly sophisticated International style building quite different from anything then existing in Australia. On a sloping rocky site Seidler supported a flat-roofed machine-made-looking box on thin pipe columns and a series of sandstone blade walls which formed a carport and the entrance. The house had a concrete slab floor and walls of flush vertical boarding painted off-white with black and primary coloured accents. He made extensive use of unshaded glass with a dramatic play of mullions and transoms to form Mondrian-like patterns in clean elongated wall openings very different from the serried row of identical vertical rectangles then used in all other Australian work. A long ramp with plain solid balustrades supported only at the ground and upper landing was a dramatic sculptural feature. The plan of the house was strongly spatial with living, eating, playing, all both indoors and outdoors, being one physically continuous space divided by changes of direction. Only the bedrooms were compartmentalized into conventional rooms.

Despite its manifest shortcomings—its ignoring of and inappropriateness to the climate for instance—it was an exciting stone to be thrown into Australian architectural waters. Imitations and virtual copies in whole or in part sprang up all around Australia immediately and for five years afterwards. The effect was

Above Hilstan Flats,
Nepean Highway, East
Brighton, Victoria: 1950.
Architect, Frederick
Romberg

Right House in Hill Street,
Toorak, Victoria: 1953.
Architect, Roy Grounds

Opposite House at
Frankston, Victoria: 1950.
Architect, Roy Grounds

least in Victoria but in the other states it swept over architecture. Until 1956 practically every architect-designed house had a flat roof and a deep plain fascia. But the importance of Seidler's Turramurra house lay not in its direct imitators but in the permanent influence that its International style had on the thinking of architects and on architecture generally. Much modified it seeped into all types of building and the ripples created by Seidler's stone are to be seen washing gently over a third of the buildings erected in the middle sixties.

During the first five years of the 1950s domestic building still held sway. In 1950, Frederick Romberg, a Swiss-trained architect, introduced a radically new concept to flat development when his Hilstan, a two-storeyed block of thirty-four flats, was built on the Nepean Highway at Brighton in Victoria. Leaving two-thirds of the site uncovered by building to provide ample garden space, it was a generous scheme built with public amenity well in mind. Six isolated block-like units of four flats each projected at right angles from, and were linked to, a long spine of abutting flats by a narrower glazed stair-well which gave direct access to each flat from the landings and thus eliminated corridors. The aesthetic flavour of the building with its square and machine-cut geometric precision was distinctly European but with its function strongly and emphatically expressed—each flat separately identifiable visually—it was a fresh and direct lesson.

The geometric qualities of Hilstan were well placed in Melbourne. In that city during the fifties a small school of thought developed which resulted in a number of houses of originality and depth in which geometry was paramount. The movement was restricted to Melbourne and found virtually no response or echo in other cities probably because, in essence, it was highly individualistic and intensely personal and, belonging to one man, could not be transmitted or imitated satisfactorily. The man was Roy Grounds. Grounds had had a deep concern with plan-form from his earliest student years. By the late 1930s this had developed into an intense pre-occupation with three dimensional form and expression. In 1940 he designed a fan-shaped block of flats called Quamby in Toorak. It was his first break from the rectangle and a development which was to culminate in a series of pure geometrically formed buildings in the fifties. In and around Melbourne he erected houses in the plan-form of circles, triangles and a square pierced by a hole in the middle. In the hands of a lesser man these would been gimcrack, artificial and showy. But Grounds was a man of measured restraint, self-sufficient order and an instinctive sympathy for materials, form and finish redolent of the Georgians. He was also a man of extraordinary inventiveness, a master of clever detailing who at the same time had a strong belief in the Classical precepts and the sensitivity of an artist. Grounds' geometric buildings were light and graceful, deceptively simple, refined and elegant yet, because of their confidence and rightness, masculine and strong.

Inevitably Grounds gathered a coterie of disciples and imitators who took the result without the understanding. They turned out houses as ovals, as triangles impaled in spikes twenty feet above the ground, as S-shapes, as waves and as spirals. But because the whole approach was uniquely and singularly the product of one particular mind the followers succeeded mainly in being exhibitionistic.

Pergolas had their strongest grip on the Melbourne houses of the early fifties. Their virtues were disseminated by Robin Boyd in his popular and professional writings and the example in his own home at Camberwell. They were used throughout Australia but in Melbourne they were *de rigueur*. Nearly every new house and, because they were cheap and their simpleness permitted erection by the home-owners at weekends, many of the existing houses were given their benefits. Because of low ceiling heights it was not usually practical to form the pergola as an open extension of the roof. It tended to be a horizontal plane springing from the eaves or attached to the wall as a separate unit below them.

Until the sixties the pergola clung to the houses but then it moved to large buildings as well. Churches, schools, halls and factories sported tacked-on grid roofs over their entrances. The pergola and its derivatives have continued to be distinctly Melbourne and an important, if minor, part of its regional style.

At the same time in Queensland where there is much more and hotter sun than in Melbourne the useful traditional features of that state were discarded from popular and many architects' houses in the chase after fashion. Roofs became low pitched, the houses were brought down off their high stumps to sit close to the ground and the wide-posted verandah shrank to narrow postless roof overhangs— thin and useless. In swaying to fashion, they became far less functional and architecturally anonymous and conventional. Even the breezeway, undeniably sensible in hot areas, was spurned as too unconventional. There were more of them to be found in the southern cities than in Brisbane. A few Queensland architects, however, strove to retain and use wide verandahs and lattice screens. Houses by Dalton and Heathwood, and Hayes and Scott built at Indooroopilly used the regional vernacular in a contemporary way, but they were a rarity in that smart and developing suburb where most of the houses were little different from their opposite numbers in North Balwyn in Melbourne. In South Australia there was, in general, far more concern for climate than in Queensland. Lawson, Cheesman and Doley, for instance, designed a beach holiday house at Grange which was a minor unspectacular masterpiece of functional and climatic design. In Western Australia during the early fifties the architectural climate went extremely International under the transmitted influence of Seidler's Turramurra house, a trend which has lasted to the present time.

Only in New South Wales was climate still seen as a major factor in architectural problems. By long experience New South Wales architects had had the problem deeply imbedded into their thinking. They had been quick to note the shortcomings of Seidler's house and either turned away from it or, if inspired to follow, had made every endeavour to supply satisfactory modifications in their own work. In New South Wales the posted verandah was recalled and developed as an integral part of domestic architecture. In houses at Wahroonga (Baldwinson and Booth) and at Pymble and St Ives (Sydney Ancher), architects designed a number of houses on which the verandah was fully reinstated as an essential and satisfactory part of domestic architecture. In their own venturesome but quite different homes, John Brindley at Castlecrag and Walter Bunning at Quakers Hat Bay allowed the climate, and to a lesser extent the topography, to be the major influences. In the Lindfield Municipal Library of Davey and Brindley the vertically louvered sunscreen was the total visual architecture.

Post-war austerity building lasted until the early 1950s. By that time finance was more liberal, the community was moving into full prosperity and the worst pinch of the housing shortage, which was to prove chronic, was passed. All these changes gradually opened a new phase of architecture. The small backyard industries which had set up in sheds, stables and garages had become established and prosperous, the factories of pre-war industries, having expanded with the general growth, were bursting at the seams, and new large industries backed by overseas capital enticed by carrots hung out by the Federal and competing State governments were moving in to partake of their share of the sweet life in a large way.

East of Melbourne, west of Sydney and north of Adelaide, industrial areas took form as large steel-framed asbestos-sheeted boxes were put up in the open, grassed paddocks near the railway lines. Most of them, like the houses which preceded them, were built to give the maximum space for the minimum cost. They wasted not a penny and accepted that factories were necessarily ugly and barren. But some, especially those backed by American money, had an American

Quaker's Hat, a house in Ryrie Street,
Mosman, New South Wales: 1952.
Architect, Walter Bunning

awareness of the fiscal value of the public image of the company. By attention to more than cheapness and mere functional efficiency, they were an advertisement for their products and a statement of the company's civic consciousness. Using new open-web steel structural members and a variety of manufactured sheet materials for walls and roofs to form plain uncluttered flat-roofed blocks adorned with strongly-coloured lettering or symbols to proclaim their identity, and with neat, precise administrative buildings set in spacious landscaped grounds, the civic-conscious factories were a new concept in Australian industrial building.

At the same time that the austerity years were passing into history and industrial building recommenced, the architectural profession was infused with the first of the post-war products of the architecture schools. Most of them were ex-servicemen who had been matured beyond their years by experience. And their years were not so few anyway. Many of them were in their late twenties or early thirties. A high proportion of them, having grasped the opportunity offered by the government's repatriation scheme to subsidize university study, came out of the university schools of architecture. Before the war only a few student architects could afford a university course and the great bulk of architects received their training by working in the architect's office during the day and attending a technical college in the evening. From 1946, the established schools at the universities of Sydney and Melbourne were filled to overflowing as enrolments increased tenfold. In 1949, the University of Queensland found the demand so great that it was forced to start a course in architecture and the New South Wales University of Technology (now the University of New South Wales) on its establishment in the same year took over the architecture course conducted by the Sydney Technical College. At the universities the architecture students, who were responsible and mature men not callow inexperienced youths direct from school, were cast into a climate in which inquiry and scepticism are of the very stuff of existence. Instead of assimilating facts they learned to question, to doubt, to analyze, to criticize and to argue. And they found that the more they did so the less were the answers. With no absolutes to cleave to, they were thrown back on their own individual and arbitrarily formed opinions. In their enthusiasm most of what existed was destroyed. The only accepted rule was that there were no rules. Naively they thought each could erect a philosophy by himself, discover all of science by himself and meld the two by himself. 'First principles' had been the catch-cry of the young Turks in the thirties. In the fifties there were no principles. Accordingly, each found himself dependent on himself alone to decide what was right and what was wrong. There were as many philosophies of architecture as there were students.

As they percolated from the schools into the profession that had been embroiled in controversy since the thirties, they injected so much disillusion with the status quo and so many fragmented convictions that architectural controversy became architectural anarchy. The effects of the plethora of disparate ideas soon showed up. Resting on self-created philosophical foundations that ranged from sound to shallow, they created a veritable menagerie of architectural answers. Rational or emotional, intellectual or intuitive, sculptural or organic, sophisticated or brutal, desperately sincere or cynically superficial, they ran the whole gamut of ideas. They began with either the structure or the materials or the function. Some started from the heart—the fireplace said some, the kitchen said others—and worked outwards to a dependent external form. Others began with a purely aesthetic form and fitted and pushed the materials and structure and the function until they fitted. Some denied history and association as being a viable factor in architecture, others maintained it was the most powerful of all influences and that churches should look like churches and factories like factories, while yet others, closer to the truth but no more helpfully, replied that each should retain its traditional emotional qualities but not necessarily its traditional physical form.

The multiplicity of creeds which gave rise to an equal multiplicity of architectural types was compounded by a host of new materials. The old range of timber, stone, brick, tile, glass, plaster and paint was increased tenfold almost every year. There were new materials and old materials in new forms. Sprayed-on plastic roof covering or screwed-on baked-enamel metal panels, extruded aluminium sections and curtain walling, rubber based paints and pressed straw panels, pressed sheets in all sorts of metals for all sorts of jobs and plastics that were said to be the perfect answer for anything from sealing openings to finishing floors—these and a thousand others claimed to have wonderful properties which made them the perfect answer to particular situations.

Technological and industrial advances indicated concrete as the coming structural material. The development of scientifically controlled factory-mixing produced concrete of reliable and uniform quality. Huge rotating drums on the back of powerful trucks could deliver up to ten cubic yards at a time. The concept had been tried in America before World War I but it was not until just prior to World War II that a satisfactory truck that could move along and rotate the drum at the same time was designed. The first successful commercial venture in pre-mixed concrete in the world was launched in July 1939 when the Ready Mixed Concrete Company was formed in Sydney. It opened a pre-mixing plant at Glebe Island. In the same way that World War I had allowed Broken Hill Proprietary to prosper, World War II encouraged and established Ready Mixed Concrete. By 1945, there were four plants in New South Wales, Victoria and Queensland. In the 1950s the company expanded overseas to take the advantages of this Australian contribution to building to the rest of the world.

But pre-mixing was only part of the story. There was new knowledge of reinforcement types and their placing, re-usable formwork, new mechanical aids to ensure denser and more reliable concrete, pre-casting and spraying, new high tensile steels which allowed post-tensioning and pre-tensioning techniques to be developed, while the mysterious but apparently limitless possibilities of thin concrete shells seemed to open an infinite new world of forms. For a while, until the new techniques and knowledge were properly understood and their limitations appreciated, it seemed that structure had ceased to be a factor in architecture. Any form that could be conceived could be built.

Architects were dazzled by the geometry of hyperbolic paraboloids and other surfaces developed from straight lines and which dipped and swooped in three dimensions. They discovered tensile forms made possible by advances in metallurgy. Catenary roofs, true hung curtain walls and stabilizing tension rods found a place in the scramble for architectural individualism.

With the solidity of the philosophical and technological bases of architecture both turned upside down and shattered, the cauldron in which they seethed spewed forth a chaotic collection of buildings. In the architects' architecture there were hard square-cut chiselled blocks, severe and mechanical, there were tents, pyramids, domes, eggs, zig-zags and wave shapes. There was geometry, and there was free form; there was violent colour and diamond shapes; there was horizontality and verticality and diagonality; there were hard artificial materials and warm natural ones. While many of those responsible were in deadly earnest and following their own particular line with consistency and sincerity, the divergence from and lack of harmony with the work of anybody else created an effect of utter confusion and lostness.

To the spectator, which included many professionals as well as the public, it seemed that all the hectic forms and colour were ruled by nothing other than a desire to be different. In following the fashions, they strove for the novel, the startling, the unusual and different for their own sake. The disturbing confusion that tormented those who were most deeply involved with the struggle to find a new direction became a sort of carnival approach for those who merely followed the trends.

This, then, was the prevailing climate of Australian architecture of the fifties. The divergent schools of thought introduced in the twenties had fermented in controversy during the thirties and borne the fruit of disintegration in the fifties. By world standards it was low on the scale. Its standing on the world scene was clearly, if rather slickly, summarized by the headline in an American journal over a short article on Seidler's Turramurra house, which read 'The Big Time Moves into the Bush League'.

When in 1955 the Royal Australian Institute of Architects in conjunction with the Federal government sponsored the first-ever exhibition in England of Australian architecture it was able to include very little work of quality that had been done since the war. The exhibition was received with typically English reserved politeness and little criticism. However, the *Observer* said the exhibition showed that while Australia had architects of quality it had no Australian architecture, while the *Times*, noting the strong American influence and the vigorous growth, said that the recent buildings bore 'a close resemblance to the routine products of the American building industry without as yet displaying the grace and maturity of the more sophisticated American architecture.' Only the houses displayed any sort of quality in their design and construction.

They were views that Australian architects themselves had somewhat embarrassedly suspected. But the exhibition, even in attempting to make the best of a poor thing, had presented a true picture. Except for some of the houses the architecture of the decade following the war was nothing to shout about.

14

The general prosperity that continued without interruption during the fifties passed into all sections of the community. Every family and every individual shared in their country's affluence. This was largely due to the acceptance of another American practice—credit purchase. Before the war the average bread-winner was prepared to borrow, and spend the rest of his life paying off, the cost of his home. To borrow more was not only difficult but was downright irresponsible and a social sin. Respectable people paid their way. But after the war the whole economy gradually changed to a credit basis. Access to the general national wealth by borrowing was encouraged by governments, financial institutions and retailers. Only in a society in which jobs and income were reasonably secure is the credit system financially sound. During the fifties the economy was set fair for stability and continuing full employment. People used it to launch a business, build a factory, furnish a home and buy a motor car. And they did so in hundreds of thousands.

As the motor car was put within the reach of every family, it became not a luxury but a necessity. The spread of the motor car changed the pattern of living and affected the face of the towns and the individual buildings. It spread the cities well beyond the reaches of public transport. The countryside was swallowed in a creeping tide of houses as orchards and market gardens were bulldozed and subdivided to become new suburbs. The increased volume of traffic caused headaches to the authorities faced with the problem of organizing and building whole new road systems and bridges. The cars caused mutations to existing types of building as well as the rise of entirely new types. It caused a flock of service stations, aimed at dispensing petrol, road maps and gimmicks, to erupt on every likely site throughout the towns and country. They were a new phenomenon, very different from the pre-war garage housed in an old shed and with its array of petrol pumps lining the footpath edge and offering a choice of brands and a blacksmith type of repair service. These were smooth, slick, efficient affairs set well back from the street with ample space for cars pulling in for the one brand of petrol they sold. Similarly, the cars caused the old corner pub to be set well back from the street to allow cars to line up at the new all-important drive-in bottle departments and to provide wide expanses of barren parking areas. The cars also caused the erection in the heart of the cities of whole buildings designed exclusively for their parking because there was no room at the cluttered kerbsides and it caused the provision in city buildings of two or three basement floors of parking area for those who worked in, or visited, the building. The car created drive-in picture theatres and by the late 1950s it had created large self-contained shopping centres designed to supply the more-than-daily needs of a whole region. The regional shopping centres offered a relaxed alternative to the ordeal and frustration of city shopping. They were large complexes of multifarious, loosely-knit, private shops clustered around a large department store. In them a customer could buy almost anything from his daily bread to a grand piano, or purchase a reel of cotton, a boat or furnish his home. Sitting grandly isolated in the middle of a hundred acres of bitumen and a sea of car roofs they created within their buildings' perimeter a wandering series of malls and courts where the pedestrian was reinstated as supreme in a dappled sunlit landscape of textured pavings, plants, seats and fountains. The car caused the proliferation of an entirely new type of building in the multi-hued motel and its later variations built as twentieth century inns for the peripatetic car-owning population.

In the suburbs the car led to a change in gardening. A day at the beach or a visit to friends which was preceded and succeeded by a long and difficult journey on public transport was an uncomfortable, full-day's effort. In a motor car it was an easy and pleasurable two or three hours. A day in the country had been impossible but was now readily available to every car owner. With these pleasures beckoning temptingly, gardening became a chore. Gardens were simplified. Flower beds were left untended or converted to lawns which could be clipped down in a few minutes with a motor-mower. Vegetable gardens in the backyard were converted to lawns and opened a market for the deep-frozen, factory-packed vegetable industry. Others turned to native plants and trees which, in their natural habitat, grew without the troubles of disease and the need for constant attention that the exotic gardens required. Many keen gardeners found a new beauty in native gardens, with their gum trees, rocks, vines and leafy ground surfaces. Instead of clean shaving their land before building commenced, as was the old standard practice, people left the native trees where there were any or planted new ones where there were not and fitted the house between them. The native garden movement was small, almost esoteric in its wholehearted form, but in a diluted form it affected a wide section of the populace who unexpectedly found the despised gum trees had primeval beauty. They planted them.

Finally, the car affected the house itself. The garage became at first attached to and then integrated into the design of the house. In the early days of the motor car, the garage had been located in a far corner of the block. Just as some of the early cars retained miniature shafts and sockets and holders for a whip, garages could not be rid of the association of the horse. Because of the swarms of flies and the smells that were an unavoidable concomitant of stables, they had been built well away from the house. For no better reason then this tradition, the early garages were similarly sited. During the twenties, when every prudent motorist had a stock of four-gallon tins of petrol in his garage, most building regulations enforced the separation of the garage from the house for fire reasons. It was not until the late forties when fundamental efficiency was being given so much attention that the bridge was closed and, over the objections of the fearful and the timid, the garage and the house were allowed to become one. Even then, when there were sufficient service stations to make it unnecessary to keep petrol in the garage and motor cars did not give off clouds of combustible fumes, inbred fears died hard and most municipal authorities required the two to be fire-isolated from each other by incombustible materials.

In lower-priced new houses and in old houses which had to provide a car shelter as an extension, the garage often took the form of an open car-port consisting basically of a roof supported on columns. The chief purpose was to protect the car from the ravages of the sun which played havoc with the highly polished paintwork. Additional protection may have been given by screening one or more of the sides but its essential character remained that of an open doorless sun protector into which the car could be driven with convenience and, incidentally, left on public display. Those who wanted security from thieves and vandals as well, built fully enclosed and lockable garages in which the old swinging side-hinged stable doors were replaced by a single large metal- or plywood-sheeted door that glided up and under the roof with the touch of a finger or slid in folds

Car Park in Kent Street,
Sydney: 1956. Architects,
Morrow and Gordon

Warringah Mall shopping
centre, Brookvale, New
South Wales: 1961.
Architects, A. Kann, Finch
& Partners

around the side. For ease of access the opening invariably faced the street. The broad expanse of the garage door formed the largest single element in the whole street front. Brightly painted and patterned with squares, diamonds, circles and zig-zags formed by planted-on mouldings, it could dominate the house and shout the resident's car-owning status. By the middle fifties, with practically every household owning a car, the single car had lost its status significance. Social position required two cars and the double garage was their symbol. The garage door became even more dominating.

The Americanization of Australian city life that welled strongly during the fifties was exemplified by the garage door but it took other forms as well. Most of it revolved around the acquisition of worldly possessions made possible by the spread of credit buying and the desire to impress by displaying it. It was much the same mood as that of the 1880s but because of different social conditions it took different forms.

All over Australia, but particularly in Sydney and areas north of it, the family took to outdoor living. Expansive paved terraces, covered with pergolas or scattered with brightly-coloured canvas umbrellas and blinds and with painted timber or wrought iron furniture, opened from glassed living-rooms. On them the servantless family sunbathed, relaxed and read, or entertained at a barbecued meal far more people than they could otherwise have done. Where the terrace was above the ground, light wrought iron balustrades, either as a row of straight rods or fancily swirled, afforded protection. Wrought iron was a material of the fifties. It was not wrought iron in its proper meaning. It was a mild steel twisted, bent and welded by machines. In a wide variety of patterns, it was used for fly-screen doors, pergola posts, screens, flowerpot holders, garden furniture and terrace and stair balustrades. It was painted black in the early fifties and white towards the end of the decade. Like the two-car garage, the harshly and artificially textured and coloured brickwork, the feature wall, the barbecue and, for a while, the television aerial, a good bestrewing of wrought iron was an essential part of popular domestic architecture. By the sixties, when an inverse sort of snobbery required television aerials to be hidden, these symbols of affluence had lost their punch. Nothing less than a private swimming pool complete with pumps, filters, lights and cleaners, and tiled or painted a delicate pale blue, sufficed to keep heads above water in the social swim.

At the time that the swimming pool became a *sine qua non* of success the affluent imitators of the architect's work had pounced avidly on a spectacular array of new cliches. While the great majority of small homes built in the outer fringe suburbs by official authorities and speculative firms remained sterile little boxes tinged with an anaemic echo of wrought iron and a car-port, the better-class suburbs were revelling in an orgy of extroverted braggadocio. The most popular form was a low single-storeyed rambling building requiring seventy feet or eighty feet of frontage. The estate agents called it ranch style but its dress varied widely. It was dreamily romantic, intellectually mechanical, aggressively brutal or desperately organic. It used a wide low-pitched or flat roof, it arranged the glass-walled rooms around courtyards decorated with exotic plants, it was surlily secretive or blatantly exhibitionistic. It used broken-faced concrete blocks coloured a murky green or khaki for walls, concrete blocks pierced in a variety of patterns to form decorative panels or screens for privacy, timber left unpainted to expose the grain and stained a rich red-brown. An unlimited Pandora's box of materials was available. And they were often put together with brassy abandon.

During the Victorian times architecture had ransacked the past and the exotic for visual forms. During the 1950s Australian domestic architecture ransacked foreign architecture for ideas and character and the principles that lay behind them. It found Colonial architecture for one thing. It was a Colonial architecture that had never been part of Australia's colonial period—it was the Americans' version of their own past. White painted brick walls had small-paned bow windows, verandahs had shallow-arched valence-boards, and roofs were decorated with a louvered ventilating fleche topped by a swinging weathercock.

Post-war architecture also discovered the warm purity of Japanese housing. It was not the first time that Japanese building had come to Australia. In Brisbane, in 1909, a house which had been designed and prefabricated in Japan was erected by a team of Japanese workmen. Brisbane architect G. H. M. Addison had thought it eminently suitable for the Brisbane climate but quite impractical for the Australian way of living. The architects of the 1950s were not so shallow as to merely imitate the form. However, the emotional quality of the Japanese house was one which they tried hard to capture in their work. The simplicity and straightforwardness of the construction, the revelation rather than disguising of the nature of the materials and the play of dark grey tiled roofs, white rectangles and plain dark lines formed by squared dark timber provided a stimulus to put into practice the first principles that were so much talked about. The houses produced were far from being copies of Japanese houses. They were soundly conceived, thoroughly understood and well worked out to suit local conditions. They were Australian through and through but the initial stimulus had come from Japan. As usual a great deal of the essential quality of the architect's original building was lost when it was imitated by others. It was the dark brown timbers and the heavy horizontality expressed in oversized fascias that gained a place on the wider domestic scene.

By 1960, then, domestic architecture, whether professional or popular, had fallen to bits in a heterogeneous welter of individualism in which every building shouted the importance of itself or its owner. Taken separately they varied from the highly sensitive even elegant statement of taste to the crude and brash display of trickery and wealth. They were not false or hypocritical in the way that Victorian buildings were. Judged by their own lights they were frankly and undisguisedly honest. But, because there were as many lights as there were people, taken together they had a disjointed stridency and diversity that was positively nerve-racking.

It was a full decade after the end of the war before conditions were right for re-commencing other than domestic and industrial buildings. From 1955, however, the gates opened and Australian building embarked on the greatest period of expansion in the country's history. It centred around an energetic surge in commercial building but it also spread to include to a somewhat less but possibly more significant extent cultural, educational, religious and medical buildings and high-density housing.

The most interesting of the new buildings were some of the churches and those built as symbols of civic culture. The best of the churches, casting off the physical symbols of Gothic architecture as well as the liturgical strait-jackets that went with them, were the combined result of new architectural and new religious thinking. Centred on the altar, the table or the pulpit, depending on the denomination, they were designed to embrace the congregation into a corporate act of worship. Many of the new churches were merely eye-catching spectacles of points, draping roofs and triangular blocks garishly coloured; but numbers of them, such as the Lutheran Church designed by Grounds, Romberg and Boyd at Canberra, a squat square building impaled at its centre on a slim soaring spire, and the Wentworth Memorial Church at Vaucluse designed by Clarke, Gazzard and Partners, were at the one time both simple and beautiful, sheltering and inspirational, close to the earth and soaring, timeless yet of the minute, strong yet sensitive. Another noteworthy church of the period was erected at Mundingburra, Townsville,

Hale School Memorial Hall, Wembley Downs, Western Australia: 1961. Architect, Marshall Clifton in association with Brand, Ferguson & Solaski

The Fisher Library at the University of Sydney, Darlinghurst, New South Wales: 1963 and 1967. Architects, the New South Wales Government Architect and Tom O'Mahony

The Lutheran Church, Canberra: 1961. Architects, Grounds, Romberg & Boyd

St Matthew's Church at Mundingburra, Townsville, Queensland: 1957. Architects, Ford, Hutton & Newell

Two views of the
Wentworth Memorial
Church at Vaucluse, New
South Wales: 1965.
Architects, Clarke,
Gazzard and Partners

The Academy of Science building, Canberra: 1959.
Architects, Grounds, Romberg & Boyd

in Queensland in 1957 by Ford, Hutton and Newell. Despite the slim aluminium needle-like spire and the corrugated asbestos cement roofing there was a strong influence of Robin Dods in the form of the heavy gable roof sweeping down to the verandah supported on thick plain square posts. As a result St Matthew's Church of England was a rare example of architects capturing a native vernacular in a type of building which had never been touched with it in all Australia's history.

More noticeable, but not necessarily more noteworthy, than the interesting parish churches were the temples built to secular culture. Canberra, in the hands of the National Capital Development Commission, which had been formed in 1957 to breathe life back into Griffin's still-born child, emerged by the sixties as one vast shrine in which university and government buildings, motels, embassies, law courts, housing and commercial building fought furiously for attention and succeeded in becoming a concentrated and somewhat expensive and sickly melange of the architectural vices and cacophony of the times. There were some buildings of quality among Canberra's marshmallow. Buildings such as the arcaded dome of Roy Grounds' captivating and modern-mediaeval Academy of Science Building displayed a depth of understanding of their job, their times and their place which made them exemplars for their colleagues. But where every building sets out to be a masterpiece and a precious jewel the result is inevitably a tawdry string of glass beads.

On a wave of cultural enthusiasm and not a little political astuteness, Sydney held an architectural competition in 1956–57 to build a so-called Opera House on Bennelong Point. The selected design submitted by Danish architect Joern Utzon was an architectural dream that turned into a political nightmare. On a rocky point of land jutting out into Port Jackson at the eastern side of Sydney Cove, surrounded by the sparkle of sunlit water speckled with curvaceous white sails and gay spinnakers, and against the magnificent backdrop of the grey arch of the Harbour Bridge, Utzon planned a piece of sculpture of almost ephemeral delight. The design and its selection were made at a time when it was believed that shell concrete could perform miracles. Disillusionment was not long in coming. Gradually, after an enormous amount of research and work, after the simple shell sail roofs were found impractical, after structural system after structural system had been investigated and discarded and after a brilliant breakthrough had been made in deciding to make the roof from surface sections of a common sphere, the building took form. Much of the grace and weightless flowing beauty of the original conception were lost as a result. The final form was somewhat heavy, static and compactly disjointed. The cost soared eightfold in the process. The building became the centre of political controversy which involved all sections of the community including the architectural profession in heated and emotional conflict. In 1966, when the main structural problems had been solved, the high-principled and strong-willed architect collided with a new government pledged to curb excessive rises in costs and resigned in frustration and anger. Despite the unfortunate and harrowing side effects the building was worth it. The Sydney Opera House was a voyage of architectural and engineering discovery in which new oceans were charted, new frontiers of knowledge and technology were conquered and the resources of science and technology were employed to solve design,

The Sydney Opera House at Bennelong Point, Sydney: 1959 —. Architect, Joern Utzon

The Olympic Swimming Pool, Melbourne: 1954-56.
Architects, John & Phyllis Murphy, Borland & McIntyre

The Civic Theatre, Canberra: 1966.
Architects, Yuncken Freeman Architects Pty Ltd

erection and quality of finish problems beyond the capacity of conventional methods; so that not only Australia's but the world's architecture was advanced and enriched by it.

In the same period the National Capital acquired satisfactory cultural trappings in the form of a fine, if conventional, Civic Theatre from the Melbourne architectural firm of Yuncken Freeman Architects Pty Ltd.

Taking warning from the unhappy lesson of the consequences of haste and lack of adequate groundwork afforded by the Sydney Opera House, Melbourne's civic fathers embarked, in 1960, on the erection of the first stage of a cultural centre at the gateway to the city at the southern end of Prince's Bridge. They entrusted the project to Roy Grounds. Working in close collaboration with Eric Westbrook, the Director of the National Gallery of Victoria, the architect designed a soaring, tapered, bellcast, copper cone opposing a low solid rectangular prism to house all the visual fine and applied arts at both the participatory and passive levels. The prism was erected as the first stage. Built of three feet by one foot blocks of rugged native bluestone, the severely plain but beautifully proportioned exterior enclosed inner courts and miles of galleries in which the drama of opening and closing, hidden and revealed space was magnificent. The first stage of Melbourne's Arts Centre proved to be more than just an aesthetic triumph for the architect. In contrast to its Sydney counterpart, it worked perfectly and its cost remained strictly within the estimates; and it was completed dead on schedule in December 1967, so that it could function as an art gallery by the middle of the following year.

Melbourne had acquired a less expensive but, in its idea, a radically different yet equally brilliant building for the Olympic Games in 1956. The Olympic Swimming Pool had been designed as a competition entry by a team of four post-war trained architects, Peter McIntyre, Kevin Borland, Phyllis and John Murphy, and a young engineer, Bill Irwin. It was a building in which a totally structural idea made practical by the latest materials was developed unswervingly to a logical conclusion.

Sydney's Opera House and Melbourne's Olympic Swimming Pool were at opposite poles of architectural philosophy—the one purely sculptural and aesthetic in which the function was subservient to the point of requiring an entirely different working building within the reef shells and in which the materials and structure were servants required to answer the demands of the artist-architect; the other a building in which the function and structure and the materials were the architecture and any other qualities were no more than inevitable consequences. Between these two extremes lay the other cultural buildings. The new Wilson Hall, designed by Bates, Smart and McCutcheon, was opened in March 1956. Erected on the ashes of Joseph Reed's Gothic Revival hall of the same name which had been destroyed by fire four years earlier, the $170' \times 63' \times 48'$ high building with its fine internal end wall by Douglas Annand and Tom Bass symbolizing Man's struggle for enlightenment cost £250,000 and was described as 'the most magnificent box in Australia'. The Sidney Myer Music Bowl in Melbourne was a prototype for eye-catching sound shells in a dozen lesser towns. Because the cultural buildings were few in number and because, individually, they were architecturally isolated (having no direct antecedents and no immediate successors) they hold no significant place in Australia's architectural evolution. But they were the concentrated essence, the spice in the whole architectural cake. In the heterogeneous welter of the cultural buildings the whole desperate egocentricity of architecture was distilled.

By 1955 housing conditions and the ever-increasing spread of the suburbs forced governments and enticed private enterprise into taking tentative steps towards inveigling some Australians out of their separate bungalows. In Sydney

The Sidney Myer Music Bowl, King's Domain, Melbourne: 1959.
Architects, Yuncken, Freeman Brothers, Griffiths & Simpson

the New South Wales Housing Commission cleared away some of the worst slums, a legacy of the post-gold era, from the south of the city. In their stead and to re-house the inhabitants of the area, long blocks of flats from three to fifteen storeys high were erected. They were spartan buildings. Shorn of anything which could be considered, even vaguely, as superflous, they were barren, dull and graceless warrens arranged, like children's blocks, in flat, green swards of grass marked with signs which ordered bureaucratically 'Keep Off'. The open areas were equipped with swings, slides, climbing bars and other things adults imagine children like; they were seldom used. To retain a little of the identifiable individuality so important to Australians in their homes the doors and balconies of the flats were painted distinguishing colours. The practice could not obviate the frightening anonymity that enveloped the reclamation schemes and their inhabitants. Whether the slum or the redevelopment was the better was a moot point. Other schemes built on abandoned racecourses at Sydney and Melbourne were equally characterless and depressing.

At the other end of the social scale private companies moved in to erect tall blocks of vertically stacked houses for people who had had enough of being in bondage to a suburban garden. With each unit in the pile having its own individual cantilevered balcony with solid concrete balustrade, they were, most appropriately, like filing cabinets with the drawers open. While some of them were rented they were generally owned by the occupants either as shareholders in an owning company or, after the law had been changed to allow title to be given to a volume of space high off the ground, outright. In the better older parts of Melbourne and Sydney, along St Kilda Road and at Toorak in the former, at Blue's Point, Neutral Bay and Elizabeth Bay in the latter, and at Eagle Farm in Brisbane, expensive human filing cabinets arose in choice areas of decayed housing or in the grounds of old mansions which had become uneconomic in the post-war world.

Between the two extremes lay a crop of three-storeyed blocks of flats erected on cheaper land in the middle and outer suburbs. They were speculative ventures. The arrangements varied but the normal practice was for a builder, who did his own designing, to finance his scheme with a high-priced loan. This forced him to build quickly, fill the building with lessees as soon as possible, at which stage having thereby proved its financial viability he sold the building, repaid his costly loan and took his profit. Flats built this way were aimed at taking advantage of a new market created by the general affluence that existed in which, for the first time in history, the seventeen to twenty-three year-old age group had fat pay packets. The money freed them from dependence on their families and enabled them to assert their freedom. Many still in their teens left home to live by themselves or with friends of the same inclinations free from parental restrictions. The money also allowed them to marry younger and with both husband and wife earning well to set up their first home in a £7–£8 a week flat furnished on credit with all the latest domestic conveniences.

Because of their speculative nature and their youthful and temporary market the three-storeyed suburban blocks of flats put their money where it counted. Aesthetically they were base and crude, incorporating individual cantilevered balconies, plenty of fancy wrought iron, gaudy colours in their brick walls, cement-tile roofs and painted windows, guttering and front doors in a parody of

A block of flats on Debney's Estate, Flemington, Victoria: 1963. Designed by the Victorian Housing Commission

Flats at Diamond Bay, New
South Wales: 1963. Architects,
Harry Seidler & Associates

Gleneagles flats at Eagle Farm, Brisbane: 1962-64. Architects, Curro, Nutter & Charlton

The MLC Building at North Sydney: 1955-57. Architects, Bates, Smart & McCutcheon

all the worst in popular taste of the time. They were jerry-built and had the barest minimum of finishes. But in their planning and use of space they were often minor masterpieces of ingenuity and compactness.

Practically none of the architects who were riding high in their profession had had experience with the size of one type of building—the city office building— that was thrown into their laps after 1955. To be sure some of them had been involved with the few city buildings and the hospitals which had been erected in the years between 1935 and 1940 but, with a handful of exceptions, even this experience had been on a small scale and not at the top level. Most architects of 1955 had been juniors before the war or had entered the profession after it. In either case their experience for the previous fifteen years had been restricted to houses and an occasional shop or factory. The architects greeted the new opportunities with an exuberance in which their hearts tended to rule their heads. The first fruits were often slick and not very sensible.

While the centres of all the capital cities were affected and transformed by the building renaissance that came after 1955 most of the important steps were taken in Sydney. For the first ten years after the war when domestic architecture was paramount Australian architecture had been led from Melbourne. There had been a high standard of thought and practice achieved in Perth also but Western Australia was still too cut off for its progress to become an influence in the eastern states. Perth received and often improved but virtually nothing flowed eastwards. While the resurgence of non-domestic building in the late fifties was Australia-wide the developments in all other states were a trailing story of what was happening in New South Wales. The lag was some eighteen months for Victoria and up to five years for the lesser states. Consequently the story of post-war city building centres almost exclusively on Sydney.

The outstanding feature of architecture after 1955 was the curtain wall. In various ways its neutral overall pattern of frame lines and infill glass was applied to factories, churches, houses and, most of all, to office buildings where it made its first and most reasonable appearance.

The first of the new commercial buildings—office blocks in Melbourne and Sydney—were conceived as blind imitations of the glass boxes which were the current vogue in America. With their structural bones kept back from the face of the building, they were enveloped in a curtain of glass and metal panels held in a light aluminium frame. Mathematically precise in both construction and form, they relied entirely on the proportions of their form and the grid pattern of the curtain framing for any aesthetic quality they had. The worst of them carried the garish colouring that was having a short popular fling in domestic work at the time and, as a result, were crude and disturbing. The best, with more sensitivity, displayed the restraint associated with self-conscious good taste and blended grey-green tinted glass with grey enamel panelling and grey wall tiling. Depending on expensive and dubiously reliable air-conditioning to make them habitable, they ignored climatic conditions as they faced tall sheets of unshaded glittering glass walls square on to the sun. Their materials, the precision required in their workmanship and the essential air-conditioning combined to make them expensive to build and maintain. Conceived as well-mannered and refined but unignorably impressive advertisements ('prestige buildings' they were euphemistically called) for the insurance companies for whom they were almost all built, the glass boxes were as much fashion buildings as any Australian buildings have ever been and were less sensible—expensive, unfunctional and, in the main, unspeakably dull. On the whole, they were bland, characterless cellophane packages which, paying no heed to either the problems or the virtues of the Australian climate, proclaimed the naive conviction that in a world of shrinking dimensions, technology had obliterated all regional distinctions as well.

That technology, or at least the architects' grasp of it, had not advanced so far was soon clear. The tinted glass was cracked by the stresses set up between its shaded and unshaded parts, large panes of the glass fell disconcertingly out of their frames and crashed to the ground, water penetrated through the mastic compound with which their cracks were sealed and which shrank and became brittle under the heat of the sun. If the air-conditioning broke down, which it sometimes did, work was impossible in these hot-houses, the glass became burningly hot and was dangerous to touch. The metal panels, warping and buckling in the heat, destroyed the essential precise smoothness of the walls by wobbling shimmering highlights and reflections.

The parade of curtain buildings was headed by the MLC building erected at North Sydney and completed in 1957. It was the first in Australia of the truly post war office blocks, the first to use a fully rigid steel frame and hollow steel floors, the first to employ 'light-weight' construction with its increase in speed of erection and consequent savings in cost, the first to use a true curtain wall filled with windows and anodized aluminium spandrels, and the first to be designed on a modular system throughout. Vermiculate plaster was used for fireproofing instead of the normal heavy concrete protection. Floors were designed on a module system to allow flexibility of use of the prefabricated and standard timber partitions, while the stamped metal ceilings, the light troughs, the power outlets and the telephone wiring were all on a module system for the same reason. As a counter to the blast of the sun the curtain wall windows were double-glazed with anti-actinic heat-resisting glass on the outer face and plate glass on the inner, set ten inches apart. The space between held venetian blinds operable from inside the rooms.

The architects, Bates, Smart and McCutcheon, clad the building in a wealth of fine facing materials—terracotta, marble, granite and mosaic tiles. In 1957 the MLC building was not only the largest (450,000 square feet of floor area in fourteen floors) office building in Australia but also in its design, construction and approach a most influential and important piece of architecture.

Close on the heels of the MLC building, curtain wall office buildings appeared in the decaying parts of the cities which were ripe for development. Around Circular Quay in Sydney and on the Western Hill in Melbourne, dilapidated masonry buildings a hundred years or more old were swept away to make way for sleek, glossy cliffs of glass. All of hem reached upwards to the maximum height permitted by the regulations. The cost of land and the building, together with an ever-increasing demand for office space and the urge for self-advertisement, created pressures to have the maximum height condition changed. Eventually, in 1957, in Sydney and Melbourne but not in the other capitals, the economic pressures and arguments had gathered such strength that the impregnability of limit heights was breached. In special circumstances and under the Control of Heights of Buildings Committees, buildings were allowed to pierce the old ceiling. With that a truly twentieth century scale came to the cities. As the first of them, the 383 feet high AMP Building at Circular Quay, deflowered the virgin purity of the skyline and the city's familiar scale was shattered, the hubbub of the 1880s was repeated. There were dire forebodings of the effect of the building's vast shadow condemning its neighbours to live in a perpetual unhealthy twilight, of the chaos that would be thrown into the city's traffic pattern, of the turbulent eddies and wind currents it would create so that to walk the surrounding streets would be to go in danger of being dashed without warning to the ground. There were aesthetic objections to placing the tallest building on the lowest point of the town instead of its high hills, and even forebodings about the risk of its concave facade concentrating the sun's rays into a focus that would literally burn the elevated concrete Cahill Expressway in front of it. But mostly the protests

Top The Council House in
St George's Terrace, Perth: 1963.
Architects, Howlett & Bailey

Below left ICI House in Nicholson
Street, Melbourne: 1960. Architects,
Bates, Smart & McCutcheon

Below right The IBM Centre in
Kent Street, Sydney: 1964.
Architects, Stephenson & Turner

were concerned with the violence being done to the scale of Sydney as it was.

Theoretically there was now no limit to the height to which a building could rise but the committee charged with pronouncing in each case seemed to decide on its own unannounced limit. In Sydney, for instance, two proposals to erect 600 feet high towers at King's Cross and Australia Square were rejected as too extreme. For five years or so the new limit appeared to be 400 feet after which it crept up a further 100 feet. By 1965, a sufficient number of tall buildings had arisen to carry the new scale satisfactorily over the cities. The tall buildings had become not merely accepted but a cause for civic pride. Erected by insurance companies, banks or the government they were, one and all, prestige buildings. Consequently, they were lavish to the point of profligacy.

All the new city buildings, whether a small twelve storeys or a mammoth thirty-five storeys, were prestige buildings. They were expensive advertisements using the costliest of materials and equipment. Extravagantly finished in costly slabs of imported marble, imported glass mosaic tiles, oiled timbers, copper; rather vulgarly paying obiesance to culture with obtrusive displays of bronze, stained glass and plastic sculpture, and gardened forecourts; furnished with marbled or thickly carpeted floors, linened or marbled walls in the public spaces; the pecking order of the occupants carefully defined by the expense and expanse of the executive areas; and with banks of silky smooth high speed apparently motionless lifts, they were no whit less ostentatious than the buildings of eighty years before.

By the late 1950s attempts were made, in a desultory sort of way, to reduce the devastating effects of the sun by incorporating sun protection devices over the walls. Large adjustable metal louvers (either vertical or horizontal depending on the orientation), projecting hoods, or overall pierced metal screens were tried. But the attempts were tentative, half-hearted and messy. With a few exceptions they were fussy in operation or design and quite out of scale with the rest of the building. The Council House, Perth, designed by Howlett and Bailey Pty Ltd for the city's administration, was one that was more successful than most when it placed a broken grid of large T-shaped pre-cast concrete hoods over its glass faces. The hoods became the butt of many jokes (the building became known in Perth as 'the tea-house') but they achieved a satisfactory scale with the building as a whole.

It was not until 1963 that the first office building which satisfactorily came to terms with the glass wall and the sun in a direct and uncomplicated way prodded into the sky at the south end of the Sydney Harbour Bridge. The IBM building, designed by Stephenson and Turner, stood on an island site high on the crown of the old Rocks area. A broad two-storeyed podium covered most of the site and supported a 220 feet high square tower. To protect its bands of glass window the architects incorporated pre-cast concrete hoods bent downwards at an angle of forty-five degrees. Stacked eighteen storeys high, the tiers of sloping hoods resulted in a most dramatic pagoda silhouette. But more important than its visual drama was its sheer sensibleness. It was a bold, simple and direct answer and, unlike any of the earlier attempts, was perfectly in scale with both the building and the city skyline of which it was a commanding part.

As well as providing tolerable working conditions and reducing the expense of installing and running air-conditioning equipment, the hoods gave a sense of enclosure and reality to the occupants. One of the psychological consequences of the glass boxes was a feeling of disembodiment on looking out through a transparent wall to an always-distant view. The hoods provided something close and immediate on the other side of the glass and the resulting relation was a reinstatement of reality.

Pre-cast concrete as used in the hoods of the IBM building gained popularity from 1960 onwards. Exposed aggregate finishes could produce a wide variety of controllable, permanent colouring with lively non-reflective textures. These virtues, combined with its precision and versatility of shape, made exposed aggregate concrete panels the distinctive material of the sixties. Quickly it replaced the pressed metal panels which had been used to sheet walls or as spandrel panels during the previous five years. Despite the impressed patterns and shapes and the dulled finishes which had been tried in an endeavour to overcome the irregularities that became so obvious in certain light, the problems of metal panels had not been conquered. Exposed aggregate concrete suffered no such troubles. It was used for paving, for internal and external walling in numerous ways, for sun-screens and for partitions. As 1946–54 had been a period of gaudy paint and 1955–60 had been a period of the curtain wall, the 1960s were the years of exposed aggregate.

The IBM building was a sensible answer to the problem of the glass box. While others, still staunchly following the fashions despite a rising chorus of professional and lay criticism, continued to erect them, an important stride in office building was taken with the administrative offices erected for the Metropolitan Water, Sewerage and Drainage Board at the south end of Sydney in 1963–65. Here the architects, McConnel, Smith and Johnson, decided with unanswerable logic to solve the problem by not creating it in the first place. The Water Board Building, its frame encased in rich sandy coloured pre-cast concrete panels, was a tall block of masonry sculptured with judiciously placed shaded window slots and draped on its northern face with a huge venetian blind of pre-cast concrete sunshades. It was an extremely sane, almost cerebral building. Each face was designed to meet its actual conditions but withal combined into a most satisfactory total unity. While it was criticized, justifiably, for a certain aesthetic flatness, in its boldness of form and precision of workmanship and finish it reflected an acuteness and clarity of thought that made it a landmark in Australian office architecture.

By the middle 1960s office buildings taller than anything seen before were reaching up with increasing speed in all the capital cities. The tallest of them was, once again, in Sydney. The Australia Square Tower, 560 feet high in fifty floors of 135 feet diameter, was only a part, but the most dramatic part, of a larger development of a city site formed by combining a number of old and small titles. The drama came not so much from its form or height, both of which were partially disguised by the site being, unfortunately, in the lowest part of the city, but from the thoroughness of its technology, the speed of its construction and its organization.

After some five years of careful preparation by the architect Harry Seidler, the Australia Square Tower began to rise with astonishing speed. On a cramped and restricted site a central core of in-situ concrete served as an ever-growing platform from which pre-cast and pre-finished concrete units were positioned to form the columns, spandrels and beams. The units were shells with the reinforcement already positioned. They served as both formwork and finish to the concrete cores which were poured in-situ. By working from the inside out the circular tower rose, free of the usual entangling cobweb of steel scaffolding, swiftly and cleanly at the rate of three floors each four weeks. As it did it convinced even the most sceptical that the single-minded and concentrated application of modern technological and management techniques yielded impressive fruit and that in this regard the Australia Square Tower was the most important building in Australia since the MLC building.

But the project of which the Australia Square Tower was a part was even more than that. It was the first practical demonstration of the precepts of architects and town planners who, for twenty years before, had been talking of the necessity of redeveloping obsolete parts of the cities by amalgamating a number of titles to

The Water Board Building
in Bathurst Street, Sydney:
1965. Architects,
McConnel, Smith &
Johnson

small portions of city land into one larger tract and erecting on it, not the site-covering block that had been the standard approach since the 1830s, but tall soaring spires containing the same total floor area but which left a half or more of the ground area open and uncluttered. The result, it was pointed out, would be better and more pleasant spaces both within and between the buildings and healthier and happier people as a consequence. It was an obviously sound idea in theory and numerous attempts had been made to try it. But the practical difficulties of finance and titles were tremendous and seemed insurmountable. In 1958, G. J. Dusseldorp, a building entrepreneur and a Dutchman who had migrated to Australia in 1951, tackled what others knew was impossible and by means of skill, courage, fortitude, psychology and determination eventually managed to acquire and consolidate the eighty-odd titles covering one and a quarter acres of land between George and Pitt Streets. The Australia Square project which eventuated was an exemplar to others and a vital milestone for Australian town planning.

By the middle 1960s Australian architects, having discovered the visual depth of the exposed aggregate panel, had also rediscovered richness and texture in other materials. Using variegated coloured rugged clinker bricks or rough common bricks painted white, imported Canadian cedar, dark stained local timber often left undressed as it came from the saw to heighten its grain, off-the-form concrete left in its raw state to show the marking of carefully constructed formwork, and by covering pitched roofs with dark grey concrete tiles, imported redwood shingles or an exaggeratedly heavy moulded Swiss pattern terracotta tile, they began to turn away from the glossy slickness and the impersonal detachment of the preceding decade to a highly textured, somewhat emotional architecture. Their buildings were richer, warmer and more human as a result.

It was a satisfactory architecture—sensitive and deep. Its principles were fundamental and basic. Its underlying qualities were timeless but its appearance was uniquely mid-twentieth century. In its development, application and appropriateness it was thoroughly and distinctly Australian.

There was nothing superficial or imitative about its best examples. The houses were real homes, protecting, sheltering, comforting, warm and relaxing without looking Colonial, Japanese or any other exotic style; the Wentworth Memorial Church at Vaucluse was at the same time human and ethereal, mundane and spiritual, knowable and aloof, comforting and inspirational without reproducing any Gothic or Spanish Mission stylism; and Goldstein College Hall at the University of New South Wales had all the emotional feeling of a great mediaeval hall at the same time that its appearance was pure 1965.

Initiated by a small coterie of Sydney architects, the style was impelled into prominence when the 1964 Sulman Award was made to the Presbyterian Church's Leppington Agricultural College designed by McKay and Cox. When over the next two years five other prizes for outstanding architecture were all awarded to buildings of the same architectural expression the idiom was established. During the same years it was disseminated widely in post-offices, court houses and schools by the work of the New South Wales Government Architect, into whose department a number of its young initiators had been gathered. For all its often rough, brutal quality the style was, in its roots, a slightly romantic reaction in the best manner of William Morris to the anaemic, spiritless sophistication and the smooth, transparent emptiness of the work of the preceding decade. The construction of the buildings, direct, simple and thoughtful, had a crafted quality and was often exposed as a powerful part of the design. It was a dense,

Above House in Mona Vale Road, Turramurra, New South Wales: 1962. Architects, Allen Jack & Cottier

Right House at Indooroopilly, Queensland: 1957. Architects, Hayes, Scott & Henderson

Below House at Brookfield, Queensland: 1965. Architect, John Dalton

Left A Pettit Sevitt project house, designed by Ancher, Mortlock, Murray & Woolley

Below House at Beaconsfield, Victoria: 1965. Architect, Charles Duncan

Below The C. B. Alexander Presbyterian
Agricultural College at Tocal,
New South Wales: 1965.
Architects, McKay & Cox

Opposite above Goldstein Hall at the
University of New South Wales,
Kensington, New South Wales: 1963.
Designed by the New South
Wales Government Architect

Opposite below The Court House at
Blacktown, New South Wales: 1966.
Designed by the New South
Wales Government Architect

tweedy architecture in which an apparently simple but actually complex arrangement of solid blocks and free-standing vertical planes of rough brickwork
penetrated by chunky planes of timber or concrete were compressed under heavy
oversized fascias into nuggety lumps. Because it contained much that was
Australian-generated it seemed to hold a promise that after a century and a
quarter Australian architecture might at last be going Australian.

During the 1960s a deal of the talk that had gone on on the architectural fringe
during the fifties began to show practical results as well. The interest in architectural history had been stimulated when in 1954 Morton Herman had published
his book *The Early Australian Architects and Their Work*. Until that time few
architects or historians had given the subject any more than a passing glance.
A National Trust had been formed in New South Wales in 1947 by a few
individuals who found a private delight in wandering around the early buildings
and delving in the various state libraries and archives; but it had remained with
them a private esoteric hobby. It had been this for Herman too until he was
encouraged to make the material of nearly twenty years' measuring, drawing and
research available to others. After a further six years of intense work the book
appeared, to receive high praise both locally and overseas. Suddenly Australians
were shown that architectural history did not lie only overseas but that they had
an interesting story of their own. A widespread interest was sparked as a result
of the book. To preserve and foster it, National Trusts were formed in all the
other states during the fifties. With only their members' subscriptions and an
occasional private donation, their activities were largely confined to planning,
talking and trying to convince governments and those with money that their
objectives were worthy. By the sixties they had made progress. The various state
National Trusts voluntarily became chapters of a national body to co-ordinate
their work. In every state they had begun to acquire properties of their own and,
at considerable expense and with voluntary contributions, had restored a number
of historically and architecturally valuable buildings to first-class condition,
furnished them appropriately, and opened them to the public. A number of smaller
local historical societies had made progress in similar ways and government
and local authorities with greater resources were both aware of the problem
and acting to meet it. One way or another the movement to preserve Australia's
architectural heritage became a viable force and its best buildings were already
being or would be saved for posterity.

Town planning and civic development grew apace as the middle sixties came
and like the historical movement began to bear fruit. Canberra became a recognizable and prideful city after Lake Burley Griffin was created. It boomed with new
buildings and changed its face so quickly that a visitor found it radically different
after only a few months. In Perth the scruffy river flats edged with dilapidated
boat sheds between Perthwater and the city were cleaned up and a sweep of
roadways and landscaping formed the beautiful first part of a bold scheme. New
roadways and new bridges gave a whole new scale to parts of the cities and country
as roadmaking authorities battled desperately to meet the problem created by a
flood of motor cars. Whole suburban areas and once secluded bushlands disappeared
as cruel gashes were torn to build high-speed roads. But the effect of the town
planners was to ensure that the results were seldom ugly and often surprisingly
beautiful. The bridges and overpasses continued the functional tradition into the
middle twentieth century. Across the Derwent at Hobart and the Narrows at
Perth fine bridges were built. But the best in their engineering and their aesthetic

The El Alamein Fountain at King's Cross,
New South Wales: 1961.
Architects, Woodward & Taranto

sensitivity were the two quite outstanding bridges built at Gladesville and Rose-ville in Sydney and the delightfully delicate and impossible spiral pedestrian-overpass ramps beside Perthwater in Western Australia. To a limited extent the taste for pleasantness in the environment spilled over into municipal authorities who made sporadic and often futile gestures to give expression to it. It took many forms; lakes, playgrounds, parks with multi-coloured seats, and bus shelters. Fountains were particularly popular and prestigious because of their patent luxury after nearly sixty years when circumstances had demanded a practical return for any money spent. Only one of the many fountains erected throughout Australia was really successful—and it could hardly have been more so. The El Alamein Fountain designed by Woodward and Taranto and erected at Kings Cross in Sydney in 1961 is a splendid sculpture in water. Its ephemeral ever-changing ever-remaining lightness dances tantalizingly in the sunshine or turns the reflections of gaudy neon lights into jewels at night. Its poetry was a sculptural breakthrough not only in Australia but in the world.

But the really significant changes that came over Australian architecture in the 1960s were not in the buildings or on the fringe areas at all but in the nature of the architectural profession itself. For over a century and a quarter from the time of the coming of the professional architects in the 1840s the idea of the architect as an artist had been assiduously cultivated. Caring little for, in fact almost despising, the mundane aspects of building, he had been superior to the need for business efficiency and the economic, legal and organizational demands they made.

The sheer size of most of the non-domestic buildings and the quantity of houses that were needed in the 1960s posed new problems that could only be solved by the introduction of modern business tools and techniques. The large buildings were exceedingly complex affairs, their parts entirely prefabricated in factories and assembled on the site, and packed with an array of mechanical services needing to be most carefully considered and designed and built-in as the work progressed. No longer could decisions be deferred or intuitive changes made on the job. When amply financed business firms moved in to offer a complete and efficient designing, building and financing service, they awoke the architectural profession to its own blatant inadequacies. At the same time, it was made painfully aware, by cataclysmic decisions in the law courts, that its claim to invulnerable, God-like authority and power was not without its responsibilities.

All of these developments came swiftly, silently and insidiously. The growth and type of work caused architectural offices to expand in size to include specialists on the staff and become technically self-contained. Small offices, which had traditionally formed the majority of practices, became proportionately fewer. In the sixties the tendency for them to disappear altogether was strongly apparent. On top of this there was a realization that self preservation in the future demanded that architects be first of all businessmen—efficient, reliable and organized in the way of the business firms who were their principal clients. The lesson was reinforced by the sobering knowledge that a professional service which had to withstand scarifying examination by devious-minded lawyers had to be thoroughly performed.

The architectural profession not only turned its attention to conducting its professional affairs in a more efficient way within the traditional framework but began to reassess the framework itself. Prevented by professional ethics from engaging directly in building operations, it nevertheless began to realize that the divorce that had taken place between the designer and constructor two hundred years before when Sir William Chambers became the first professional architect was an illogical and artificial bifurcation of what was essentially one operation. By means of tight specifying, which set out not only what was to be done but also how it was to be done and in what, and by breaking the whole building operation into a number of smaller specialized packets, many architects became virtually builder-architects erecting their work by means of a number of sub-contractors.

By the middle sixties the architectural profession was making hurried, almost desperate revolutionary efforts to fit itself to take its place in the modern high-pressure business world. The old individual gentleman-artist-architect offering a highly personal service to his client had been dehumanized and was almost dead. The future, unknown and, as always, a cause for trepidation, appeared to belong to the impersonal, conglomerate architecture-building-business corporation.

TAILPIECE

In following the progress of architecture in Australia we have seen not only the ups and downs and the changes of direction but also the major reasons why they happened. Some of the changes in direction such as that during the late Victorian period were steady and gradual—reflecting the steadiness of those stable years; some of them such as those of 1838 in Sydney, the gold-discovery years in various separate places and the 1930s throughout the whole nation were hard and abrupt—reflecting the conditions of which they were a part. The ups and downs had their causes too. The 1850s and early 1860s were a down as were the late 1920s and early 1930s; the 1830s were an up as are the 1960s to a lesser extent. The architecture that has been created in Australia since 1960 has had much dross in it as architecture anywhere in the world has had in the same period; but Australian architecture has had more than the usual number of nuggets. Many of the recent buildings are equal in architectural quality to their opposite numbers overseas and just as frequently to be found. Numbers of them have a distinctive and unique flavour and give rise to a justified hope that the Architecture in Australia of the future will be a truly Australian architecture.

RECOMMENDED FURTHER READING

Birrell, James	*Walter Burley Griffin*, Brisbane, University of Queensland Press, 1964
Boyd, Robin	*Australia's Home*, Melbourne, Melbourne University Press, 1952
Ellis, M. H.	*Francis Greenway*, Sydney, Angus and Robertson, 1953
Freeland, J. M.	*Melbourne Churches 1936-51*, Melbourne, Melbourne University Press, 1963
	The Australian Pub, Melbourne, Melbourne University Press, 1966
Herman, Morton	*The Early Australian Architects and Their Work*, Sydney, Angus and Robertson, 1954
	The Blackets, Sydney, Angus and Robertson, 1963
Robertson, E. G.	*Victorian Heritage*, Melbourne, Georgian House, 1960
	Sydney Lace, Melbourne, Georgian House, 1962
	Early Houses of Northern Tasmania, Melbourne, Georgian House (limited edition in 2 Vols. 1964, second edition in 1 Vol. 1966)
	Ornamental Cast Iron in Victoria, Melbourne, Georgian House, 1967
Smith, Roy	*John Lee Archer*, Hobart, Tasmanian Historical Research Association, 1962
Verge, W. G.	*John Verge*, Sydney, Wentworth Books, 1962
Wardell, V. A.	*Architecture and Engineering Works of W. S. Wardell*, typescript in Mitchell Library, 1940

GLOSSARY

acanthus A formalized ornament of Greek origin based on the leaf of the acanthus plant.

acroterion A formalized ornamental upstand placed on the gable apex in Classic architecture.

antefixae Formalized upstanding decorations spaced along the horizontal edge of a roof eaves overhang.

arch A structure forming the head of an opening and in which all the materials are in compression. It is usually curved (partly circular or elliptical) but sometimes flat.

architrave (a) The main beam spanning between the columns of a colonnade: (b) The moulding around a doorway, window or arch.

arris The sharp edge or salient angle formed by the intersection of two planes.

awning A roof of a light or temporary nature with at least one open side supported either on posts, brackets or tie rods or by cantilevering.

balcony A balustraded platform with access from an upper floor level.

baluster A post between the newel posts of a staircase helping to support the handrail; a pear or urn shaped pillar usually of stone supporting a railing.

balustrade A series of balusters and a capping rail or coping.

bargeboard A board running up the exposed end of a gable roof for the purpose of covering the roof constructional timbers.

bellcast A flared concave upwards shape in which the slope of the surface from the horizontal increases with height, as in the shape of the lower portion of a bell.

bond The method of overlapping bricks or stone to bind them together in a wall. There are a number of usual methods (English b., Flemish b., Colonial b., with stretcher b. being the most common in present day work) which are recognizable from the pattern of header and stretcher bricks on the wall face.

boss A plain or decorated knob at the intersection of ribs, the termination of a moulding or even by itself on a wall or ceiling surface.

bressummer A beam supporting a superstructure and spanning a broad opening normal to the two parallel supports from which it springs, e.g. across a shop front or the outer edge of a stair landing.

bullnose A convex outwards shape.

buttress A support against a wall to carry a thrust—usually from the roof load.

cantilever A horizontal projection supported not by posts, brackets or rods but by the rigidity of the connection with the vertical surface from which it springs.

capital The top elaborated part of a column.

casement A window in which the opening sash is hinged at the side and opens like a door.

Classic Of Greece or Rome.

Classical In the manner of Classic.

clinkers Bricks from the hottest part of the kiln which have been overburnt and vitrified. They are usually extremely hard, dark in colour and often, having fused together in the firing, have to be broken apart leaving jagged surfaces.

colonnade A series of columns and their superstructure.

contour A line joining the points on the ground surface which are the same height above a fixed datum.

coping A capping course at the top of a brick or stone wall, a balustrade or similar.

corbel A higher course of brick or stone work projected beyond the line of the face of a lower course for the purpose of supporting a load.

cornice Externally: a horizontal projecting moulding crowning the top of a building or a similar moulding above the frieze in Classical buildings. Internally: a moulding at the junction of a wall and ceiling.

dado The lower part of an internal wall especially when faced or coloured differently from the upper part.

dentil One of a series of small separated rectangular blocks forming a part of a Classic cornice.

diaper An ornamental diamond pattern in a wall often created by differently coloured bricks.

dormer A vertical window with its own small roof and side walls projecting from a larger sloping roof.

double-hung (window) A window with two glazed sashes both of which slide vertically within the window frame.

doughboys Bricks from the coolest part of the kiln which have been underburnt as a result. They are usually soft and pale in colour.

dressing The elaborated surround to windows, doorways and other special parts of a building which have been worked and finished to a higher degree than the rest of the building.

egg and dart A moulding of alternating egg-like and sharp dart- or tongue-like forms forming part of a Classic cornice.

entablature In Classic architecture the superstructure above the column consisting of the architrave, frieze and cornice.

entasis The convex swelling of the shaft of a column beyond a straight line joining the vertically corresponding points on the circumferences of the bottom and top of the shaft. It is generally at its maximum about one-third of the way up the column shaft.

fanlight The glazed part of a doorway above the door. While in Colonial architecture it was often in the shape of a fan being either elliptical or semi-circular and with radial glazing bars the term applies to a sash of any shape whether fixed or openable.

fascia A flat on-edge member finishing the edge of a roof.

finial The ornamental finishing piece, usually spiky in general form, at the top of a spire, buttress, roof, gable, corner of a tower, etc.

flagging Paving with flat slabs of split or sawn stone (flags or flagstones).

gable The upper triangular part of an external wall which carries a pitched roof.

gablet A small gable roof.

galvanize Strictly to coat a metal by electrical-chemical action. When used as 'galvanized iron' it is to coat iron with zinc usually by dipping or spraying rather than by galvanic action.

half-timber A type of construction in which a large proportion of the building consists of a heavy timber frame with the spaces between the framing members filled in with brick, wattle-and-daub or similar.

header A brick laid so that an end of the brick forms part of the face of the brickwork.

hip The sloping arris of a hipped-roof running from the ridge to the eaves and formed by the intersection of two roof planes.

hipped-roof A roof which is wholly pitched from horizontal eaves. Salient changes in wall direction are accommodated by hips, not gables.

jalousie A swinging external window- or door-shutter with louvered slats sloping upwards from the outside.

joist The immediate supporting member of a floor or ceiling.

keystone The central stone or brick of an arch.

label mould A continuous projecting weather moulding or dripstone running across the top of a window or doorway opening for the purpose of diverting water running down the wall face away from the opening.

ledged-and-braced The simplest form of door construction in which vertical boards are nailed to cross timbers (ledges) near the top and bottom of the door and a diagonal strut (brace) is run from the outer end of the top ledge to the inner end of the lower ledge.

lintel A structural piece of timber, concrete, stone or metal spanning a flat-headed doorway or window opening.

loggia An open-sided arcade.

louver Overlapping slips of timber, glass or other thin material arranged with spaces between to exclude rain but to admit air.

mansard A roof in which each roof plane has two slopes, the lower portion being the steeper.

mortar A mixture of sand, lime, cement and water laid between bricks and stone.

mortice A hole in a frame intended to receive the end or tenon of some other part.

mullion The vertical part of a frame between the lights in a window or in a doorway between the door and sidelight.

neck (a) The S-shaped part of a stair handrail between abrupt changes of rail height: (b) The part of a column between the shaft and the capital.

newel The main supporting post of a stair handrail at the top or bottom of each flight.

nogging A piece of non-structural framing fixed between the studs of a timber frame.

ogee A moulding which in section is a double continuous S-shaped curve, concave below turning into convex above.

open-couple A form of roof framing in which the feet of pairs of rafters are not joined with joists or timber ties.

Order The architectural style and the proportions between the parts of a complete column and its entablature. The Classic Orders are either Greek (Doric, Ionic, Corinthian) or Roman (Tuscan, Doric, Ionic, Corinthian, Composite).

oriel A polygonal projecting alcove on an upper floor and usually supported on corbels.

oriel window A window in the form of an oriel.

parapet A low solid protection wall at the edge of a roof, formed by carrying the main wall past the eaves line.

parge To plaster a wall with mortar as the erection of the wall proceeds. Particularly used in connection with fireplaces and chimneys.

party-wall A wall built on the boundary line between two adjacent properties with the costs, rights and responsibilities shared by the property owners.

pediment (a) A gable in a Classic building: (b) A triangular, partly-circular or other geometrical shaped decoration crowning a window, doorway, archway or other wall opening.

pergola An open trellis-like roof intended for supporting climbing plants.

pilaster Any column with a shaft rectangular in plan but particularly one which is attached to a wall as though the column were half buried in the wall.

pisé Rammed earth or clay.

pitch The slope of a roof measured either in degrees above the horizontal or as a ratio of the vertical rise of the roof to its span.

plate Any load carrying member in which two dimensions appreciably exceed the third and which is laid on the flat. Particularly used for the horizontal piece of timber at the top of a wall to provide seating and fixing for roof and ceiling timbers, a similar piece to connect the bottom of the studs of a frame wall and for pieces at the bottom of posts and stumps to spread the load being carried.

plinth The slightly projecting base of a column or a building.

quirk A deep groove, cut or notch.

quoins Corner stones at the angles of a building.

rafter A sloping member of the framework of a pitched roof.

reveal The side face of a window, doorway or other wall opening.

ridge The high-line of a roof formed by the junction of two oppositely sloping roof surfaces.

riser The vertical part of a step between the treads.

roundel A round or oval-shaped medallion-like ornament.

rusticate To finish stonework with a very rough surface but with deeply cut, precise and accurate joints.

sash In a window the framework which holds the glass.

scotia A concave moulding.

shingle Strictly a rectangle of split wood used overlapping like tiles for a roof covering; now a flat unit of any material used in the same way.

shutter Any removable panel covering the inside or outside of a window either to provide protection or privacy or to exclude light. In Australian Colonial architecture shutters were made of wood and were either hinged at the side like a door and arranged one pair to a window, or slid into a wall cavity at the side or below the sill, or folded into the internal reveal of the opening. External hinged shutters were usually jalousies.

sidelight The glazed part of a doorway at the side of the door and below the fanlight.

skilling (a) A lean-to extension at the rear of a hut or house: (b) A rude shelter with a skillion roof supported on posts.

skillion A one-way pitched roof of even fall running from a highest point at one side of a building to the lowest point at the opposite side.

skirting A board along the bottom of a wall at the junction with the floor.

slab A broad length of timber, a sector in section, split from the side of a log by wedges and mauls.

spandrel Originally the triangular part between the tops of arched columns or between a stairway and the ground; now also applied to any 'fill-in' panel intended to provide closure or hide an unsightly part of the building.

stallboard The vertical part of a shop front between the bottom of the window and the ground.

stretcher A brick laid so that a side of the brick forms part of the face of the wall.

stringer The sloping part of a staircase running between landings and carrying the outer loads and ends of the treads.

stucco To plaster externally with a special gypsum-lime-cement plaster suitable for modelling and moulding.

stud A vertical load bearing piece of the wall framing of a timber framed building.

stylobate Strictly the three-stepped base of a Greek building; now the tiered base of any colonnade.

tenon The end of a piece of wood shaped to fit into a corresponding cavity or mortice.

tensioning The application to a structural member of a permanent stress opposite to that to be expected from the working load. The technique is usually used in, but not confined to, reinforced concrete work. The tensioning can be applied either before (pre-t.) or after (post-t.) the concrete is poured, set and cured.

thatch To roof with rushes, grass, straw or similar.

transom The horizontal part of a frame between the lights of a window or, in a doorway, above a door and below its fanlight.

tread The flat horizontal part of a step.

truss A load bearing structural frame built up of comparatively light members.

tympanum The triangular area of a pediment.

valence (board) A decorative panel between verandah posts and on the underside of the awning.

valley A re-entrant angle formed by the intersection of two roof planes; the opposite of a hip.

verandah An external floor attached to a building and covered with an awning supported on one side by a wall of the building and on its outer edge by posts.

wattle-and-daub A type of wall construction in which slim pliable pieces of wood (wattles) are fixed to or between framing timbers and thickly plastered, usually with mud (daub).

INDEX